A Summary of Christian History

ROBERT A. BAKER

A SUMMARY OF

CHRISTIAN HISTORY

BROADMAN PRESS • Nashville, Tennessee

Dedicated with love
to
the REVEREND FRED A. and
MRS. ONA HARRIS McCAULLEY,
faithful witnesses of Jesus

© 1959 • BROADMAN PRESS
Nashville, Tennessee

423–08041

Library of Congress catalog card number: 59–5852

Printed in the United States of America

5.JUL58K.S.P.

Preface

For sixteen years a part of my work has involved the teaching of a rapid survey of church history to a group who has had little previous background in the field. While it was in print, W. J. McGlothlin's book *The Course of Christian History* was used. The present summary was begun a decade ago as a temporary makeshift until a suitable text could be located. The fine one-volume texts that have appeared in the meantime have been too encyclopedic and full for this group.

I have tried to tell this story as briefly as possible. Brevity, in fact, is at the same time the merit and the weakness of the summary. It has been most difficult to distinguish between the necessary and the desirable. Here the main stream of Christian history is greatly telescoped, and many important fringe areas are omitted altogether. It may be that my surgery was too radical, but, if so, perhaps the bibliographies will provide the remedy.

The material in this work is the common stock of all church historians. I am indebted to everyone for it. An effort has been made to incorporate as far as possible the results of the latest research in the various periods, but generally speaking, this same story in more detail and larger sweep is found in every standard history. For that reason documentation would be superfluous, although the interpretations have an undeniable evangelical bias. The bibliography following each period will provide additional help for the student desiring to secure more knowledge of that section. These works in turn have detailed bibliographies for additional study, if desired. From this general summary, then, a student may step through additional doors to specialized study of almost unlimited extent. On the other hand, if the reader is the average "man in the street" who simply wants a glimpse of the general stream of Christian history, this work may be useful to him.

One change has been introduced in the general outline. Usually the Reformation period is dated from 1517 when Luther prepared his Ninety-five Theses, but one cannot properly understand the Reformation without a great deal of background before 1517. This background has been inserted into the Reformation section. Since the radical collapse of papal prestige in the Avignon visit and papal schism, along with the almost universal clamor for reform, followed nearly immediately the achievement by the Roman Church of its highest pre-eminence as exemplified in the Fourth Lateran Council of 1215, that date has been chosen as the dividing line between the height of Roman Catholic domination and the antecedents of reform. It makes the picture clearer.

Contents

List of Maps

I. PERIOD OF CHRISTIAN BEGINNINGS (4 B.C. to A.D. 100)

Introduction to the Period

Jesus Christ was born between 6 and 4 B.C. The error in dating his birth occurred because time was not calculated according to Christ's birth until the sixth century. A mistake of several years was made during the process of numbering back. The Mediterranean world was ruled by the Roman Empire at the time of Jesus Christ's birth. Their armies had overrun Palestine about sixty years before. For most of that time the ruler of Palestine was Herod the Great. When Herod died in 4 B.C., Palestine was divided so that his three sons might share authority. Philip ruled over the extreme northeastern area east of Jordan; Herod Antipas ruled in Galilee and Perea. Both of these men were in office during Christ's ministry and are referred to in the Scriptures. Archelaus, the third son of Herod, received the large central section of Palestine (Judea, Idumea, and Samaria), but was removed from office by the Roman emperor in A.D. 6. Roman governors or procurators were appointed to rule this portion of Palestine. During the entire ministry of Christ the procurator was Pontius Pilate (A.D. 26–36), also mentioned in the Scriptures.

Christianity spread rapidly during the first century. The end of the period (A.D. 100) finds it growing, pure in doctrine, and relatively unaffected by the destruction of what had been its home base.

Points of Special Interest

The student should notice the divine preparation for the revelation in Christ, not alone in Judaism but in other great races also. He should also keep in mind the New Testament pattern of a functioning church, its local character, its officers, its organization, and its autonomy. It is in these matters, as well as in doctrine, that later developments turn away from the original pattern.

1

1

The Beginnings of Historical Christianity

Aɴʏ ᴛʜᴏᴜɢʜᴛꜰᴜʟ ᴘᴇʀsᴏɴ will look with real curiosity at the description of the apostle Paul in Acts 21:37–40. Paul had stirred up his customary riot, this time in the Temple at Jerusalem, and was only saved from severe injury at the hands of the Jewish mob by the intervention of the Roman soldiers patrolling the city. As Paul endeavors to speak to the people from the stairs of the prison castle, four aspects of his life are presented in quick succession: (1) He spoke the Greek language and was a citizen of a city noted for its Greek culture. (2) He was a Roman citizen (notice Acts 22:25–29, along with 21:39). (3) He was a Jew and was fluent in the Hebrew tongue. (4) He was a Christian, bearing testimony of the Master to his own race.

The diverse racial, linguistic, and religious elements reflected here are intelligible only as the background of Paul is understood. Here is the function of church history—to explain *why* and *how*. It is impossible to interpret Paul or any part of Christianity without an understanding of the historical background. For the New Testament period this includes Greek, Roman, and Jewish influences. Customs, parties, traditions, and allusions that are meaningless unless they are explained in historical terms constantly crop up in the New Testament.

Greek Influence on Christianity

The Greek elements in the world into which Christianity came may be traced to the conquest of Palestine (and almost all of the known world) by Alexander the Great in the last half of the fourth century before Christ. This Macedonian soldier scattered into almost every part of the known world the tremendous culture and spirit of the Greeks. After Alexander's death his military generals and their successors ruled Palestine for over a century and a half. Without attempting to relate the remarkable history of Greek life and development, the outstanding contributions of that race to the Christian movement may be summed up under three heads.

First, Greek philosophy, some good and some bad, was scattered everywhere. Strangely enough, God used both the good and the bad to prepare for the coming of Christ. The atheistic and skeptical philosophy of the Greeks turned many in the Gentile world away from the superstitious worship of false gods and intensified their heart-hunger for the true God. The good Greek philosophy, on the other hand, prepared the world for the coming of Christ by magnifying the worth of the human spirit and by placing high value upon spiritual and moral truth.

In the second place, the Greek language became the common tongue throughout the whole Mediterranean world. Even in Palestine good Jews were forced to learn the Greek language in order to carry on trade in the markets. The fact is of more importance than might appear at first glance. For one thing, the missionaries of Christ could begin their work immediately without waiting to learn a new language. Furthermore, the presence of a common language brought a sense of unity to the various races. Compare the present-day slang expression "he speaks my language," suggesting a basic unity. Finally, the language itself was marvelously adequate. The Greeks had developed a language that made it possible to express clearly and precisely the great truths of the Christian revelation. Greek was the language of most (if not all) of the New Testament.

Third, the Greek spirit made its contribution to the Christian movement. It is difficult to put this spirit into words, but it included an intense love for truth, vision that encompassed large sweep, and initiative that was bold and daring.

Roman Influence on Christianity

The constant protection afforded Paul because he was a Roman citizen suggests the contribution of the Roman Empire to the Christian movement. Historically, Greek rule in Palestine ended about 167 B.C. when the Jewish patriots under Judas Maccabeus defeated the Greeks. In 63 B.C., after Jewish independence of about a century, the soldiers of Rome took possession of Palestine. A glance at the New Testament reveals evidence of Roman rule. It speaks of Roman centurions, Roman guards, Roman jailers, Roman castles, Roman governors. One of the questions which the Pharisees asked Jesus concerned whether a good Jew could serve God under Roman rule. The unpopularity of Matthew, the publican, grew out of the fact that he was collecting taxes for Rome.

Roman rule in the world when Jesus was born was not altogether good nor completely bad in its effect upon Christianity. The strong centralized government of Rome provided a measure of peace and protection. Rome would not permit any sort of violence to take place within the borders of her empire, lest the uproar should serve as a cloak for political revolt. This made it possible for Christian missionaries to move among the various races of the Mediterranean world with a minimum of political friction. Roman citizens like Paul were protected from unjust treatment by local officers. The network of Roman roads and ship routes made travel less hazardous and more convenient. Two hundred years later the language of the Romans would be adopted as the principal medium for religious expression.

On the other hand, the world government of Rome became the great enemy of Christianity before the end of the first century. It will be noted that the Roman mind had little conception of the value of an individual soul, choosing, rather, to exhaust religious devotion in the service of the state. The Roman armies adopted the false gods of every nation whom they conquered, only requiring that in return the subjugated nation accept Roman gods, including the Roman emperor. When Christians refused to worship the Roman emperor, severe persecution was inflicted.

Jewish Influence on Christianity

The third racial influence upon the Christian movement was the most significant. The Jewish nation provided the immediate background of Christ and all of his early disciples. The history of the Jews as related in the Old Testament is too well known to be repeated in detail. God chose a family of faith which, under divine care, developed into a nation. Several factors combined to bring political division about 975 B.C. The Northern Kingdom was carried into Assyrian captivity about 722 B.C. The Southern Kingdom stood until about 587 B.C. when it officially fell to the Babylonians. After about seventy years, remnants of the Southern Kingdom were permitted by the Persian empire to return to Palestine. They remained subject to the Persians until about 334 B.C., when Alexander the Great conquered them. The Greek period (334–167 B.C.), the century of Jewish independence (167–63 B.C.), and the beginning of Roman rule (63 B.C.) bring the history of the Jewish people to the New Testament era.

During this long history the Jewish people were, to some extent unconsciously, making preparation for the coming of Christ. They carefully preserved the revelation which God had given them. Through adversity and captivity two great truths were burned into their souls: first, that there is only one God for men; and second, that the relationship of God to men is personal, not national. Before the Babylonian captivity the Jews had often fallen into idolatry and polytheism, but after their return to Palestine they became zealous teachers of the truth that God is one (monotheism). While residents of Palestine, the Jews had sometimes conceived of God in national terms, but in captivity their isolation from every material reminder of a national deity brought them to realize that the *individual* must commune with God through the spirit. It was worth the experiences of the Babylonian captivity to learn this lesson.

Although some, like Jonah, were reluctant to witness to Gentiles, the entire world became familiar with the beliefs and practices of the Jews. Early in the Greek period a movement known as the

Dispersion began. This was the voluntary movement of great numbers of Jews from Palestine to almost every part of the Mediterranean world. Wherever they went the Jews made numerous proselytes to their religion, establishing synagogues for teaching God's revelation, witnessing to the sovereignty of one God, and looking into the heavens for the Messiah. This leaven prepared the world for Christ's coming.

The Jewish institutions and parties that form so much a part of the New Testament story have their background in these historical experiences. The synagogue was developed as a place of teaching and worship during the Babylonian captivity when there was no temple available. The prominent place that it held after the return of the Jews from the exile brought into existence the groups known as scribes and lawyers. Their chief duty at first was to copy Scriptures; because they became experts in what the Scriptures said, their duties were enlarged to include scriptural interpretation and instruction.

Perhaps the contact between the Jews and the Persian religious ideas helped to produce the party known as the Essenes, which probably arose about 150 B.C. This group numbered about four thousand at the time of Christ and was characterized by rigorous orthodoxy, celibacy, communal ownership, and the elimination of animal sacrifices in worship. The Pharisees doubtless grew out of the separatist tendency when the overtures of the Samaritans were rejected during the days of Ezra and Nehemiah (about 500 B.C.). During the Maccabean struggle (beginning about 167 B.C.), this party took distinct form. In the New Testament they are pictured as narrow, bigoted, and to some extent hypocritical. They were numerous and popular in the time of Jesus, rallying to traditional supernaturalism and ceremonial exactness. The Sadducees probably arose during the second century before Christ. Friendly to Roman and Greek culture, they represented religious and political liberalism. Their rationalism led them to deny the resurrection and divine providence, to refuse all tradition, and to magnify the freedom of the human will.

The Samaritans arose through the intermarriage of Jews who

6

had been left in Palestine after the beginning of the Babylonian captivity with Gentiles who had been brought into the land. The Herodians were the Jewish political patriots who supported the Herod family against Rome. The Zealots were probably the heirs of the Maccabean tradition of fervent zeal to throw off the yoke of foreigners.

Jesus Christ (4 B.C.–A.D. 30)

Into this sort of world Jesus Christ was born. Practically all that is known of his earthly life may be found in the Synoptic Gospels (Matthew, Mark, and Luke) and in John. John's Gospel describes Jesus' eternal nature and preincarnate existence; Matthew and Luke record his human genealogy. It is likely that Matthew gives the genealogy of Joseph while Luke deals with the genealogy of Mary. Matthew and Luke alone recount the birth and childhood of Jesus and of John the Baptist, the forerunner of Jesus. All of the Gospels speak of John's ministry and look from different points of view at the life of Christ.

The birth of Jesus Christ occurred about 4 B.C. This means that Christ actually began his public ministry about A.D. 27 and was crucified about A.D. 30. The Lord's ministry may be conveniently divided into seven sections. (1) His early Judean ministry, described principally in John's Gospel, includes the calling of the first disciples and the first cleansing of the Temple. (2) The great Galilean ministry covers the principal period of Christ's work and lasted about a year and a half. During this time the Lord was rejected at Nazareth, moved to Capernaum, chose the twelve apostles, set forth the Sermon on the Mount, and toured Galilee three times. (3) His several withdrawals from the press of the crowds gave opportunity for special instruction to the disciples, for securing the great confession at Caesarea Philippi, and for the transfiguration experience. (4) His later Judean ministry continued for about three months and is described by Luke and John. It centered on the attendance of Jesus and his disciples at the Feasts of Tabernacles and Dedication in Jerusalem. (5) His brief Perean ministry is spoken of by all four of the Gospels and

7

is characterized by final miracles, parables, and prophecies of his resurrection. (6) The last week in Jerusalem is treated in great detail by John's Gospel. It begins with the triumphal entry and closes with the crucifixion. (7) The postresurrection ministry of Jesus for about forty days before his ascension marks the close of the Gospel accounts.

The teachings of Jesus are remarkable both in their method and content. He drove home truth through parables, questions, discourses, and debates. God's person and purpose were revealed in Christ's life and teachings. Love is to be the dominant theme of the Christian's life. Because God loved men, Christ died on the cross for man's sins; by personal trust in Christ, men could receive a birth from above and assurance of eternal life. The conquering power of the cross and the ultimate triumph of the kingdom of God were central in Christ's teachings. He established his church, a local autonomous body where two or three gathering together in prayer could find his presence and power.

After the death and ascension of Christ, the disciples whom he had chosen and instructed set out on the seemingly impossible task contained in the Great Commission. Despite efforts of many other religions to attract men, Christianity began growing like a mustard seed. From a human standpoint, many reasons may be advanced for this tremendous development. (1) Heathenism was bankrupt and could not answer the call of hungry hearts. (2) The great welter of religions of every description clamoring for devotees could not compete with God's revelation in Christ. (3) Every Christian became a missionary; the sacred fire leaped from friend to friend. (4) The Christians had a burning conviction that Christ alone could save the lost world about them and that since the return of Christ was imminent, there was no time to be lost.

The seventy years of Christian growth from Christ's death to that of the last apostle may be divided into three periods.

Period of Local Witnessing (A.D. 30–45)

The first twelve chapters of Acts describe the history of the Christian movement during the first fifteen years after Christ's death and resurrection. The Holy Spirit was given in accordance with the promise of Christ, providing power for witnessing in a hostile world, bringing the presence of Christ for fellowship and strength, and giving leadership from Christ in the initiation of important movements. At Pentecost men from every part of the world were saved and doubtless went back to their own cities to establish Christian churches. Persecution, want, and internal bickering were only temporary hurdles (see Acts 3–6).

The martyrdom of Stephen marks a turning point in two respects: it began the persecution that drove the Christians out of Jerusalem into all Judea and Samaria in their witness; and it profoundly moved Saul the persecutor in the direction of personal conversion to Christ. The local witness was expanded by the preaching of Peter to a Gentile (for which he was required to give explanation to the church at Jerusalem), the founding of the Gentile church at Antioch, and the martyrdom of James, son of Zebedee. The conversion of Saul, his preparation for service, and his ministry at Antioch provide the background for the second stage of Christian development.

Period of Missionary Expansion (A.D. 45–68)

Under the leadership of the Holy Spirit a new direction of witnessing was begun with the inauguration of the missionary tours of Paul and Barnabas. Paul is the central figure in at least three great missionary tours between the years 45 and 58, when he was seized in the Temple at Jerusalem. During these thirteen years he wrote two letters to the church at Thessalonica, two to the Corinthians, one to the Galatians, and one to the Romans. After his imprisonment in Rome about A.D. 61 he wrote the letters known as Philemon, Colossians, Ephesians, and Philippians. He probably was released for four or five years, but the extent of his travel during this time is not known. His two letters known as 1 Timothy and Titus were prepared in this interim. Tradition suggests that he may have gone as far west as Spain on one journey. He was imprisoned again about 67 at Rome. Just before his death at the hands of Nero he wrote 2 Timothy.

9

It is quite possible that tradition is correct in speaking of extensive missionary activity by other apostles, but such accounts are too meager and too far removed from the occasion to be of much value. It is known that Paul's missionary activity accounts for the rise of practically all of the important Christian centers of the first century. Churches were established through his efforts in some of the strongest cities of the empire.

Between the first and second missionary journeys, Paul and Silas attended a conference at Jerusalem (about 50). James presided at the meeting, and several discussed the question of whether a man needs to become a Jew first in order to become a Christian. After some, including the apostle Peter, had spoken, James gave his decision that any Gentile could find salvation by simple faith in Christ without going through Judaism.

During this period, which closes with the death of the apostle Paul at Rome in A.D. 68, nine other books that form the New Testament were written. These were James, Mark, Matthew, Luke, Acts, 1 Peter, Jude, 2 Peter, and Hebrews, perhaps in that order.

Period of Westward Growth (A.D. 68–100)

After Paul's death the center of Christian strength moved toward the western section of the Mediterranean area. Although the material for this period is scarce, it is not difficult to find reasons to substantiate the tradition of the westward move. About the year 66 the Jewish War broke out in Palestine, resulting in the complete destruction of Jerusalem in 70 at the hands of the Roman Titus. This catastrophe marked the end of Herod's Temple and the sacrifices of the Jews; at the same time it uprooted the Christian church in Jerusalem and scattered the people abroad. In which direction should Christianity move? Tradition reports that the apostle John went to Ephesus about the time Jerusalem was destroyed. This is plausible, since the most logical move would be toward the great church centers in the West established by the apostle Paul. Here and there in later literature are hints that Christians may have gone to every part of the western Mediterranean. The tradition of Christianity in Britain is very early; perhaps one of the soldiers chained to the apostle Paul was won by him to Christ and then transferred to the British garrison, there to witness and organize a Christian church. Possibly a similar situation sent the good news to central Europe, North Africa, and elsewhere to the fringes of the Roman Empire.

Conservative scholars assign five books by the apostle John to this period. Written by a "son of thunder," these books contain warnings against diluting Christianity and minimizing either the humanity or the deity of Christ. The advocates of such heretical views cannot be identified, but their presence is significant in view of the rise of these very doctrinal aberrations in the next century. Apparently John was exiled to the Isle of Patmos from Ephesus during the course of a severe persecution by the Roman Emperor Domitian (81–96). The book of Revelation, defying the effort of the Roman Empire to require Christians to worship the Roman emperor, was written in the closing decade of the apostolic period.

Concluding Summary

The literature that became the New Testament canon had not as yet been brought together into one book. The various churches used the Old Testament, together with such Christian writings as they might possess. The evidence shows that at the close of the century the Christian movement was pure in doctrine and growing in numbers. It is true that there were efforts on every hand to dilute the nature of Christianity, but apostolic leadership helped to maintain a strong internal unity.

The functioning New Testament church showed no signs of developing into an ecclesiastical hierarchy or spiritual despotism. It was a local autonomous body with two officers and two ordinances. The two officers were pastor (sometimes called bishop, presbyter or elder, minister, shepherd) and deacon. These leaders usually worked with their hands for their material needs. There was no artificial distinction between clergy and laity. The pastors had no more authority in offering salvation through Christ than

11

did any other member of their body. Their distinguishing marks were the gifts of leadership given them through the Spirit and their willingness to be used of God. In view of the later pretensions of the Roman pastor or bishop, it should be mentioned that each church was completely independent of external control. There is no indication anywhere in the literature of this period that the apostle Peter ever served as pastor in Rome; nor, for that matter, is there any basis for believing that the church at Rome was founded by any apostle. Doubtless it was organized by men converted at Pentecost.

The two ordinances were baptism and the Lord's Supper. These were simply symbolical memorials. Salvation or spiritual gifts did not come through either one. The transference of spiritual regeneration and spiritual merit to these ordinances is a development that comes through later corruptions. Worship was simple, consisting of the singing of hymns, praying, reading of Scriptures, and exhortations.

BIBLIOGRAPHY

ANGUS, SAMUEL. *The Environment of Early Christianity*. New York: Charles Scribner's Sons, 1920.

BETTENSON, HENRY (ed.). *Documents of the Christian Church*. New York: Oxford University Press, 1947.

BOUQUET, A. C. *Everyday Life in New Testament Times*. London: B. T. Batsford, Ltd., 1953.

GRANT, CHARLES M. *Between the Testaments*. New York: Fleming H. Revell Co., n.d.

HESTER, H. I. *The Heart of the New Testament*. Liberty, Missouri: William Jewell Publishers, 1950.

LATOURETTE, K. S. *A History of Christianity*. New York: Harper & Brothers, 1953.

NEWMAN, A. H. *A Manual of Church History*, I. Philadelphia: American Baptist Publication Society, 1953.

STEVENSON, J. (ed.). *A New Eusebius*. New York: The Macmillan Co., 1957.

II. PERIOD OF PAGAN DOMINATION
(A.D. 100–325)

Introduction to the Period

The story of Christianity between 100 and 325 reveals a period of extreme peril to the movement. Two dangers confronted it: (1) hostility and violence from the pagan government; (2) corruption and division within.

From the outside the principal danger came from the Roman Empire. After the close of the apostolic era (A.D. 100), Roman emperors viewed Christianity as an outlaw. It meant death to bear the name Christian. On two occasions during the period determined efforts were made to exterminate Christianity throughout the world. Relief came when Constantine espoused the Christian cause—perhaps from political motives—and fought his way to the place of sole emperor in 323. This period closes with the first world council of Christians at Nicea in 325, when Christianity began to develop in a new direction.

Within Christianity the danger of corruption and division grew out of its close relationship with Jewish and pagan movements. Christianity was influenced internally by its environment. Sometimes the reaction from fighting heresy was as harmful as the corruption.

This period is discussed in three chapters—one describing the struggle against outside forces, one describing the struggle against internal corruptions, and one summarizing the condition of Christianity in 325.

Points of Special Interest

Several matters should claim the student's attention and interest in the study of this period. He should notice the sort of response that was made by the Christians when they were persecuted—no military action like that of the Jews, no general compromise of principle to the pagan state, but the development of an effective literature to enlighten the persecutors, and the display of Christian fortitude and constant testimony. He should notice also the gradual infiltration of error, as displayed in the writings of the second century. No violent change can be dated, but the Christian vocabulary began to take on new meanings

13

and to be enlarged rapidly, marking radical changes from the New Testament pattern and innovations in all Christian areas. He should carefully weigh the influence of the various parties in the pagan environment of Christianity, noticing the transferring of ideas.

2

Pagan Opposition to Christianity

THE PRINCIPAL OPPONENTS of Christ in the New Testament were Jews. His followers during the next several centuries found their most formidable foes to be Romans. It may be noticed that the writings of Paul do not speak unfavorably of the Roman government. This does not mean that Rome was friendly to Christianity. It is doubtful that Rome at first even recognized that Christianity would develop into a movement separate from Judaism. The Jewish War of 66–70 accentuated the difference between the two, however, for the Christians refused to join in the Jewish insurrection. Christians were never in doubt about the fact that their worship of Christ was completely incompatible with the demands of the Roman government for all faithful citizens to worship the Roman emperor.

The death of Paul was occasioned more by the caprice of the Emperor Nero than any policy of persecuting Christians. Nero (54–68) had set fire to Rome. In order to shift blame from himself, he accused Christians of burning the city and brutally slaughtered them. The second pagan persecution, under Domitian (81–96), was not a universal movement against Christianity as such but was directed against anyone who would not worship the emperor, which, of course, included the Christians. The last book of the New Testament, written in the closing decade of the first century, names the Roman Empire with its emperor worship as the very opponent of God.

After the first century the opposition to Christianity took three general forms—popular antagonism, intellectual assaults, and physical persecution.

Popular Antagonism

Despite its remarkable growth, Christianity was not a popular movement in the second century. Its character, so altogether different from anything known by the people of the Roman Empire, made it an object of suspicion and hate. It offended the people religiously, ethically, and economically. The religious aspect of Christian unpopularity took strange forms. During the second century an unusual number of floods, earthquakes, and other natural catastrophes occurred. Immediately the populace cursed the Christians. The old gods are displeased with us and are punishing us, they said, because of this new religion. Either wilfully or ignorantly, the pagans twisted the vocabulary of the Christians to involve atheism (no idols), cannibalism (eating the Lord's body and drinking his blood), immorality (growing out of a sensual conception of the word "love"), and magic and sorcery (in the Supper and baptism).

The large gulf between the ethical ideas of the Christian and those of the pagans constantly exposed Christianity to the ire of the people. Christians refused to attend the immoral and brutal shows and contests, refused to murder their young children by abandoning them in a lonely place, refused to live by standards which magnified lust and material possessions.

The exclusiveness of Christianity caused it to become an offense economically. Christians refused to recognize any other gods. In so doing they struck at several well-established types of business in the communities where they lived. Those who manufactured pagan idols or raised animals for pagan sacrifices found that Christianity was hurting their business. Like Demetrius the silversmith (Acts 19:24), they opposed vehemently the movement that touched them at such a sensitive point.

Intellectual Assaults

The intellectual assaults on Christianity represent one of its severest struggles and greatest victories. Pagan writers, skilled in logical argumentation and trained in the best scholarship of

16

the revived classical era, leveled against Christianity every criticism that modern infidels and agnostics have used. With ridicule and sarcasm they scornfully attacked Christian beliefs about the person of Christ and his miracles and resurrection, the truth and authority of the Christian Scriptures, grace, regeneration, heaven and hell, and immortality. The principal names in the attack were Celsus and Porphyro, Greek philosophers of the second and third centuries respectively.

In a sense these literary attacks were disguised blessings to Christianity. They stirred up the Christians to produce literary monuments to second-century Christianity. Christians had already produced some literature. The edificatory writings of the second century will be discussed in the next chapter. The external attacks upon Christianity called forth a group of writings known as apologies; the internal struggle for purity resulted in writings known as polemics; while both the external and internal struggles helped to bring forth the systematic expositions of Christian beliefs. In this chapter the apologetical writings only will be discussed.

The Apologists.—The group of trained writers in the second and third centuries who endeavored to justify the doctrines of Christianity against the attacks of the pagan philosophers were called "apologists." In general, the apologists defended Christianity from charges of atheism, licentiousness, and cannibalism; they linked Christianity with the prophetic Scriptures of the Old Testament to show that the movement was no innovation but was very ancient and respectable.

The principal apologist of the second century was Justin. He was slain as a marytr in 166. Justin was a Samaritan philosopher who was converted to Christianity in his maturity. He retained his philosopher's garb and traveled as an evangelist to the educated class. His great *Apology* was addressed to Emperor Antoninus Pius and adopted son Marcus Aurelius and was prepared about 150. In its first section the *Apology* argues that Christians should not be condemned without a hearing, for they are innocent; they are not atheists, but true worshipers of the true God; they are not dangerous to the political safety of the Roman Empire,

17

but with a wonderful ethic constitute its strength, and their doctrine of the resurrection is most reasonable and glorious. In the second section Justin asserts that Christianity alone has full truth; that in Jesus Christ the Son of God actually became incarnate; and that paganism consists of fables invented by demons. The final section of the *Apology* describes the religious practices of Christianity.

In his imaginary *Dialogue with Trypho the Jew* Justin defends Christianity against Jewish attacks, especially attacks upon the person and work of Christ.

Other prominent apologists of the second century were Quadratus, of Athens, who addressed Emperor Hadrian; Aristides, who addressed the same emperor; Athenagoras, of Athens, who addressed Emperor Marcus Aurelius and the emperor's son Commodus; and Melito, of Sardis, and Apollinaris, of Hierapolis, who addressed Marcus Aurelius.

Although not generally considered apologists, Tertullian (160–220) prepared apologies against paganism and Judaism in behalf of Christianity, and Origen (185–254) wrote his apologetical work *Against Celsus,* probably the ablest production of early Christianity against paganism.

Other results of intellectual assaults.—There were other results from the intellectual assaults against Christianity. For one thing, Christianity became intellectually respectable in a world in which that was very important. Again, these assaults, together with the internal controversies described in the next chapter, helped to show the necessity for an authoritatively recognized canon or collection of inspired writings. For generations the churches had been testing the writings which now comprise the New Testament. Through the leadership of the Holy Spirit and in the crucible of Christian experience they had already indicated their conviction that these writings were inspired of God. It took many decades for the external ecclesiastical machinery to place its official stamp of approval upon the books so collected, but it would seem that this action constituted simply a formality anyway.

18

Physical Persecution

Jesus had warned his disciples that the world would treat them as it had treated him. If tradition can be trusted, most of the disciples experienced martyrdom. Unnumbered thousands of Christians were slain at the hands of the imperial soldiers during the second and third centuries. The popular hatred of Christianity can be understood in the light of religious, social, and economic tensions. The intellectual assaults on Christianity are understandable, since pagan philosophers attacked any system that differed from their own. But why, it may be asked, should the government of Rome engage in the destruction of its own citizens simply because they were Christians?

The answer is found in the Roman conception of religion. As suggested in the first chapter, Romans practiced religion mainly for political reasons. The religious department was one of the branches of government. Through it attempts were made to appease known and unknown gods and to foretell the future. Christian ideas of morality and personal immortality had no counterpart in the Roman view of religion. Gods were numerous, the Roman state itself claiming deity in the person of the emperor. Conquered nations were required to worship Roman gods, including the emperor. At the same time Rome "legalized" any local gods in these nations so long as the local worship did not interfere with loyalty to the Roman state.

The Jews had been excepted from this general rule because of their spirited refusal to worship any god but Jehovah and because of respect for their great antiquity. When, therefore, Christianity separated itself from Judaism and refused to worship Roman deities, it was officially entitled "an illegal religion." As such, the laws of the Roman Empire demanded prosecution, even though the action seemed to the Christians to be persecution. When the Christians, fearing violence, met secretly for worship, they were accused of the worst crime a Roman could imagine— plotting the overthrow of the government.

Before the close of the apostolic period the Roman government

19

had moved against the Christians. The caprice of Nero brought the persecution in 67–68, which included Paul among its victims. The persecution by Domitian in the last decade of the first century did not constitute a general policy against Christianity but was an attempt to make them conform to the ancient laws. After the close of the apostolic period two types of physical persecution may be identified.

Local and intermittent persecution.—The period from 96 to 180 was one of outward prosperity in the Roman Empire. The five "good" emperors (Nerva, Trajan, Hadrian, Antoninus Pius, and Marcus Aurelius) were comparatively diligent in government and had considerable success in meeting contemporary problems within and without the empire. During the reign of Emperor Trajan (98–117) the imperial pattern for the persecution of Christianity was developed. In 112 Pliny, the Roman governor in the Asia Minor province of Bithynia-Pontus, wrote Trajan a description of how he was handling the superstition known as Christianity. By the use of torture he had learned that the movement was rather harmless, involving mainly the worship of Jesus Christ as God and a resolution to live nobly. Pliny's method had been to demand that Christians deny Christ and leave the sect. Should they refuse after three such requests, they were executed because of their "obstinacy." If they should agree, they were released without further punishment. Trajan's reply commended Pliny's conduct, suggesting that no effort be made to search out the Christians but that if responsible men brought charges, the death penalty should be pronounced upon those who refused to deny the Christian faith. This comparatively lenient pattern was followed in the empire generally for over a century.

The kind of persecution that could have been leveled against Christianity may be glimpsed in the imperial persecution of the Jews. By specific law the Jews were forbidden to practice their religion, including such vital features as the observance of the sabbath and circumcision. As a direct blow at the Jews, the site of Jerusalem was to be made into a Roman city with pagan temples. Enraged beyond reason, the Jews proclaimed a messiah about 132

20

in the person of Bar Cochba (Son of the Star), and making the destroyed city of Jerusalem their rallying point, they attempted to throw off the Roman yoke. It took the Romans three years to crush the movement, during which about half a million Jews were slaughtered.

So far as the Christians were concerned, however, the policy of the Emperor Trajan was continued under Hadrian (117–38), Antoninus Pius (138–61), and Marcus Aurelius (161–80). Under each of these emperors Christians were slain, in particular under Marcus Aurelius, but there was not yet a worldwide effort to exterminate the Christian movement as such.

Universal attempt at extermination.—Political conditions played a large part in the two efforts by the Roman government to destroy Christianity. The severest persecutions ever directed against the Christians grew out of attempts to restore the ancient glory of the Roman Empire. The "golden age" of the empire was experienced under Augustus (31 B.C.–A.D. 14). Various relatives succeeded him in the office but could not match his accomplishments, and this method of securing an emperor was discontinued with the death of Nero in 68. Vespasian seized the throne as the strongest military commander in 69, and his two sons ruled after him until 96. The Roman senator Nerva was elected by his fellow senators and introduced a new method of imperial succession, not of blood or election but personal selection. Each of the five emperors following Nerva selected his own successor. Following the death of Commodus in 192, the Roman armies named his successor and continued to name the emperors for about a century.

Although all of the reasons for the striking decline of the Roman Empire after the death of Marcus Aurelius (161–80) are not clear, one very important contributing factor was the breakdown at the top—the weakness of imperial leadership. Almost all of the "barracks emperors" secured the throne by violence and were themselves the victims of violence. Internal decay and external aggressors combined to tear away the foundations of the empire.

Christianity entered into this picture because it was conceived as an innovation that in some way had contributed to the general decline of the glory of Rome. Religious pagans attributed all of their ills—natural calamities, heavy taxation, invading barbarians —to the anger of the pagan gods because Christianity was allowed to continue. Some political thinkers, influenced by these attitudes, wondered if the extermination of Christianity would help restore the glory of Rome that had existed before the Christian movement began. These ideas were discussed widely in 248 when the Roman Empire celebrated the one-thousandth anniversary of the founding of the city of Rome. The new emperor, Decius (249–51), decided to attempt a revival of the empire's ancient glory and, among other things, determined to destroy Christianity and restore the worship of the spirit of the Roman state. In 250 an edict was prepared requiring every Christian to deny the faith or be subject to extreme penalties, including death. His successor Valerian (253–60) continued the effort. Many Christians were slain, many were tortured, many compromised. The continued decline of the empire, despite the effort to exterminate Christianity, contributed to the cessation of active persecution after the death of Valerian.

A similar persecuting effort was made under Emperor Diocletian (284–305). Desiring to stop the evident decay of the Roman state and conceiving that a restoration of the ancient state worship would bring unity and political strength, Diocletian issued a series of edicts, beginning in 305, which ordered Christian churches destroyed, all bishops and presbyters imprisoned, and all Christians to choose between denying Christ or suffering death. Again the fires of persecution took the lives of many Christians and forced others to compromise.

Results of physical persecution.—In general, the periods of persecution greatly affected the nature of Christianity. Abnormalities developed which are common to repressed minorities or underground movements. On the one hand, the situation caused many to center their religious devotion in relics of former martyrs and to magnify the magical efficacy of the vehicles of worship; on the other hand, some became fanatical in their desire for martyrdom and ascetic sufferings. A serious problem arose after each

persecution concerning what to do with those who had denied
Christ or had in some other way compromised with the Roman
power. Furthermore, the person of the bishop acquired an unusual prestige and sanctity during this experience. The bishops
had become to the Roman state the symbol of the Christian
movement and were sought out for special persecution. The many
courageous bishops who died for the faith enhanced the office of
bishop as a rallying point for Christian faithfulness.

The Decline of Imperial Opposition

Political factors finally brought an end to the long struggle of
Christianity against the Roman state. Emperor Diocletian determined to set up a system of imperial succession that would insure
capable leadership for the empire and at the same time prevent
revolution from occurring whenever the emperor's throne became
vacant. Consequently, he appointed Maximianus as co-emperor
and, in addition, appointed two subordinate rulers with the title
"caesar"—Constantine Chlorus in the West and Galerius in the
East. His theory proposed that whenever an emperor died, the
co-emperor would immediately become the sovereign, thus preventing an effort to seize the office by violence. One of the subordinate caesars would then theoretically be elevated to the co-
emperor's place and a new caesar would be appointed. The system
appeared to be foolproof. However, in 305, when Diocletian
retired, the various armies nominated their caesars to be not only
co-emperors but sole emperor. Military considerations again determined who should rule as emperor.

The rise of Constantine.—The soldier who finally conquered
all his rivals and became also the sole ruler of the empire was
Constantine, son of Caesar Constantine Chlorus in the West. Constantine's mother had been a Christian and his father had looked
tolerantly upon Christians, refusing to enforce the edict of Diocletian for their persecution. Copying his father's attitude, Constantine, upon succeeding his father as ruler in the West, gladly
united with the eastern rulers Galerius and Licinius in an edict
in 311 which provided limited toleration for Christians. In the

following year Constantine fought a crucial battle with Maxentius and claimed that he had seen a vision in the heavens which caused him to adopt Christianity and win the victory. In 313 Constantine and the eastern Emperor Licinius issued the Edict of Milan, granting full toleration to Christianity. In 323 Constantine defeated Licinius in battle and became the sole ruler.

Constantine and Christianity.—Constantine's adoption of Christianity was more of a political than a religious decision. The Roman Empire was fast declining. Its greatest need was a strong, internal unity that could both engender loyalty within and beat off attacks from without. Constantine proposed to attain this unity by making Christianity the cement of the empire. This would supply a double bond for the citizenry—political loyalty supplemented and strengthened by religious unity. At the same time Constantine did not divorce himself from religious support of the pagan devotees; he retained the title of chief priest of their system and became one of their deities after his death in 337. It is hardly conceivable that Constantine really became a Christian. His considerable crimes, including murder, long after his alleged vision, could hardly be the acts of a Christian. Thinking that baptism washed away sins, he delayed receiving this rite until he was at the point of death.

He did shower favors upon Christianity. Almost without help he secured the cessation of persecution. He destroyed pagan temples and filled official positions with Christians. Christians were exempted from military service, their churches were allowed to hold property without taxation, their day of worship was made a civil holiday, and their growth was encouraged. In 325 Constantine issued a general exhortation to his subjects to become Christians.

The effect of Constantine's adoption of Christianity upon the movement itself has been widely debated. It led directly to the official declaration that Christianity was the state religion at the time of Emperor Theodosius (378–95). Constantine was not responsible for all of the corruptions of Christianity from the New Testament pattern, for these had developed long before his day.

24

He did, however, introduce many new elements of corruption and greatly contributed to the rise of the Roman Catholic Church. It is impossible to know how Christianity would have developed had it not been adopted by the imperial authority, but doubtless it would have escaped many of the most hurtful evils which now beset it.

Concluding Summary

The Christian movement developed during its most crucial period in the midst of an unfriendly environment. The literary attacks upon Christianity during the period were not an unmixed evil, for they made it clear to Christian leaders that an authoritative canon and a definition of beliefs were necessary. Physical persecution by the Roman Empire was local and intermittent until the middle of the third century when two worldwide efforts were made to exterminate Christianity. The opening years of the fourth century witnessed the rise of Constantine, a friendly emperor, who turned the Christian movement in a new direction by providing secular support.

The Struggle for Purity

AT THE SAME time that Christianity was meeting its severest test from the outside it was also struggling to retain its original purity of doctrine and practice. Of the two battles the second was more important; yet, while the first was won, the second, though not entirely lost, inflicted great and terrible wounds upon Christianity.

Early Purity

The earliest Christian writings outside of the New Testament are of interest because they reveal the internal condition of Christianity and indicate the direction of thinking. Six early writings (apart from several fragments) have been preserved. (1) A letter written about A.D. 96 by Clement, pastor at Rome, in reply to one addressed to him by the church at Corinth, is probably typical of a great many such letters written by the various influential bishops over the empire. It appears that the Corinthian church had deposed some presbyters who had been appointed by the apostles. Clement urges the church to return these men to office and comments at length upon the evils of jealousy and faction. (2) A letter entitled the "Epistle of Barnabas" (but probably not written by Barnabas, the fellow laborer of Paul) has been preserved. Its main emphasis is upon the superiority of Christianity over Judaism. This writing may be dated between 70 and 135. (3) A great deal of controversy has arisen over the epistles of Ignatius. Scholars disagree about how many epistles Ignatius wrote, about the genuineness of many references within the epistles, and about the correct text of the letters. Some assign twelve epistles to him, some seven, and some follow a Syriac version which allows only three epistles. If authentic, these letters would appear to have been written about 115 after Ignatius had been condemned to death by the Emperor Trajan. These letters contain many exhortations to the churches to be faithful to the bishops, presbyters, and deacons whom God had given them. The letter to the church at Rome, in particular, constantly reiterates the desire of Ignatius to be devoured by the wild animals in the arena as a martyr for Christ. (4) A religious allegory called the *Shepherd of Hermas,* written about 140, was quite influential in the second century. It is made up of five visions, twelve commands, and ten similitudes, endeavoring to promote purity and faithfulness. (5) The Epistle of Polycarp dates from about 116. Polycarp was pastor at Smyrna; he was quite important in that he was an intimate disciple of the apostle John and the teacher of Irenaeus, a prominent writer of the second century. Polycarp's epistle consists mainly of scriptural quotations designed to inculcate purity in doctrine and steadfastness in service. (6) The *Didache* or *Teaching of the Twelve Apostles* was not discovered until 1883, but many have accepted it as being a genuine writing of the first or second century. It seems to have been a manual prepared by a Jewish Christian for use in a Jewish Christian community. The most controversial section is its seventh chapter, which describes baptism as trine immersion but allows pouring if there is not sufficient water to immerse.

These early Christian writings reflect a healthy and pure Christianity. The strong emphasis upon obedience to the church officers in Ignatius (if these are actually the letters of Ignatius in 115 and do not contain interpolations by a later hand) shows a tendency that later became an actual corruption of the New Testament pattern. Other later writings than those ascribed to Ignatius, however, show no evidence of that tendency. In the main, these writings show the extensive use of the Scriptures as authoritative, give a great deal of good advice, and aim at producing purity of life and faithfulness in service.

Later in the second and in the third century Christianity was faced with several internal struggles, which may be outlined under four heads, as follows: the struggle against diluting Christianity; the struggle against inadequate views of Christ and the Trinity; the struggle against pagan corruptions; and the struggle against lowering Christian standards.

The Struggle Against Diluting Christianity

Christianity would have been destroyed had it, like the Roman religious system, incorporated other religions within it. There were several efforts to alter the character of Christianity by attempting to add other religious systems in part or in whole.

Attempt to dilute with legalism.—The first of these efforts attempted to combine Judaism with Christianity. Such a move began during the life of Jesus Christ, and he emphasized the impossibility of putting new wine into old wineskins. The Judaizers who hounded Paul endeavored to mingle the legalism of the Jews with the spiritual Christian movement. How does a person become a Christian? The Judaizer would answer that he must first become a Jew, meeting certain legal requirements, then move on out into the realm of what Jesus had added to Judaism. This perversion, which Paul answered in the book of Galatians, was the occasion of the first church council in Jerusalem in the year 50. At this council Paul boldly asserted that a person need not become a Jew before becoming a Christian and produced Titus, one of his converts, as proof. The council agreed that Paul was correct, and a decree to that effect was prepared by James, who presided at the council. The Judaizers paid no attention to the council. A number of parties sprang up, taking such names as Ebionites, Nazarenes, and Elkesaites. They insisted upon regarding Christ as simply a Jewish prophet and Christianity as an extension of Judaism. Because Judaism had been badly scattered in the destruction of Jerusalem (70) and in the Jewish War (132–35), and because Gentiles soon dominated Christianity, these various Jewish-Christian sects died out within the first few centuries. The influence of their legalistic thinking, involving the merit of obedience and works, has not yet died out.

28

Attempt to dilute with philosophy.—A second effort to dilute Christianity had its source in Jewish speculation, although it was adopted by Gentile philosophers and in its developed state actually became anti-Jewish in its teachings. This movement took the name Gnosticism, which means knowledge, because its followers claimed to have a special knowledge about God and the world which the remainder of mankind did not possess. Its roots may be found in Jewish writings like those of Philo of Alexandria (20 B.C. to A.D. 40). As a fully developed system by Gentile philosophers, Gnosticism laid stress on the nature of evil, the nature of God and his relation to the world, and on the meaning of the present order of existence. The definition of the nature of evil forms a central idea in Gnosticism. An effort was made to isolate evil by affirming that it resided in matter or material things. If a thing had mass, it was evil; goodness was found in spirit. Thus it followed that a chair is evil, a house is evil, the physical world is evil, the physical body of man is evil.

Some far-reaching inferences, decidedly anti-Jewish in nature, followed this definition of evil. If the physical world was evil and the Jewish Old Testament taught that in the beginning God had created this physical world, then the nature of God was compromised, for how could a perfect God create an evil world? In reply the Gnostics took the position that the Jehovah of the Old Testament was not the true God but was a lower creation of the true God.

At this point the many Gnostic systems offered various explanations of the creation. Most of them taught that evil broke into the completely spiritual existence before the creation of the world, growing out of envy and spiritual pride and resulting in the imprisonment of men's pure souls in evil bodies. The good God, they continued, was too holy to create an evil world, but in order to provide a place for human habitation, this good God formed a divine being a little less holy than himself, this process continuing until finally, after a series of descending gods or aeons, the Jehovah of the Old Testament was created. He was so much less holy at this stage that he found no difficulty in creating

29

an evil world. In this way the Gnostics magnified the complete holiness of God and yet accounted for the creation of an evil world by the ultimate authority of the true God.

Applied to Christianity, this system affirmed that Christ was the highest of the aeons—the divine being which the true God himself had created. Christ did not have a real body in the incarnation, they said, since he was too holy to be attached to an evil substance; rather, Christ was just a spirit who appeared to be in human form. The Gnostics twisted the idea of Christian redemption in accordance with their peculiar idea of sin as residing in all material substances. Salvation, they said, consisted of freeing the spirit from the evil body in which it resided. Christ's redemptive work was to come from the true world of spirit into a material, and thus evil, world in order to teach men this true knowledge. Of course, Gnosticism denied the fundamental Christian doctrines of an actual incarnation, an actual physical ministry, and an actual death on the cross. Any idea of the resurrection of the body was in their thinking ridiculous, since every material body was completely sinful. This conception of the sinfulness of the body resulted in a twofold attitude toward morality. Some Gnostics said that since the body was sinful anyway and would be cast away at the time of death, it was not wrong to live in a most licentious way; the soul would remain pure in the midst of any physical debaucheries. Others said that since the body was sinful, it should be starved, neglected, and mistreated. Thus licentiousness and asceticism branched out from the same tree.

Evidences of the struggle by Christianity to keep this philosophical system from swallowing up the Christian message are found in the New Testament itself. Tradition has it that John the apostle had this group in mind when writing his Gospel and first epistle. His Gospel graphically describes the actual physical ministry of Jesus, particularly emphasizing the story of the cross. His epistle speaks of Christ as the One whom the disciples had "seen with our eyes, which we have looked upon, and our hands have handled" (1 John 1:1), and he identifies the Spirit of God as the one that "confesseth that Jesus Christ is come in the flesh"

(4:2). The book of Colossians combats the doctrines of the Gnostics, and the Nicolaitanes condemned in Revelation were probably Gnostics (2:6, 15).

During the several centuries after the apostolic era Christian writers fought savagely against this system which would deny the true deity as well as the true humanity of Christ. The principal writers against it were Irenaeus (about 130–202) and Tertullian (160–220). Irenaeus had been a disciple of Polycarp in Asia Minor, who in turn had sat at the feet of the apostle John. Perhaps some of the fire which burned against the Gnostics in the heart of Irenaeus had been kindled secondhand by John. Irenaeus moved from Asia Minor to France and in 177 became the bishop at Lyons. In 185, out of wide experience and painstaking scholarship, he wrote his principal work entitled *Five Books Against Heresies,* directed almost wholly against the Gnostics. His refutation of the Gnostic system was thorough and effective. Tertullian was a hot-blooded Roman lawyer in North Africa before his conversion to Christianity about 180. He became a Montanist about 200. His writings are pungent and thought provoking. He attacked practically every opponent of Christianity—the pagans for their idolatry, persecution, and bloodshed; the heretics for holding inadequate views of the Trinity; the Jews for not coming to Christ; and the Gnostic systems described above.

The influence of Gnosticism upon Christianity was tremendous. On the surface the very fact that Christians answered the attacks of Gnosticism provided a valuable source of literature which mirrored the condition of Christianity in the second and third centuries. Beyond this literary interest, Gnosticism required that Christianity define itself. If, said the Gnostics in effect, Christianity is not what *we* say it is, then what is it? Thus it became necessary for Christianity to define its essential elements. This was done in several ways.

In the first place, under the leadership of the Holy Spirit the various churches gathered together the writings of the apostles and primitive Christians and formed the canon (rule), or the inspired writings. These writings had been tested in the crucible

31

of daily living. It is true that a council of churches did not recognize this collection officially until some time later, but from the writings of the various Christian leaders it is apparent that Christians of this period recognized as inspired the books that are now included in the New Testament.

In the second place, Christians began preparing short statements of faith which could be memorized easily. One of the earliest creeds or statements of faith dates back to about the second century, and it reads as follows:

I believe in God the Almighty Father,
And in Christ Jesus his Son,
Who was born of the virgin Mary,
Crucified under Pontius Pilate and buried,
Who arose from the dead on the third day,
Ascended into the heavens,
Sits at the right hand of the Father,
From whence he shall come to judge
   living and dead,
And I believe in the Holy Spirit,
   [and] the resurrection of the flesh.

It may be observed that this statement is a direct answer to the claims of the Gnostics, in that it emphasizes the actual earthly body of Christ, his crucifixion, and the resurrection of the body of the Christians—all of which were completely antagonistic to Gnostic doctrine.

In the third place, Christians began formulating the entire Christian teaching into systematic form as a means of answering Gnostic thinkers and began establishing Christian schools for teaching Christian doctrine. Clement of Alexandria (born about 160) was one of the first systematizers of Christian doctrine. He was trained in a Christian school formed by Pantaenus at Alexandria and succeeded his teacher as head of the school when Pantaenus was forced to flee from persecution in 190. Clement's principal writings illustrate the importance of this type of literature. He prepared an elementary book of Christian instruction for children or new converts; on a higher level he addressed an eloquent work to the Greeks in an effort to win them to the gospel; and, finally, he prepared some speculative discussions of the profound truths of Christianity as a challenge for philosophers to accept the Christian faith.

The other important systematizer of Christian doctrine was Origen (about 185–254), who succeeded Clement as head of the Alexandrian school. Origen gathered texts of the Scriptures in various languages, wrote commentaries on almost the whole Bible, fought literary battles with paganism, set forth devotional and practical exhortations on many aspects of Christian life, and prepared the first systematic theology. His work abounds in speculation, some of which is quite unsound. In particular he went astray in teaching the eternity of matter, in advocating a sort of human pre-existence of each individual soul, in supposing that everyone (including rebellious men and the devils themselves) would finally be restored to divine favor, and in holding several Gnostic ideas concerning man and creation. Origen's two disciples, Gregory Thaumaturgus and Dionysius of Alexandria, did much to popularize Origen's theology.

In addition to causing Christianity to define itself, the Gnostic movement set in motion ideas and methods of argument that greatly influenced Christianity. Philosophy and religion were wed. Intermediary beings between God and man were suggested. The authority of the Gnostic came, they said, from a secret knowledge, not written but brought down from primitive times by tradition. In answering this allegation, Irenaeus replied that true Christianity also had a tradition given by the Lord through the apostles and preserved by many churches which could trace their history back to apostolic days. Thus the Gnostic movement led to a veneration of tradition and antiquity; succession, more than conformity to the revealed Word of God, became the ultimate proof of authority and orthodoxy.

Finally, the Gnostic movement, along with other heresies, so emphasized the worthlessness of the material body that it paved the way for asceticism and monasticism. Asceticism refers to the view that the soul may be purified and merit gained by punishing

33

the body through neglect, isolation, or some positive discomfort. Monasticism, in effect, organized ascetical tendencies so that the individual might cut himself off from all social intercourse with the outside world and systematically discipline his body for the benefit of his soul. This movement will be discussed in a succeeding chapter.

Attempt to dilute with other religions.—The third effort to dilute Christianity is known as Manichaeanism. Christianity had been preached in Persia quite early in the Christian era. In the middle of the third century a Mesopotamian known as Mani felt the influence of the many religious movements about him, and from them he compounded a composite religion which took his name. It included elements from the older pagan religions of Persia, from Judaism, and from Christianity. The vocabulary of Christianity and a few of its teachings were incorporated into the movement. Many of the Gnostic interpretations of Christianity were adopted. This religion did not have a great deal of influence upon orthodox Christianity as a whole.

The Struggle Against Inadequate Views of Christ and the Trinity

The question of Jesus to the disciples at Caesarea Philippi, "Who do men say that I the Son of man am?" was not answered in such a way as to preclude a similar question during the succeeding several centuries. The shibboleth of Judaism for over a millennium had been their Shema, "Hear, O Israel, the Lord thy God is one God." The New Testament describes Christ as God and the Holy Spirit as God. Second-century Christianity pondered a good deal over the question of how the incarnate Christ could be God without affecting the oneness of God. Five principal views that attempted to answer this question may be briefly summed up.

One view solved the problem by denying the eternal sonship of Christ. This group was known as the *alogoi* (which means literally "not the Word"—referring to John 1:1). As their name suggests, they denied that Christ was the Word, the expression of God, insisting that there was no Trinity since God was one. Christ, they said, was a great teacher, but not divine.

34

A second view asserted that Christ was born simply as a man but that God adopted him. The principal tenet accounts for the name "adoptionism" given to this theory. Although agreeing in the idea that Jesus was adopted of God in a special way, the followers of this view differed at various points from one another. A popular viewpoint asserted that Jesus was adopted at his baptism when the dove descended from heaven and God's voice announced, "This is my beloved Son, in whom I am well pleased." At this time divine power descended upon Jesus—for that reason the view is sometimes referred to as "dynamism," meaning "empowered"—and remained with him as a teacher and healer until the experience of the cross. His cry, "Why hast thou forsaken me?" was interpreted as indicating that at this time the divine power had departed from him. After all, it was argued, God could not die on a cross, so whatever deity Jesus received at his baptism was taken from him at the cross before his death. In this sense, then, Christ became the adopted Son of God only for a brief season of earthly ministry, and no doctrine of the Trinity was necessary.

A third view said that Christ was divine but subordinate to the Father. Such a view would eliminate the necessity for a doctrine of the Trinity, for while Christ was divine, he was less than God the Father and thus could not be one with the Father in essence.

One group advanced the idea that Christ was just another name for God. This school of thought argued that when Christ was born into the world in the incarnation experience, it was God the Father being born; there was no Father left in heaven. When Christ ascended again into heaven, he became God the Father. And when the Holy Spirit was given in power at Pentecost, heaven was emptied again. In other words, this view said that the Son and the Holy Spirit were simply God the Father in another mode or function; from this idea the movement was known as "modalism."

Many followed the orthodox view that Christ is of one essence with God and that the identification of the three persons in the

Godhead in no sense affected the basic monotheism of the Old Testament.

These several views relative to Christ and his relation to the Trinity were gathered up in the Arian controversy which will be discussed later.

The Struggle Against Pagan Corruptions

The principal converts to Christianity after the first century were Gentiles or pagans, most of whom were won to Christianity from other religious backgrounds. It is not surprising then that many of the corrupting ideas of these contemporary religious systems were reproduced to some extent in the Christian movement. Several of these pagan tendencies are as follows:

Fetishism.—All forms of paganism magnified the vast importance of religious externals, things and acts. The early Christians were scornfully referred to as atheists because they had no material evidences of their religious zeal. Such externalities began to be added to Christianity in the second and third centuries. Bones of saints began to possess a sanctity; religious possessions and the sign of the cross began to give outward evidence of piety. True religion began to be judged by participation in religious acts and possession of sacred relics.

Sacramentalism.—Closely akin to this development was a new attitude toward the ordinances. The two symbolical ordinances of the New Testament were baptism and the Lord's Supper. These were given the name "sacrament" (from the Latin military oath of loyalty), which carried with it the idea that the physical elements themselves were judged to possess salvation and spiritual grace. The water of baptism began to have a saving efficacy. According to Justin Martyr (about 165), baptism completes salvation; Irenaeus (about 185) boldly asserted that baptism is the new birth and brings regeneration. In Irenaeus' writings is the first hint that perhaps infants were now subjects of baptism, which would confirm the conception that water baptism without reference to repentance brings redemption. The bread and wine of the Lord's Supper were called the "medicine of immortality" by

36

Ignatius (about 115)—perhaps in symbolical language, but by the time of Irenaeus the assertion is flatly made that after the bread has been consecrated it is no longer common bread. In some sense it has been given a new character that enables it to convey spiritual grace to men.

Sacerdotalism.—This word means "priestism." Not only the Jewish system but all of the ancient pagan cults required priests and ritual as a part of their religious worship. The introduction of pagan ideas of external magical efficacy into the rites of baptism and the Supper demanded that such "magic" must be preserved by securing men who were trained and qualified to administer them. The view became current that only the bishop or those trained and authorized by him could effectively call forth the grace resident in these rites. Thus salvation became identified with the rites of baptism and the Supper, and these were effective only under the supervision of the bishop.

A female deity.—Every pagan religion in the ancient world had its female deity. Even Gnosticism posited a female counterpart to their deity. Converts from these systems quickly magnified the place of the virgin Mary until she became an object of adoration and worship.

Professionalism.—Jesus said that the kings of Gentiles exercise lordship over them, but that among Christians service and humility were to characterize the leaders. This Scripture was forgotten as bishops began to seek lordship and authority in the ecclesiastical sphere. Copying from practically every pagan religion, the Christian leaders began to make a distinction between the sacred character of the inner group who dispensed religion and the rest of the mortals. The very names adopted in Christianity show the official attitude of superiority, for clergy means "those who have been called of God," while laity means "the people."

The Struggle Against Lowering Christian Standards

There were three movements during the first several centuries which, although separate and distinct, yet overlapped and to some extent included one another. All of them accepted the contemporary corruption that viewed baptism as a saving ordinance, but all protested against allowing the unworthy—whether these had denied Christ in the persecution or had surrendered sacred Scripture to be destroyed—to receive or administer the benefits of a saving church and saving sacraments.

Montanism.—The first of these was known as Montanism. Between 135 and 160 Montanus, apparently a recent convert from the heathen priesthood, suddenly began to upbraid the Christians in Asia Minor where he lived, charging them with accepting Gnostic ideas, with following human leadership instead of the Holy Spirit in church life and organization, and with becoming criminally lax in Christian discipline. With two female helpers, Priscilla and Maximilla, he denounced the bishops in his area for their unspirituality and asserted that they were not qualified for office since they lacked the proper gifts of the Holy Spirit. Montanus magnified two distinctive doctrines. The first was an emphasis upon the Holy Spirit. At times the preaching of Montanus suggests that he himself was the Holy Spirit promised by Christ. He claimed an immediate inspiration for himself and his assistants so that their words were authoritative, even beyond the written Scriptures.

An emphasis upon Christian discipline was the second of the doctrines. Montanus predicted that Christ was coming shortly to begin the millennial reign in the little Phrygian village where Montanus was preaching. Because this was true, Christians ought to be completely separate from the world and ready for Christ's kingdom. He drew up a list distinguishing between mortal sins (which bring condemnation) and venial sins (which are forgivable). The clergy, in particular, must follow a stricter ethic than the ordinary Christian. At a time when Christians were being persecuted to the death, Montanus warned that if a Christian fled from suffering or denied the faith, it would bring total and final condemnation. Physical suffering and similar hardships for Christ purified and strengthened the spirit. Such a rigid screening of worldliness, punctuated by the example of Montanus, had great influence in forwarding the monastic movement a little later. The outstanding convert of Montanus was Tertullian, the great writer of North Africa, about 200. Tertullian did not accept all of the doctrines of Montanus but saw the inroads of worldliness and laxity on the Christian movement as most perilous.

Novatianism.—In many respects Novatianism was the reappearance of Montanism. When Emperor Decius (249–51) attempted to root out all Christianity from the world, there were two ideas about the treatment of those who had fled from persecution, surrendered sacred Scriptures, or denied the faith. One party allowed these people to return into the bosom of the saving church after certain conditions had been met; the other party said that these should never be allowed to return. Since it was conceived that salvation outside of the church was impossible, this question was of more than academic importance. In 251 Cornelius, the leader of the lenient party, was chosen bishop at Rome after considerable controversy; whereupon, Novatian, leader of the strict party, withdrew from fellowship with the lenient party on the ground that they were no longer the true church. He was elected bishop by his followers. Churches following his leadership sprang up in various parts of the empire, particularly in North Africa and Asia Minor. Many Montanists saw in this movement the revival of their own ideas and flocked to Novatian. There are evidences that this movement persisted until almost the fifth century.

Donatism.—The severe persecution by Diocletian brought the same problem to the fore in the opening years of the fourth century. During the crisis Bishop Mensurius of Carthage and his deacon Caecilian made themselves quite unpopular by attempting to discourage overzealous Christians from seeking martyrdom. After the death of Mensurius in 311, Caecilian was ordained bishop of Carthage by Bishop Felix of Aptunga, who was accused by the strict party of having surrendered Christian Scriptures during the persecution. The strict party objected to this ordination on the ground that Felix was a heretic and asserted that a heretic's ordination did not transmit power to perform saving baptism or other episcopal act. In 312 a council of about seventy bishops of the strict party assembled at Carthage and elected Majorinus bishop, causing a schism quite similar to that of Novatian. The name of this controversy was that of Donatus, who was ordained bishop of the strict party after the death of Majorinus in 313. The doctrinal position of both sides was about the same, save that the strict party insisted that when a bishop is personally unworthy (having denied the faith under persecution or surrendered Christian Scriptures) or has been consecrated by an unworthy bishop, any ecclesiastical acts of that bishop are invalid. In other words, he is unable to administer saving baptism. The Donatists, on the other hand, claimed that they represented the true line of episcopal succession and thus were qualified to administer such saving baptism and perform other episcopal rites.

The Donatists attempted to consolidate their position by requesting an ecclesiastical hearing before disinterested bishops. In 313 before six bishops (including the bishop of Rome) the case was heard, but the decision favored Caecilian. The next year the Donatists appealed the case to a council, but again the decision favored Caecilian. The Donatists then appealed to the Roman emperor who had become sole ruler in the West. Constantine, however, in 316 decided against them and threatened them with banishment if they did not cease this schism. Only after the Donatists had appealed to the secular power and been spurned did they finally come to the position that there ought to be no civil interference with religion. This movement gathered strength and continued until about the fifth century.

Concluding Summary

During the period from 100 to 325, the Christian movement faced various internal forces that threatened to move it away from the New Testament pattern. Some of these internal problems were caused by the external forces of persecutions and corruptions. Christianity was affected in some instances by the very machinery it set up to deal with these problems. The next chapter will discuss some of the changes in character that came to Christianity because of the struggle against external and internal forces.

4

The Close of an Era

THE SECOND PERIOD of church history (A.D. 100–325) closes
with the meeting of the first universal council. The occasion for
this council was a doctrinal struggle over the person of Christ.
That story will be told in the next chapter since it inaugurates a
new direction on the part of Christianity—the beginnings of the
Roman Catholic Church. The close of this very crucial period of-
fers an opportunity to examine Christianity in 325 and to compare it with the kind of Christianity taught in the New Testament.

New Testament Christianity taught that salvation came through
simple faith in Jesus Christ. Nothing is required for salvation,
declared Paul, but the regenerating work of the Holy Spirit that
comes when one confesses Jesus as Lord and acknowledges Jesus'
resurrection from the dead. Saving faith is an immediate experience with Christ, and all men are capable of coming directly to
Christ. No external institution, good work, human priest, or religious rite is required to qualify a man for coming to Christ and
receiving the free gift of salvation. New Testament Christianity
also taught that a New Testament church is a body of persons
who have been born again, baptized, and possess the Spirit of
Christ. The officers of the local body were two—pastors and deacons. The pastor has various names in the New Testament; he is
called the bishop, the shepherd, the presbyter or elder, and the
minister. The ordinances were two—baptism and the Lord's Supper. All churches were on the same level, and each one possessed
authority to govern its own affairs without outside interference.

By the close of this period (325) it is difficult to look at the general state of Christianity and recognize a picture such as the one

drawn from the New Testament. No longer were the people the church; now the pastor or bishop, given a new office, is viewed as constituting the church. The word "church" had come to mean not a local body or a local institution, but the totality of bishops. Salvation was viewed as coming through the bishop as the custodian of the saving sacraments of the church. He alone is qualified, it was believed, to administer or authorize saving baptism and to serve the "medicine of immortality," the Lord's Supper. No longer were all churches and pastors equal under God and before men. Territorial divisions had been marked off to show the boundaries of the authority of various strong bishops.

By 325, then, the very nature of Christianity had been corrupted. Changes had come in several overlapping areas.

Change in the Nature of Faith

By 325 faith had lost its personal character as being the whole dependence of a person immediately upon the person and work of Jesus Christ. Rather, while Christ was a part of the system, faith was to be directed toward the institution called the Church; and salvation did not result from the immediate regenerating power of the Holy Spirit but was mediated by the sacraments of baptism and the Lord's Supper. Since the sacraments were under control of the Church and since salvation came through them only, it followed that a person must join the Church in order to be saved. That is exactly what Bishop Cyprian meant in 250 when he said that no man can have God for his Father who does not have the Church for his mother. No wonder those who denied the faith in the time of persecution were so extremely anxious to be forgiven by the Church, for they believed that salvation outside of this institution was impossible.

During this period personal faith was eliminated entirely in some instances. In the writings of Irenaeus (about 200) there is a hint that perhaps in his generation infants were baptized in order to save them. Under these circumstances individual faith becomes unnecessary. With someone to act as proxy for the infant in order to make pretense of faith, the "saving water of baptism" was applied. Furthermore, there is evidence that the first instance of pouring for baptism took place about this time. Novatian, leader of the strict ecclesiastical party at Rome, became quite ill, and it was feared that death was near. He had never been baptized. Since he was not strong enough to permit immersion in water, it was decided to pour a quantity of water upon his body. This was done and marked the beginning of a change in the form of baptism. Sprinkling soon developed, for if the water does the saving, a little water can be as effective as a great deal. It was more convenient also.

With this view of church and sacraments, it is evident that complete dependence upon Christ, clearly the only requirement for salvation in the New Testament, was modified to require obedience to the institution and reception of the sacramentals. Thus faith alone, without church and sacraments, cannot save; church and sacraments alone, as in the case of the infant, can save without faith by the individual.

Change in the Nature of the New Testament Church

Sacramentalism made a vast difference in the conception of a New Testament church. In the New Testament period the church consisted of the people in a local body; the leaders were on the same level with the people but served because they had been given special gifts by the Spirit. The ordinances were not magical but symbolical. Now, however, this view was entirely changed. For one thing, the original equality among the several pastors, bishops, or presbyters serving in a church began to disappear. In the New Testament church there was no difference in office between a bishop and a presbyter, the two names simply describing functions of the one office (see Acts 20:17–35). But quite early in the second century it became common for one of the ministers to assume leadership, sometimes because of unusual scholarship, strong personality, or maturity.

As early as 150 one of the writers speaks of a president of the ministers in a single church. There were several reasons why such an officer should develop rapidly. The earliest bishops or presbyters engaged in secular labor to make their living and performed the duties of their church office when not at work. As Christians increased in number and financial ability, one man, the best qualified, was asked to resign his secular labor and give full time to the religious task. It became his business to "oversee" (the word which means "bishop") the work of the Christian community. He received the title of bishop in a special sense and finally claimed the name as a unique dignity. The other ministers were now called "presbyters" in distinguishing them from the overseeing minister, the bishop. Early in the second century the churches at Antioch and in Asia had developed such a leader over all other presbyters, although this had not yet manifested itself in Rome, Philippi, or Corinth.

Another factor that brought authority and prestige to the new officer known alone as the bishop was the development of local councils for advice and discussion. Leaders of the several churches in a given geographical area began to hold such councils or synods, and because of his place in the local congregation, the new bishop acted as spokesman for his church. It was he who brought word back to the congregation concerning the united action of all Christians in fighting heresy, in exercising discipline, and in other matters of common action. By the end of the second century, generally speaking, the office of bishop had become a third church office. This meant that in each local church, or diocese, there were three grades of ministers: one bishop to oversee all and exercise total authority, many presbyters, many deacons.

The office of bishop soon developed beyond the confines of a single congregation. When Christians were comparatively few, one church could serve an entire city. As new congregations were organized in different sections of cities where a bishop was already serving, a significant departure from the New Testament conception occurred. The New Testament plan called for each congregation to have its own leadership and to be independent of any authority from another congregation. What actually happened was that in these cities the bishops already serving were influential enough simply to extend their jurisdiction to include new congregations. New presbyters were ordained to provide workers for the new congregation, all under the authority of the bishop of that city. In Rome, for example, by the end of the third century there were forty congregations; each congregation or parish had its own presbyter or—as he came to be known—priest. And over the entire city was a single administrative officer who bore the title of bishop. Influential city bishops soon extended their authority in this fashion to include villages around the large cities.

Although, therefore, there are late writings that identify the bishop with a local congregation, by the fourth century the separation of the office of bishop from that of the presbyters and the development of a territorial authority over a large area was the normal situation. The strongest bishops (assuming additional titles such as archbishop—ruling bishop, or patriarch—ruling father, or pope—papa) presided at large councils attended by bishops and presbyters from adjacent territory and began looking toward extending their jurisdiction even further. The extent of such development is indicated by the sixth canon of the first universal council at Nicea in 325, which asserted that according to custom the bishop of Alexandria shall exercise authority over Egypt, Alexandria, and Pentapolis; the bishop of Antioch shall have similar authority in the area adjacent to his city; and the bishop of Rome shall exercise a dominant influence over the territory around his city.

The influence of the bishop developed in other directions also. The church was conceived now as a saving institution because it possessed the saving sacraments of baptism and the Lord's Supper. But who within the church controlled these sacraments? The bishop, of course. The view became current that only the bishop could authorize or perform the sacraments; thus the bishop personally possessed the essential power of the church. Such a view was greatly forwarded during the persecutions and the heretical movements. The bishop had been thrust into the position of embodying the Christian faith. The strongest Christians had been placed in that office. During the persecutions the bishops bore the brunt of the attacks; during the conflicts with heresy they had been looked to as the bulwark of orthodoxy. As a result, the bishop became the church both in popular conception and in authority to wield her sacramental powers. Bishop Cyprian of Carthage could say in about 250 that where the bishop is, there is the church, and there is no church where there is no bishop.

Thus it may be seen that the original nature of a New Testament church was completely corrupted. It no longer consisted of the congregation, for the bishop was the church. It was no longer a fellowship; it had become a saving institution. Its ordinances had become saving sacraments, not symbolical reminders of Christ. Its ministry was no longer in two offices but in three. It was no more a democracy in government but a hierarchy.

Change in the Nature of Ecclesiastical Authority

Conforming to the historical developments described in the previous section, the literary remains of ancient Christianity show clearly a shift from the New Testament conception of the final authority of a local church to the idea that the final word of authority in all matters religious was the bishop. It has been pointed out that Christianity produced four general types of literature in the two centuries following the apostolic period.

The earliest chronologically was primarily *edificatory* in nature. In none of the writers of this early type of literature is there any evidence that the New Testament pattern for ecclesiastical authority has been altered. The letter of Clement of Rome to the Corinthians urges the church to restore some officers who had been disciplined, even though they had originally been appointed by the apostles. This means that the Corinthian church exercised authority even beyond apostolic appointment. Clement's letter gives advice but shows no authority to require the Corinthian church to follow it. The writings of Ignatius (about 115) place great emphasis upon the necessity for obedience to the pastor and the deacons and are morbidly ascetical. Because of the emphasis upon these two ideas, there is considerable suspicion that interpolations by later hands have endeavored to give early authority to matters developed later. However, at this early period the bishop was simply one of the pastors of a local body. Although later than the writings of Ignatius, the Epistle of Polycarp and the *Shepherd of Hermas* reveal no episcopal development.

The second type of Christian literature was *apologetic* in nature. Its main purpose was to defend Christianity against such charges as atheism, licentiousness, and cannibalism, leveled against it by the pagans. In the doctrinal discussions of this literature the ground of authority was the Scriptures, primarily the Old Testament. There was no appeal to episcopal authority.

The third type of Christian literature was *polemical.* Its purposes were to fight heresy that threatened to break out within the Christian ranks. Two important writers in this field were Irenaeus (about 130–202) and Cyprian (195–258). In the course of his arguments to discredit Gnosticism around 185, Irenaeus first refutes their doctrines from the Christian Scriptures. He then proceeds to say that the continuous existence of the various churches from the days of the apostles proves that they have not erred in the interpretation of the apostolic teachings. Referring to Rome as an example of one of such churches, Irenaeus names its bishops in succession back to apostolic days (but his list poses problems in its disagreement with other lists). In other words, Irenaeus makes historical succession of the bishops the basis for confidence that orthodox Christianity was true Christianity while Gnosticism was a false perversion. Basically, then, the authority cited by Irenaeus was the Scriptures; the correct interpretation of the Scriptures he attempted to prove through succession.

The other important polemical writer was Bishop Cyprian of Carthage (195–258), who did more than any other individual to forward the office of bishop as the ultimate Christian authority. Cyprian's theory grew out of practical problems in administrating his diocese. In his struggle over what to do with those who had denied Christ or surrendered Scriptures under persecution, he finally rested his argument on the fact that he as the bishop had authority over all churches and individuals in his diocese because he was the successor of the apostles. He conceived of one universal (Catholic) church in the world, composed of many bishops, the successors of the apostles. The unity of all the various bishops constitutes the unity of the catholic (universal) Church. Only those who are in fellowship with this universal episcopal unity (the Catholic Church) are saved. Thus if any person in any diocese anywhere refuses to be obedient to his bishop, that person forfeits his salvation.

The interesting paradox about Cyprian is that while he firmly taught that all bishops were of equal rank (and practiced it when he fought the Roman bishops and told them to quit meddling in his diocese), yet he called the Roman church the "mother and root of the catholic church." When the Roman bishop attempted to instruct Cyprian on the validity of heretical baptism and to exercise whatever authority was involved in the title Cyprian had applied to the Roman church, Cyprian vigorously denied the right of any bishop, even the Roman bishop, to exercise jurisdiction in the diocese of another bishop.

It was Cyprian, then, who corrupted the New Testament pattern of authority. Instead of the local church, the territorial bishop became the final word of authority. The universal (Catholic) church rested upon the sole sovereignty of the bishops as successors of the apostles. Local churches lost every vestige of authority.

The fourth type of Christian literature—*systematic* development of doctrine—does not concern episcopal development.

Change in the Nature of Worship

In the New Testament the pattern of worship consisted principally of singing, Scriptures, prayer, and preaching. The service required no altar or ritual, for God was recognized as spirit and could be reached through spirit. But a change had occurred by 325. The idea that the sacraments were magical brought a change to the nature of worship. Instead of magnifying his prophetic or preaching ministry, the local presbyter began to function as a priest. In fact, after the fourth century the very name "presbyter" began to drop out, and the title of this office became "priest." This development could be expected when the sacraments became magical; it required a priestly qualification to administer this sort of rite. Consequently, the center of worship became the observance of the Lord's Supper, which was already being called "mass" (from the Latin word meaning "dismissal," when those not qualified to partake of the Supper were asked to leave the church).

The magical nature of the sacraments also brought emphasis upon the proper form, words, and materials used in administering them. In the Roman religion great stress was laid upon pronouncing the ritual exactly as a means of making the service effective. If a word was mispronounced or omitted, the magical nature of the religious service could not be appropriated. This spirit began to prevail in Roman Christianity; the ritual must be repeated exactly according to formula in order to be efficacious. Furthermore, this corruption in the nature of the worship services contributed greatly to the development of the catechetical means of instruction in religious doctrine. Since the worship service was dedicated to a priestly ritual, it became necessary to instruct children and new converts in the proper ritual as well as in the rudiments of Christian doctrine on some other occasion than in the church services. Summaries of the ritual and of the doctrines were prepared, and newcomers were required to memorize these as a prerequisite to admission.

Finally, the purely spiritual nature of religious services was changed. Magnificent processions and external splendor, after the manner of pagan parades, became popular. Places identified with early Christianity became holy and were accorded unusual reverence. Bones of martyrs and other material remains were sought and attributed magical power. Holy days were named and observed. Easter had been set apart from the time of the apostles, but new days were added. Both the baptism and the birth of Jesus had been celebrated in January during this period; but in an effort to win the pagans, the celebration of Christ's birth was changed shortly after the close of the period to December 25, a Roman and Scandinavian feast day.

Reasons for Extensive Corruption of Christianity

It is impossible, of course, to plumb entirely the various interacting factors that moved Christian development in the direction that it took. The several suggestions that follow simply mention the most obvious of the elements that turned Christianity away from its original purity.

The tremendous growth of the Christian movement.—The growth of Christianity in the three centuries following the death of Christ was phenomenal. Figures cannot be given with any accuracy, but some think that Christians numbered from five to ten millions by the time of Constantine (323). From a human standpoint this tremendous growth may be explained by three general factors.

First, heathenism had failed as an answer to the needs of man. Greek rationalism had emptied the pagan heavens. Men thoroughly disbelieved the superstitious legends that had power neither to affect their daily lives nor promise good things to come. In the dizzy maelstrom of social, economic, and political foment which threatened men in the early Christian centuries, pagan religious systems were silent.

Second, the Christian message was positive and effective. The content of Christ's teachings tugged at the hungry hearts of men everywhere. The pagans could see what Christianity meant by observing the lives of the Christians. Love was the theme of their living. When called upon to die during the various periods of severe persecution, the Christians responded with faith and courage. Such a spirit the pagans could account for only in terms of the power of God.

Finally, the zeal of the Christians in witnessing for Christ was overpowering. Unlike the pagans about him, the Christian insisted that all religions were not of equal value; either accept Christ as Saviour or be lost was the conviction of the Christian. Every Christian was a missionary, every crossroad a pulpit, every person a prospect. There was a sense of urgency in the Christian witness. Conscious of Christ's injunction to be watchful and busy, the Christians worked with a feeling that the Lord might return at any time. As a consequence they pleaded with unction and personal conviction.

The remarkable growth that followed was one of the factors that helped corrupt the original purity of the Christian movement. Without question it promoted the development of the power of the bishop. His prestige was enhanced when large numbers of converts made Christianity the religion of a majority of the people in many areas. These converts were not drawn entirely from the lower class of people. Education, wealth, and civil rule soon were enlisted in the Christian cause, bringing to the overseeing bishop powerful new weapons and influential friends.

This growth also enhanced the danger of sacramentalism. Large numbers of pagans flocked to the doors of the Christian church and were admitted through the use of magical sacraments. Great masses of unregenerated pagans were brought into the churches in this way. Thoughtful Christians watched uneasily as these pagans introduced ideas from the background of their early religious training. With other factors, this situation led to monasticism, as Christians fled from the paganized churches to find purity and spirituality in the caves of the desert.

Finally, the influx of large numbers into the Christian churches furthered the institutional development of Christianity. Young children and uninitiated pagans required extensive instruction in ritual and doctrine. The sprinkling of water upon them could not bring a new heart; it was hoped that extensive instruction would make them good Christians.

Pagan persecution.—The external opposition to Christianity described in the second chapter was also a contributing factor in the changes that occurred in Christianity. What should be the attitude of a church toward a member who, when brought to physical torture by secular authorities, denies Christ and surrenders precious Christian Scriptures to be destroyed? This happened many times in periods of severe persecution during the first three centuries. The two severest trials came about 250 and about 300 during the Decian and Diocletian persecutions. Many nominal Christians defaulted during these periods. In general, after each period of persecution five rather distinct groups could be named. (1) There were *martyrs,* who had refused to put a pinch of incense upon the altar of the Roman emperor and to deny Christ and were slain.

(2) There were *confessors*, who were true to Christ but because of local influence or leniency were not put to death. Sometimes they were blinded or maimed. (3) There were *apostates*, who denied Christ and offered incense upon the altar of the emperor. (4) There were *falsifiers*, who by bribes or passive compromise received certificates from the imperial officers stating that they had offered pagan incense and had cursed Christ, although this was not actually the fact. (5) There were the *unfaithful*, who surrendered true Christian Scriptures to the officers.

The early leaders divided over how to treat the apostates, falsifiers, and unfaithful. Some, like Montanus, Novatian, and Donatus, wanted to bar them forever from the church; others, like Caecillian and Callixtus, wanted to let them return to the church after evidence of repentance. Various plans were suggested for bringing such offenders back. One system permitted them to kneel outside the church and give evidence of grief for a full year—these were called *weepers;* the next year they were allowed to come into the church and hear the service, hence were called *hearers;* the next year they could kneel during the service until the time for the Lord's Supper, when they must leave—these were called *kneelers;* the fourth year they were allowed to stand during the service— they were called *co-standers;* and finally, they were admitted to the Supper and restored to fellowship.

It can easily be seen how such a system would magnify the nature of the church as a saving institution; else such strenuous efforts to get back into its fellowship would hardly be worth the protracted ceremonies. The persecution also fostered other elements that contributed to the corruption of Christianity, such as the deterioration that always comes from literary warfare, the centralizing of ecclesiastical authority in the bishop to meet the threats of the persecutors, and the development of the attitude that physical coercion was the best means of dealing with dissenters.

Internal conflicts.—One of the most important factors in the corruption of Christianity was the series of internal controversies described in the previous chapter. While officially condemning many of the heretical perversions, Christianity unconsciously imbibed some of the teachings that were so widely propagated through these controversies. The doctrine of mortal and venial sins was lifted from Montanism, as well as ascetic and monastic emphases. Gnosticism had taught that there was a series of mediating persons between man and God; the idea of mediating saints for invoking the blessings of God grew up in Christianity. The magical power of the ordinances that changed them to sacraments came unrefined from paganism. Jewish ideas hastened the development of the priestly system. The secular Roman government provided a pattern for organization that was duplicated by the ecclesiastical monarchy which grew up in later centuries. The expression of Christian truth in philosophical terminology was inevitable in the course of the various controversies, but it served to glaze over spirituality with argumentation. The various internal struggles played a large part in enlarging the stature of the bishop, since he was called upon to be the champion of orthodoxy.

Ecclesiastical rivalry.—It will be remembered that the office of bishop had been separated from that of the presbyter or priest and had successively become the governing power in a local church, the ecclesiastical head of a diocese (a city) and the spiritual prince of a territory, sometimes an entire province. The development of councils or synods for mutual help and advice had introduced the bishops to one another and encouraged the opportunity of larger leadership by the more gifted bishops. One of the common practices during the controversies was for one of the parties to secure favorable response from one or more of the strong bishops before the outbreak of the conflict. This insured allies. But it also enhanced the prestige and influence of the bishops to whom appeal had been made, for it gave them opportunity to act as judge. By 325 the three most influential bishops in the Mediterranean world were those in Rome, Antioch, and Alexandria. Already these bishops were sparring for the chief place, and other bishops were striving to elevate themselves to the place occupied by these bishops. This intense rivalry fanned the flames of ambition that normally did not lack fuel. Recrimination, condemnation, and outrageous forgery of official documents in an effort to attain first place characterized this struggle between bishops. What a contrast with the teachings of the humble Galilean!

Concluding Summary

By 325, then, tremendous changes in the nature of Christianity had taken place. The developments brought a new movement that did not greatly resemble Christianity except in terminology. There was no Roman Catholic Church as yet, for the bishop of Rome was only one of several powerful bishops; but the direction had been taken. The church had become a saving institution centering in the bishops. A small group of strong bishops had been elevated into world leadership. One of them was already claiming first place and was working feverishly to secure it.

BIBLIOGRAPHY

BAKER, G. P. *Constantine the Great and the Christian Revolution.* New York: Dodd, Mead & Company, Inc., 1930.

BETTENSON, HENRY (ed.). *Documents of the Christian Church.* New York: Oxford University Press, 1947.

CADOUX, C. J. *The Early Church and the World.* Edinburgh: T. & T. Clark, 1925.

GWATKIN, H. M. *Arian Controversy.* London: Longmans, Green & Co., Inc., 1896.

HARDY, E. G. *Christianity and the Roman Government.* New York: The Macmillan Co., 1925.

LATOURETTE, K. S. *A History of Christianity.* New York: Harper & Brothers, 1953.

NEWMAN, A. H. *A Manual of Church History,* I. Philadelphia: American Baptist Publication Society, 1953.

RAMSAY, WILLIAM M. *The Church in the Roman Empire Before 170 A. D.* Grand Rapids: Baker Book House, 1954.

ROBINSON, JAMES HARVEY. *Readings in European History,* I. Boston: Ginn & Co., 1904.

STEVENSON, J. (ed.). *A New Eusebius.* New York: The Macmillan Co., 1957.

UHLHORN, GERHARD. *The Conflict of Christianity with Heathenism.* New York: Charles Scribner's Sons, 1891.

WORKMAN, HERBERT BROOK. *Persecution in the Early Church.* Cincinnati: Jennings and Graham, 1906.

III. PERIOD OF PAPAL
DEVELOPMENT (A.D. 325–1215)

Introduction to the Period

From 325 to 1215 the Roman Catholic Church, under the headship of the pope, developed and reached its height. The opening date is that of the first world council, which initiated a new direction; the closing date of the period marks the meeting of still another council—the Fourth Lateran Council (also called the Twelfth Ecumenical Council by the Roman Church). The Fourth Lateran Council represents the highest pinnacle attained by the Roman Catholic Church. Thus between the Nicene Council of 325, when the new direction was taken, and the Fourth Lateran Council of 1215, the Roman Catholic Church developed, expanded, and reached its height.

The large historical movements of this period were political and military. In the fourth and fifth centuries the German barbarians from the north and northeast overran the Western world, bringing what has been called the Middle Ages. The old Graeco-Roman culture and economy were overwhelmed, but the tribes in general were either won from paganism or indoctrinated away from Arian Christianity through efforts of the Roman Church. One of the tribes, the Franks, became the dominant military power, and with them the Roman Church made alliance. One of the Frankish kings, Charlemagne, was crowned in 800 as the Holy Roman Emperor. The Holy Roman Church and the Holy Roman Empire struggled for mastery—the "spiritual" against the secular—throughout the remainder of the period.

The Eastern world was not invaded by the Germanic hordes but was overwhelmed by an even worse fate. The Mohammedans of Arabia began their conquest for world domination in the middle of the seventh century. Almost the entire eastern section around the Mediterranean fell to the Saracens in little over a half century; by 732 they had conquered all of North Africa and Spain and were menacing France. In that year Charles Martel defeated them at Tours. The threat which these Mohammedans and their successors offered to western Europe played a large part in the movement of history.

The next seven chapters will describe this period from the viewpoint of ecclesiastical history. The first chapter in this section will introduce the student to the new direction which was begun in 325, and the last one will review the ecclesiastical development of the nine centuries. The five chapters within this framework describe the laying of Roman Catholic foundations between 325 and 451; the expansion of the Roman Catholic Church between 351 and 1050; the religious and secular opposition to this Roman Catholic expansion between 451 and 1050; and the attainment of complete supremacy, both secular and religious, by the Roman Catholic system between 1050 and 1215.

Points of Special Interest

The student will notice several significant matters during this period. (1) The Roman Catholic development was gradual and slow, but effective. Two groups opposed autocratic power: those within the church who rejected Roman pretensions and the secular governments without the church which resented Roman domination. These two elements of opposition were never completely overcome. A special chapter has been devoted to each; although overlapping somewhat, they present in unified and topical form the struggle against the expansion of Roman power. (2) The records of dissenting movements are very meager. The nature of the religious spirit would demand dissent. Laxity always develops asceticism of some kind; rigor and repression always breed disobedience or dissent. (3) The long-range program of the Roman Church represents its greatest strength. The ups and downs of Roman ecclesiastical power sometimes made it seem doubtful that world domination would ever come. The historic policy of the papacy never to retract one of the claims made in earlier centuries, however preposterous and arrogant it may be, and to assert that claim when the occasion is favorable, contributed directly to the world domination of the twelfth and thirteenth centuries.

5

A New Direction

THE DEVELOPMENTS SKETCHED in the previous chapters represent more than a departure from the New Testament pattern; they also constitute a preparation for further significant changes. Church government no longer proceeds from the people but from the officers; the two sacraments, endowed now with magical efficacy, have made the church a saving institution; salvation now comes through admission into this saving institution, not from the power of a message by the institution; the bishop has been separated from other local church officers and now rules as a monarch, not only in the local church, but in large areas contiguous to his own. The new direction of the development that begins with the first world council at Nicea in 325 leads directly to the Roman Catholic Church. Such a development would have been impossible without the friendly attitude and strong arm of the secular power. These elements were secured when Constantine chose to link up his future with the growing, dynamic movement called Christianity.

Constantine's Purpose

Constantine was a political genius. From his comparatively meager understanding of Christianity and his brief contact with it he concluded two things: that Christianity would become the dominant religious system of the world, and that the dying Roman Empire could be saved, or at least prolonged, by a union with this dynamic religion. Constantine wanted Christianity to become the cement of the Empire; he wanted religion to act as a unifying factor in the political system. This was not an altogether new idea, for religion had been a part of the Roman system of government through the centuries. The innovation consisted in the kind of religion that was not a state-projected syncretism that invited all who would to join, but a widespread and powerful movement which was exclusive in its view of God and its requirements for admission.

Such a union of forces was something new, both for the Empire and for Christianity. Each developed differently because of their alliance. Christianity was not able to save the Roman Empire—it was too far gone; and Constantine was wrong, also, in supposing that Christianity would act as cement for the Empire. How could Christianity bring unity to the political world when Christianity itself did not possess unity? Already three schools of thought had developed and displayed antagonism to one another.

Alexandria formed the center of the earliest of these schools. A converted philosopher, Pantaenus, organized a school for instructing Christian converts. He was succeeded by Clement, and Clement by Origen—both of whom have been mentioned in connection with the literary monuments of the second period of church history. These men looked upon philosophy as the means of interpreting Christianity. In the best philosophical tradition, the Bible was read allegorically. Great emphasis was placed upon redemption as a mystical union with God through Christ.

Antioch was the second center. This school was founded by Lucian in the closing quarter of the third century. Representing the tradition of the apostle John, this school of thought magnified the Scriptures as their own best interpreter. Because of the intensive struggle with the Gnostics, philosophy was mistrusted. The literal meaning of a text, as understood in the light of its grammatical and historical background, was sought.

The Western school of thought claimed writers from both the Continent and North Africa. Like the Antiochian center, it also mistrusted philosophy and placed its principal emphasis upon the practical application of Christianity.

The controversies that begin to arise in Christianity will follow the pattern of thought represented in the various schools; that is, with the same facts and Scriptures the followers of the Alexandrian school, using the philosophical approach, reached different conclusions from the Antiochian school and the Western school. Many times the search for truth was simply a secondary stimulus to the controversy; the intellectual rivalry spurred on the adherents of each type of thought far beyond the limits of Christian charity.

With this sort of disunity in the Christian movement, there was considerable doubt that it would bring unity to the Roman Empire when they formed the alliance. It was not long before this fact rudely awakened Constantine. Gathering up historic schismatic movements like Montanism and Novatianism, the Donatist split in North Africa thrust itself upon Constantine at almost the time he had decided to make Christianity the cement of the Empire. Constantine's treatment of Donatism was, of course, motivated by political factors. He did his best by appeal, argument, threat, and finally, physical persecution to close the ranks of Christianity, all without success. This problem for Constantine was just a taste of what was yet to come. The cry of the Donatists later on, "What has the emperor to do with the church?" was one that symbolized the greatest dilemma of the new alliance between church and state. What should an emperor do in order to maintain political control when his Christian citizens insisted upon forming hostile theological camps on the basis of their scriptural interpretations? Whether it was his original intention to relate himself in such fashion or not, Constantine was forced to become "bishop of the bishops" in an attempt to restore unity. This position was accorded him by the ecclesiastical princes of the Empire.

The controversy that brought Constantine into this place of doctrinal and ecclesiastical leadership was called the Arian controversy and concerned the interpretation of the person of Christ in relation to God.

The Beginning of the Arian Controversy

It will be remembered that one of the earliest doctrinal discussions in Christianity centered in the nature of Christ and his relation to God the Father. Was Jesus Christ completely God or was he less than God? This question had never been adequately answered. Many outstanding Christian writers had wrestled with the problem. If Jesus were completely God, it was asked, then do Christians have three Gods (including the Holy Spirit) ? But, came the response, could Jesus bring salvation to men if he were not God, as he had claimed? Origen of Alexandria had probed deeply into this question in the third century. His writings contain two different views. In one place Origen affirmed that Christ is subordinate to God, is less than true God. In another he asserts that Christ was the eternally generated Son of God; Christ had always existed as the divine Son, both before time and since the temporal creation. Strange as it may seem, these two positions in Origen form the center of the Arian struggle, the first view precipitating the controversy and the second view finally resolving the conflict.

Arius, the man responsible for beginning the controversy, was a presbyter under Bishop Alexander of Alexandria but had been trained at Antioch to interpret the Scriptures in a literalistic sense. About 318 Arius decided that it would compromise the dignity and honor of God the Father to say that Jesus Christ was of the same divine, eternal essence as God. Consequently, he worked out a system which declared that Christ was a being who had been created before time and that through Christ God had created all other things. His theory made Christ greater than man and less than God—somewhere between the two, but fully neither.

The controversy spread rapidly beyond Alexandria and soon gripped the entire Eastern world. The Antiochian school of thought could see nothing wrong with the interpretation and added intellectual rivalry to the issue. Arius was a popular and able preacher and gained much support through his personal charm. As the controversy grew, Constantine acknowledged that some sort of action would have to be taken. After becoming the sole emperor in 323, following the experience he had gained in dealing with the Donatists, he directed that a meeting of all Christian leaders be convened to settle the issue. This universal (the meaning of the Greek word for catholic) council met at Ni-

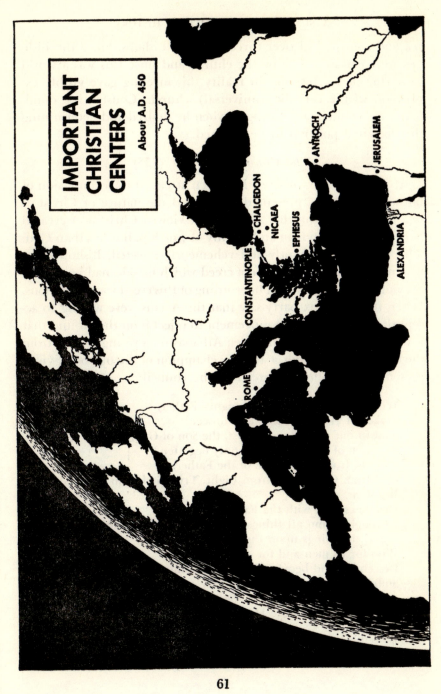

IMPORTANT CHRISTIAN CENTERS
About A.D. 450

ROME

CONSTANTINOPLE

CHALCEDON

NICAEA

EPHESUS

ANTIOCH

JERUSALEM

ALEXANDRIA

cea and consisted of over three hundred bishops. Since the bishops were considered to be the church and since this was a world gathering of the bishops, in reality this meeting gave visible expression to the catholic (universal) church. Constantine dominated the council, addressing it when he desired and determining the doctrinal position to be adopted.

The Council of Nicea (325)

After preliminary matters had been attended to, a confession of faith by Arius was presented. It defined the nature of Christ as being different from that of God and viewed Christ as a created being, greater than man and worthy of worship, but less than God. This creed was promptly and vehemently rejected. Bishop Eusebius of Caesarea then offered a creed which he said had been used previously in his church. The wording of this creed was ambiguous. When the orthodox party saw that the Arians were willing to accept the creed, they led a movement to reject it on the ground that it was not explicit enough. Then Athanasius, a young deacon from the church in Alexandria and the champion of the orthodox view, presented the following creed to the council:

> We believe in one God, Almighty Father,
> Maker of all things seen and unseen,
> And in one Lord Jesus Christ, the Son of God,
> Begotten of the Father and only begotten
> That is, from the essence of the Father,
> God from God, Light from Light, True God from True God,
> Begotten, not made,
> Of one essence with the Father.
> Through whom all things were made, both the things in heaven
>   and the things upon the earth,
> Who for us men and for our salvation,
> Descended and became flesh and became man,
> Suffered and arose on the third day, and ascended into the heavens,
> And is coming to judge living and dead.
> We believe also in the Holy Spirit.

Following this creed was the condemnation of anyone denying its doctrine, mentioning specifically the assertion by the Arians that Christ did not exist in all eternity. It should be noticed that this creed emphasizes the oneness of Christ with God the Father. The key words were "of one essence with the Father." Constantine decided that this creed would bring political and religious peace, doubtless at the advice of Bishop Hosius of Cordova, his ecclesiastical adviser. Therefore, with his approval the creed was adopted, and a decree of banishment was issued against Arius and those who followed his view. Christians who had been victims of imperial power just a few years before now utilized imperial power to persecute one another. Constantine later changed his mind and recalled Arius, banishing Athanasius. The complete doctrinal reversal meant nothing to his political mind. It is likely that Constantine had little grasp of Christian principles of doctrines. His deferred baptism, moral and ethical standards, and retention of the pagan office that guaranteed his place as a Roman god after death were in themselves evidence of his spiritual character.

Later History of Arianism

There was much dissatisfaction within Christianity after the decision of the Nicene council. The language of the creed led some to fear tritheism (three gods) and others to fear modalism (the loss of individual personality). By political maneuvering and playing upon the fears of sincere thinkers in the religious realm, Arianism gained the upper hand for a generation. A semi-Arian school developed which took a position halfway between that of Athanasius and the Arian view and asserted that while Christ was not of one essence with God, yet he was similar to God. This drew many followers from the strict Athanasian party. Athanasius himself was repeatedly banished for holding to the views of the Nicene Creed.

The political scene aided in bringing temporary Arian triumph. When Constantine died in 337, his three sons, Constantine II, Constans, and Constantius, divided up the Roman Empire. However, Constantine II was slain in 340 in a battle with Constans, and Constans committed suicide in 350. These two men favored the Nicene view. The third son, Constantius, was an Arian. His reign from 337–61, as sole ruler after 350, provided opportunity for Arianism to develop with the blessing of imperial authority.

In addition to banishing Athanasius, Constantius dealt severely with pagan and Jewish adherents. The death penalty was enacted for offering pagan sacrifices and for becoming a Jewish proselyte. Partly because of this severity, a pagan reaction took place. Constantine had slaughtered his relatives, other than the three sons, in order to insure proper succession. He missed two intended victims. One of them, Julian, the son of a brother whom Constantine had slain, secretly embraced paganism and in 361 wrested control of the Empire from Constantius. He did everything he could to increase divisions in Christianity. Athanasius was brought out of banishment, and the other dissenters were encouraged. Julian also endeavored to introduce a reformed and refined paganism— adopting many Christian elements—as a rival to Christianity. After his death in 363, however, the succeeding emperors favored Christianity of the Nicene type. Arianism slowly receded in influence through the succeeding centuries. The second universal council of 381 at Constantinople reaffirmed the position of the first council relative to the person of Christ.

Results of Arianism

One important result of the Arian movement was the spread of its doctrine of Christ through missionary activity. In 340 while Arianism enjoyed imperial favor, a young missionary called Ulfilas, trained in the Arian doctrine, was sent to the Visigoths. He served until his death in 383, apparently receiving much assistance that cannot now be determined. Ulfilas himself labored diligently, but the conversion to Arian Christianity of great masses of Visigoths and neighboring tribes could hardly have been the work of one man. Ulfilas is best remembered for reducing the Gothic tongue to writing through the translation of the Scriptures. As a result of his work and that of others, when the Roman Empire was finally overrun by these German tribes in the late fourth and fifth centuries, the task of Roman Catholic Christianity was made easier. A remarkable number of the invaders had already embraced Arian Christianity and required only indoctrination into Nicene formulation.

Another result of the Arian movement was the adoption by Constantine of the general policy of physical persecution against ecclesiastical dissenters. It is true that the Donatists had suffered physical persecution at the hands of Constantine in 316, following their refusal to accept the decision of the Council of Arles. After five years Constantine ceased closing Donatist churches and banishing their bishops, feeling that the results of this use of force were unsatisfactory. With this experience there was some question of whether Constantine as sole emperor would continue such a policy. His determination to continue it suggests his deep desire to secure at least external conformity.

Furthermore, the Council of Nicea provided a precedent and pattern for future councils of this sort. Everyone knew that the decision of the council had been arbitrary. Constantine had determined what the council should decide. Yet at the same time decrees of the council were recognized as authoritative Christian pronouncements. Thoughtful leaders pondered this new development. Christian motives and conduct were secondary; decisions were the authoritative matters and the goal to be attained. Apparently the lesson was learned. Many of the later universal councils reached their decisions through physical coercion and rough-and-tumble tactics. It is difficult to see what part genuine Christianity had in some of them.

Finally, the Council of Nicea gave visible form to the catholic church. It will be remembered that in the writings of Cyprian in the previous century it was asserted that the church existed in the bishops. The catholic church (universal Christianity), then, could become visible when all the bishops gathered in council. This was effected at Nicea. It completed the ecclesiastical machinery for universal domination by a spiritual monarch.

The New Relationship

The beginning of an alliance between Christianity and the Roman Empire under Constantine profoundly influenced the history and development, both of the religion and of the state. Christianity was officially decreed the religion of the Roman state under Emperor Theodosius (378–95).

A new area of controversy.—Before Nicea Christianity had really had no occasion to ponder what its relations to the state should be. Centuries of secular persecution had followed the original antagonism of the Empire against an "illegal" religion. The attempt to adjust the relations between Christianity and the secular power forms a large part of the history of Christianity in the centuries to come. Some felt that the state should control the church. Roman history recommended this view, for religion had been a department of the government long before Christianity had been established. Constantine assumed this attitude, as did his sons. The emperor was the "bishop of bishops." Such a relationship became known as Caesaro papacy—state domination of the church. Others felt that the church should be above the state. This became the ideal of the developing Roman Catholic system. Still others looked upon each institution as having a peculiar stewardship from God and believed that the two should work alongside one another without undue interference. It should be said that this problem has never been settled to the satisfaction of all. A new direction, tremendously significant in the history and development of Christianity from Nicea to the present, was begun.

The increase of secular influence.—It is difficult to conceive how much secular influence was exerted upon Christianity through the alliance between church and state under Constantine. In the area of organization, for example, Christianity made use of the imperial pattern. In the terminology of American geography, Christianity organized on the basis of city, county, state, sectional, and national political divisions. After the development of the office of pope in the next century, the imperial organization and that of Christianity were strikingly similar.

The very motives of Constantine in adopting Christianity indicate the direction to be taken. He wanted to use Christianity as a political and social factor in building the state. This meant the use of secular power, as has been seen, in establishing uniformity.

Dissent must be stamped out. It meant imperial settlement of doctrinal and ecclesiastical disputes. The administrative officers of state found themselves advising ways to increase efficiency in Christian administration; Christian officers under Constantine began to use methods and ideas in church life that they had learned in government service.

Nicea also brought with it the problem of secular authority in the filling of important ecclesiastical offices. The Christian movement was too important politically to allow radicals of any kind to hold high office. A bishop must now be pleasing to state as well as to God. In this sphere secular influence was widely exercised.

The influx of the unregenerate.—All historians speak of the mass movement into Christianity after it had come into imperial favor. While Christianity was not officially termed the religion of the state for about half a century, yet Constantine's appeal to his subjects to become Christian, his generous gifts to those who were Christians, and the ease with which Christianity could be embraced aided many to make their decision. The similarity between the magical sacraments of Christianity and parallel rites in paganism gave the prospective members a feeling of familiarity in their initiation. In the army, especially, the influence of some sagacious leader might result in the winning of all his loyal followers within a short time.

An example of the ease with which this could be accomplished may be seen in the conversion of one of the Frankish chieftains in the next century. Clovis faced a crucial battle on the following day. He made a solemn vow that if the Christian God of his wife would give victory in battle, then he would become a Christian. Having won the victory, he kept his vow. When his army learned what was happening, they also wanted to join. It was accomplished rather easily. The soldiers marched alongside a river where priests stood with branches from trees. As the soldiers went by, the priest dipped the branches into the river and flung baptismal water upon them, all the while repeating the proper formula. As soon as the water touched the soldiers, of course, they supposedly were made Christians. It is not surprising that when these sprinkled pagans entered the membership of the Christian churches, they brought pagan ideas with them. Consequently, Christianity was more and more infected with pagan corruptions as it became a popular movement.

Impetus to the rise of monasticism.—The gorging of Christian churches with sprinkled pagans was responsible in part for the rapid development of asceticism. Laxity in Christian life and ethics has always brought reactionary movements. Sometimes these did not develop into parties or schisms but brought expression in individual remorse that led to ascetical practices. Remaining within the regular churches, conscientious Christians found relief of soul through fasting, long hours of prayer, and rigorous spiritual discipline. Others, however, chose a more radical method. In the East, where the climate was inviting during most of the year, men left the churches and their homes and became religious hermits. They took literally the injunction of Jesus to the rich young ruler to "leave all and follow me." They felt that by burying themselves in a cave away from men and engaging in prayer and spiritual contemplation they could "lose their lives in order to save them."

One of the most famous of these hermits was Anthony of Thebes in the middle of the third century. Fleeing from men at about the age of twenty, he spent the next eighty-six years in a cave. He was venerated as a very holy man, and his cave became a place for blessing. Others began leaving their homes and following his example. Before long there were so many hermits in the desert that the caves were all taken. Soon there came the formation of community or cenobitic groups. A number of hermits banded together under a common rule of organization. The earliest known movement of this kind was that of Pachomius which took place about 335 in Egypt.

From the East this movement spread into Asia Minor. The Western practical mind and the rigorous climate discouraged those who would flee to caves, but by the sixth century an orderly and effective movement was begun in Italy by Benedict of Nursia. This will be discussed in a succeeding chapter.

Concluding Summary

A new direction had come. The problem of imperial persecution had been replaced with the problem of imperial favor. The Christian ideal was greatly influenced by the pattern and patronage of the Roman government. The development of the universal council as an authoritative legislative body for all Christianity, coupled with the intense desire of Constantine for universal conformity to a single Christian pattern of doctrine and practice, was a large stride in the direction of a monarchial government in Christianity. Christians had learned to persecute fellow believers in an effort to secure uniformity.

The succeeding chapters will tell the story of the rise of the Roman Catholic Church. All of the ingredients necessary to make up such a system were now assembled—sacramentalism, sacerdotalism, episcopal government, Roman ambition, ecclesiastical rivalry, an authoritative world gathering, and the pattern and power of the secular state. All of these elements were utilized fully by the Roman bishop in the next period.

6
Roman Catholic Foundations

By 325 WHEN THE first catholic (universal) council met, Christianity had assumed several characteristics that were distinctively nonscriptural and may be called by the name "Catholic." These include the idea of a visible universal church composed of the bishops, the belief that the sacraments (as they will now be called) carried with them a magical kind of transforming grace, the employment of a special priesthood (the clergy) which alone was qualified by ordination to act in the administration of those sacramentals, and the recognition of the bishops as the ruling officers (episcopal government). All of these characteristics may be seen at the present time in the Christian groups which call themselves Catholic—Roman Catholic, Greek Catholic, and Anglican Catholic.

After 325 came the foundations for a new advance in hierarchal development. The oligarchy, the rule of many bishops, began to change into a monarchy, the rule of one bishop—the bishop of Rome. This does not mean that the Roman bishops were not among the outstanding bishops of all Christianity before 325; for as early as 58 the apostle Paul had complimented the church at Rome for her excellent reputation through the whole world. The earliest noncanonical writings tell of the great influence of the large, wealthy, and generous body of Christians at Rome. The church had benefited from the illustrious name and history of the city in which it was located, for Rome had been the center of the world for centuries. It was customary, furthermore, for churches having problems to write larger and more experienced churches for advice in matters of discipline and doctrine; it is known that the Roman Church received many such appeals for help. A good example is the letter which the church at Corinth addressed to Rome in the last decade of the first century. The Corinthian church, exercising her prerogatives as an autonomous body, had removed several presbyters who had been appointed by the apostles, and in the controversy someone had written to the church at Rome for advice. The reply by Clement, a pastor or bishop at Rome, is probably typical of letters written by many bishops to churches asking for advice in such matters. The Roman Church was later than some of the others in setting forth a single bishop above the remainder of its officers, apparently Bishop Anicetus (154–65), being the first monarchical head of the Roman congregation.

The reference of Bishop Irenaeus of Lyons to the apostolic tradition of the Roman bishop carried with it an emphasis on the doctrinal rightness of Rome rather than the ecclesiastical authority of Rome. Irenaeus, like Cyprian, could write more eloquently about the eminence of the bishop of Rome than he could act out. In the middle of the second century a quarrel broke out between Rome and certain of the leaders in Asia Minor involving the proper date for observing Easter. The Eastern practice was to celebrate it according to the moon, regardless of what day of the week the celebration came on, while the Roman practice was to wait until the following Sunday. Bishop Polycarp (a disciple of the apostle John), representing the East, and Bishop Anicetus, representing the West, could not agree, and each continued to observe Easter according to his own practice. The controversy was taken up in every church and threatened the peace of the Christian world. Synods (or councils) were called at Rome and in Palestine, in particular, which debated the merits of each side, and the practice of observing Easter on Sunday was generally favored. When the Ephesian bishop and many churches in Asia Minor refused to change their ancient practice, synods or no synods, Bishop Victor of Rome (189–98) declared them excommunicated. Promptly Irenaeus rebuked Victor for this action, raising a doubt as to what Irenaeus actually believed relative to the orthodoxy and authority of the Roman bishop.

Tertullian, the Carthaginian presbyter who has been called the father of Latin Catholic theology, had no sympathy with claims by the Roman bishop and in 207 broke with him and joined the Montanist movement. His pupil Cyprian also could write eloquently about the unique place of the Roman bishop, but about 250 he vigorously told the bishop to quit meddling outside of the Roman diocese. The only superiority he would allow to the Roman bishop was in dignity. It is significant that the fourth-century Donatists addressed their appeal to a council, then to the emperor, not to the Roman bishop.

By 325, then, the Roman bishop, although undoubtedly considered to be one of the strongest bishops and viewed by some as possessing an unusual dignity among bishops, yet was but one of many bishops, all of whom, according to Cyprian, possessed equal and apostolic authority. The sixth canon of the Council of Nicea (325) recognized the Roman bishop as being on a par with the Alexandrian and Antiochian bishops. It is significant that a forgery was inserted into the copy of this canon in the possession of the Roman bishop, which alleged that Rome had always held the primacy. This pious fraud was later discovered when the Roman copy was compared with other copies of the Nicene records. It suggests the mind of those in Rome as they sought by every means, fair or otherwise, to claim pre-eminence. It is no wonder that many scholars today doubt the texts of some of the older writings which have been preserved by Rome; forged insertions and false decretals appear throughout the history of the Roman Church in an effort to forward their position.

Between the first universal council of 325 and the fourth held at Chalcedon in 451, however, the Roman bishop laid the foundations for the ecclesiastical monarchy now known by his title. There were many outstanding factors that entered into this development.

Able Men

One of the most important reasons for the rise of the Roman bishop is the type of men who held the office. They recognized the dignity of their position and sought in every way to forward it. As evidenced by the forgery mentioned heretofore, they wanted first place and actively sought it. Their immediate territory was well organized so as to consolidate their holdings. The marvelous organizational skill of the Romans was turned into ecclesiastical channels. A whole series of subordinate officers guaranteed discipline and uniformity.

Two of these men were quite vocal in their claims. Innocent I (402–17) was the first bishop of Rome to claim universal jurisdiction by the Roman bishop on the basis of the Petrine tradition. Leo I (440–61), who may be rightly called the first pope, asserted scriptural authority for Innocent's claims, secured imperial recognition of his claims to primacy, and by a confluence of political and ecclesiastical interests was able to dictate the doctrinal statement of the Council of Chalcedon, the fourth universal council in 451. "Peter has spoken," cried the bishops when Leo's *Tome* was read; and such recognition, imperial and ecclesiastical, laid the foundations for the papal system.

Geographical Position

The bishop of Rome had no rival in the Western world. Rome had been the ecclesiastical mistress of the West long before the rise of strong bishoprics in North Africa and Europe. This was not true in the East. Ancient and powerful bishops in cities like Alexandria, Jerusalem, Antioch, and Ephesus disputed constantly. Rather than choose an umpire among themselves, these bishops regularly appealed to the sole Western bishop. By so doing they unconsciously increased the Roman bishop's stature. Furthermore, the movement of history was westward. The eastern Mediterranean was surrendering its place in the sun. With the stirring of the German tribes in central and northeastern Europe and the westward surge of empire, Rome was in the center of advance.

Move of the Imperial Capital

In 330 the Emperor Constantine moved the capital of the Roman Empire from Rome to Byzantium, which became known as

Constantinople. Instead of weakening the position of the Roman bishop in so doing, the emperor unknowingly aided the growth of the bishop's prestige. As long as the emperor resided in Rome, the bishop must take second place. As "bishop of bishops," the emperor could overshadow his political subject and dominate the ecclesiastical policies of the bishop. The removal of the emperor to a new city in the East emancipated the Roman bishop from the secular influence and allowed him to develop without restraint. As a matter of fact, with the move of the emperor the bishop became both ecclesiastical and secular sovereign. The Roman bishops became administrators of the secular affairs of the city, defending it against military aggressors, maintaining internal order, supplying its physical needs, and initiating its foreign policy.

Political Prestige

Rome had been the center of the political world for several centuries when the last of the apostles died. How much prestige this political situation brought to the church of the city cannot be estimated. The importance of such political centrality is seen in the fact that Constantinople, location of the new capital, had no other claim to ecclesiastical prestige than that it was the seat of the emperor; yet in a little over a century it was Rome's greatest ecclesiastical rival because of its political importance.

History and Tradition

It has been pointed out that the church at Rome had a long and honorable history. It is impossible to find evidence of the present Roman claim that Peter was bishop of Rome for twenty-five years. The Scriptures connect Paul, not Peter, with the church at Rome. The tradition that Peter was pastor at Rome for a quarter of a century is very late, and outstanding Roman Catholic writers admit that it can never be proved. Furthermore, Roman claims of authority based upon this tradition were not made until the fifth century. That is, after the Roman bishop had become powerful, the right to wield such power was claimed in terms of the Petrine succession.

The whole theory was given scriptural basis by Bishop Leo I
(440–61). He claimed that Peter had been the first bishop of Rome
and then interpreted three Scriptures to prove that Peter was
given the authority to rule all Christendom. The first passage is
found in Matthew 16:18–19. This was interpreted to mean that
Christ would build his church upon Peter personally and that
Peter was given authority to bind and loose souls in a spiritual
monarchy. The second scripture is John 21:15–17, which was interpreted to mean that Peter was to be the chief shepherd and have
the task of feeding, tending, and caring for all of Christ's sheep in
the world. The third scripture is Luke 22:31–32, which was con-
strued as meaning that Peter, after having been turned from his
errors by Christ, would become the chief teacher of Christendom.
The theory alleged that Peter wielded this authority over the
other apostles; that he passed this same authority down to his successors in the office of bishop of Rome; and that other bishops,
like other apostles, were subject to the authority of the Roman
bishop.

Doctrinal Wisdom

The bishop at Rome was able to strengthen his position as
leader of other bishops by his ability to handle himself well during the doctrinal scuffles between 325 and 451. There were three
controversies in the East (Apollinarian, Nestorian, and Eutychian)
and one in the West (Pelagian) during this period. The speculative nature of the Eastern mind and the practical nature of the
Western mind may be glimpsed in these controversies.

Was Christ human?—Apollinaris was bishop of Laodicea in the
middle of the fourth century. In his effort to understand how
Christ's nature could be viewed as both divine and human, he
eliminated a rational human spirit in Christ and substituted the
divine Word, taking literally John 1:14, "And the Word was made
flesh." This protected the deity of Christ but eliminated his true
humanity. Bishop Damasus of Rome condemned this view in 377
and gained added prestige when the second universal council at
Constantinople took similar action in 381.

Was Christ's human nature separate from his divine nature?—
The Nestorian controversy grew as much out of the ecclesiastical
rivalry between the bishops of Rome, Alexandria, and Constantinople as it did from an effort to find the truth. Nestorius became
bishop of Constantinople in 428. Shortly thereafter he strenuously
objected to the name given to the virgin Mary—the mother of God.
He asserted that Mary might be called the mother of Jesus' human nature but certainly should not be viewed as the mother of
Christ's divine nature, as the term might suggest. Bishops Cyril of
Alexandria and Celestine of Rome promptly condemned Nestorius. Their doctrinal objections were based upon the feeling that
the view of Nestorius disrupted the unity of Christ's person and
so separated Christ's nature into human and divine as to deny the
deity of Christ. By physical and political force Bishop Cyril controlled the third universal council (at Ephesus in 431), which
pronounced Nestorius guilty of heresy and deposed him. His followers fled to Persia and established a separate church which has
continued through the centuries.

Did Christ have one nature or two?—The Eutychian controversy
followed as a reaction to the Nestorian controversy. Eutyches, a
zealous monk near Constantinople, profoundly moved by the differences between Bishop Cyril of Alexandria and the Nestorians,
took the position that after the incarnation Christ had only one
nature and that it was divine. Bishop Leo I of Rome sided with
Bishop Flavianus of Constantinople in condemning Eutyches. In
a long letter to Flavianus, Leo insisted upon two natures in
Christ. In 449 Bishop Dioscurus, who had succeeded Cyril at Alexandria, caused a synod to be assembled at Ephesus in which by
threat and violence the theory of Eutyches was approved. Leo of
Rome called this the "robber synod" and refused to accept its
findings, but because Emperor Theodosius supported Eutyches,
the Roman bishop was powerless to act. In 450, however, Theodosius died, and his sister was favorable to the Roman view.

With her approval another council was summoned (recognized
as the fourth universal council) and met at Chalcedon in 451. During the meeting the letter of Leo to Flavianus was read, and the as-

sembled clerics cried out, "God has spoken through Peter; the fisherman has spoken." Leo's view was followed in the doctrinal definition of Christ's nature. The nature of Christ, said the council, was the same as that of God as to his deity and the same as man as to his humanity; Christ is one person in two natures united "unconfusedly, unchangeably, indivisibly, inseparably." The feeling of superiority over even a universal council was revealed by Bishop Leo of Rome. In deference to the political power of Constantinople, the bishop of that city, although without apostolic tradition, had been recognized as a patriarch by the council of 381 in Constantinople, and the Chalcedonian council of 451 asserted in its twenty-eighth canon that the bishop of Constantinople had authority equal to that of the Roman bishop. Leo refused to accept this decision by the ecumenical council, declaring that he would not recognize the bishop of Constantinople as his peer. He preferred to rule alone.

How is man saved?—The one Western controversy of this period centered in a very practical question and one which influenced the machinery of the church. The Western world did not argue over speculative matters, but when it came to a practical question that affected their program, they promptly and effectively dealt with it.

Could man have been saved without the special revelation in the Bible and through Christ, and does it require a special divine grace working upon the soul in regeneration to attain salvation? The controversy raising these questions began when Pelagius, a British monk, and his disciple Coelestius fled from Britain to Italy, then to North Africa about 411. Their teachings quickly came into conflict with the beliefs and practices of the churches in North Africa, for the Pelagians taught that it was not necessary that a child be baptized, since he had no original sin to be washed away. Such a direct denial of one of the important tenets of the Catholic churches brought prompt bickering. The Pelagian group said that every man could either choose to sin or choose to be righteous. They considered all of man's environment to be God's revelation, including creation, friends, circumstances, and

77

insisted that no special regenerating grace was necessary for salvation. It was quite possible to be saved without the Scriptures and Christ's revelation, although these should not be minimized since they provided inspiration and guidance. There was no such thing as original sin for, they said, God creates each soul at the time of birth and endows it with purity and freedom. After the child is able to make his own choice, God expects him to use his environment, friends, education, and intellect to choose righteousness; and the child is capable of doing it.

Because of these views Coelestius was excluded from the church at Carthage in 412 and fled to Palestine to rejoin Pelagius. Here in 415 an interesting incident occurred which illustrates the general attitude toward the Roman bishop by Eastern bishops. Bishop John of Jerusalem and his presbyters were assembled to hear charges against Pelagius. After the evidence had been presented, John gave the decision that since Pelagius was from the West, he came under the authority of the bishop of Rome. That is, all *Latin* Christianity was viewed as coming under the sway of the Roman bishop.

The Roman bishops intermittently took both sides of the controversy. In 416, Bishop Innocent condemned the movement. After his death, in that year Bishop Zosimus publicly approved the teachings of Pelagius and Coelestius. In the following year, not accepting the idea that the Roman bishop might be infallible, the North African bishops condemned the Pelagian movement. Even the Roman Emperor Honorius in Constantinople issued an edict condemning the Roman bishop and any others holding to this heresy. Finally, Bishop Zosimos of Rome changed his position and approved the African view, ordering all Western bishops to make the shift in doctrine at the same time. Many eminent bishops refused to condemn entirely the views of Pelagius. At the universal council in 431 at Ephesus the Pelagian view was officially condemned, along with the Nestorians with whom the Pelagians had been friendly. A semi-Pelagian position was maintained by many of the bishops, laying emphasis upon man's good works and initiative in salvation. This position was taken in opposition to the alternative theory by the great opponent of Pelagius, Augustine of Hippo.

Augustine was the great theologian of the fourth and fifth centuries. He was born in North Africa in 354. Turning successively from philosophy to Manicheanism to skepticism to Neoplatonism to Christianity, he became the dominating figure in Christian thinking for a millennium. His profound experience of finding God and his deep devotion to God gave richness to his theological ideas. His *Confessions,* deeply personal and mystical, explain his doctrinal point of view.

In the Pelagian controversy Augustine asserted that Adam had been created faultless and with freedom, but that in Adam's fall all mankind had lost its purity and freedom. Augustine felt that the baptism of babies or adults washed away the guilt of original sin but not sin itself, and he taught that the sacraments of the Church were necessary to preserve the individual from additional guilt and penalty of this sin. He insisted that men cannot work for salvation, that even the ability to accept salvation is a gift of God. The helpless condition of man requires that God do everything. God both chooses those who should be saved (predestination) and enables them to be saved. Augustine's inconsistency may be glimpsed at this point. In his emphasis upon God's sovereignty Augustine left nothing for man to do in salvation; yet he demanded that infants be baptized in order to be saved from inherited guilt. If God predestinated a child to be saved, it would appear that baptism would have little effect in attempting to accomplish the same thing. Augustine's strong emphasis upon God's total sovereignty repelled some of his contemporaries as much as Pelagius' doctrine of man's ability to co-operate with God in attaining salvation, thus giving rise to the semi-Pelagian and semi-Augustinian views mentioned before.

In addition to his *Confessions* and his opposition to Pelagius, Augustine made two other distinct contributions. He established the official doctrine of the Roman Catholic Church relative to the Donatist controversy. The Donatists had said that when a bishop's character is unchristian or unrighteous, all the sacramental acts of that bishop are invalid. Thus, they had said, Bishop Felix could not properly ordain Caecillian and Caecillian could not administer saving baptism, because these two men were heretics; they had delivered up Scriptures to be destroyed during the time of persecution. Augustine reinterpreted the issue by teaching that a bishop's character made absolutely no difference in the validity of his acts, since the authority or insignia of the church guaranteed the validity of any official acts that a bishop might perform. This marked a great advance in the idea of an authoritative Church.

Augustine also put into written form the ideal toward which the Roman Catholic Church was struggling. Although unfinished, his twenty-two books entitled *City of God* sketched the conflict between earthly rule and the heavenly rule. It should be remembered that Augustine was writing at the time when the Germanic barbarians were overrunning the Western world. In the very year that he died these pagans were pounding at the gates of Hippo, his own city. Augustine described the earthly city, maintained through war, hate, and evil; in contrast he pictured God's city, slowly but surely growing to cover the earth and overcome the secular rule of the earthly city. This idea of a conflict between the spiritual—identified with the ecclesiastical system—and the secular was a prophecy of events to come and did much to fashion the thinking of Augustine's era and the Medieval period.

Concluding Summary

Thus from 325 to 451 the foundations for the Roman Catholic Church were laid. The world councils had provided an arena where the Roman bishop was able to exert growing authority. Arguing on the same grounds that had proved so effective against the Gnostics, the Roman bishops said that their tradition of succession to the apostle Peter endowed them with a continuing authority, and they quoted Scripture texts to prove that Peter had such authority. When wrong doctrinally, and even when snubbed by an ecumenical council, the Roman bishop showed his tremendous prestige and sagacity by shifting his position or standing firm, as circumstances warranted, and in it all maintaining his powerful place. The recognition by imperial and ecclesiastical authorities of Bishop Leo's pretensions to primacy, based upon the Petrine tradition, provides grounds for believing that Leo was the first of the Roman Catholic popes.

Roman Catholic Expansion

BETWEEN 325 AND 451 THE FOUNDATIONS of Roman papal control of the Catholic Church were laid. Roman claims were given a scriptural tone through the alleged primacy of Peter and the alleged apostolic succession through the Roman bishop. The period from 451 to 1050 was one of confusion and violence, but the very historical movement that brought the crisis to Roman Christianity—the barbarian invasions—also provided the opportunity for the papacy to expand its claims to include authority over secular powers and to widen the geographical extent of papal control.

Invasion by the Germanic Tribes

Even while Bishop Leo I of Rome (440–61) was securing recognition of some of his claims at the Council of Chalcedon (451), great racial migrations were taking place. During the second century it had been necessary for the Roman government to maintain large garrisons across central Europe to keep the German tribes from spilling over into the Roman Empire. As other tribes wandered south and west from the broad steppes of what is now Russia, additional pressure was put upon the tribes facing the Roman garrisons to move on into the empire. Throughout the third and fourth centuries of the Christian era the Roman rulers fought continuously to stem the invasion of the various tribes known as Goths, Visigoths (western Goths), Ostrogoths (eastern Goths), Vandals, Franks, Burgundians, Lombards, etc. The tribes began moving in during the fourth century. The date when the Ostrogoths finally overthrew Rome is usually given as 476, but Rome had fallen as early as 410 to Alaric the Goth. Attila (452) and Geisric (455) were subdued only by the sagacity of Pope Leo I.

Some of these tribes were already nominal Christians. Ulfilas and his movement had reached many of them with Arian Christianity. As these Germanic tribes overran the old Roman Empire, it is true that they broke down the old Graeco-Roman civilization. But it is also true that they provided an opportunity for the Roman Catholic Church to mold a new civilization and to be elevated by it. These tribes did not destroy and slay as they advanced into Roman territory. Rather, they adopted whatever elements of the old culture appealed to them and intermarried with the population. Because of these factors, the power of the Roman Catholic system was not harmed permanently by the invasions.

Lasting benefits were secured. At least five of these benefits stand out. (1) The Germanic tribes provided new and numerous subjects for Roman Catholic control. They were awed by the beautiful and solemn services in the orthodox churches and were delighted with the magical sacramental system that provided for all of their needs. The Arian Christians among the tribes were unskilled in doctrinal matters, and it was not difficult to win all of them to the orthodox point of view on the person of Christ. (2) The tribes gave an opportunity to enlarge and tighten the machinery of the Roman Church. New churches were established, new priests trained, new catechisms provided. The untutored Germans brought no new doctrinal problems to complicate this tremendous expansion. (3) The Germanic tribes were rulers over the domains which they had conquered but became subjects of the religious training of the Roman system. This meant that the Roman hierarchy quickly attained great prestige and extensive influence. In addition, it gave the point of view suggested by Augustine's *City of God:* that the heavenly city was superior to the secular and would one day become dominant. (4) The Western world was cut off from the influence of the Roman emperor in Constantinople. Except for a brief period, the entrance of the Germanic tribes made it impossible for the emperor to exercise secular or ecclesiastical power over the Roman Church. Before

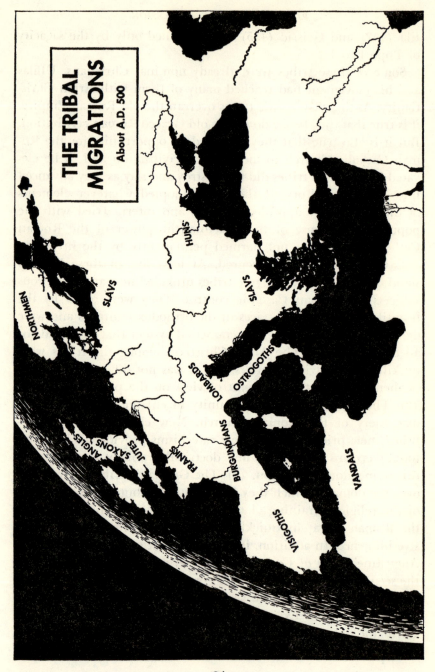

THE TRIBAL MIGRATIONS

About A.D. 500

NORTHMEN

SLAVS

HUNS

SLAVS

OSTROGOTHS

LOMBARDS

ANGLES

SAXONS

JUTES

FRANKS

BURGUNDIANS

VANDALS

VISIGOTHS

the invasion the emperor had still viewed himself as bishop over all bishops and with his army had held a threat over the Western world. But with the barbarian wall surrounding the West, the emperor was helpless to interfere. (5) The winning of these barbarians to a recognition of the spiritual sovereignty of the Roman Church was a deathblow to the ambitions of any other Western bishop and brought gifts of territory and military protection.

Monasticism in the West

The barbarian invasions probably gave impetus to the monastic ideal in the West. It will be remembered that in the Eastern world Anthony and Pachomius had begun hermit life and cenobitic organization. In the West the movement developed more slowly but became more influential. The example of the East doubtless offered incentive to Western leaders to emphasize ascetical life. Men like Athanasius, Jerome, Ambrose, Augustine of Hippo, Martin of Tours, and Eusebius of Vercelli strove to convince many of the superior virtue of losing their lives monastically that they might save them. The cessation of persecution by the state also helped to popularize the monastic movement. Martyrdom was now rarely possible; the most rigorous means of self-denial and suffering for Christ came now through monasticism. The triumph of the "lax" party over the "strict" party in dealing with those who had been untrue to Christ caused many to look askance at the regular means of worship and service and to betake themselves to the caves or to monastic seclusion. Some viewed the Germanic invasions as the wrath of God upon Christianity for leaving its early purity and passion and determined to flee for safety into the rigorous movement that was developing in the West. Still others were dismayed by the pagan corruptions which were introduced into the thinking and practice of the churches. Another group bewailed the formalism in worship that now characterized Western Christianity and sought in monasticism a more personal communion with God. These and other factors help to explain the growth of the movement in the West.

Historically, the Western movement modified the character of monasticism. Although monasticism had originally been a lay-man's movement, Western monasticism made priests of all those taking the monkish vows. Furthermore, the Western movement magnified monasticism as an instrument to advance the very church system against which it was in part a protest. Monks became the missionaries and front-line soldiers of Christianity. As a matter of fact, monastic orders have been at the forefront of every victory achieved by the Roman Church since the Middle Ages.

The outstanding name of Western monasticism was that of Benedict of Nursia. About 500 Benedict became a hermit and in 529 founded a monastery at Monte Cassino, south of Rome. His system emphasized worship, manual labor, and study. In less than three hundred years monastic houses following his rule covered the European continent. More than any other man, Benedict was responsible for molding the monastic movement into practical lines and reconciling its ideals with those of the Church.

The most important monastic reform occurred in the opening years of the tenth century. Duke William of Aquitaine provided for the founding of a new monastery at Cluny in eastern France in 910. In an effort to free this monastery from corruptions which had entered into many others because of secular control and ecclesiastical interference, William provided that this house should look immediately to the pope for protection. Heretofore, under the Benedictine system, the various monasteries were controlled by the bishop in whose diocese they were located. Now a new type of monasticism was begun as a reform movement, which brought the institution into direct loyalty and obedience to the pope. The rule of this monastery was that of Benedict, interpreted strictly. This type of reform became popular and spread rapidly.

A development of the next century transformed even more the new type of monasticism. The abbots of Cluny began to assume jurisdiction over the new monasteries founded by Cluniac followers, as well as those embracing reform after Cluniac principles; consequently, the abbot of Cluny became the head of an extensive network of monasteries whose aims he could dictate and whose abbots he could appoint. Such an organization, whose head swore allegiance immediately to the pope, was greatly influential in undermining episcopal and secular authority opposing the papacy.

Missionary Expansion

Rome did not foster missions to any extent until the sixth century. Reference has been made to the work of Ulfilas in the fourth century under the auspices of Eastern Christianity. Bishop Martin of Tours vigorously assailed paganism in his country during the fourth century. Missionary work had been carried on in the British Isles. A Scotchman named Patrick, whose Christianity was not of the Roman Catholic type, evangelized Ireland in the early part of the fifth century, and an Irishman named Columba preached extensively in Scotland in the latter part of the same century. Another Irishman, Columbanus (543–615), began to preach in south Germany but was diverted into France, thence again into south Germany, to Switzerland, and finally to Italy, where he died.

The work of these missionaries, while not under the direction of Rome, prepared the way for Roman Catholic domination. In 596 at the direction of Pope Gregory I (590–604), a Benedictine monk named Augustine and forty companions went to England as missionaries. After a struggle with the different type of Christianity from Ireland and Scotland already there, the Roman Catholic type of organization and worship prevailed. At the Synod of Whitby (664), it was decreed that Roman Christianity should be practiced in all of England. The older type of Christianity was dispersed.

From England, Roman Catholic missionaries moved to the Continent. Wilfrid, a Benedictine monk who had been influential in establishing Roman Christianity in England, began mission work in what is now Holland about 678. He was followed there by Willibrord about 690. The greatest of the Roman Catholic missionaries from England was Boniface. During the first half of the eighth century Boniface worked tirelessly in northwestern

Europe to bring existing churches under Roman Catholic authority and to win the pagans. Other Roman Catholic missionaries pushed toward the north and east. Early in the ninth century Ansgar reached Denmark and Sweden. Cyril and Methodius, sent out by the Greek Church but voluntarily transferring to the Roman Church, worked extensively in the Balkans in the same century.

As a result of this missionary activity the Roman Catholic Church brought vast areas of population under its tutelage, instilling in them a loyalty that knew no ecclesiastical rivals.

Military and Political Aid

In the long run the barbarian invasions of the West brought new and important allies to the Roman Catholic Church. It is true that for a period the various marauding tribes caused considerable trouble, fighting with one another and with the Romans. By skilful and armed opposition, the popes at Rome were able to maintain some semblance of order during the death of one culture and the molding of another. As secular rulers of the city of Rome, they gained prestige and power. Many of the barbarians were won quickly. When Clovis, the great Frankish chieftain, decided to cast his lot with the Christian God in the closing years of the fifth century, his entire army made the same decision, although hardly on religious grounds. Furthermore, several of the popes, such as Gregory I (590–604), made alliances with tribal leaders nearby and secured a measure of political freedom.

The story of the alliance of the papacy with the Frankish kingdom will be told in more detail later. It should be noticed here, however, that papal alliance in the eighth century with the strongest military power in Europe aided greatly in the expansion and the development of authority by the Roman Church. First, the immediate crisis was met when the Frankish kings defeated the Lombards who were threatening Rome. Second, the Frankish leaders gave to the papacy a large territorial domain in the vicinity of Rome, marking the beginning of what is known as the "papal states" during Medieval history. And in 751 the pope crowned Pippin, the strong military leader of the Franks, to be king instead of one of the hereditary line. What Pippin had asked for was simply the moral support of the papacy to forestall revolution in the Frankish kingdom during the change of the ruling house, but the prestige of a pope who could dispense, or at least insure, kingdoms was greatly exalted. When the pope crowned Charlemagne as Holy Roman Emperor in 800, there was a feeling that the papal office had the authority to make or unmake emperors.

Charlemagne

The greatest of the Frankish rulers was Charles the Great (771–814). As a military and political leader he had no peer in the Medieval era. He doubled the geographical extent of his empire. More than that, the empire was consolidated and well administered during his reign. His contribution to the expansion of the Roman Church was greater than that of any of the popes. As he pushed his secular military conquests, Charlemagne carried Roman Christianity with him. By 777 he had utterly destroyed the kingdom of the Lombards in northern Italy, replacing it with inhabitants who recognized the authority of the pope. He forcibly required the Saxons in northwestern Germany to accept Christianity. When he moved against countries already nominally Christian, he required them to come into the orbit of the Roman pope, as in the case of the war against Bavaria.

One of Charlemagne's important contributions came in the fields of education and literature. He combed Europe to secure scholars who would found schools and produce literature. Priests were encouraged to widen their learning, in some cases to begin it. From Charlemagne's hand the Roman Church received many gifts and great prestige.

It is clear that Charlemagne viewed his relation to the Church much as Constantine had. Even in matters of controversial theology he felt free to summon synods and issue authoritative decrees. At the Synod of Frankfurt in 794 Charlemagne took a position opposite to that of a general council—that of Nicea in 787—

and also to that of the pope by forbidding image reverence and worship.

In all, however, the secular support of Charlemagne probably did more to advance the papal cause than any other single factor in this period.

Forged Documents

Two important forgeries were effectively used by the Roman popes during this period. The first was known as the *Donation of Constantine*. This spurious document asserted that when the Emperor Constantine had moved his capital to Constantinople in 330, he had donated to the bishop of Rome sovereignty over the Western world and had ordered all Christian clergy to be obedient to the Roman bishop. The forgery was a crude one, for it had literary and historical reflections of the eighth century. It probably was produced about 754 in an effort to induce Pippin the Short and his successors to recognize the secular claims of the papacy in the West. It was a successful forgery, for not only did Pippin give to the papacy the land in Italy conquered from the Lombards, but his successors recognized the *Donation* as genuine and based their conduct upon it. The forgery was not discovered until the fifteenth century, after the document had served well its purpose.

The other documents involved in the same forgery were known as the "Pseudo-Isidorian Decretals." Isidore of Seville had collected genuine ecclesiastical laws and decretals in the seventh century and published them as a guide for future action. The forgery of some additional decretals took place about a century later. Its effort was to magnify the office of the pope against the claims of the archbishops and metropolitans by quoting the primitive documents in papal favor. It was officially used by the popes after the middle of the ninth century. By the time that it had been proved to be a forgery in the eighteenth century, this pious fraud also had been effective in establishing the power of the pope over the Church.

Feudalism

Charlemagne's son and three grandsons continued his kingdom, but decay had begun to undermine it. The rule of the Carlovingian line (the line of Charles) broke down in the closing years of the ninth century. With the decline of a strong central government, the movement known as feudalism developed. It was a simple and natural process. When there was no central king, local strong leaders organized themselves and those whom they could control into small armies and small kingdoms. The size of the kingdom depended upon the strength of the leader. Sometimes it consisted simply of a city; sometimes it included large areas. Each kingdom became a complete monarchy. The sovereign or ruler required that all in the area of his kingdom swear personal fealty to him.

The lowest class in this system was that of the *serfs*. These men and women were the slave laborers and were treated as chattel, bound to the soil. Above them in dignity were the *freedmen,* who were not slaves but had no privileges and very little liberty. The *leudes* were holders of land by the favor of the sovereign, administering sometimes small tracts and sometimes vast areas. It was they who exercised complete supervision over the freedmen and the serfs beneath them. The more important of the leudes served as a sort of advisory council to the sovereign and assisted in community functions, such as administration of justice and community enterprises. When enemies threatened, all of these vassals took up arms to protect the rights of the sovereign.

At first glance it might appear that feudalism would greatly harm the interests of the Roman Catholic system. Some of the petty sovereigns might be unfriendly to the pretensions of the pope. As a matter of fact, the immediate result of feudalism was the decline in authority and prestige of the papal office. Bishops were leudes in many of these small kingdoms and were forced to take the oath of allegiance to the secular sovereign. Religious work was neglected in the press of secular duties.

However, when measured in terms of centuries, the papal system was not permanently injured by feudalism. Bishops sometimes became sovereigns in small kingdoms or as vassals were sometimes given large grants of land by the sovereign. Subsequently, much of this land fell into the hands of the Roman Church. In addition, a popular reaction against secular authority resulted in a zealous devotion to spiritual things on the part of the bishops. Furthermore, the kindly treatment accorded to vassals by bishops in places of authority, contrasting considerably with the treatment accorded by secular sovereigns in many cases, resulted in a feeling of affection and loyalty among the lower classes for the religious leadership. All of these factors in feudalism worked to the advantage of the Roman system, even while papal prestige and authority were at a low ebb.

Internal Developments

Worship.—During the period from 451 to 1050 the Roman Catholic method of worship began to be copied throughout the West. Variations in language, order, and liturgy were eliminated as much as possible. Worship was centered in the observance of Mass (the Supper) which, as described previously, had become more than a sacrament to bring grace to the one partaking; it was now looked upon as the "unbloody" sacrifice of Christ again, the shedding of his blood and the breaking of his body. The symbolism had become completely literal. The wine was not yet withheld from the people. Although not defined, it was generally conceived that something happens to the bread in the Mass to change it into the body of Christ. An extensive system of mediating saints had grown up. Martyrs were invoked by name to ask their intercession. The worship of the virgin Mary also increased considerably during this period. The story was spread that she had been taken immediately into heaven at her death. Prayer was offered to Mary for help and intercession. Relics became an increasingly important part of the religious life. The number of sacraments was not yet fixed; some theologians argued for simply two (baptism and the Supper), some insisted upon five, while some would have a dozen. Auricular confession had been well established, and the idea of merit from external works became widespread. Monasticism of the Benedictine type covered Europe.

Doctrinal controversies.—The doctrinal controversies in which the Roman popes engaged had their source, as might be supposed, primarily in the speculations of the East. These controversies were influential, however, in establishing ecclesiastical and secular relationships. In this period the papacy moved directly to assert its authority, not only over ecclesiastical rivals, but over secular powers as well.

One of the first disputes occurred when the patriarch of Constantinople refused to banish a heretic. Pope Felix III (483–92) attempted to excommunicate the patriarch, dismissing him from the priesthood, cutting him off from Catholic communion and from the faithful. Felix asserted that his authority as the successor of Peter enabled him to do so. However, even the Eastern bishops who had been loyal to the papacy informed Felix that he had no power of this kind, and they chose communion with Constantinople rather than with Rome. For thirty-five years this schism continued. Through political sagacity, a succeeding pope healed the schism with no loss of dignity.

A very important doctrinal controversy was brought over from the previous era—the question of the nature of Christ. The Council of Chalcedon (451) had defined the nature of Christ as being twofold—completely divine and completely human. Conciliar action did not convince many in the East. The opponents of this decision took the name of Monophysites (one nature). Practically all of Egypt and Abyssinia, part of Syria, and most of Armenia took up Monophysitism and have retained it to the present. In an effort to mollify this large section of the Eastern World, Emperor Zeno (474–91) at Constantinople issued a decree that practically annulled the definition of Chalcedon, but the only result was to alienate the West.

In another effort to placate the Monophysites, Emperor Justinian (527–65) issued a series of edicts in 544 which also compromised the Chalcedonian definition in favor of the Alexandrian interpretation so as to mean that the human nature of Christ was subordinate to the divine. Pope Vigilius (538–55), who owed his office to imperial influence, at first refused to accept the action of Justinian, but imperial pressure in 548 induced him to consent. Two years later he changed his mind and refused to attend a council to discuss the question. At the conclusion of the council in 553, Pope Vigilius was excommunicated and Justinian's edicts were given conciliar authority. The pope then apologized and accepted the council's action, and the excommunication was lifted.

Still another attempt was made to conciliate the Monophysites. Through the influence of Patriarch Sergius of Constantinople, Emperor Heraclius set forth a doctrinal interpretation which in 633 brought favorable response from the Monophysites. This interpretation shifted the area of discussion from the *nature* to the *will* or *energy*, asserting that Christ had one divine-human energy or will. Pope Honorius (625–38) was consulted and replied that Christ had one will but that the expression "energy" should not be used since it was unscriptural. Succeeding popes took the other side of the question. One of them, Pope Martin I (649–55), defied the order of Emperor Constans II (642–68) not to discuss the question and assembled a Roman synod in 649 which, among other things, condemned the emperor's order. The emperor promptly seized the pope and sent him into exile to die. However, the Monophysites meanwhile had been overcome by the Mohammedan invasion; so to please Rome and restore unity, Emperor Constantine IV (668–85) summoned the sixth universal council at Constantinople in 680–81, which asserted that Christ had two wills. Interestingly enough, this council condemned the so-called infallible Pope Honorius as a heretic.

Probably the bitterest of the doctrinal controversies began in the eighth century and is known as the "iconoclastic [image-destroying] controversy." The use of images in worship had become quite popular in both Eastern and Western Christianity since the time of Constantine, who had died in 337. The primitive Christians had refused to keep any kind of idol or image either in the home or at church and for that reason were called atheists by the pagans of the second century. However, the influence of paganism brought the extensive use of images, ostensibly at first for the sole purpose of teaching through pictures and statues. These images soon began to be looked upon as possessing divine qualities. They were venerated, kissed, and, in some cases, worshiped by enthusiastic supporters. The Mohammedans objected strenuously to this idolatry and, partly as a political move to conciliate the Mohammedan Caliph, Emperor Leo the Isaurian (717–41) issued an edict in 730 against the use of images. Despite the fanatical opposition of the monks, the images were removed from Eastern churches.

When the emperor commanded the churches in the West to remove images, he met further opposition. He argued with the pope that image worship is prohibited by both the Old and New Testament and by the early fathers, that it is heathenish in its art and heretical in its doctrinal ideas. In reply Pope Gregory II (715–31) said that God had commanded the cherubim and seraphim (images) to be made; that images preserve for the future the pictures of Christ and the saints; that the commandment against images was necessary to prevent the Israelites from heathenish idolatry, but this danger no longer existed; and that adoration and prostration before the images do not constitute worship, simply veneration. The controversy continued for more than a century.

Through political maneuvering by the regent Irene, the seventh universal Council of Nicea in 787 upheld the right of image worship. Charlemagne, emperor in the West, flatly opposed the decree of this council and the position of the popes, insisting that images were for ornaments, not worship. During the controversy Pope Gregory III (731–41) pronounced the sentence of excommunication against anyone removing, destroying, or injuring images of Mary, Christ, and the saints. This attitude was continued by the popes, despite the opposition of Charlemagne. Emperor Leo the Armenian (813–20) voided the decrees of the second Nicene Council of 787 as soon as he had taken office, but image worship achieved final victory when the regent Theodora

(842–67) ordered the images restored and the iconoclasts persecuted. A limitation was placed upon images in the East, permitting only paintings and mosaics in the churches. Statues project-
ing beyond the plane surface were forbidden. No limitation of this
kind was made in the West. Images were even more venerated
and widely used there as a result of the controversy.

Strong popes.—The expansion of papal authority during this
long period (451–1050) rested, in the final analysis, upon the able
men who occupied the chair at Rome. The work of Leo I
(440–61) has been mentioned. During the last years of his pontificate he showed his growing power by humiliating Archbishop
Hiliary of Arles through restoring a bishop whom Hiliary had
deposed legally and by having Hiliary imprisoned for disobedience. He meddled with ecclesiastical rivalries in Greece and
North Africa and claimed final authority in everything Christian.

Gelasius (492–96) asserted the primacy of the Roman pope in
every church in the world; Symmachus (498–514) claimed that
no tribunal on earth could try a pope. Gregory I (590–604) was
probably the ablest pope of the Medieval period. By careful diplomacy he wooed imperial support. He established the practice
of bestowing the pallium upon every bishop, making the pope's
consent necessary to a valid ordination or consecration. A part of
his program emphasized the need for a celibate (unmarried)
clergy. His theology summed up the sacramental system of the
Medieval period and was notable especially for its emphasis upon
good works and purgatory. His missionary interest in England
caused him to send Augustine the monk in 596. He revised church
music and ritual and worked toward making Rome's pattern uni-
form throughout the world. His encounter with the patriarch of
Constantinople was not entirely successful (as will be seen in succeeding pages), but he did not allow this to diminish his exalted
view of his office. Nicholas I (858–67) was the last outstanding
pope before the deluge of anarchy. He magnified the missionary
program, excommunicated the patriarch of Constantinople during a brief schism, required the Holy Roman Emperor, Lo-
thair II, to take back a divorced wife, and humiliated those

archbishops who were tardy in obeying his instructions to the letter.

Anarchy and Confusion

The closing two centuries of this period provided a crucial test for the papacy. The events of this era will be discussed in more detail in chapter 9. It may be sufficient to note that Europe was in anarchy after about 880. The turmoil in Italy turned the papal office into a petty political prize. Between 896 and 904 there were ten popes, murder and treachery disposing of most of them. The period from 904 to 962 is known as the "pornocracy," connoting lewdness and immorality, because the papal office was controlled by unscrupulous and wicked men and women. From 962 to about 1050 the popes were named and controlled by the German emperors of the re-established empire. The papacy had reached its lowest point in prestige and authority, but a new day was dawning. Through an effective internal reform, the rise of orderly central governments, and the ability to use ecclesiastical weapons, the papacy soon reached new heights of power in both ecclesiastical and secular realms.

Concluding Summary

Between 451 and 1050 the Roman Catholic Church and the papacy which directed it made remarkable advances. The barbarian invasions were disguised blessings. Monasticism provided militant and trained soldiers. Missions expanded Roman Catholic influences even beyond the widely extended boundary of the new Holy Roman Empire under Charlemagne. The doctrinal controversies generally worked to the benefit of the papacy, although Honorius was condemned as a heretic and Vigilius was humiliated by Eastern councils. The alliance of Rome with the Franks during the eighth and ninth centuries brought it land, prestige, and authority. The breakdown of that central government brought loss and humiliation to the papacy. The Church had become so dependent upon the military and political strength of the state that it could not stand without them.

The struggle of the papacy to dominate both ecclesiastical and secular authorities has been described in this chapter in terms of papal expansion. There was another side that should also be noticed. The succeeding two chapters will deal with opposition from ecclesiastical rivals and from secular powers. The overlapping in the story will be justified by the different point of view which will be presented in these two chapters.

8

Religious Opposition to Roman Authority

THE ROMAN CATHOLIC Church did not attain its dominant position without encountering strong opposition from other Christians. This would be expected. The dignity of the Roman see had always been recognized, but to create an ecclesiastical monarchy with the Roman bishop as its head was hardly in accord with the thinking of early Christian leaders. The earliest Roman bishops about whom there is direct historical information were rebuked by neighboring bishops for breaches in ecclesiastical and doctrinal matters. Before the close of the second century Roman bishops were condemned because they followed the Montanist heresy and were excommunicated for ecclesiastical laxity. Men familiar with this history could hardly be expected to accept at face value the arrogant claims that later developed.

Weakness in Rome's Claims

There were several definite weaknesses in the claims for primacy by the Roman Church. Some of these may be noted.

Relative to apostolic succession.—Rome was not the only church with a strong tradition. Both Irenaeus (185) and Tertullian (200) point out that many churches were founded by the apostles and had apostolic writings. Corinth, Philippi, and Ephesus were mentioned in particular. More than that, Gregory I (590–604), one of the greatest of the Roman popes, admitted that the churches at Alexandria and Antioch had the same apostolic background as Rome. His letter said, "Like myself, you who are at Alexandria and at Antioch are successors of Peter, seeing that Peter before coming to Rome held the see of Antioch, and sent Mark his spiritual son to Alexandria. So, do not permit the see of Constantinople to eclipse your sees which are the sees of Peter." In other words, if the basis of Roman authority, as claimed, is succession from Peter, then Antioch and Alexandria should have a claim prior to that of Rome. As a matter of fact, if tradition constitutes the basis of authority, then Jerusalem, where Jesus established the first church, should have the primacy.

Relative to Peter.—It should be noted in particular that the claims of the Roman Church to universal dominion because of the alleged primacy of Peter were made very late. Innocent I (402–17) was the first Roman bishop to base his authority on the Petrine tradition. By that time, due to the influence of many other factors, Rome was already recognized as one of the principal bishoprics in Christianity. Leo I (440–61) prepared the first scriptural exposition of later papal claims about the primacy of Peter, basing them, as previously discussed, on Matthew 16:18–19, Luke 22:31–32, and John 21:15–17.

In the first passage the important words are "upon this rock," since the promise of binding and loosing is repeated to all the disciples on other occasions (see Matthew 18:18 and John 20:23). What is the rock upon which Jesus would build his church? The greatest theologians of the first four centuries did not agree with the Roman view. Chrysostom (345–407) said that the rock was the faith of the confession; Ambrose (337–97) said that the rock was the confession of the universal faith; Jerome (340–420) and Augustine (354–430) interpreted the rock as Christ. If one desires to be literal in the interpretation of this passage, he should continue his literal view to verse 23 where Jesus names Peter as Satan. The passages in Luke and John must be utterly twisted out of their meaning to buttress universal papal domination.

Furthermore, a reading of the New Testament fails to give the impression of any primacy on Peter's part. Apparently Peter did not recognize it; he gave a labored explanation to the Jerusalem church for baptizing Cornelius. The other disciples apparently were ignorant of it, for James, not Peter, presided at the Jerusalem conference. Paul's sharp rebuke to Peter and Peter's admission of error suggest that Paul had not been informed of Peter's primacy.

The Roman Catholic claim that Peter was the first bishop of Rome and served in that capacity for twenty-five years is completely unsupported by Scripture or primitive tradition. It is most difficult to see how this position can be sustained in view of Paul's letter to the Romans (about 58), which makes no mention of Peter, and the account of Paul's residence in Rome in the Acts of the Apostles. An agreement was made at the Jerusalem conference that Peter should limit his ministry to the Jews and Jewish Christians. It seems probable that the Roman church was predominantly Gentile, and it would be quite unlikely that Paul's letter to the Romans could have contained some expressions that are there had Peter founded the Roman church and been serving as bishop.

Relative to primacy of the Roman bishop.—If antiquity and tradition possess any authority, the principle of the equality of all bishops should claim a primary place. This was a very ancient and universal belief. The New Testament shows that even the apostles themselves respected the authority of the churches which they had established. Antioch did not ask Jerusalem for permission to begin the missionary movement, and Paul did not first consult Peter before preaching salvation to the Gentiles throughout the Roman Empire.

In the second century the same principle was followed. Bishop Irenaeus of Lyons condemned Bishop Eleutherius of Rome (174–89) for following after heresy and rebuked Bishop Victor of Rome (189–98) for intolerance, but still recognized their ultimate right to hold their own opinions. Origen (182–251) denied that the Christian church was built upon Peter and his successors; all the successors of the apostles, said he, are equally heirs of this promise. Cyprian (200–258) emphatically asserted the equality of all bishops, stating that each bishop holds the episcopacy in its entirety. Even Jerome (340–420), famous as a papal proponent and translator of the Greek and Hebrew Scriptures into the Vulgate (the official Latin version of the Bible), acidly remarked that whenever a bishop is found, whether at Rome, Constantinople, Eugubium, or Rhegium, that bishop has equality as a successor of the apostles with all other bishops. Pope Gregory I could use such an argument when protesting against the ecclesiastical pretensions of his rivals. If the patriarch of Constantinople is the universal bishop above all others, then bishops are not really bishops but priests, wrote Gregory. In other words, Gregory based his argument on the fact that all bishops are equal, and if one is exalted above the others, then the others cease in reality to have the episcopal office.

The victory of Leo I at Chalcedon in 451—which, in the thinking of many, established him as the first Roman pope—grew out of the recognition of Leo's claims concerning Peter's primacy and the transference of that primacy to the Roman bishops through historic succession. Even this achievement did not break down the ancient belief that one bishop is equal to another. Had it not been for the political and military support of the secular powers, the Roman bishop could never have asserted his claims, even in the West. Bishop Hiliary of Arles fought strenuously to maintain this principle, but Leo humiliated him through political power. The same thing was true with Bishop Hincmar of Rheims in his struggle with Pope Nicholas in the ninth century.

Opposition to Roman Pretensions

Since Rome was the earliest and strongest bishopric in the West, opposition in that section of the Mediterranean world was nominal. It is true that Tertullian and Cyprian, bishop of Carthage, defied the Roman bishop, and through the Medieval era many efforts were made by various bishops to resist the encroachments of papal power. Invasions by the Germanic tribes in the third and fourth centuries provided the opportunity for Roman Christianity to gain great multitudes of new followers who knew no rival loyalty; the Mohammedan seizure of North Africa in the seventh and eighth centuries eliminated any rivals from that area.

In the East the situation was different. Two outstanding religious centers vied for supremacy: Antioch, famous for its Pauline tradition, and Alexandria, viewed as Petrine in origin since it was thought that Peter had sent John Mark to that city as leader. Even before the founding of Constantinople in 330 as the capital of the Roman Empire and before the bishop of Jerusalem was strong enough to be recognized as a patriarch, these two cities had been ecclesiastical rivals. Mention has been made of the varying points of view in the doctrinal interpretation between the two cities. One of the causes for the influence of the bishop of Rome was that each of these rivals sought Roman support for his position against the other side. Consequently, appeals to the Roman bishop came frequently.

The Council of Nicea (325) recognized the equality of the bishops of Rome, Antioch, and Alexandria. The Council of Constantinople in 381 raised the bishop of Constantinople to the dignity of a patriarch, and the Council of Chalcedon in 451 gave that position also to the bishop of Jerusalem. Thus there were five strong bishops who were potentially rivals for first place. The Roman bishop had the great advantage. He was the only candidate from the West; sharp and ancient rivalry kept the Eastern patriarchs constantly vigilant lest one should gain some favored place; constant controversy and schism prevented careful organization and ecclesiastical consolidation in the East. The principal opposition to Rome came from Constantinople for two reasons: first, the political situation of Constantinople insured its prestige and power; and second, all of the rivals except Constantinople were overwhelmed by the Mohammedan invasion of the seventh century. These two elements deserve a brief discussion.

The rise of Constantinople.—The move of the imperial capital from Rome to Constantinople in 330 brought it important ecclesiastical influence promptly. Within a half century after the establishment of the city as capital, Constantinople was elevated to the place of chief rival of Rome, mainly through the work of Emperor Theodosius (378–95), who made Christianity the official state religion. The Council of Chalcedon in 451 reasserted the dignity of Constantinople and naïvely remarked that such eminence was due because of the *political* importance of the city. Evidently it took neither apostolic tradition nor religious orthodoxy to attain such a high place. By this time the bishop of Constantinople was simply a tool of the emperor in most respects. This situation is known as Caesaro-papacy, the domination of the church by the emperor. The several controversies of the Eastern world made Christianity a potential political danger. So it became necessary, in order to preserve unity in the political sphere, for the emperor to keep his finger constantly upon the Church. Doctrinally, Eastern Christianity developed the same sort of sacramentalism and sacerdotalism as Western Catholicism, although it practiced trine immersion for baptism.

Despite the inevitable clash between the strongest power of the East and that of the West, the day of reckoning was delayed because of invasions in each area. The Germanic invasion of the West and its far-reaching consequences have been described in chapter 7. The Mohammedan invasion of the East did not begin until the seventh century. Even before the Eastern collapse, it became apparent that the bishops in Alexandria, Antioch, and Jerusalem would not be able to stand in ecclesiastical conflict with Rome and Constantinople. Civilization was moving westward, and these cities lived in the glory of the past.

The bishop of Constantinople, however, challenged the pretensions of the Roman bishop, particularly after the Council of Chalcedon (451) had spoken in such exalted terms about the place of the Constantinopolitan office. Reference was made in the previous chapter to the effort by Pope Felix III to excommunicate Patriarch Acacius of Constantinople in 484 and to the refusal of the Eastern world to accept such authority on the part of the pope. The story of Pope Vigilius and his humiliation by the East (through imperial power) in the Council of 553 has been told. The claims of the patriarch at Constantinople became more extravagant when Emperor Justinian (527–65) recaptured Italy from the barbarians in about 536 and began to control the pope. The ambitions of Constantinople were not different from those

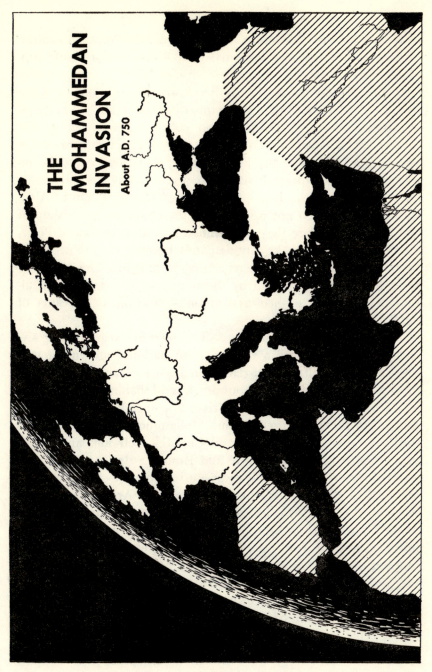

THE MOHAMMEDAN INVASION

About A.D. 750

of Rome. No longer would Constantinople, the imperial capital, be second to Rome or even equal with Rome, but it would supplant Rome.

In the last decade of the sixth century Bishop John of Constantinople claimed the title "ecumenical patriarch." The pope at Rome, unaided by military and political power, could only protest and scheme. He, Gregory I (590–604), circulated letters among the bishops of the East, arguing that there could be no such thing as a universal bishop or pope, basing his statements on the equality of all bishops. He begged the patriarchs at Alexandria and Antioch not to recognize the claims of the bishop of Constantinople since they, like himself, were successors of Peter. The pope did not make any demands because of his succession from Peter, nor did he excommunicate anyone. The battle of titles was temporarily won by the bishop of Constantinople, although Gregory assumed a new one—"servant of servants of God."

The Mohammedan invasion.—The opening years of the seventh century produced a religious and national movement that was destined to affect Christianity in both East and West for almost a thousand years. Its founder was Mohammed (570–632), who in his youth was a camel driver and merchant of Mecca in Arabia. In his trips into Palestine Mohammed had ample opportunity to observe the Jewish and Christian religions and to see the influence of Greek culture and Roman rule. In 610 he proclaimed a new religion which was a mixture of Jewish, Christian, Greek, and Roman elements, together with Arabian ideas and emphases. His system included prophets from Judaism (like Abraham and Moses) and Christianity (Christ) and outstanding military leaders from pagan history. The last and greatest prophet of God, however, was Mohammed, who supposedly was the Holy Spirit promised by Christ.

The Mohammedan system was completely fatalistic—all things are already determined. An individual's good works prove that he is elected to a paradise of sensual and fleshly enjoyment. These good works include prayer, fasting, almsgiving, and war against the unbeliever. After Mohammed's death in 632, his followers planned a conquest of the world. Striking westward, the Saracens overran Palestine and practically all of the East except Constantinople. Within a hundred years they had conquered all of North Africa, had crossed the Straits of Gibraltar into Spain, and were arrayed for battle near Tours, France. In 732 Charles Martel engaged them here in battle and defeated them in a crucial encounter that determined the culture of Europe. Again, seven years later, Charles inflicted a severe defeat upon them to save continental Europe from their devastations.

As a result of this movement, all of the Eastern rivals to Rome were swept away except Constantinople, which was under constant threat of capture. Wherever the Mohammedans ruled, Christianity became stagnant through rigorous repression. Priceless Christian manuscripts and books were destroyed by the invaders in Palestine and Alexandria.

Renewed Controversy Between East and West

The several doctrinal controversies of this period were discussed in the previous chapter. The bitterness of these struggles served to accentuate the ecclesiastical rivalry between Constantinople and Rome. Added to these factors were racial differences, political distrust (especially after Charlemagne was crowned in Rome in 800), and doctrinal and ceremonial variations. It appeared that a permanent schism would occur in the ninth century. Patriarch Photius of Constantinople (858–67 and 878–86—twice in the office) rejected the claims of the Roman popes and instituted a vigorous program to win the bordering Slavic states to Greek Christianity. Photius charged that the Roman Church was heretical in doctrine and practice, particularly in amending one of the ancient creeds without calling a universal council to discuss the matter. Pope Nichols I (858–67), however, was one of the ablest of the Medieval popes and maintained the Roman prestige. The issue was temporarily straddled by the Synod of Constantinople in 869.

The controversy was renewed in the eleventh century, resulting in a permanent schism between Latin and Greek Christianity. Patriarch Michael Cerularius (1043–58) of Constantinople deliberately provided the occasion for the schism. He was ambitious to forward the office which he held and felt that a break with the West would offer the greatest opportunity for advancement. Without too much difficulty he was able to stir up the wrath of Pope Leo IX (1049–54).

In the conferences to discuss the situation, the ancient differences between Eastern and Western worship were debated. Rome used unleavened bread; Constantinople, leavened bread. Rome had added a word to the Nicene Creed which taught that the Holy Spirit proceeded from Father and Son; Constantinople denied that additions could be made to the creed without an ecumenical council. Rome required clerical celibacy; Constantinople allowed the lower clergy to marry. Rome allowed only bishops to anoint in confirmation; Constantinople allowed priests to do so. Rome allowed the use of milk, butter, and cheese during Lent; Constantinople said no. These differences, however, were not the cause of the schism which came. By deliberate design the Roman representatives were irritated to the breaking point, and on July 16, 1054, the schism was begun. East and West formally excommunicated one another. Such is the situation at the present time, although efforts have been made to heal the break.

Dissent from Catholicism

Reference has been made in the previous period to dissenters from the general movement toward Catholic and Roman Catholic Christianity. Montanism, Novatianism, and Donatism maintained themselves through several centuries of struggle. Nestorian, Monophysite, and Monothelite parties, denouncing both Roman and Greek Catholicism, have continued to the present time in considerable strength.

Jovinianus and Vigilantius.—Two distinctly antipapal movements appeared within the Roman Church in the fourth and fifth centuries. One was headed by Jovinianus of Rome (about 378), who bitterly denounced the movement toward asceticism and

108

righteousness by works. His main tenet asserted that a saved man does not need merits from fasting, withdrawal from the world, and celibacy. A similar movement was begun by Vigilantius (about 395), who protested strongly against the honoring of relics, asceticism, and image worship. The first of these movements was condemned by Bishop Siricius of Rome (384–98) in a local synod, while the second was swallowed up in the barbarian invasions of the fifth century.

Paulicians.—One of the important dissenting minorities during the Medieval period was called the Paulicians. The origins of this group are obscure. Its general doctrinal position suggests that it grew out of primitive Armenian Christianity. Its name came either from veneration for Paul the apostle or from Paul of Samosata, bishop of Antioch until about 272. It is generally admitted that in the seventh century Constantine introduced a reform to a much older movement and was not the founder. The Paulicians bitterly opposed the Roman, Greek, and Armenian churches as "satanic." They viewed Christ as the adopted Son of God. Their emphasis upon the power of Satan has brought charges of dualism. It is uncertain whether they observed the ordinances or viewed them as completely spiritual elements. The apostle Paul was greatly venerated, and his ethical and moral teachings were emphasized and practiced. Their history has been a tragic one. Except under emperors Leo the Isaurian (717–41) and Constantine Copronymus (741–75), they were rigorously persecuted. In their zeal against images they took the side of the Saracens and assisted in destroying and pillaging. In the eighth and ninth centuries many Paulicians emigrated to Thrace and Bulgaria, thence on to the lower Danubian regions. It is thought that the Bogomiles of the Balkans and the Cathari of southern France gathered up their teachings and continued their movement. Some think that the Anabaptists were a product of these influences.

Concluding Summary

Ecclesiastical opposition to Roman pretensions had Scriptures and primitive principles in their favor. Apostolic and even Petrine succession were not confined to Rome. The scriptural evidences of Rome's primacy were developed late and are unconvincing. The ancient principle of equality of bishops was overcome by Rome only through severe struggle and the use of military and political coercion.

Constantinople, the principal opponent of Rome, made a determined bid for first place. After numerous and bitter controversies, a permanent schism was effected in 1054. Other ecclesiastical rivals of Rome were overwhelmed by the Mohammedan invasion of the seventh century. The Mohammedans succeeded in pushing into southern France before their defeat by Charles Martel in 732.

The record of ecclesiastical opposition to papal authority is very sketchy. Those within the hierarchical system who might oppose the domination of Rome would think twice before making outward protest or recording literary dissent. The only records were kept by those who looked upon the dissenters as heretical schismatics. There must have been much dissent that had no voice, for during the centuries immediately following the eleventh, opposition to papal authority sprang up in every part of Western Christianity.

Secular Opposition to Roman Authority

WHEN CONSTANTINE ASSUMED a friendly attitude toward Christianity and became sole emperor in 323, it was hoped that tension between the secular state and Christianity was a thing of the past. It is true that Constantine passed imperial edicts making it possible for Christianity to develop in a favorable atmosphere. One reason for the removal of the capital of the empire to Constantinople was that Rome was crowded with pagan temples and memorials. At the Council of Nicea (325) Constantine displayed a paternal attitude and until his death in 337, whatever his motives may have been, maintained a singularly constant devotion to the Christian movement. After Constantine's death some segment of Catholic Christianity was conscious of the antagonistic or repressive aspect of secular power throughout the remainder of the period. Before discussing specific instances of this, it is well to give a résumé of why secular opposition arose.

Reasons for Secular Opposition

Various reasons caused secular powers to struggle against Christianity. (1) *Religious antagonism* motivated a man like Emperor Julian (361–63) in his opposition to the Christian movement. It will be recalled that his family was slain by the order of his uncle, the Christian emperor. His personal resentment was transferred to the religion which his uncle professed, although Julian was enamored with paganism while a student. Upon becoming emperor, Julian attempted to reintroduce a refined paganism, but the attempt failed. (2) *A desire to control* Christianity for political or selfish purposes led many secular rulers, both East and West, to impose severe restrictions upon Christian leaders. As has been mentioned, this condition was known as Caesaro-papism. (3) *Material possessions* in the hands of Christian bishops provided an excuse for attempts by some of the Germanic tribes to seize the land and goods of the Church. (4) *Rivalry with secular powers* constituted another reason for secular opposition. By the fifth century the Roman popes were beginning to assert their right to rule not only the spiritual world but the secular world as well. Such assertions, supported later on by ecclesiastical weapons, kept the papacy in constant struggle with secular powers. (5) *Internal controversies* added another reason for secular restriction and repression. Religious controversy, particularly in the East, could be very dangerous politically. Secular rulers felt that it was a political necessity to maintain control over Christianity. (6) *Corruption and decay* in Western Christianity brought the strong arm of imperial rule. Sometimes for religious reasons and sometimes for political considerations the late Medieval emperors appointed the occupants of the papal office and dictated their policies.

A brief summary of relations between the various secular powers and the developing Roman Church will provide historical examples of these several reasons for secular opposition.

Opposition from the Roman Empire Before 476

The three sons of Constantine succeeded him in 337. One was killed in battle, one committed suicide, and the third, Constantius, ruled until 361. Constantius was an Arian Christian, and his long rule brought repressions and antagonism to Nicene Christianity, which included Rome. It is significant that Athanasius, not the Roman bishop, was singled out as the target in the persecution of Nicene Christianity.

Emperor Julian (361–63) was anti-Christian in his attitude and actions. Had Constantine been a consistent Christian (or even a Christian at all), Julian might well have been reared to respect

112

Christianity and to embrace it. Julian's brief reign and the fundamental weakness of the refined paganism which he tried to introduce blunted the force of his antagonism.

The basic rivalry between church authority and secular authority was made clear in this period. Augustine's very influential
writing, the *City of God,* set secular and religious authority over
against one another and magnified their incompatibility. Fifth-
century popes grasped the ideal, soon beginning to describe the
relationship between the two powers as two swords—the *spiritual*
sword as greater than the *secular* sword.

Struggle with the Germanic Tribes (476–800)

It is difficult to describe in a few words the complex story of the
barbarian invasions of the West. Perhaps as a summary the movement can be divided into six general periods.

The breakdown of old Roman authority (about 392).—It has
already been mentioned that since primitive times the Germanic
tribes north and east of the Empire had only been restrained from
overrunning the southern area through the establishment of strong
garrisons across the northern frontier. In the third century the
Gothic tribes almost succeeded in invading the Empire on two
occasions. Finally, because of the increasing pressure of less civi-
lized and stronger tribes pushing south and west from central Asia,
the Visigoths were allowed to cross the Danube and secure refuge
within the Empire proper. Aroused in 378 by alleged mistreatment, the Visigoths met the Roman army in the Battle of Adrian-
ople and inflicted a severe defeat. Emperor Theodosius (379–95)
was able to control them, but at his death the deluge began. The
Visigoths were beaten away from Constantinople but moved westward to capture Rome in 410, Gaul two years later, and then
settle down to rule in what is now France and Spain. The dikes had
been breached, and barbaric tribes of every sort flowed into the
Western empire. Vandals, Alans, and Suevi entered Gaul and
Spain; the Franks and Burgundians settled in Germany; the Angles, Saxons, and Jutes occupied England; the Spanish Vandals
conquered North Africa.

113

The rule of the army (until about 493).—The century after the barbarian invasions was one of confusion and conflict. Army chieftains became rulers. In 476 a mutiny by the Germanic tribes within the army resulted in the overthrow of the nominal Roman government and the elevation of a German general to the kingship, but this event was of no special significance.

The rule of Theodoric the Ostrogoth (493–526).—In 493 a new wave of barbarians invaded Italy—the Ostrogoths, the eastern Goths from Russia. Their chief, Theodoric, ruled from Ravenna in northern Italy and was successful in maintaining order.

The re-establishment of imperial control (535–72).—Justinian the Great secured the emperorship in Constantinople in 527 and immediately made plans for reconquering the West. By 534 the Vandals of North Africa had been defeated and the Ostrogoth kingdom in Italy had been attacked. During the lifetime of Justinian, imperial control of the West was maintained.

The kingdom of the Lombards (572–754).—More barbarians bearing the name Lombards swept south into Italy and captured the northern section. Although they did not take Rome, their strong military power prevented any other tribes from doing so. They were a constant threat to Rome's security, but on the other hand, their presence guaranteed a certain amount of freedom from Constantinople to the bishops of Rome.

The rise of the Franks (754–800).—The tribe known as the Franks was destined to become the dominating power in all Europe. The Romans had fought to hold this tribe, along with the others, from crossing the Rhine in northern Germany as early as the second century. With the breakthrough of the Visigoths in the fourth century, the Franks had fought their way into southern Germany and eastern France. An event of great significance for Christianity occurred in 496. Influenced by his wife, who was an orthodox Christian, and his great victory over the Alemanni at Strassburg in 496, the Frankish chieftain Clovis (481–511) adopted Christianity and with his army was baptized. Succeeding kings enlarged the Frankish kingdom until it included most of what is now France.

114

When the Lombards in northern Italy threatened the capture of Rome itself in 739, Pope Gregory III appealed for help to Charles Martel, the military dictator (although not the king nor of the kingly line) of the Franks, without success. Charles' son, Pepin the Short, on the other hand, entered into friendly relations with the papacy after the death of his father. His plan was to seize the kingship from one of the weak descendents of Clovis who had succeeded to that office by right of inheritance. In order to forestall serious opposition and perhaps revolution, Pepin desired to secure ecclesiastical approval, along with the good will of the Frankish nobility. In return, Pepin could offer ample protection against the Lombards. Gladly the papacy entered into this trade and Pope Zacharias (741–52) arranged for the anointing of Pepin as king of the Franks in 751. The new line was known as the Carolingians, after either Charles Martel or Charles the Great.

Pepin kept his part of the bargain. By 756 he had forced the Lombards to recognize the pope as the sovereign over a large area of land in central and northern Italy. This was the beginning of the papal states which the Roman Church held until 1870. Perhaps the desire to secure those lands motivated the forgery at Rome known as the *Donation of Constantine* just at this time, by which it was asserted that the emperor Constantine in 330 had given to the Roman bishop all of the western lands. At any rate, Pepin and his successors were greatly influenced by this forgery.

Holy Roman Empire versus Holy Roman Church (800 On)

Pepin's son was Charles the Great (Charlemagne). His aid to the Roman Catholic Church has been described in the last chapter. He dominated the Western world ecclesiastically, in addition to ruling it as sovereign. The climax, not only to his rule but to the Middle Ages, came in 800 when Pope Leo III (795–816) crowned him as Holy Roman Emperor. This act, apparently by the initiative of the pope, shaped ideas and history for a millennium. For one thing, it was popularly looked upon as the reestablishment of the old Roman Empire in the West, an office unfilled since Constantine moved the capital to Constantinople in

115

330. Racial and sectional patriotism immediately hailed the beginning of a day that would restore the ancient glory to Rome and the West. In the second place, this restoration was viewed as proceeding from divine purpose. The title "Holy" called attention to the fact that God now had provided a secular power that was the counterpart to the spiritual power in the Roman Church. In the third place, papal prestige was lifted to new heights. Following up the antecedents laid in the crowning of Pepin the Short, the bestowal of the imperial title marked the pope as the giver of the greatest secular blessings of the earth. This prestige was enhanced when the Eastern Emperor Leo V (813–20) later recognized the validity of the transaction. Finally, unknowingly the papacy had given birth to its greatest rival throughout the remainder of the Medieval period. Perhaps Pope Leo had in mind the ideal described in Augustine's *City of God,* but, if so, the results must have been most disappointing. The earthly ruler controlled the heavenly; Charlemagne dominated the Church, appointing bishops at will and for the most part dictating papal policy.

After the death of Charlemagne, his weak son Louis ruled until 840; his three grandsons divided the empire in 843. The three divisions that were carved out at this time became roughly the states of Germany and France and the intervening strip.

Anarchy and Papal Degradation

The Carolingian line collapsed about 880. Strong nobles ruled feudal kingdoms and the Church as well. After the pontificate of Nicholas I (858–67), the papal office sank to indescribably low depths. Violence, murder, and mutilation were practiced on its occupants as various political factions intermittently seized control. New invasions terrified and devastated the population. Northmen and Hungarians swept the northern plains. The Mohammedans in North Africa and Spain were on the verge of winning the victory which they had been unable to accomplish because of Charles Martel in 732. From bases in Africa, Egypt, and Spain, these raiders captured Corsica, Sardinia, and Sicily, then Palermo and Messina in Italy proper. Rome was sacked in 841.

The German Re-establishment of the Empire

A new direction was taken in the middle of the tenth century when Pope John XII (955–64) appealed to the German king Otto I (936–73) for aid against the military attacks of Berengar II, an Italian noble seeking the imperial title. Otto had already invaded Italy in 951 with considerable success; ten years later, complying with the pope's request, Otto completed the task. In 962 Otto was crowned Holy Roman Emperor by John XII. He and his successors exercised complete control of the papacy for a century. Otto III (983–1002) appointed the first German pope in 996 and the first French pope in 999.

Before the middle of the eleventh century even the emperors were looking longingly for a church reform. Henry III (1039–56) attempted to introduce such reform by brusquely ending a papal schism involving three claimants and appointing German popes who agreed to reform measures. His last nomination was his cousin, a zealous reforming bishop, who became Leo IX (1049–54).

Thus at the close of this period the papacy was under the complete domination of the secular authority. However, this situation was about to be remedied. The reforming work of Leo IX and the rise of Hildebrand, who became Pope Gregory VII (1073–85), began the movement to rid the Roman Church of secular control.

Concluding Summary

In its relations with secular power the Roman Catholic Church came out second best during this period. Even when such power was friendly, as in the case of Charlemagne, it reserved the right to handle Christianity as a part of imperial administration. The various popes strongly asserted the ideal introduced by Augustine —namely, that the spiritual power in the world is superior to secular power and one day will completely overcome it. This ideal was not attained during the period from 325 to 1050.

The papacy made significant advances, however, despite many

hardships. The forgeries of the eighth century greatly increased papal prestige. The *Donation of Constantine* was doubtless influential in causing Pepin to make his donation of large areas of land in central and northern Italy to the pope. The forged decretals which bore the name of Isidore of Seville had their bearing upon the relations of the papacy to the secular power in that they established Rome as the focal point of the Christian movement.

The papacy was undergoing one of its greatest humiliations during the immediate centuries preceding the close of this period. However, the end of this situation was near. Within a century the papal office had regained its dominant place in ecclesiastical life and was well along toward dominating secular authority.

10

Roman Catholic Domination

THE AUTHORITY AND prestige of the Roman Catholic pope reached their height in the period from 1050 to 1215. Building upon the claims made before the deluge of anarchy and feudalism and the domination of the two empires (800 and 962), the Roman Church not only regained its power but was victorious in new and greater conquests. There were many contributing factors that made this possible. One principal factor was the attitude of the people everywhere. Tired of war and violence, men were ready to follow any leader that promised peace and justice—the key words of the papal promise. There was universal rejoicing when the spiritual weapons of the papacy began to overpower the familiar swords and spears. Secular unity had been destroyed in feudalism, and the hope of one universal spiritual government, resting upon sure and eternal foundations, provided an almost irresistible appeal.

The Roman Catholic revival began from the inside with a thorough reform and regrouping of papal forces; the revived papal monarchy then achieved domination of the Western world, both secular and spiritual. The most important movements contributing to this revitalization of the papacy and the Roman Church will be briefly discussed.

Monastic Reform

The Benedictine monks had been one of the foremost factors in the expansion of the papacy and the Roman system. They were skilled both as missionaries to carry the gospel and farmers to till the soil. The success of Augustine the monk in winning England is more spectacular than the work of many of his brethren who formed small bands and conquered nature in large sections of the European wilderness, but the accomplishments of the latter were almost as important. Monasteries sprang up all over Central Europe, providing large tracts of land under the control of the Roman Church, as well as a place of refuge for the needy, a retreat for the scholars, and a conservatory of learning through the period of the Dark Ages. These monasteries, however, did not escape the secular spirit of their times. Even though a monk must take an oath of poverty, for example, nothing was said about the material possessions of a monastery. Through valiant community of effort, through gifts of admirers, through special religious offerings for services, and by other means, monasteries became extremely wealthy. The monks could not *own* possessions but they could *use* them, and this distinction made it possible to circumvent entirely the idea of personal poverty. Other abuses crept into the system. Feudal lords sometimes lavished goods upon the monasteries, demanding (and securing) in return the right to name the abbots and direct their policies. Monasteries became the places of pleasant and leisurely service by the closing years of the ninth century.

A reform was needed and soon came. Under the leadership of its strong abbot, the monastery at Cluny began such a reform in the opening years of the tenth century. Strict ascetical living again was magnified. Complete separation from secular favors and control took place. The pope became the immediate superior rather than the local bishop. Several monastic communities banded together under the leadership of the Cluniac abbot to forward this reform. The religious sincerity and fervor of such a movement was bound to induce support and admiration. Even the secular rulers in Germany, the emperors themselves, encouraged the reform after 962. It is a revealing commentary upon the decayed condition of the papacy in these centuries to notice that the popes in Rome opposed this movement, even though a main purpose, through spiritual reform, was to magnify the papacy. Emperor Henry III (1039–56) would allow no Roman opposition to the Cluniac movement to blunt the reform, however, and in 1049 appointed his cousin, one of the Cluniac reformers, as Pope Leo IX. Without delay Pope Leo began reform in Rome along the lines of the Cluniac movement, choosing as one of his assistants a young and zealous reformer named Hildebrand. These men brought the reform into the papacy and made possible the tremendous upsurge of the Roman Church during the succeeding centuries.

The Crusades

Another factor that greatly aided in the rapid rise of the papacy is known as the Crusades. This movement began as an effort to capture Jerusalem from the hands of the infidels. The Roman Church had for centuries laid great emphasis upon pilgrimages as a means of securing forgiveness for postbaptismal sins. A pilgrimage to Jerusalem was considered the great satisfaction for sin. In the seventh century the Mohammedans captured the Holy Land but allowed pilgrims to visit Jerusalem for religious purposes. In the eleventh century the land was overcome by the Seljuk Turks, a new Saracenic power from Asia Minor. These Turks were completely unsympathetic to any pilgrimages by Christians. For centuries Western Europe had played with the idea of a vast attack upon the Mohammedans to rescue the Holy Land. Great impetus had come from the conversion of the Normans in 911, a warlike people who enjoyed nothing more than fierce fighting. They had conquered areas of France, England, and southern Italy. They had been particularly effective in driving the Mohammedans out of Sicily, Sardinia, and Corsica. Because they were seafaring people, the Normans were especially equipped to attack the Holy Land; they could sail the Mediterranean almost to within striking distance of Jerusalem. Furthermore, the conversion of Hungary had provided a point of departure at the very edge of the Turkish empire and had shortened the distance through hostile territory by thousands of miles.

The popes had hinted at the idea long before it was carried out. Pope Silvester II (999–1003) had spoken of such a grand crusade against the Turks; Gregory VII (1073–85) had actively planned the attack but because of his struggle with Emperor Henry IV was unable to secure the secular support necessary for such an undertaking. In 1095 the Greek emperor Alexius appealed to the West not to delay such a crusade any longer. The Turks were threatening to take Constantinople. In that year Pope Urban II (1088–99) called upon secular powers to devote themselves to this divine crusade, promising forgiveness of sin to those dying in the effort. Europe was swept with the passion of slaughtering for the cross (the word "Crusades" comes from the word "cross") .

In 1096 the first crusade began. About half a million soldiers moved toward Jerusalem. As this enormous and undisciplined army moved eastward, it lived on the countryside, completely devastating the areas through which it moved as though it were a hostile army. About forty thousand finally reached Jerusalem and captured it. There were about eight other crusades, including a children's crusade in 1212—a tragic, evil thing in every respect.

The results of the Crusades were manifold. In a sense they worked toward the immediate strengthening of the papacy. They brought an immediate prestige to the papacy which could give orders to princes everywhere and assume such international leadership. The papacy profited enormously from a financial standpoint. The people lavishly bestowed gifts upon the Roman Church and arranged to give their possessions to the Church in the event they did not return. The papacy used the Crusades as an excuse to levy a new ecclesiastical tax, which continued to be sought long after the crusading movement had ceased.

Papal methods were both aided and shaped by the Crusades. The idea soon became widespread that the pope could call upon all faithful secular rulers to march against heretics anywhere, including minority religious dissenters in Europe and secular princes who refused to be obedient to papal orders. A new and powerful weapon for coercion had been formed.

The Crusades were based upon the idea that had brought relics and fetishism into popularity. Extreme reverence for, and even actual worship of, physical remains followed the struggle to recapture the greatest of all relics, Jerusalem. During the period of the Crusades almost every sort of relic was allegedly brought back from Jerusalem. When Jerusalem was recaptured by the Turks, the market value of relics went out of sight; cutting off the source of relics brought inflation. Fraud and misrepresentation were the rule in trafficking in these items. The use of the Rosary increased considerably in the Roman Catholic system during this period.

On the other hand, from the long look of history the Roman Catholic Church was harmed by the Crusades. The popes weakened their prestige by continuing to press for new crusades after the fad had gone out of style. The continuance of the crusade tax did not increase papal popularity either.

The Crusades opened the eyes of many to a new world. New literature, new interests, and new ideas crowded upon those who had invaded the Eastern world, and they brought these things back with them. Even some of the popes became enamored with the ancient literary remains and forms and emphasized culture more than Christianity. The Renaissance was not far when the minds and hearts of the people were stirred and enlightened. Such general diffusion of enlightenment could not fail to undermine an institution which was based upon superstition and fear.

The Crusades introduced new economic and social reforms. Commerce and trade were fostered, and new items for manufacture called for industry. The middle class—neither peasant nor prince—developed. Those returning from the wars flooded the cities and changed social and economic forms.

Politically the papacy was not permanently forwarded. The breakdown of feudalism resulted in the rise of the nations, a potential threat to papal power. As the strong nobles were slain in the struggle, the monarchs in the various states increased in power. Even the opposite situation in the German states did not work out to papal advantage. The German knights refused to go on the Crusades. The tardy decline of feudalism in the German states may have been an immediate help to the papacy in its effort to divide and conquer; but this situation brought general unrest among the Germans, and when the struggle came, the papacy had to fight individual battles in scores of small feudal areas instead of simply winning over the monarch in a large domain.

Scholasticism

The third movement that made a distinct contribution to the rapid recovery of the Roman Church has been called "scholasticism." The term refers to the teaching of the schoolmen. It will be remembered that Charlemagne had encouraged the education of the clergy and the upper class. Perhaps from this inspiration the universities of the twelfth century arose, principally in order to teach civil and ecclesiastical law. These institutions of learning became small, self-governing cities within cities. Every European city ardently longed for its own university during the thirteenth and fourteenth centuries. Two types of universities developed: in Italy, growing out of considerable political freedom, the students organized their own schools and administered them; in France, following the monastic system, the faculty constituted both the teachers and the administrators of the school. The curriculum included theology, medicine, canon and civil law, and the liberal arts (grammar, logic, rhetoric, music, arithmetic, geometry, and astronomy).

The religious scholars of these schools developed the system known as "scholasticism." It was based upon a method of thought (deductive reasoning) and a preconceived conclusion (the intellectual proof of papal doctrine). Deductive reasoning begins with a general truth that is authoritative and develops subsidiary refinements through the application of valid principles. The important factor, then, is the starting point. Scholasticism, magnifying the thought forms and philosophy of Aristotle and Plato, started with the Bible, the decrees of popes, the canons of councils, and tradition as authoritative; from these it reasoned out the doctrines of the Roman Church. Although the various schools of thought differed in their viewpoint relative to the place of reason and revelation, the total result of scholasticism was to undergird with philosophy the Roman Catholic system. Bible and tradition are so inter-

THE TERRITORIAL DIVISION
OF THE EAST-WEST SCHISM
A.D. 1054

GREEK CATHOLIC CHURCH

ROMAN CATHOLIC CHURCH

125

mingled in the doctrinal development of the Roman Church that any attempt to eliminate tradition would require a complete re-definition of every doctrine.

Some of the leading scholastics were Johannes Scotus Erigena (about 800), Anselm (1033–1109), Roscellinus (about 1090), Abé-lard (1079–1142), Alexander of Hales (about 1245), Albertus Magnus (1206–80), Thomas Aquinas (1225–74), John Duns Scotus (1265–1308), and William of Occam (about 1349).

Strong Papal Leadership

Even beyond the contributions of monasticism, the Crusades, and Scholasticism, the spectacular rise of the Roman Catholic papacy to the height of power in the period from the eleventh to the thirteenth centuries was the work of three strong popes. Had all the contributory factors existed, the Roman Church could not have attained the place that it did without the initiative and determination of the strong men who headed it.

Gregory VII (1073–85) .—The first of these popes was Gregory VII, who is better known as Hildebrand. Under the reforming program of Leo IX, Hildebrand was appointed a cardinal in 1049. Before long he assumed leadership in the policies of the papal government and did not relinquish it until his death in 1085. He endeavored to carry out three principles: (1) to eliminate internal opposition to papal rule within the Roman Church; (2) to free the papacy from external influence in the appointment of bishops and the election of popes; (3) to secure co-operation from secular rulers in attaining the ideals of the papacy.

The weapons used by Gregory to accomplish his program were both spiritual and secular. In dealing with secular opposition, the spiritual pre-eminence of the papacy was fashioned into a political club. It was generally accepted that there was no salvation outside the external Church, that salvation came through the sacraments, and that no Western church could properly observe the sacraments unless it was in communion with Rome. Thus for all practical purposes, the pope controlled salvation. The manipulation of this power formed the basis of papal coercion. When any person, for example, refused to obey the Roman pontiff, an edict of excommunication was prepared and published. This officially cut off the person from the Church; this separation would include salvation. A total excommunication was a fearful thing. Not only was the individual deprived of salvation, but he infected those about him. Mass could not be held in his presence; those giving him refuge of any kind were subject to severe discipline by the Church. If the one excommunicated was a ruler, it was within the power of the Church to release his subjects from all loyalty to him, thus opening the way for general political revolt. Loyal Catholic rulers were invited to crusade against the heretic and seize his kingdom for themselves, which gave double incentive.

A second weapon based upon control of the sacramental vehicles of salvation was called the "interdict." In a sense, the interdict was excommunication applied to a community, whether a small town or a large kingdom. An interdict closed the churches, which were viewed as the only means of salvation for the people. The only ministry that was carried on provided baptism (to bring babies into the Church and salvation) and extreme unction (the sacrament at death to prepare the individual for judgment). It will be noted that the giving of these two sacraments during the period of interdict was a means of maintaining the strength of the Church if the interdict was applied for a long period.

By these weapons—excommunication and interdict—papal power could be applied quickly in a practical and political way. Furthermore, when civil rulers were friendly, the popes used their influence to secure still another coercive weapon. This was known as the "ban," by which the civil rulers made an outlaw of the person involved in ecclesiastical disobedience. The machinery of secular punishment could then be applied to the heretics.

Freely using these weapons, reasserting the claims of the pseudo-Isidorian decretals and the *Donation of Constantine,* and invoking the authority of the apostle Peter, Gregory VII quickly brought an effective internal reform of the papal government and soon began speaking with an authoritative accent to all secular rulers.

Under his leadership Roman synods took the right of nominating or appointing popes completely out of secular hands and placed it in the power of the cardinal bishops and cardinal clergy. In addition, kings and secular princes were denied the power of appointing or installing any bishop. These measures looked to the elimination of all secular power in the appointing of church officials and placed that power directly in the hands of the papal government.

Furthermore, under Gregory an edict requiring clerical celibacy was ratified. This meant that deacons, priests, and bishops could not take wives. It eliminated the financial burden upon the Church of providing for the families of its officers; it enlarged the distinction between the clergy and the laity; it made the clergy more mobile, for without wife and family the priest or bishop could move quickly to whatever place he might be sent; it insured the right of the Church to appoint a bishop's successor without family influence in case the bishop's son should be an ecclesiastic and desire the post; and it made the Church heir to the possessions of most of its clergy, for they had no one else to whom they might leave their worldly goods when they died.

Pope Gregory used the interdict freely in an effort to establish papal power. He sent legates (or representatives) to every civil government in order to guard papal interests in the various countries. Perhaps the greatest triumph came in his enforcement of the synodical decrees relating to the appointing and installing of a bishop by secular powers. In this struggle the pope fought against an ancient and popular practice. In feudalism, it will be recalled, the sovereign, or lord of the manor, was the sole ruler in his own domain. If a bishop happened to serve in that domain, the bishop must swear allegiance to this secular ruler. Should the bishop die, the sovereign usually appointed someone else to that office from his own domain. Since papal power was greatly compromised during the several centuries of anarchy and feudalism following the breakdown of the Carolingian line, no protest was voiced over this situation for generations. But now Pope Gregory refused to allow the bishop to be appointed, installed, or con-

128

trolled by the secular power. The Roman synod of 1075 reiterated this principle, denying the right of the emperor himself to appoint and invest bishops.

A test quickly came. Henry IV (1056–1106), the German emperor, could not discern the changed situation. Had not his predecessors appointed even the popes less than a century before? Had not the popes agreed solemnly that the emperor should forever have the right to appoint even the bishop of Rome? So when a bishopric became vacant in the northern part of Italy, the emperor immediately appointed a successor and installed him in office. When Pope Gregory denied the validity of the action, the emperor declared the papal office empty. But a century had made a great difference. Now the pope, prestige restored, hurled the dreaded weapon of excommunication against the emperor, freeing that sovereign's subjects from allegiance. More from a political than a religious standpoint, the emperor made a pilgrimage southward to ask the pope's forgiveness and secure restoration to the Church. Meanwhile, the pope had started northward toward Germany to carry on the struggle. They met at Canossa, where the emperor stood outside the castle in the snow, barefooted, for three days, begging the privilege of asking the pope's forgiveness. Upon being admitted, he made promises to be obedient and was restored to fellowship.

The emperor's humiliation strengthened his influence with his people; despite his reinstatement, the emperor declared war on the pope and succeeded in driving him into exile to die in 1085. The successors of the emperor and the pope continued the battle. In 1122 an agreement was reached known as the Concordat of Worms. This provided that the Church should have control of the election of bishops and abbots but that the emperor should exercise supervision over the elections. In case of a dispute the emperor would have the deciding vote. The pope should invest every bishop or abbot with the spiritual symbols of office—the ring and the staff—while the emperor should be allowed to touch the candidate with sceptre to indicate imperial approval. Neither popes nor emperors were true to this compromise.

Alexander III (1159–81).—The second of the strong popes who were responsible for bringing the papacy to the height of its power was Alexander III. He entered into the papal office under fire. The cardinals elected him by a small majority. The minority of the cardinals, with the support of the Roman clergy and of the imperial authority, elected a rival pope called Victor IV. The emperor, Frederick Barbarossa (1152–90), disliked Alexander and supported Victor, even going so far as to summon a church council, which obediently voted in favor of Victor. Alexander was supported by England, France, Spain, Hungary, and Sicily, however. For almost twenty years Emperor Frederick tried to force his way to Rome in order to set up Victor as pope, without success. In 1177 he submitted to Alexander.

Meanwhile, Alexander had continued the work and spirit of Gregory VII. Typical of his efforts to advance the power and prestige of the papacy were his dealings with England. In 1163, after the death of the archbishop of Canterbury, King Henry II of England (1154–89) forced the appointment of Thomas à Becket, one of his cronies. To the king's dismay, Becket became a champion of the pope against the king. In 1164 the king called a national council in an effort to eliminate papal influence in England. This council passed all of the king's measures, known as the Constitutions of Clarendon. Ecclesiastical courts were shorn of extensive jurisdiction; no appeal could be made to Rome without the king's permission; the king could appoint abbots and bishops in England; the revenues from vacant episcopal offices in England would revert to the king. Because of strong opposition to King Henry over this program, the archbishop was assassinated. Popular feeling was so aroused by this act that Henry was forced to submit to the pope and renounce the Constitutions in 1172.

The Third Lateran Council was convened by Pope Alexander in 1179, and decreed that the cardinals alone should elect the pope, that Roman Catholics should take arms against heresy with the promise of full forgiveness of all sins if death should result, and that secular authorities may not meddle with internal affairs of the Church.

Innocent III (1198–1216).—The third and greatest of the popes of this period was Innocent III. Gregory VII had made exalted claims concerning the dignity of the pope and the Roman Church: God alone had founded the Roman Church; the pope's feet shall be kissed by all princes; emperors may be deposed by the pope; the pope may be judged by no man; and the Roman Church has never erred, nor will it err in all eternity. But Innocent III magnified these pretensions to make the pope alone God's authoritative representative upon the earth. With the work of Gregory VII and Alexander III to prepare the way, with the continuing spirit of the Crusades to foment religious passion and fanatical loyalty, and with doctrine and organization perfected, Innocent was able to dominate the entire world, secular and ecclesiastical.

Through his influence he deposed emperors, forced heads of states such as Spain and France to submit to his authority, required states to pay annual tributes of money, and most spectacular of all, humiliated King John of England. The English king had tried to defy Innocent and found himself excommunicated and his kingdom under interdict. Without papal support, King John was captured by his nobles in 1215 and was forced to grant the Magna Charta, a bill of rights for protection against oppression by the crown. The pope refused to admit the validity of the document because, he said, it was secured under duress. Meanwhile, by interdict and other coercive measures, Innocent brought every secular government into his orbit. He put into practical operation the claim that he was the immediate instrument of God for world rule.

The Fourth Lateran Council of 1215 marks the height of official Roman Catholic domination. This council is unrivaled as a picture of universal subjection to the pope by every ecclesiastical and secular power. The bishop of Constantinople, once a strong rival, was there to bow his knee. The spectacle of this tremendous pageant was more important than what was done. A new crusade was discussed, union with the Greek church was looked into, the punishment of heretics by the state was arranged, and a number of canons were enacted providing for ecclesiastical discipline. The doctrine of transubstantiation, which affirms that the bread and wine of the Mass lose their character and become actually the body and blood of a newly crucified Christ, was officially defined.

The universal dominion of the papacy was an accomplished fact. Between the Council of Nicea of 325 and the Fourth Lateran Council of 1215 the Roman bishop had become master of the world, spiritual and secular. The structure was complete. Its builders thought that it was eternal. In less than a century it began to crumble.

Concluding Summary

The papacy accomplished a spectacular revival of authority and prestige in the eleventh and twelfth centuries. An internal reform through the agency of monasticism began the recovery. Papal prestige skyrocketed as a result of the Crusades under their leadership, but the long-range results were not favorable. Scholasticism provided intellectual justification for papal doctrines. Three outstanding popes, using the ecclesiastical weapons of excommunication, interdict, and crusade, humbled every secular power.

Retrospect and Prospects

THE ROMAN CATHOLIC papacy had now reached its height. Secular and ecclesiastical princes bowed to its authority. Until the closing years of the thirteenth century it appeared that a new and permanent world order had been created. It is instructive to compare the Christianity of this golden age of Roman Catholicism with the Christianity of the New Testament. Even beyond the strange externals of glittering wealth, false pride symbolized in the kissing of feet and the holding of stirrups by earthly princes, and the kneeling of men to men, a vast difference in character between the movement described in the New Testament and that in the Roman Catholic Church of the thirteenth century had developed.

Roman Catholic Domination

The New Testament picture of ministers (bishops) serving in an autonomous local church, theoretically equal with all other bishops everywhere, has disappeared. Out of the circumstances which have been sketched in previous chapters a few important bishops began to shape the policies of all Christianity. One of these bishops, that of Rome, was able to impress upon all other Western bishops not only his example but his authority. In addition, the Roman bishop, through spiritual and political coercion, had managed to assume control over secular kings. Sometimes retreating, sometimes compromising, sometimes demanding, the Roman bishops constantly kept in mind their ultimate aim of universal rule, both ecclesiastical and secular, and attained it after about a millennium of struggle.

Roman Catholic Organization

The simple local church government of the New Testament days was gone. In its place was the Roman hierarchy. The Roman bishop headed a vast network of ecclesiastical organization that manipulated the sacramental vehicles commonly supposed to bring salvation. Such a widespread function demanded a strong central organization. In the fourth century Rome was divided by the bishop into twenty-five parts, each headed by a presbyter or priest. Each of the twenty-five divisions was called a parish or *titulus*. Furthermore, in order to provide for the administration of charity, seven deacons were appointed for the city of Rome, each with a specific geographical section under his responsibility. This scriptural number of deacons was later augmented by seven subdeacons.

In the eleventh century these twenty-five priests, the seven deacons, and several bishops from the area about Rome formed the basis of what is known as the College of Cardinals. The name "cardinal" developed from a Latin word which means a hinge, and although the play on words has nothing to do with the original application of the word, it is true that the Roman system hinges on cardinals. Since the time of Gregory VII (1073–85), the cardinals have been entrusted with the most important organizational tasks of the Roman Church. At the present time it is their duty to elect and advise popes and to determine administrative policy through committee functions. Because of the historical developments related above, there are three types of cardinals: the cardinal bishops, the cardinal priests, and the cardinal deacons. The original names of these three types are now without meaning, for cardinal priests are usually strong bishops from various parts of the world, while cardinal deacons are usually priests. The total number of cardinals has varied from about thirteen to seventy-six. At the present time the maximum is seventy—fourteen cardinal deacons (the original seven plus the seven subdeacons who were elevated), fifty cardinal priests (doubling the original number), and six cardinal bishops who are still the bishops of dioceses in the immediate vicinity of Rome. The cardinals are appointed by the pope, and he could depose them, although that would be quite unusual.

The committee work of the cardinals developed rapidly after the thirteenth century. Probably the most important committees, or congregations (in their terminology), are the Sacred Consistory, a rather full cabinet meeting to consider matters of policy and those of high importance; the Congregation of the Inquisition, that watches for heresy and deals with it; the Congregation of Rites, that deals with liturgy and ceremonies; and the Propagation of the Faith, the missionary organization. In addition, the cardinals also constitute the principal members of ecclesiastical tribunals. Ecclesiastical appeals are handled by seven tribunals, each with jurisdiction over certain classes of litigation. The supreme court of appeal is the Rota Romana, consisting of twelve members.

All of these committees and tribunals—the central core of Roman Catholic organization—are termed the Roman Curia.

Roman Catholic Doctrine

Attention has already been directed to the corruption of New Testament teachings in the developing Roman Catholic system. The New Testament pattern of salvation emphasized faith in Jesus Christ without the mediation of any person or institution. The ordinances of baptism and the Supper were symbolical, not magical. In the Roman system the ordinances became sacraments, vehicles of grace. Salvation was conceived as coming from the Catholic Church alone through the administration of the sacraments. The question of the number of sacraments, argued by Catholic theologians for centuries, was finally resolved. Chief credit for establishing the official position should probably be given to Peter Lombard in the twelfth century. About 1150 he prepared his *Four Books of Sentences,* the last division of which discussed sacraments. Over against earlier theologians like Augustine (who died in 430), who felt that all ministries of the Church were sacraments, and later theologians like Hugo of St. Victor and Abélard (contemporaries with Peter Lombard), who emphasized five sacraments, the *Sentences* named seven sacraments. Peter Lom-

135

bard's *Sentences* were taught in practically all of the schools for theological training during the succeeding several centuries. It is likely that Thomas Aquinas (1225–74), who provided the most influential synthesis of Catholic doctrine for the modern period, followed Peter Lombard in asserting that the Church has seven sacraments.

As developed by Peter Lombard and Thomas Aquinas, the seven sacraments were baptism, confirmation, penance, the Lord's Supper (Mass), extreme unction, ordination, and matrimony. A word of description about each will suffice.

The sacrament of baptism is the initiatory rite. By it, the Church taught, original sin and all acts of sin committed up to the time of baptism are forgiven. Sprinkling became the general mode of baptism in the West after about the ninth century, and infants began to be subjects of baptism in the second or third centuries. In order to maintain the appearance of baptism as profession of faith, the use of sponsors developed quite early after the adoption of infant baptism. The priest administering baptism asked the infant if he were willing to renounce Satan, if he believed the various points of the creed, and if he were willing to be baptized. The sponsor, or godparent, answered all such questions for the undiscerning infant. The catechism says that this ceremony makes the child a Christian, a child of God, and an heir of heaven.

The sacrament of confirmation claims to impart the Holy Spirit. Its scriptural basis is usually given as Acts 8:17 and 19:6. In the Western world this sacrament could be administered only by a bishop. Until about the thirteenth century it was conferred shortly after baptism; then the time was changed to allow the subject to reach his twelfth or thirteenth year. The age does not matter, since a sponsor is required and the sacrament works without reference to any understanding by the subject. In this sacrament, which in a sense inducts the child into the duties and responsibilities of church life, the bishop anoints the subject with oil which has been blessed.

The sacrament of penance provides forgiveness of sins committed after baptism. Scriptures like 1 John 1:9 are used to buttress this doctrine. The earliest confessions of sin were made to the congregation, but such a practice manifestly could not continue. The very volume of such confessions would make it difficult to have any other type of service. The intense persecutions of Christianity under Emperors Decius (249–51) and Diocletian (284–305) caused many nominal Christians to deny the faith. To meet this need, as well as the normal demand, a division of functions was required. Through successive developments, auricular confession (confession in the ear of the priest) became the custom. Not until the Fourth Lateran Council in 1215 was confession to the priest made a Church law.

Under the theory developed by Aquinas and now generally accepted, the subject of this sacrament must first be moved by contrition, sorrow for sin, or attrition, a fear of the punishment of sin. With this motive, confession is made to the priest who in turn requires that the subject must give "satisfaction." This idea probably also grew out of the rigorous persecutions of the early period. The original purpose of satisfaction was to give evidence that the subject was really contrite and willing to do what he could to show this spirit. In a sense this satisfaction originally had a twofold function: it provided a basis for the forgiveness of eternal and deadly sins, and it displayed contrition for sin in the temporal order. In other words, sin was viewed as having eternal consequences and temporal disabilities.

This distinction became very important in view of the development of various methods of making satisfaction and the exceptional extent of the effectiveness of such satisfaction. The method of making satisfaction before the tenth and eleventh centuries had been primarily through making religious pilgrimages to some shrine or through other channels of revealing personal piety. In the eleventh century, however, the temporal penalties could be remitted in whole or in part by the use of indulgences. "Indulgence" was the name given to the remission of punishment due to temporal sins. After the eleventh century, instead of taking pilgrimage as a part of penance, it was possible to purchase an indulgence in order to give satisfaction for temporal sins.

In addition, the interpretation of the large area in which temporal sins brought hurt increased the importance of the distinction between temporal sins and eternal. Temporal sins, it was taught, must be paid for in purgatory after death, if they were not completely expunged through satisfaction. The Church, it was further taught, could issue these indulgences for temporal sins because of the possession of a treasury of merits bequeathed to it by the good works of Christ and the saints. This development was reflected in the order of the elements of penance. Earlier the order consisted of contrition, confession, satisfaction, and then absolution or forgiveness by the priest. That is, satisfaction was given before the priest pronounced absolution or forgiveness. The developed order was changed somewhat; contrition and confession formed the first part, but absolution came after confession, and satisfaction was placed last. Thus after confession the priest, in his authority of the keys granted him by the Roman bishop, would forgive the eternal sins of the subject; then there was imposed upon the subject the necessity of giving satisfaction for the temporal guilt which, if not expiated, required suffering in purgatory. It should be said that the doctrine of purgatory was first taught as a matter essential to the faith by Gregory I (590–604).

The sacrament of the Lord's Supper, or Mass, is described as the unbloody sacrifice of the body and blood of Christ. According to Roman Catholic catechism, Christ is slain again in every church each time Mass is performed. By this means Christ's soul and divinity are reproduced in both bread and wine. This is the theological reason why the Roman Church refuses to allow the people to partake of the wine; they get all they need in the bread. The Mass has become the central feature of Roman Catholic worship services, for through partaking of the bread, which allegedly has been changed into the broken body of Christ, and witnessing the transubstantiation of the wine into the blood of Christ, the subject actually partakes of Christ's body, which gives spiritual merit.

The sacrament of extreme unction is, as the name indicates, the last anointing. Its practice is based upon James 5:14. In the administration of this sacrament the priest anoints the eyes, ears, nose, lips, palms of the hands, and feet to expiate sins contracted through any of these organs. A plenary, or full, indulgence is granted but does not take effect until the time of death.

The sacrament of orders applies only to those entering upon the service of the Roman Catholic Church. It sets them apart and qualifies them for the task which they have assumed.

The sacrament of matrimony consists of the union of a man and woman in marriage. Of course, ordinarily the sacraments of orders and matrimony mutually exclude one another.

Thus the Roman Catholic sacramental system, which had developed its present features by the thirteenth century, aimed to control the life of the subject. It touched the individual at birth, in childhood and adolescence, and at death. It required regular confession of sin and absolution at the hands of the priest as a means of escaping the purgatorial sufferings which the earthly Church could remit. The Roman Church utilized every means of influence; an appeal was made through beauty to the eyes, through melody to the ears, through incense to the nose, through participation to the hands and knees. Solemn rites and incantations brought a sense of belonging and initiation, and a common language spoke of unity.

Roman Catholic Monasticism

Throughout the Medieval period the monastic movement retained its great popularity. It was universally felt that the perfect life could only be found in monasticism. The monks were viewed as men who had lost their lives to save them again, who had given all to follow Christ. Papal advance insured great encouragement for monasticism, for the monks were the strongest supporters of papal supremacy. Particularly after the new type of monasticism inaugurated by the Cluniac reform had developed, the pope was able to undermine the power of any antagonistic bishop. Since these monks were no longer under the control of the local bishop, the pope could send them into any diocese to hear confessions, forgive sins, baptize and bury, bless or condemn. As a consequence, the bishop of that diocese would find himself bypassed and his functions taken over by the monks.

Furthermore, the monasteries provided a place of refuge for many—for the scholar who desired peace and quiet for study, for the pious who wanted a haven from worldliness, for the fearful who would flee from the misery and disorder of society. In a sense, monasteries also provided a place for minor dissent. Some might disagree with the papal program, yet desire to remain within the ecclesiastical structure from either conviction or fear. The various monastic orders, magnifying different emphases in doctrine and practice, offered a choice of minor variations from the normal pattern. Many a monk doubtless found himself in a congenial atmosphere for ideas which would not have been generally acceptable outside his haven.

From the eleventh to the thirteenth centuries several new monastic orders arose. The Cistercians were one of the reform movements and became famous because Bernard of Clairvaux, maker of popes, joined it in 1113. The Augustinian canons represented an effort to bring monastic discipline into the parish clergy. In 1119 an order known as the Premonstrants was founded, providing for communal living in a monastic house by the several priests of a particular parish. Another type of monasticism grew out of the Crusades. Three outstanding military orders developed. The Knights of St. John, or the Hospitallers, were organized in the twelfth century to aid sick and helpless pilgrims on their way to Jerusalem; the Knights Templars were a lay order organized in 1119 to protect Jerusalem pilgrims; and the Teutonic Knights, with a similar mission, date from 1190. The two most important orders of these centuries were the Dominicans and the Franciscans. Dominic (1170–1221) organized an order for the purpose of winning heretics back to the Roman Church through preaching. Recognition was obtained in 1216 from the pope, and the movement spread rapidly. Before Dominic's death, his order numbered sixty houses, situated in every part of Europe. Doubtless copying the Franciscan movement, the Dominicans became mendicants, or beggars. Because of their emphasis upon education and preaching, the Dominicans have produced some of the greatest theologians and scholars of the Roman Church.

Francis of Assisi was born about 1182. At about the age of twenty-five his military and business pursuits were changed by a conversion experience, and two years later he determined to form an order which would endeavor to reproduce the spirit and work of Christ. This order was approved by Pope Innocent III in 1216. The inclinations of Francis himself turned away from formal and effective organization, but through able friends, especially Pope Gregory IX (1227–41), the Franciscan movement developed and spread rapidly. After Francis' death in 1226 his followers divided over the interpretation of his teachings.

Both the Dominicans and the Franciscans included provision for nunneries, where women might serve the cause. These two mendicant orders have been a tremendous force in the development of the Roman Catholic system.

The Inquisition

The several elements of Roman Catholic strength which have been mentioned—prestige, organization, doctrine, and passionate defenders—seemed to give promise of the continued domination of the world by the papacy. But the picture would not be complete without a word concerning factors which threatened and finally overthrew universal papal domination. One of these factors was the extraordinary spread of religious dissent. In a succeeding chapter, specific instances of dissent will be described. It is significant that the very pope who symbolized the complete domination of Roman Catholic power should find it necessary to institute special ecclesiastical machinery for the suppression of dissent.

The inquisition of heresy had at first been under the supervision of the local bishop. With the rise of the Roman bishop to power, it became his prerogative to ferret out those who refused to follow the pattern. The founding of the Dominican order followed directly the discovery of the strength of the Albigenses in southern France and constituted an effort to win these dissenters back to the faith. The Fourth Lateran Council of 1215 passed new decrees designed to compel the various bishops to seek out heretics in their own dioceses. A new direction was taken in the thirteenth century. Emperor Frederick II (1215–50) offered the services of the civil government to the papacy for the suppression of heresy, and in 1252 a papal bull directed that civil magistrates be utilized in the detection and punishment of heresy. After 1233 the Dominicans were given the task of searching out dissenters and handling them. In 1262 the office of inquisitor general was set up at Rome to spearhead the fight against heresy.

The inquisitorial methods have been publicized. Despite lurid descriptions, it is doubtful that any of the stories exceeded the horrors of the actual movement, particularly in the Spanish Inquisition. Christians were very adept in devising ways to torture Christians. Informers were secured by promising them a part of the estate of the condemned. Torture was the principal method of securing evidence. No person was safe. Simply the accusation of heresy by anyone, whether through personal hatred, greed, or other motive, was sufficient to start the machinery of torture, under the pains of which almost anyone would confess almost anything. Cynicism and bitterness filtered into all parts of the Continent. Things were not well with the dominating ecclesiastical system.

Political Developments

A new set of strong rulers was arising, supported by the zeal of nationalism. Drawing new strength by the destruction of many of the nobility in the Crusades and enriched by the increase of trade and the development of industry following the Crusades, these new secular sovereigns prepared to challenge the supremacy of the pope over civil government. That story will be told in a succeeding chapter.

The Diffusion of Light

The Roman Catholic system reached its height through coercion because it allegedly controlled the only front of salvation. Superstition and fear played a large part in this sort of Christianity. The entrance of light of any kind constituted a threat to the system.

And the light was growing. The movement called the Renaissance was not far. Here and there in the thirteenth century were signs of spiritual awakenings and intellectual advance. When once men learned that God was a Saviour as well as a Judge, that they could find his love and blessings apart from the ecclesiastical organization known as the Church, and that the service of God was not bound up with merits and penance, then the great sacramental system of the papacy was undermined.

Concluding Summary

The difference between the New Testament pattern and that of the Roman Catholic Church in the thirteenth century was great. The Roman bishop had become dominant. His authority was recognized in spiritual and secular areas. His organization was strong and well disciplined. The doctrinal definition of Rome's principal tenets was almost complete. New monkish orders provided recruits for every kind of special service. The future seemed bright. But there were elements that would have disturbed an observant onlooker. Dissent was widespread. The methods that were adopted to combat dissent only scattered the spirit across the Continent. New secular rulers were developing who were not afraid of the papal excommunication and interdict. The foregleams of the dawn were casting light against which the Roman system could not continue to dominate the minds and hearts of men.

BIBLIOGRAPHY

BETHUNE-BAKER, J. *An Introduction to the Early History of Christian Doctrine to the Time of the Council of Chalcedon.* London: Methuen & Co., Ltd., 1951.

BETTENSON, HENRY (ed.). *Documents of the Christian Church.* New York: Oxford University Press, 1947.

FOAKES-JACKSON, F. J. *An Introduction to the History of Christianity A.D. 590–1314.* New York: The Macmillan Co., 1921.

LATOURETTE, K. S. *A History of Christianity.* New York: Harper & Brothers, 1953.

NEWMAN, A. H. *A Manual of Church History,* I. Philadelphia: American Baptist Publication Society, 1953.

ROBINSON, JAMES HARVEY. *Readings in European History*, I. Boston: Ginn & Co., 1904.

STEVENSON, J. (ed.). *A New Eusebius*. New York: The Macmillan Co., 1957.

SULLIVAN, JOHN F. *The Visible Church*. New York: P. J. Kenedy & Son, 1920.

WORKMAN, HERBERT BROOK. *The Evolution of the Monastic Ideal*. London: The Epworth Press, 1927.

IV. PERIOD OF WESTERN REFORM
(A.D. 1215–1648)

Introduction to the Period

The papacy could attain no higher prestige than it displayed in the Fourth Lateran Council of 1215. For a comparatively brief period it seemed that the papacy would be able to maintain its imposing position indefinitely. The claims of the popes who succeeded Innocent III (1198–1216) sounded like him, but there developed a difference in the ability to enforce these claims. The removal of the papal throne to France from 1305 to 1378 made it a tool of national interests; the papal schism from 1378 to 1409 (with two popes) and from 1409 to 1415 (three popes) stripped the office of much of its prestige and authority. Strong attempts were made to reform the Church in "head and members," but these failed. From the Council of Constance (1414–18) to the theses of Luther (1517), papal abuses became even more flagrant.

The various types of revolt against the Roman Church occurred between 1517 and 1534. The Council of Trent (1545–63) represented the Roman Catholic reform. The Reformation period closes with the Thirty Years' War (1618–48), which in a measure brought mutual toleration between the Roman Catholics and their opponents.

Points of Special Interest

The student should notice that the roots of reform were imbedded deeply in medieval Christianity. For that reason it has been thought wise to push back the traditional date of 1517 to the date at which the Roman Church reached its highest peak—the Fourth Lateran Council of 1215. Widespread dissent, the Avignon papacy, schism and confusion, and attempts to reform in the three centuries before Luther's theses justify the inclusion of that period.

The student should notice carefully the interaction of all factors in the Reformation—political circumstances, for example.

It should not be overlooked, also, that the Roman Catholic reform looked primarily toward modernizing its machinery to meet the threats of the schismatics. There was no attempt to continue the radical reforming measures taken by the councils of the fifteenth century.

Collapse of Papal Prestige

IT IS SIGNIFICANT that the factors which helped to establish the prestige of the Roman papacy also co-operated in bringing its downfall. The very height which the papal monarchy attained for a few centuries was a guarantee that a decline must take place. Secular rulers could not fail to see that the papacy was an institution of this world, not of the next. Papal policies were ofttimes greedy and vicious. Despite assertions that the Roman leadership could not err, civil sovereigns saw many examples of mistakes in doctrines and in policies. Papal avowal of the Crusades and the Inquisition were examples. The tragic slaughter of untold hundreds of thousands of men, women, and children in the fruitless march toward Jerusalem brought many to their senses. What could the will of God have to do with this sort of political undertaking?

The German nobles bluntly refused to go, papal promises of complete forgiveness of sins notwithstanding. The popes were slow to see that the aroused passion had died down, and their continued pleadings for new crusades and their collections of gifts and taxes, ostensibly for such crusades, disgusted thoughtful and spiritual people. Furthermore, the Roman slaughter of the Albigenses and their appropriation of the crudest tortures in the Inquisition were a shocking disclosure of the character of the papacy. As the Inquisition spread into all parts of Europe, the tyranny of the Roman system became more and more visible. Fear had always been a major part of the hold upon the people by the Roman Church; and now to the fear of purgatory, excommunication, interdict, ban, and zealous crusaders the nightmare of accusation of heresy, against which there was no defense, was added. The brutality of the whole movement prophesied the downfall of such tyrannical monarchs, whether in the ecclesiastical or the secular sphere.

Financial Exploitation by the Roman Catholic Church

An important area of rising resentment against the papacy was their financial demands. The tremendous expansion of the central organization demanded immense revenues. One example will suggest the picture. When Rome set up the Rota Romana in 1234, constituting the supreme ecclesiastical court in Christendom, sufficient personnel was required to handle appeals from every part of the world. Subsidiary courts for special appeals were necessary. An army of clerks was required to maintain the records. Worst of all, flagrant abuses characterized every step of the legal proceedings. Official records show that in some cases simply securing the briefs cost approximately forty times the legitimate amount. Furthermore, litigants from all over the world were encouraged to appeal their cases directly to Rome, and it was well understood that the highest bidder won the case.

The financial gain secured by this fashion was not sufficient to care for the vast expenditures, legitimate and otherwise, of the papacy. Especially during the fourteenth century the papacy utilized every possible means for increasing its revenue. Some of these methods were through annates, collations, reservations, expectancies, dispensations, indulgences, simony, commendations, the *jus spoliorum,* tithing, and special assessments.

Annates refer to the gift by a newly appointed bishop or abbot of his first year's income in the office to which he was appointed. Collations refer to the practice of shifting several bishops or abbots in order to secure annates from each one. For example, if the archbishop of Cologne were to die, the pope would not appoint simply one person but would shift, let us say, the archbishop of Mainz to the open place, then appoint the bishop of Trier to the Mainz office, another bishop of Trier, and so on. An effort would be made, of course, to give each man a better situation, which would be possible when a strong prelate died. Before exhausting his possibilities the pope could have a dozen annates paid in through one vacancy.

Reservations refer to the practice of reserving the best and richest offices for papal use. The pope himself did not, of course, serve the particular bishopric or archbishopric but would send a priest to minister to the needs of the people while the revenue was sent to Rome. Expectancies mean the practice by papal authorities of selling to the highest bidder the right of nomination to an unusually desirable benefice before the person filling the office had yet vacated it. It became the practice of ambitious men to keep a watchful eye on the health of the incumbents of the various desirable offices, and when there was any encouragement that one might not continue long, the bidding began. Occasionally some embarrassment was experienced when it was found that several men had paid huge sums in anticipation of securing the same office. In reality, then, expectancies became almost a bid for the right to bid again when the incumbent of the desired office actually did die.

Dispensations has reference to the papal practice of excusing ecclesiastical violations upon the payment of the proper amount of money. In one of his outbursts against the Roman Curia, Luther wrote that it was a place where vows could be annulled, monks could get permission to leave their orders, priests could buy a dispensation to get married, the illegitimate might be legitimatized, and where evil and disgrace were knighted and ennobled. His closing sentence, in typical impetuous language, declares that at the Roman Curia there is "a buying and a selling, a changing, blustering and bargaining, cheating and lying, robbing and stealing, debauchery and villainy and all kinds of contempt of God that Antichrist could not reign worse." Even allowing for Luther's usual enthusiasm, it is evident that considerable income was secured by allowing dispensations for breaking canonical restrictions.

Indulgences have been described before. They were the pardons for temporal sins. Individuals might buy them instead of taking a pilgrimage or showing some other evidence of contrition. The revenue from this one source alone was considerable because of the widespread fear of spending a season in purgatory.

Simony refers to the sale of a church office. It takes its name from Simon Magus (see Acts 8:9 ff.), who tried to buy the power of the Holy Spirit with money. Closely associated with simony was the practice of nepotism. This word refers to the installing of relatives in lucrative church offices.

Commendations has reference to the practice of paying an annual tax to the papacy in return for a provisional appointment year by year to a desirable benefice. The *jus spoliorum* was the name applied to the papal practice of demanding that any property secured by a bishop or other officer during the tenure of office should, upon the death of the person, become the property of the Church, since such property was judged to come to the deceased individual in consequence of holding the office.

Tithing applies to a levy against church property, the value of which formed the basis for the amount demanded. Special assessments were made under any pretext. The Crusades opened the way for an annual tax. Unusual blessings, unusual sins, or any other situation might call for such assessments.

Even beyond these various methods of raising money, gifts of every kind were solicited. Gifts for approving relics, for permission to view the papal rooms, for jubilees, for charities, etc., swelled the revenue of the Roman Church almost beyond computation.

There were other factors that brought resentment. The Roman system was reasoned out carefully and made a distinct appeal to philosophical minds, but it was not meeting the needs of the people's hearts. Dissent was spreading. There was disaffection in the monastic system, as well as among the clergy. Some were openly skeptical. The enforcement of celibacy upon the clergy brought immorality and concubinage. The doctrinal teaching that the character of a priest or bishop was of secondary importance and did not affect his ability to forgive sins and administer valid sacraments played havoc with the morals of many.

It was the political aspect, however, that brought an end to the universal sway of the papacy. As on previous occasions, it became evident that papal prestige and authority could not yet be divorced from secular power.

The Beginning of Papal Humiliation

Pope Innocent III died in 1216, one year after the spectacular Fourth Lateran Council which marked the height of papal pretensions. For about seventy-five years no direct challenge was made to papal domination in both ecclesiastical and secular spheres. But with the election of Pope Boniface VIII (1294–1303), the new order of things began to appear. Not that Boniface was less vocal in his claims for the papacy nor less aggressive in his demands upon secular and ecclesiastical princes; if anything, he was more vociferous and more arrogant than previous popes. But his claims and demands were not heeded in the way that those of his predecessors had been. In his meddling with the political affairs of the Italian states he was less than successful. He attempted to force an end to the Hundred Years' War between France and England but was ignored by both nations. Enraged, he threatened both England and France with interdict and excommunication should they continue to levy war taxes upon the Roman Church in their realms. King Edward of England simply disregarded the pope; his parliament voted the taxes. King Philip of France, on the other hand, was not so kind. He promptly forbade the exporting of any revenues from France to the papacy. Hurt at a sensitive point and with morale shaken, Boniface canonized Philip's grandfather in an effort to placate the French king. But the war had begun. In 1302, after a preliminary skirmish, Boniface issued his bull entitled *Unam Sanctam*—named, as usual, after the first two words of the bull—excommunicating Philip and placing France under interdict. This famous bull plainly states that every man must obey the pope or forfeit his salvation. Philip was undisturbed, however; the weapons that had brought Gregory VII and Innocent III to power had lost their sting. Philip had the pope seized and imprisoned. The death of Boniface occurred in the following year.

150

The Babylonian Captivity and Papal Schism

The successor to Boniface, Benedict XI (1303–4), lived only nine months after his election to the office. Benedict's successor, Clement V (1305–14), was appointed through the influence of King Philip of France. In his pontificate papal headquarters were moved from Rome to Avignon, France, in 1309. During the next seventy years seven French popes filled the office. Because the papacy was absent from Rome for about seventy years (just as the Southern Kingdom was in Babylonian captivity for about that length of time), this period of papal residence in France has been called "the Babylonian captivity of the Church."

Clement showed his subservience to Philip of France by acquiescing in the destruction of the Knights Templars. There can be little doubt that this action was dictated by the French king. The Templars had constantly opposed Philip, and he was fearful lest the order should become a military rival. Through promises and torture, enough evidence was secured to convince Pope Clement. In October, 1311, he convoked an ecumenical council (the fifteenth in Roman records), which voted to suppress the order because of corrupt and immoral practices and other crimes, including blasphemy.

The events of the next seventy years convinced the states of Europe that the papacy had become a French institution. French cardinals were appointed in sufficient number to constitute a majority. Many new methods of raising money were fashioned, particularly by John XXII (1316–34).

The return of the papacy to Rome became an issue in each papal election. It was recognized that identification of the papacy with French interests was a serious blunder, particularly in view of the rising tides of nationalism on every hand. Finally, in 1377 Gregory XI ended the fiasco by returning to Rome to die. Urban VI (1378–89) was elected to succeed Gregory upon a promise to return to Avignon, but after his election Urban decided to remain in Rome. The cardinals met again and elected another pope, Clement VI (1378–94), who returned to France. Now there were two popes, each claiming to be validly elected—and each was. For a quarter of a century rival popes at Avignon and Rome anathematized one another and sought to undermine the work of the other. Of course, there had been antipopes before. In 251 Novatian had been elected bishop of Rome by a rival party. Other rival popes include Felix II (355–65), Boniface VII (974), and John XVI (997–98).

Probably the strangest papal schism had occurred in the middle of the eleventh century. Benedict IX had been placed on the papal throne in 1032. In 1044 he was driven out of Rome and certain of the local nobles placed Silvester III in the papal chair. Benedict returned to Rome, however, and sold the papal office for about a thousand pounds of silver to an archpriest in Rome, who took the name of Gregory VI. Benedict refused to abide by the bargain, and as a result there were three popes, each with enough strength to resist his opponents but not enough to conquer them. The situation was finally cleared up by Emperor Henry III.

The presence of two popes in the fourteenth century over a long period of time created a number of problems. The validity of almost every ecclesiastical act was brought into question. Which one should bestow the pallium upon newly consecrated bishops? To which should the monastic orders swear their solemn vows? Which should be recognized by the various states? From an organizational standpoint, the situation was almost intolerable. Theoretically each pope, if he were the correct one, should oversee the appointment of bishops in every diocese, fill the numerous vacancies in the archbishoprics, maintain the number of cardinals, appoint administrative heads in the Curia, and carry on the other multitudinous duties required in the operation of a widespread ecclesiastical monarchy. With two popes there were likely to be two appointments to the various positions, rivalry in ecclesiastical law cases, and overlapping in jurisdiction. The Christian world was aghast. Protests came from everywhere.

In 1409 an ecumenical council was called by cardinals of the two popes to meet at Pisa. This council in a rather hasty fashion declared the papal office vacant and elected a new pope, who took the name Alexander V (1409–10). To the dismay of all, the two incumbents refused to recognize the authority of the council, and now there were three popes. By political maneuvering and liberal bribery, the several strong states were induced to support a new council, called this time by one of the popes. The Council of Constance (1414–18) deposed all three of the popes and elected another, who took the name of Martin V (1417–31). This time, however, by political means the task was accomplished. Once again the secular sword controlled the spiritual. The schism was ended, but the prestige of the Roman papacy had been brought low. Voices everywhere were calling for a drastic reform of the whole system. The next chapter will discuss in some detail this clamor for reform.

Concluding Summary

The Roman papacy had exercised world domination through the imposing ecclesiastical structure built up between 1050 and 1215; but the building could not stand. Its essentially tyrannical and non-Christian character was seen in its initiation of movements like the Crusades and the Inquisition. The great increase in central organization, together with the squandering proclivities of the papal court, demanded vast revenues. Every papal policy appeared to be designed to raise money. Religious disaffection was widespread. The popes could not read the signs of the times, and endeavored to speak arrogantly to the strong monarchs of the developing states. Nationalism, however, had blunted the force of the ecclesiastical weapons wielded by Gregory VII and Innocent III, and the states paid little attention to papal demands.

King Philip of France gained control of the papal office, and for over seventy years papal headquarters were at Avignon. During this time the papacy was completely subservient to French interests, causing the alienation of the political rivals and enemies of France. The attempt to return the papacy to Rome in 1378 brought schism, which continued until 1417, when it was finally healed by conciliar action.

Clamor for Reform

THE LONG "BABYLONIAN captivity" of the Church and the disastrous papal schism of about forty years dramatically symbolized the need for papal reform. Many recognized that these tragic events were symptoms of the trouble, not its cause. Certainly the financial, political, and moral abuses by the papacy did not help the situation, but the basic problem was not the abuse of the system but the system itself. The clamor for reform did not refer simply to the immediate problem but challenged conceptions advocated by the popes for centuries. Some calls for reform had a distinctly biblical basis. The doctrinal and ecclesiastical tenets built up by the Roman Church over a long period were compared with the Scriptures and criticized from that viewpoint. Patriotic motives impelled some to demand reform. The rising nationalism of the late Medieval period brought conflicting loyalties into the hearts of men everywhere. Not a few of the protests against Roman domination grew out of the resentment against French control of the papacy during the "Babylonian captivity." Wretched economic and social conditions and the poised Turk on the very border of the Empire in the Balkans led many to think that God was punishing the world because of the misdeeds of the papacy. Finally, spiritual men in all countries were sincerely grieved to see the low state to which Christianity had come. Mysticism and dissent increased as men sought to find communion with God apart from the prevailing ecclesiastical system.

One of the greatest antecedents of reform was the movement known as the Renaissance. The throbbing of new intellectual life and the discovery of new worlds profoundly prepared the way for reformation. The resulting movement known as "humanism" brought the refocusing of men's eyes, and their new vision discerned many of the superstitions that characterized the Medieval Roman Catholic system. Some writers have minimized the scope of the Renaissance, insisting that Western culture required no rebirth. However, the very theological system of the Roman Catholic Church was partly responsible for the slow recovery from the barbarian invasions and the Dark Ages that followed. Because Medieval theology rested upon the extensive unraveling of established propositions through the use of deductive reasoning, it follows that the sources of Roman Catholic doctrine were completely authoritative and traditional. There was very little new grist for the mill but a constant regrinding of the old. For this reason, truth and progress were actually impeded by the scholastic systems of Roman Catholic theology.

But the Renaissance came. The Arabic scholars who followed the Mohammedan invasion of Spain in the eighth century helped to pry open the doors of learning in the West. Classical culture and the study of antiquity became the vogue. The Crusades helped to introduce a new world. The fall of Constantinople (1453) gave impetus to the movement when Greek scholars fled to the West for haven. A score of other factors—Italian nostalgia for the ancient glory of Rome, the appearance of genius in artistic and literary forms, economic developments, geographical discoveries, revolutionary inventions—made up what has been called the "rebirth" (Renaissance) of the West.

This awakening touched Christianity at many points. The movement known as "humanism," which will be discussed in the next pages, sprang directly from these elements. Humanism was greatly influential in preparing the way for reform. The excellence of the ancient literary forms brought contempt for scholastic writings. The revival of interest in the ancients also brought the study of Hebrew and Greek texts making up the Christian Scriptures, as well as the careful perusal of the ancient Christian writings. The eyes of men, so long focused only on the heavens, began to turn toward the world about them and upon themselves. The very foundations of Roman Catholic authority were undermined by the new thought forms.

The centuries just before the sixteenth resounded with calls for reform. Perhaps the best picture of this clamor for reform can be secured by discussing it from a geographical standpoint.

Italy

The strongest protests from Italy against the papal system were based upon the intellectual revival and the resulting humanism. Humanism was the name arbitrarily given to the classical and literary revival which began in Italy about the fourteenth century. It was largely patriotic as well as cultural. It was hoped that the glorious history of past days, spread before the eyes and minds of the present generation, might bring inspiration to attain a new unification of Italy and secure again Roman supremacy in the secular sphere. No little part in creating this longing was due to the removal of the papal chair from Rome to Avignon, France.

The humanists collected manuscripts of classical writers of antiquity, learned to criticize ancient texts through internal study, reveled in imitating the literary style and social manners of the ancients, and viewed the world in which they lived from a rich historical and literary background. Societies were organized to study the Greek language, to read Plato and Cicero, and to gather libraries of the ancient authors. The movement spread from Italy rapidly into northern Europe through religious, intellectual, social, and even economic ties. The development of the printing press helped to spread the gospel of humanism, just as half a century later it reproduced the writings of the Christian reformers for transmission to every part of the world.

It should be noted, however, that the emphasis of humanism took a different turn in northern Europe. In Italy the interest was primarily cultural and patriotic, resulting in disdain for religious ideas and activity. It bred actual cynicism in many cases. Northern humanism, on the other hand, channeled its literary and cultural interest into religious antiquities. The study of Hebrew and Greek looked to better interpretation of the Scriptures; the recovery of the best text of the Scriptures encouraged the critical examination of ancient manuscripts; while those interested in historical investigation republished the ancient Christian writings with critical interpretations. That is, the northern emphasis looked toward uncovering the ancient origins of the Christian faith and restoring the primitive purity of the movement.

So far as reform was concerned, then, the influence of humanism in Italy and in the northern areas performed different services. In Italy its contribution was mainly negative; in the remainder of Europe it was more nearly positive. The negative factors of humanism in Italy that encouraged the reforming spirit were twofold. First, humanism brought a widespread neglect of Christianity and enthroned ancient vices as well as virtues. Even the papacy was infected after its return from Avignon. In 1447 an out-and-out humanist scholar was elected pope and took the name of Nicholas V (1447–55). Religious matters became secondary; libraries, poems, and classics became the foremost items of business. Pius II (1458–64) was an outstanding versifier before his election as pope.

Humanism also encouraged the application to Christian documents of the critical methods used on ancient classical manuscripts. Under Nicholas V, Lorenzo Valla, a young humanist scholar, was brought to the papal court to assist in the translation of Greek classics. While in and out of papal service he wrote a great deal about Christianity from the humanist viewpoint. His study of the Greek text of the New Testament was of great value to the reformers half a century later. He scoffed at the monastic movement and handled roughly the Vulgate translation, which is the inspired Latin version for the Roman Catholics. One of his most spectacular feats was his convincing proof of the spurious nature of the *Donation of Constantine* by the application of internal criticism.

A product of this Italian patriotic revival was the celebrated poet Dante. Exiled to Ravenna in North Italy in the fourteenth century, Dante longed for the restoration of the glory of ancient Rome. His work entitled *On Monarchy* discusses the proper relations between the papacy and the empire. God has given each a sword, said Dante, and neither should control the other. The papacy should not control the empire or meddle in secular matters. While this idea was not new, its application would move the papacy back to an earlier stage of development. The fact that it was suggested by a thoroughly orthodox Catholic, in opposition to papal claims of several preceding centuries, together with the fact that Dante used biblical exegesis to controvert the papal interpretations, made the ideas of Dante quite significant.

The Empire

The loose collection of German states known as the Empire added their protest. Humanism played some part as the background for reform demands. The work of men like Rudolph Agricola, teacher of Greek at the University of Heidelberg, Sebastian Brant of Basel, Johann Reuchlin, and others was mainly negative. Their writings helped to undermine the Roman system with both the populace and the thinkers. Satirical verse and scholarly research joined hands in the protest. Some of the German humanists like Ulrich von Hutten, Franz von Sickingen, and Pirkheimer of Nuremberg actively supported the reform movement when it came. Philip Melanchthon, nephew of Reuchlin and himself an accomplished humanist, became Luther's righthand man.

The political situation provided the principal protest against papal power, however. In 1314 Duke Louis of Bavaria became emperor following his military victory over a rival candidate. Louis became embroiled in a dispute with Pope John XXII at Avignon over the right of the pope to sanction the election of every emperor. Among other things, French control of the papacy made it quite distasteful for Louis to submit. In 1324 the pope excommunicated Louis. Two scholars, Marsiglio of Padua and John of Janduno, collaborated to prepare one of the most unusual treatises of the day. It was known as the *Defensor Pacis* (Defender of Peace).

This document asserted that the people are the final authority in all things, whether secular or ecclesiastical. Thus in ecclesiastical matters the whole body of Christians, following the principles of

158

the New Testament, constitute the highest power. This remarkable document undermined the papal theory of government. Arguing from the New Testament, it denied that the pope had superior power over any bishop and remarked that there was no scriptural evidence that Peter was ever in Rome. All spiritual power rests in the body of Christian believers, not in priests, bishops, or popes. Furthermore, in a Christian state, reflecting the character and will of the people, the civil ruler has the right to control ecclesiastical affairs, including the calling of ecumenical councils and the appointment of bishops. The ultimate authority resides in a general ecclesiastical council of the people, not simply the bishops.

Another powerful voice that supported Emperor Louis was that of William of Occam, the great English theologian, who took refuge with the emperor. Occam also insisted that the true church did not reside in the bishops but in the believers. He denied the infallibility of the pope and magnified the Bible. The papacy should never deal in secular matters and should be subordinate to a general council of all Christians.

France

French humanism made a distinct contribution in the protest against the unreformed papacy. The movement was late in its beginnings in France but quickly gained strength. Through it the upper class in particular received considerable enlightenment as to the abuses of the Roman system. Jacques Lefèvre Étaples (1455–1536) became an accomplished biblical scholar and antedated Luther in his advocacy of salvation by faith alone, without sacraments, and his emphasis upon the authority of the Scriptures.

The University of Paris provided the early center calling for reform. William of Occam had taught there and expressed his views. Jean de Gerson (1363–1429) and the chancellor of Notre Dame, Pierre d'Ailly (1350–1420), inheritors of Occam's attitude and outlook, headed a scholarly group of men in the university who desired earnestly to reform the papacy in head and members. This group finally succeeded in ending the papal schism through the use of general councils.

England

Resentment against papal claims had deep roots in England. William Rufus, successor to William the Conqueror, notified the pope that he was unwilling to bow the knee, since his predecessors had not done so. The humiliation of England by Innocent III in 1215 produced a reaction against papal absolutism. One of the great reforming churchmen of England was Robert Grosseteste, who became bishop of Lincoln in 1235. Besides reforming his own diocese, Grosseteste addressed Pope Innocent IV about 1250 relative to the corruptions of the Roman Curia and of the Roman Church in general; eight years later Grosseteste refused to accept Innocent's appointment of a relative to the Lincoln diocese. In the struggle between Boniface VIII and King Edward I in 1299, the English Parliament upheld their king and defied the pope. The "Babylonian captivity," which brought the papacy under French domination, occurred just at the time France and England were engaged in war. King Edward III (1327–77) secured the passage of two legislative blows against the papacy. In 1350 the Statute against Provisors was enacted, which provided English free elections of archbishops and bishops—an attempt to eliminate foreign influence in the filling of high church offices. Two years later the Statute of Premunire was enacted, which made it treason for any English subject to accept jurisdiction of papal courts outside of England or to appeal cases to them.

John Wycliffe and the Lollards.—One of the outstanding opponents of the papacy in the latter years of his life was the patriot and preacher, John Wycliffe (1320–84). Before about 1376 Wycliffe withheld his attacks against the papacy, but the disreputable conditions surrounding the closing years of the Avignon papacy and the beginning of the papal schism in 1378 touched off his violent protests. Wycliffe urged that both of the popes be deposed. In his lectures at Oxford he advanced the idea that if any secular or ecclesiastical prince were not faithful to his task, his right to hold the office was forfeited. If bishop or even pope proved unworthy, civil rulers, as agents of God's will, had the right to despoil him of his temporal property. Probably encouraged by the protection given him by powerful English patriots, Wycliffe boldly continued his criticism of the papacy. Using the Bible—which he helped translate into English about 1382—as final authority, he vigorously attacked the Roman Catholic sacramental system, particularly the doctrine of transubstantiation. He also asserted that the New Testament made no distinction between the bishop and the presbyter (priest) and that consequently the Roman bishop had wrongfully usurped power which was not his. Wycliffe's views were greatly colored by his patriotism—he objected to papal extortion of English funds, to papal appointments of foreigners to English benefices, and to papal encouragement of mendicant monks in England who, said he, robbed the poor.

To give scriptural instruction, Wycliffe organized a group known as the "poor priests" who wandered about two by two (following scriptural injunctions), preaching and teaching. They were received joyfully by the people. Wycliffe was condemned by the pope in 1377 but was protected until his death in 1384 by political influence. The Lollards, as his poor priests were called, continued to increase in number and influence until 1399. In 1395 they delivered a bold memorial to Parliament denouncing Romanism. However, the accession of King Henry IV (1399–1413), an ardent papist, was the signal for persecution. Scores of Lollards were burned at the stake and their churches suppressed. Lollard followers went underground after 1431 and doubtless provided a fertile soil for the reform movement which came about a century later.

English humanism.—English humanism also played a part in increasing antipapal sentiment. John Colet (1467–1519), dean of St. Paul's Cathedral in London, was an outstanding humanist. With William Grocyn and Thomas Linacre he formed a nucleus for the school of thought that despised the scholastic methods and theology. Colet, a deeply spiritual and capable leader, was especially skilled in biblical interpretation. His eloquent voice constantly called for reform. He greatly influenced Erasmus, the outstanding continental humanist, between about 1498 and 1514.

Bohemia

The clamor for reform in Bohemia was partly religious and partly patriotic. Bohemia was under German domination. Her Christianity had originally been received from the Greek Church, but the great Magyar invasion of the thirteenth century had forced the nation into a German alliance, and through the Germans the Roman type of Christianity had been introduced. The University of Prague was the center of religious and patriotic opposition. A number of eloquent preachers and teachers advocated stringent religious reforms. Among these were Conrad of Waldhausen, who openly denounced the Roman monks and clergy; Milicz of Kremsier; Matthias of Janow, a remarkably able teacher and writer; and Thomas of Stitny, a very popular preacher. Two events brought great impetus to the reform movement. One was the marriage of Ann of Bohemia to King Richard II of England in 1382; the other was the exchange of scholars and correspondence between the universities of Prague and Oxford, resulting from the closer ties between the two nations because of the marriage. The exchange of scholars and correspondence between the universities brought Bohemia into familiarity with the writings of John Wycliffe.

The man who inherited these factors and headed up the reform movement in Bohemia was John Huss (1369–1415). Huss was a native of Bohemia, educated at the University of Prague. A careful student of the Scriptures and of Wycliffe, he filled some of the highest offices in the University of Prague. By his struggle against the Germans in the university he was able to secure from the king a change in the constitution of the school in January, 1409, which brought the native Czechs into a favored position over the German majority. As a consequence the German teachers and students withdrew.

Huss became increasingly bolder in his attacks against foreign and papal usurpations. In 1410 he was excommunicated and his teachings were condemned. Huss then published his treatise *Concerning the Church,* in which he repeated the views of Wycliffe,

162

sometimes copying page after page from Wycliffe's writings. His preaching was directed against papal abuses and demanded reform. He was summoned to the Council of Constance in 1415 to discuss his views and was promised his safety if he would attend. The Roman bishop violated the promise, however, remarking that the Church did not need to keep its word with heretics. Huss was condemned by the Council and was burned at the stake in 1415. A follower, Jerome of Prague, suffered the same fate months later.

The burning of Huss and Jerome aroused Bohemia to open revolt. The Hussite wars, both political and religious in nature, lasted only until about 1435, but the influence of the strict party, the Taborites, led to the formation of the Bohemian Brethren.

The Netherlands

Probably the greatest continental humanist was Desiderius Erasmus of Rotterdam (1465–1536). The son of a priest and gifted in many ways, his life was profoundly affected by the death of his parents when he was but thirteen. For a brief time he attended the school of the Brethren of the Common Life at Deventer but was shunted to a monastic school when his guardians squandered the money left for him. After splendid training at Paris and Cologne, he took his place as the outstanding humanist of his day, making his living by dedicating his works to the patrons who supported him. He had little inclination to break with the Roman system, but his writings are filled with ridicule of the abuses and superstitions that prevailed in the papal Church. His publication in 1516 of a critical edition of the Greek text of the New Testament was of double value—the text itself was quite helpful to reformation scholarship, and the Preface spelled out the need for reform. His hope for reform was through the process of education and infiltration. If men simply knew the gospel of primitive Christianity, the prevalent ills and abuses would be corrected.

Mysticism

A number of groups not specifically confined to one geographical area provided great impetus toward the reform movement. The mystics were one of the most important. Mysticism viewed man as having within him an affinity with God that does not require ecclesiastical machinery to make the contact. God's presence could be felt in the heart and soul without reference to sacraments. It may be observed that this attitude could completely bypass all of the machinery of the Roman Church, for if one could have an immediate and intuitive vision of God, it would be unnecessary to use the services of the priest and the Church. Most of the mystics, however, did not actively oppose the external spiritual exercises of the Roman Church. They were willing to utilize these as aids to supplement their own consciousness of the nearness of God. They had a real concern over the corruptions and schisms in the visible institution.

The principal leaders of this group were Meister Eckhart (1260–1327) in Germany and Jan van Ruysbroeck (1293–1381) and Gerhard Groote (1340–84) in the Netherlands. Eckhart's theology was simple: men should allow God to fill them until they are actually absorbed into God and become Godlike. The modification of this central idea into orthodox harmony with the sacramental system of the Roman Church accounts for differences in the thinking of Eckhart's successors, such as Johann Tauler (1290–1361) and Henry Suso (died 1366). The influence of these men and many other mystics went far beyond simply producing additional mystics. In fundamental conceptions their thinking modified the crass sacramentalism and formalism of many continental theologians. One anonymous writer produced a work which Martin Luther, the great German reformer, later published and prized highly and which Luther termed "German theology," as over against scholastic theology of the Roman Church. This writing was deeply influenced by German mysticism and scriptural theology.

The system of Ruysbroeck in the Netherlands magnified the study of the New Testament and was quite influential in preparing the way for the reform movement that broke out later. Gerhardt Groote, a layman mystic of the Netherlands, led in the formation of the organization called the Brethren of the Common Life, whose purpose was to forward the mystical and pious conceptions of

Ruysbroeck and make them available to others. They established several schools in the Netherlands and Germany. Erasmus attended one of these schools for a period, and Luther himself did likewise. Thomas à Kempis is credited with writing a devotional guide that is still valuable, the *Imitation of Christ*.

Many of the mystics were found in the monasteries. Meister Eckhart was a Dominican monk. Doubtless the long hours of reflection and contemplation gave ample opportunity for the development of mystical tendencies or, as a matter of fact, for the rise of extreme ideas for ceremonialism. The tendency would be to reach either extreme—to attain a passionate love for excessive sacramentalism or a genuine attachment to God apart from any externals. One large party from the Franciscans broke with the majority in an effort to follow more closely the simple ethic of their founder. Their mystical and scriptural simplicity abhorred the luxurious and schismatic Christianity of the papacy. They joined so zealously in the clamor for reform that they were condemned as heretics and many were martyred.

Popular Calls for Reform

The papal schism, extending as it did into every diocese and raising serious questions in the mind of every Roman Catholic concerning which pope (and which bishop) was the valid one, stirred up on every side a popular desire for reform. The immediate motive was to secure the unity of the papacy. Since the rival popes anathematized one another and all supporters of one another— which really negated the effectiveness of any sacraments and official acts of the false pope and his followers—and since no one knew which was the correct pope, utmost confusion and widespread fear prevailed among the masses. Lay organizations sprang up, and orders of women arose whose main emphasis was upon the necessity of reform.

Concluding Summary

The desire to reform the Roman Church sprang from various motives. The study of the Bible, intellectual awakening, patriot-

165

ism, economic and social conditions, military considerations, and religious hunger combined to seek reform. Voices could be heard from practically all of the principal countries. Mysticism and dissent increased considerably.

The next chapter will discuss the effort to bring reform, primarily by the conciliar method. This did at least heal the papal schism, although no progress was made toward reforming the papacy itself.

14

Efforts at Reform

THE DOMINATION OF the papacy by French interests from 1309 to 1378 and the scandalous schism for almost forty years after the attempt to return the papacy to Rome emphasized the necessity of reform. But circumstances and traditional beliefs seemed to make any sort of reform completely impossible. In the first place, there was no way to determine just who was the proper occupant of the papal chair. Each of the popes was supported by a legitimately appointed and properly consecrated group of cardinals. Each had declared himself the rightful pope and had anathematized his opponent. Even worse, each had sufficient political backing to maintain himself in office. In the second place, what could be done against a pope, assuming that one of the two or three was the proper one? As early as the fifth century, Pope Symmachus had set forth the theory of papal irresponsibility. By 503 this idea had received dogmatic approval. As enlarged through the centuries, this doctrine taught that even if the pope were in complete error, he could not be tried by any but God; no tribunal on earth could challenge the doctrines, morals, motives, or decrees of a pope. How, then, could there be any action taken to heal the schism?

Individual Protests

In the previous chapter some of the protests from every part of the Roman Church were sketched. Plans of reform were urged; severe criticism was directed against the papal government and papal doctrines. But in view of the traditional notion that no one may correct a pope and the doubt concerning which claimant actually was the true pope, no practical move was taken.

The Opinions of Scholars

Despite repeated appeals to both popes after 1378, neither would take the initiative to restore papal unity. The scholars in the various theological schools, whose views had often borne great weight in doctrinal controversies, were consulted about the best way to end the schism. It was inevitable that the idea of Marsiglio of Padua, written in 1324 into his *Defensor Pacis*, should be asserted, namely, that a general council possesses supreme authority in Christianity. This same suggestion was made by two other scholars, Conrad of Gelshausen in 1379 and Heinrich of Langenstein in 1381. By 1408 most of the scholars in the great universities of the Continent agreed that the only method of healing the schism was through a general council. The scholars could not agree as to the makeup of the council. Some thought that all true Christians should constitute the membership; others would favor the precedent of the earlier general councils and limit the membership simply to the bishops who, they said, constituted the visible Church. But there were other problems. Who should call the council? The emperors had called some of the early councils, but the popes had claimed that prerogative for many centuries. Neither of the popes was willing to call the council; however, the cardinals of the rival popes were convinced that a general council was necessary to restore peace and unity.

The Council of Pisa (1409)

At the call of the cardinals a general council was assembled at Pisa in March, 1409. The council attempted to solve three problems: the papal schism, reform, and heresy. The first of these problems was viewed as the principal purpose of the council. It was well attended and took definite action by declaring the papal throne vacant. Cardinals representing both popes united to elect a new one, who took the name Alexander V. Since neither of the two existing popes, Gregory XII and Benedict XIII, recognized the council as validly assembled or authoritative, the net result was simply the addition of another pope.

The Council of Constance (1414–18)

The mistakes of the Council of Pisa were evident. For one thing, many of the bishops desired more information about the authority of a council, particularly in deposing a pope. Others felt that the council should have been summoned by a pope, not by the cardinals or by a secular power. Furthermore, it was apparent that political factors would determine whether or not any action of a future council would be effective. As it was, each of the three popes had enough political and military support to maintain himself in office. The new pope, Alexander V, was recognized by England, France, Hungary, and parts of Italy; Benedict XIII was called pope by Spain and Scotland; while Gregory XII had most of the Italian support and that of Germany.

Two men remedied these defects. John Gerson, one of the champions of the conciliar idea after 1408, determined to clothe a future council with express authority to take action in dealing with schism, reform, and heresy. The other, the German emperor Sigismund (1410–37), determined to provide political support sufficient to make the decrees of the council effective. Sigismund had the first task, and he worked diligently at it. He induced Pope John XXIII (successor to Alexander V) to call a general council to convene at Constance. By clever political tactics he secured the support of the Spanish, English, and Burgundian rulers for the council. He had chosen Constance in Germany as the place of meeting in order to neutralize the influence of the Italian clergy, practically all of whom favored John XXIII. In addition, arrangements were made for the council to vote by nations rather than by individuals, in this way circumventing plans by some of the incumbent popes to "pack" the meeting. Thus each of the five nations— England, France, Spain, Germany, and Italy—had one vote and must vote as a unit.

Gerson and his supporters did their part. Through Gerson's influence the council passed a decree in April, 1415, defining its own authority. It claimed to represent Jesus Christ and asserted that its decisions on all religious matters were binding upon every

Christian, including the pope or popes. This decree, of course, cut directly across papal claims for centuries. Passed unanimously by the ecumenical council, it challenged ancient dogmas of the Roman Church which were alleged to be incapable of change and provided an example of an alleged infallible council and infallible papacy in conflict. Acting upon this decree, the council forcibly seized Pope John XXIII and deposed him in May, 1415; Gregory XII then resigned; Benedict XIII was twice deposed, although he refused to accept this action.

Another innovation occurred. Instead of having a new pope elected by the cardinals, it was agreed by the council that those cardinals present at the council, supplemented by thirty members of the council, should elect a new pope, with only a two-thirds majority required for election. They chose one who took the name Martin V. He took office immediately, possessing sufficient political support to guarantee his universal acceptance. The schism was almost over. Benedict XIII had refused to resign, but after his death in 1424, his successor was recognized only by Aragon and Sicily; and in 1429 the schism was completely ended.

The second problem of the Council of Constance was reform. After the election of Martin V the council passed another decree which denied papal claims of almost a millennium. This decree provided that general councils would meet again in five years and in seven years, and that thereafter such councils would meet every ten years. Future popes would be subject to instructions from these councils. The ancient papal claims of superiority to councils seemed doomed. However, the attitude of the new pope should have warned the conciliar leaders. Martin V had supported the conciliar idea until his election as pope; then he immediately became anticonciliar. When the council endeavored to bring reform, the new pope worked feverishly to prevent the adoption of antipapal measures. This he was able to do.

The problem of heresy also occupied the attention of the council. The burning of John Huss and Jerome has already been mentioned. The outbreak of the Hussite wars shows that the council was not only religiously suspect but was also politically unwise.

Council of Pavia and Siena (1423)

The papal schism had been healed, but reform still was not begun. Martin V (1417–31) asserted traditional papal claims in an effort to neutralize the decrees of the Council of Constance, which claimed to be the supreme authority in Christendom. However, the pope felt it necessary to carry out the decree of Constance providing for the calling of a general council in five years, especially since the Bohemians were still threatening and the Ottoman Turks were winning new military victories. The plague at Pavia caused the removal of the council to Siena. The pope dismissed the council soon, however, alleging poor attendance as the reason.

Council of Basel (1431–49)

It had been planned at the Council of Constance to call another general council seven years after the Council of Pavia. Pope Martin V had agreed to call this council but died before it assembled. His successor, Eugenius IV (1431–47), had promised to support the conciliar program as a condition of election but violated his promise. When the council met and showed the spirit of the Council of Constance, Eugenius tried to dissolve the assembly before any action was taken. Political pressure dissuaded him. Three problems faced this council: how to deal with the warring Hussites; what to do about a reform of the Church; and how to effect a reunion of Eastern and Western Christianity, desired by some of the Eastern leaders as a means of driving away the Ottoman Turks who were threatening to capture Constantinople.

The council was partially successful in dealing with the Bohemians. By appeasing the moderate party (the Utraquists or Calixtines), a division was caused between them and the more radical Taborites. The result was another civil war in Bohemia, but the Catholics were able to defeat the Taborites and repress the spread of their ideas.

For a brief period it seemed that some effective ecclesiastical reforms might result from the deliberations of the council. However, as soon as the council touched the person of the pope and his authority, papal influence blocked further progress. Eugenius decided to deal with the council as the council had dealt with the Bohemians—to divide and conquer. The question of union between East and West was pressed upon the council. When sharp differences appeared, the pope denounced the council and in 1437 removed it by papal bull to Ferrara, thence to Florence in 1439. A substantial party refused to abide by the papal edict and continued to meet at Basel. They voted to depose Eugenius as pope and selected another who took the name of Felix V (1439–49). Now there were two popes again, but Felix had no political support, and there was widespread revulsion at the thought of another papal schism. Consequently, the Basel council was discredited and in 1449 surrendered to Nicholas V (1447–55), who had succeeded Eugenius. The conciliar efforts to reform the papacy had failed.

Council of Ferrara and Florence (1437–39)

The principal reason of Pope Eugenius for moving the council from Basel to Ferrara and then to Florence was to discredit the Basel reforming party. The pope was determined that there would be no reform by a council. Because of this fact, considerable responsibility for the schismatic movement known as the Reformation must be laid at his door. The Council of Basel was eager to make reforms and doubtless would have done so along the lines of the Pragmatic Sanctions of France, which will be mentioned hereafter.

It is true that the representatives from the Greek Church preferred to meet in an Italian city, but this was of small moment. As a matter of fact, the question of uniting East and West was doomed before the Greek delegation arrived at Ferrara in 1438. A majority of the East definitely opposed the union under any circumstances. The minority desired union simply to secure military and political assistance against the Turks. In the council the pope agreed to organize a new crusade against the Turks, in return for which the East would recognize the universal supremacy of the pope. This agreement, however, was promptly repudiated by the Eastern clergy.

Reasons for Failure of Conciliar Efforts

The collapse of the Council of Basel in 1449 brought to an end the movement begun about forty years before in the Council of Pisa. Some reasons for the failure of this effort to reform the Church in head and members are apparent. For one thing, there was a lack of unity in motives for reform. Some were interested in reform only from a political standpoint, some were seeking to fish in troubled waters in the hope of personal advancement, while some were willing to go along with the movement so long as it was popular.

A partial solution of the immediate problem at hand, the papal schism, blunted the desire for thorough reform. When the Council of Constance solved the most pressing problem facing it in 1417, even the brave statement of the authority of the council did not hide the fact that in the minds of many the council had gone as far as it should. With a single pope to deal with, leadership in a stringent reform brought danger of effective reprisals.

The active antagonism of the popes predestined to failure any attempts at reform. The several popes of the first half of the fifteenth century agreed in principle with the efforts of the conciliar reformers until they had been elected to the high office. Their sympathy for reform and their recognition of the authority of a council then vanished immediately. The comparatively long period of time between the meetings of the reforming councils gave the papacy an opportunity to recoup much of its strength and prestige.

After the Reforming Councils

Although an effective program of reform was not accomplished, the battle had not been lost entirely. The various nations represented in the councils had seen at first hand the need for reform and the attitude of the papacy toward reform. They had also caught a glimpse of the authority that political and military strength carried. Consequently, England, Spain, and France, already strong and unified, were able to secure important concessions from the papacy with reference to the control of the Church within their boundaries. France, in fact, shortly after the failure of the Council of Basel assembled a meeting of the clergy and enacted the Pragmatic Sanctions of 1438, which accomplished the very thing for France that the conciliar proponents had hoped would come for all of Christianity from the general council. These Sanctions asserted that a general council was the supreme authority in Christendom and, among other things, claimed French autonomy in filling its ecclesiastical vacancies. It is just as significant that the loosely organized German states, where the reform movement subsequently broke forth, were unable to secure any such concessions and consequently felt even more heavily the burdens of papal financial and ecclesiastical tyranny.

The failure of the conciliar movement seemed to increase the arrogance of the Roman popes. The religious and moral tone of the papacy from the close of the Council of Basel until the Lutheran Reformation was indescribably low. Two of the popes were out-and-out humanists (Nicholas V, 1447–55, and Pius II, 1458–64) ; one of them a second-rate despot (Sixtus IV, 1471–84) ; two were shameless in their immorality and vice (Innocent VIII, 1484–92, who openly acknowledged and promoted his seven illegitimate children, and Alexander VI, 1492–1503, noted for his immorality, vice, and violence) ; one should have been an army officer (Julius II, 1503–13) ; while the pope of the Reformation, Leo X (1513–21) , reportedly called Christianity a profitable fable and spent his time in his hunting lodge. Had there been wise and upright popes in this period, it is very likely that the next effort at reform would have been different in its direction and consequences. The succession of men of this calibre guaranteed the certainty of the deluge to come.

Concluding Summary

The ticklish problem of ending a papal schism was finally accomplished by the authority of a general council, buttressed by political and military support. Such action marks the council as superior to popes, a fact which was subsequently denied by succeeding popes but which established them in their office and succession. To deny the authority of a council to depose popes would appear to deny the validity of their own succession.

The thorough reform of the Roman Catholic Church in head and members, however, could not be accomplished by reforming councils, despite many efforts during forty years. The occupants of the papal office in the half century immediately before the Reformation constitute ample evidence of the need for reform.

Ecclesiastical Dissent

ONE FACTOR OF great importance relating to the papal decline and the clamor for reform was the presence everywhere of anti-papal dissent. It is difficult to lump together into one descriptive term all of the extensive movements which existed just prior to the Reformation. The only record of so many of them comes from their persecution in the Inquisition. Some of the movements were distinctly medieval in their religious conceptions. Others held evangelical tenets. It is hard today to interpret contemporary religious movements correctly despite the possession of extensive literature by their own adherents. The problem of attempting to give a true picture of movements whose only records are those of one man, an enemy to the cause and one unversed in differentiating objectively between evangelicalism and heresy, is far greater.

The same situation renders most difficult the matter of determining the relations and history of any such movement. Were these antipapal dissenters isolated and separate in their several movements, or was there correspondence among them? Did they represent the fruits of earlier movements, or did they spring *de novo* from the earth? Such questions have passionate defenders at both extremes and cannot be settled completely. Conclusions, therefore, in many cases are a matter of personal attitude and judgment.

Evidences of Unity and Continuity

Literary remains of concerted opposition to the Roman Church would naturally be quite scarce. There is indisputable evidence, however, that many of the movements which were at one time thought to be isolated and separate were, in reality, in close fellowship and correspondence. For example, evangelical parties in Germany, Austria, and Italy assembled in convention as early as 1218 to discuss points of mutual belief. Constant correspondence had taken place also long before the Reformation between evangelical dissenters throughout Germany and those in Bohemia. In the thirteenth century Pope Innocent III denounced the translation of the Scriptures into the language of the people, and the possession of Scriptures in the vernacular tongue was looked upon as heresy. Even before Wycliffe's version in English in the late fourteenth century, dissenters were translating the Bible into the language of the people. Dozens of German translations existed in the fifteenth century, some showing evidence of independent work while others, betraying a common source, turned up among widely separated groups. Long after the Reformation had begun, the Anabaptists of Germany used these ancient translations rather than the translation of Luther. An interesting reflection of connections among the dissenters is seen in the fact that the Waldenses of Italy and France, the Brethren of the Common Life in the Netherlands and Germany, and the United Brethren of Bohemia used the same catechism for the instruction of the children in their movements. Editions of the identical catechism are found in French, Italian, German, and Bohemian.

It is not difficult to find convincing evidence that many of the dissenting movements of the thirteenth and fourteenth centuries were the successors of more primitive groups. Peculiar doctrines, noticeable in the system of the Eastern Paulicians of the early Middle Ages, for example, are reproduced in the Bogomiles of the Balkans and the Cathari of France and Germany. The Western dispersion of the Paulicians is a historical fact. The name of the Cathari (Greek both in form and in spirit) marks them as an Eastern movement transplanted to the West, probably a reappearance of the Paulician and Bogomile dissenters. There are evidences of the persistence of the older Christianity of Britain (discountenanced by the Synod of Whitby in 664), as well as older Christianity upon the Continent proper. The rapid spread of Luther's reform and the sudden appearance of organized Anabaptist congregations all over the Continent in the sixteenth century testify to a widespread evangelical background.

Handicaps to Historical Certainty

It is impossible to be dogmatic about the history of dissent in this period. The sparsity of historical material would forbid it. Most of the literary remains were prepared by the enemies of dissent, secured through the most excruciating torture by the inquisitors. Before the suppression of dissent through the central organization of the Roman Curia, this work was carried on locally by bishops or crusading preachers like Bernard, the Cistercian monk. Under these circumstances even inquisitorial records are lacking, and there is practically no evidence of any kind about the dissenters and their beliefs.

For example, although the Bogomiles of the twelfth century may have numbered as many as two million, one of the principal records of their beliefs comes from a Byzantine monk named Euthymius who died in 1118. He gave an account of how, among other things, they rejected the Lord's Supper as the sacrifice of demons, called the churches the dwelling places of demons and the worship of images in them idolatry, and termed the "Fathers of the Church" false prophets against whom Jesus warned. Such charges doubtless were similar to the charges brought against the early Christians: they were called atheists because they had no idols, cannibals because they partook of the body and blood of Christ, and immoral because they spoke of Christian love. Perhaps the Bogomiles did reject the Mass, reject the orthodox churches, and oppose idolatry. From the entire description given, the Bogomiles seem to have been the product of missionary work by the Paulicians among the Bulgarians. At least, their alleged doctrines reflect some of the peculiarities of the Paulicians, modified by dualistic and Manichean tendencies.

Another example of the sparsity of records is seen in the story of the Petrobrusians and Henricians. These movements were begun separately but coalesced. Much of what is known about the Petrobrusians comes from the pen of a Roman Catholic enemy.

Peter de Bruys was a priest of the Roman Church in the twelfth century. He had been a student of Abélard, the great freethinker. About 1104 he began a career as a reformer in southern France and was widely influential until his martyrdom about 1126. Henry of Lausanne was a Roman Catholic monk who associated himself with Peter as a reformer. After a long and active ministry he died as a martyr in 1148. The evangelical nature of the things these men taught is evident in spite of the denunciation of their doctrines by their enemy biographer. (1) They denied that the christening of infants was baptism and said that only an intelligent profession of faith by a person for himself (without proxy) brought salvation. (2) They vehemently rejected crosses in worship, since Christ was slain upon one. Even temples and churches were unnecessary for the worship of God. (3) They denied the doctrine of transubstantiation and perhaps refused to observe the Supper at all. (4) They recognized the Scriptures alone as authoritative, denying the authority of the early Fathers and of tradition.

Innocent III and Dissent

The pope who both closed the previous period and opened the present one (Innocent III, 1198–1216) had contact with two dissenting groups, the Waldenses and the Cathari. Both of these movements had a long history before that time. The origin of the Waldenses is disputed. Even the source of their name is in doubt. Perhaps it was begun by Peter Waldo of Lyons, France, in the closing years of the twelfth century. He headed a movement in which laymen wandered about teaching and singing Scriptures. The group was excommunicated in 1184 but continued to spread rapidly through southern France, Italy, Spain, and the Rhine Valley.

The inquisitors who sought out information on the beliefs of the Waldenses testify that they had about the same doctrines as the Petrobrusians: the sole authority of the Scriptures, the necessity for believer's baptism, the denial of the authority of the Roman Church, the denial of purgatory and the merit of praying to the saints, and refusal to believe that the bread and wine are changed

179

into the body and blood of Christ by the priest. In addition, it was alleged that the Waldenses permitted men to preach without proper ordination, vilified the pope, refused to make canonical confession, and rejected oaths and war. About 1212 Innocent III was approached by some of this group for permission to assemble and read the Scriptures. The pope gave this permission but three years later initiated a decree of condemnation against all Waldenses. In an effort to cripple the movement, two successive Catholic synods forbade the reading of the Bible in the language of the people, either by laymen or clergy. Although severely persecuted, the Waldenses continue to the present time.

The group known as the Cathari came to light in France in the eleventh century. Their doctrines were quite similar to those of the Bogomiles. As a matter of fact, the Cathari of France looked toward Bulgaria as their source and recognized a Bogomile leader as their spiritual head. Their dualistic view of God and Docetic Christology suggest a strong Manichean influence, another indication that perhaps their doctrinal system originated in the East where Manicheanism was strongest.

The dissenters known as the Albigenses (because they lived near Albi in southern France) were Cathari. Innocent III (1198–1216) decided, in view of the great strength of the movement, that strong means must be taken to root it out. Accordingly, Innocent sent two legates to France to begin the effort. They were persuaded by the bishop of Osma and by Dominic to try religious measures first. Assuming the garb of beggars, the legates and others wandered about barefooted and presented an example of humility and poverty. Few Albigenses were convinced. Violent measures soon followed.

Count Raymond of Toulouse was the nominal ruler over the area where the heretics lived but was indifferent to their religious views so long as they were good subjects. One of the legates was murdered in 1208, and Raymond was suspected of complicity or at least accused of it. Innocent III proclaimed a crusade against Raymond and the Albigenses. Whoever conquered them should have both territory and spoils from the war. For twenty years the war raged. As cities were captured, their inhabitants were either slaughtered or sold into slavery. The Albigenses fled throughout Europe, and others of the Cathari followed their example. Pope Innocent pushed through the Fourth Lateran Council in 1215 three canons relating to heretics: secular rulers must not tolerate heretics in their domain; secular rulers refusing to uproot heretics must themselves be driven out, either by their subjects or by crusaders from the outside; crusading against heretics at home brings all the sacramental privileges and indulgences which accrue from crusading against the Turks in Jerusalem.

The Extent of Ecclesiastical Dissent

One method of noting the wide extent of dissent against the Roman Catholic system is geographical. Between 1215 and the theses of Luther in 1517 it is possible to find sizable groups of dissenters in almost every section of the Western world. Dissent was also strong in the East, but that area was not involved in the domination of the papacy after 1054 and did not share in the Reformation.

England.—In England the Lollards (the name given to the "poor priests" of Wycliffe) constituted a large and aggressive dissenting movement. A Roman Catholic writer of the late fourteenth century said that one out of every two men seemed to be a follower of Wycliffe. The Lollards were strong enough in 1395 to present a memorial to Parliament attacking the Roman Church and its doctrines, in particular condemning the Roman priesthood, Roman celibacy, Roman transubstantiation, Roman liturgies and prayers for the dead, auricular confession, and Roman crusades. Four years later, with the accession of Henry IV who was under the influence of Archbishop Thomas Arundel of Canterbury, persecution of the Lollards began. After 1417 they were driven underground, but their influence and doctrines were not destroyed.

France and Spain.—Reference has already been made to the dissenting movements of Peter de Bruys and Henry of Lausanne and to the Cathari. Some historians believe that through these

181

groups almost the whole of southern France was antipapal during the twelfth century. When the Albigensian persecution came in the thirteenth century, many of the Cathari fled into Spain and became victims of the Spanish Inquisition. One of the letters of Bernard, the outstanding preacher of the twelfth century, remarks that the churches were without congregations because of the heretical movement.

Italy.—Reformers were not unknown at the very door of the papal see. One of the outstanding reforming figures was Arnold of Brescia in northern Italy. His strictures against the papacy were aimed mainly at the secular and financial activities of the clergy which, he said, should not occupy their attention. Freewill offerings alone should provide for the support of all religious leaders. He fled from Italy in 1139 to escape charges of heresy but in 1145 assumed leadership of a popular movement which expelled the pope and looked to the restoration of the ancient Roman republic. Ten years later, overwhelmed through the military alliance of Pope Alexander III, Arnold was martyred.

It is likely that Arnold was the founder of the group known as Arnoldists and the inspiration of the movement developing later known as the Poor Men of Lombardy. Not a great deal is known about these two sects, except that they are frequently mentioned as heretics in the Roman Catholic writings of the thirteenth and fourteenth centuries. They seem to have opposed vigorously the Roman Catholic system, to have denied that water in baptism brings forgiveness, and to have excoriated the Roman clergy for secularization and corruption.

Another Italian group known as the Humiliati arose in the twelfth century; about them little is known, except that they were classed as heretics and mentioned in such fashion that they seem to have been associated with the Waldenses.

The influence of these dissenters was extensive in northern Italy. In a document written about 1260, an anonymous author remarked that in northern Italy the Waldenses had more schools than the orthodox Church and also had more hearers. He further asserted that because of their large numbers, these heretics held public disputes against Catholicism and services in the market place or the open field.

The Germanic states.—The Waldensian movement also infected many areas in the Germanic states. The same author who describes the large number of Waldenses in Italy speaks of the extensive spread of the Waldenses around Passau on the Danube River. He named forty-two places in the Catholic diocese of Passau which were affected by the heresy. In twelve of these places the Waldenses had schools and in one of them a bishop. Roman Catholic documents a century and a half later (1389) describe ninety-two points of papal doctrine and practice rejected by the Waldenses and provide evidence that this movement had become thoroughly evangelical in its doctrinal views.

In the fourteenth century two theologians in German schools openly taught doctrines at variance with the teachings of the Roman system. One was John of Wesel. He placed the Scriptures alone as the final authority in Christianity. He rejected the priestly pretensions of controlling salvation and denied the doctrine of transubstantiation. Imprisoned by the Roman authorities at Mainz, he died in 1482. The other theologian was Wessel Gansfort, who died in 1489. He proclaimed the doctrine of justification by faith and attacked the doctrine of indulgences. Luther later confessed that his entire Reformation doctrine was so evident in the writings of Wessel Gansfort that had Luther been acquainted with these writings, his enemies might have charged him with securing material from that source.

Netherlands and the Rhine Valley.—The records speak of heretical movements in the twelfth century in northern Europe also. In the Netherlands, Tanchelm (1115–24) strongly denounced Roman Catholic churches and sacraments as pollutions and in general followed the teachings of Peter de Bruys, with whom he was a contemporary. At about the same time Eudo de Stella carried on a similar ministry in the Rhine Valley. His followers were so aroused by his preaching that they destroyed Roman Churches and monasteries. He was seized by the Roman Church and died as a martyr about 1148. Other dissenters, quite evangelical and antipapal, left a record of their work along the Rhine Valley. They clearly denied the Roman doctrines of transubstantiation and infant baptism.

Bohemia.—Perhaps of all the areas of Europe, Bohemia had been most completely infected with dissent. Historically, of course, Bohemia had looked to the Eastern world for her religious pattern and had only accepted the Latin Church because it was brought by the Germans who protected Bohemia against the Magyar invasions of the eleventh century. Resentment against foreigners politically and religiously formed a background of Bohemian dissent. It is known that the Waldenses were quite strong in southern Bohemia—so strong, in fact, that in about 1340 they threatened to destroy their Catholic foes should an attempt be made to coerce them religiously. Out of the Hussite wars, following the burning of John Huss in 1415, came the two parties, the strict one (the Taborites) holding views much like those of the evangelical Waldenses. They fiercely opposed the Roman Catholic Church in every point save one, the retention of infant baptism. One of the outstanding leaders of Bohemian dissent in the fifteenth century was Peter Chelicky, a native Bohemian, born about 1385. He, too, followed closely the doctrines of the evangelical Waldenses; he would allow infant baptism in practice, although denying its validity in principle.

The Bohemian Brethren constituted the evangelical wing of the Hussite reform. It was organized in an effort to bring a general reform within the national church so as to restore to Christianity the original purity which had been lost. In its practical aspect this movement formed a community which endeavored to live according to the law of Christ. Specific organization was effected about 1457. Before the Reformation crisis of 1517 this movement had spread throughout Bohemia and Moravia and had become a considerable force for reform. Through extensive use of the newly invented printing press, the organization of schools, and the wide dissemination of their doctrines through Austria and Germany, the Brethren played a large part in preparing for the events of the sixteenth century.

Concluding Summary

It may be seen, then, that dissent of some sort appeared in almost every section of Europe in this period. The sparsity of records makes it difficult to judge accurately either the doctrines or the extent of the movements. It should be remembered that this description of these movements is not exhaustive. The myriad of reformers who lingered just below the surface of recorded history can never be known. But they were there. The rapidity with which the Reformation developed in the sixteenth century provides evidence of this. How else is it possible to explain how a large part of the Continent and England embraced the reforming movements so rapidly between 1517 and 1534? Such widespread defection from the Roman Church demanded widespread dissent as an antecedent.

16

The Fulness of Time

THE WORD "REFORMATION" describing the revolution of the sixteenth century is, in a sense, a misnomer. The principal events did not center in reform but in schism. Certainly those who participated in the organization of new ecclesiastical bodies conceived of their movements as true Christianity moving into, or toward, its primitive channel. In that sense there was a reformation of Christianity, not of the Roman Curia, for the Curia refused to be reformed.

In the latter months of 1517 a monk named Martin Luther, incensed by the recent sale of indulgences in a nearby German town, gave public notice on the door of the church at Wittenberg that he desired to debate what the Catholic Church actually taught about indulgences. In this rather ordinary fashion the Lutheran Reformation began. What was it that brought comparative success to Luther's efforts when so many previous efforts had failed? Was it in the monk, in his environment, in the circumstances of his life, in his inheritance from previous generations? It was in all of these.

Political Factors That Aided the Reformation

Practically every political body in Europe contributed in some way to the progress of the reform movement. In most cases it was done unwittingly. The strongest state in Europe during this period was Spain. The peninsula had been unified politically by the marriage in 1469 between Ferdinand of Aragon and Isabella of Castile and by the subsequent conquest of contiguous areas. The grandson of this couple, Charles I, became king in 1516 and in

1519 was elected Holy Roman Emperor of the German nation. The latter succession titled him Charles V, by which he is best known. He inherited a strongly Catholic nation, made so by the work of Cardinal Ximenes, principal adviser of Queen Isabella. Ximenes had instituted a reform of the Catholic Church in Spain which abolished papal abuses and much papal control; consequently, neither Charles nor his people were sympathetic with the continental reform movements. Emperor Charles V was the principal enemy of the Lutheran Reformation and was more powerful and apparently more interested in suppressing it than were the popes. Only nineteen when elected emperor, his youthfulness was not marked by frivolity but by a zeal to restore to preeminence the ancient Catholic faith which his forebears had followed.

The principal rival of Spain during the Reformation period was France. This nation had achieved a strong centralized government through a succession of able kings. The rivalry between Spain and France flared up before the outbreak of the reform. Both King Ferdinand of Spain and Charles VIII of France had claims in the Kingdom of Naples in southern Italy. In 1495 Charles VIII was crowned king of Naples after leading a French army through the center of Italy and defeating the Aragonese claimant. King Ferdinand of Spain decided to assert his claim in Naples and in 1504 drove Louis XII (1498–1515), successor to Charles VIII, out of Naples and eight years later drove him completely out of Italy. This marked the beginning of a series of wars between France and Spain, which in a sense saved the Lutheran Reformation. The chief opponent of Luther, Emperor Charles V of Spain, became so busy fighting France and the Turks that he could not devote himself to smothering out the religious revolt until it had become strong enough politically to offer formidable opposition. The king of France during most of the Reformation was Francis I (1515–47), who did not favor the reform movement as such but helped it considerably by his political and military feuds with Spain.

The third of the centralized monarchies of this period was Eng-

EUROPE
at the Time of the
REFORMATION

Finland

Russia

Mohammedans

Ottoman Empire

Norway

Sweden

Lithuania

Poland

Denmark

The Empire

Bohemia

Switz.

Hungary

Naples

Papal States

Sicily

Ireland

England

Scotland

France

Spain

Portugal

● ● ● ● line shows the extent of Mohammedan infiltration

land. A military struggle among the nobles for royal succession almost eliminated them as a political factor, allowing the new king, Henry VII (1485–1509), to rule with a free hand. His son, Henry VIII (1509–47), was the sovereign during the principal portion of the continental movement. Henry VIII was a bitter opponent of the Lutheran reform during its early stage. He inaugurated a schism with the Roman Church in 1534 which was primarily external and governmental. He did not depart from most of the doctrines of Rome.

The fourth political power in Europe during the reform movement was the Empire. It will be remembered that the Western Empire was restored under Charlemagne in 800 and again under Otto the Great in 962. After about the middle of the thirteenth century the Empire began to decay again. A literary struggle over the right to bestow the imperial dignity (pope versus German electors) led to the *Defensor Pacis* of Marsiglio of Padua. The elective system won out. Although there were scores of small German states, seven strong sovereigns (three ecclesiastical and four secular) had named the emperor since 1356. The ecclesiastical electors were the archbishops of Mainz, Trier, and Cologne; the secular electors were the king of Bohemia, the elector of Saxony, the elector of Brandenburg, and the count palatine on the Rhine.

For generations the emperor had been chosen from the family of Hapsburgs. In the opening years of the Reformation the emperor was Maximilian I (1493–1519). Maximilian's son Philip was married to Joanna, the daughter of Ferdinand and Isabella of Spain. Through the efforts of Maximilian, his two grandsons, Charles and Ferdinand, controlled practically all of central Europe and Spain, excepting only France. Charles became king of Spain through his mother's succession and from his father inherited the Netherlands and large portions of northern and eastern Europe. Ferdinand was married to Anne of Bohemia, by which the Hapsburgs acquired rule over Bohemia and Hungary. In a strong shuffling of political interests both the popes and the king of France, through their efforts to undermine the Hapsburg power heading up in Emperor Charles V, were enemies of their own religious cause. It should be pointed out that the actual authority of the emperor over this loose confederation of German states was quite limited. The strong princes within the Empire ruled their own states as completely sovereign, many times circumventing the desires of the emperor through political sagacity. Such a situation allowed the elector of Saxony, for example, to protect Luther from the anger both of popes and of the emperor.

Another political and military power that played a large part in affecting the progress of Western reform was the group known as the Turks. After the capture of Constantinople in 1453, the Turks drove north and westward through the Balkans with an avowed purpose of overrunning all of Europe. During the Reformation the emperor's desire to stamp out Lutheranism was greatly affected by the Turkish menace. He could hardly afford to start a civil war when the Turks appeared to be on the verge of breaking into central Europe.

Italy had little political significance during the Reformation. Russia was rapidly becoming a strong political power but played no part in the Western reform. Christianity from the East had begun work in Russia, and later on Russia formed her own national church, loosely in fellowship with Constantinople. The Eastern world from Palestine to the Balkans had been overrun by the Mohammedans in the Medieval period, and it neither influenced nor was affected by the Western reform. Although not directly related to the movement, the states of Transylvania on the southeast of the Empire and Poland on the northeast were involved indirectly, since these areas, lying outside of the boundary of the Empire, were havens for dissenting leaders.

Economic and Social Factors That Aided the Reformation

New economic and social patterns were greatly influential in fostering the reform movement. The German states entered into a period of economic and social transition in the fourteenth and fifteenth centuries. The merchant or capitalist class had arisen because of trade and commerce in the Mediterranean area. Geographical discoveries of the period opened a new world economically. The Portuguese discovery of a new route to India and the development of colonies provided new opportunity for the profitable investment of capital.

Furthermore, the discovery and development of German mineral resources threatened to supplant the agrarian interests, pyramiding economic and social problems. With the withdrawal of many peasants from agricultural labor and the increase of mineral production, the natural economic consequence of inflationary prices for food followed. Worse yet, harvest failure over Germany occurred for almost thirteen successive years, beginning about 1490, bringing starvation and malnutrition on every hand. There was universal discontent. Because of the necessity for harder work on the part of the peasants still working the land, resentment by the middle and upper classes at the sudden skyrocketing of food prices which nobody could explain or control, and the devaluation of wages incident to the economic inflation, the entire social and economic attitude was antagonistic. Peasant revolts became common, particularly after the attempt to supplant the old German legal customs by principles of Roman law. It is no wonder that the inordinate avarice of the Roman Church in demanding annates, tithes, indulgences, etc., was looked upon as tyranny.

Intellectual Factors That Aided the Reformation

One reason for failure of earlier reform movements was the general lack of intelligence. Fear and superstition were obstacles too great for any antipapal movement to hurdle. The intellectual renascence that followed the Crusades gave a great deal of impetus to popular enlightenment. The development of the printing press in the middle of the fifteenth century made it possible to reproduce the spoken message for thousands of audiences. Luther's reform could not have been so effective had there not been widespread information and interest through the use of pamphlets and books. Furthermore, the movement known as "humanism," while not always religious in its emphasis, provided enlightenment and leadership that contributed greatly to Luther's reform.

191

Finally, the attitude of the common man toward the papacy had undergone a profound transformation. It is quite doubtful that Luther or anyone else would have dared to take the steps which might sever them from the visible Roman Catholic Church if it had been believed that such a schism would result in the loss of salvation. Foreign to philosophical realism and the claims of the Roman Church, there had developed a widespread conception that salvation could be attained apart from the Roman system.

It is true that some followers of Luther forsook him when he deliberately turned away from the Roman Church; but the very fact that the German multitudes followed him in a schismatic movement, sharing with him the anathematizing by the Church, speaks of a new point of view. The principal events that inculcated such a conception may only be guessed, but it is likely that the recollection of the papal schism had shaken the implicit faith of many in a visible and unrent body of Christ. The defiance of papal excommunication by the secular states both revealed the popular mind and strengthened the idea that salvation did not rest only with the Roman system; the presence for centuries of strong movements of dissenters like the Waldenses and Bohemian Brethren discounted Roman claims; and the constant conflict between the Church and the Empire, each conceived as a divine institution, brought confusion and doubt concerning the claims of the former. Whatever the reasons may have been, it is evident that millions were willing to leave the body which claimed to be the only font of salvation. They were convinced that salvation could be found elsewhere.

Religious Factors That Aided the Reformation

Almost inseparable from the intellectual factors described were the religious elements that moved the multitudes toward reform. Some of the dissenting movements have been described in the previous chapter. It is impossible to measure the influence exerted by these groups, but it must have been tremendous. Whether judged from the meager records that are available or from the attempt to explain the sudden widespread support of the reforms of Luther and others, it must be plain that either a great historical phenomenon occurred without sufficient antecedents or that the masses of people were extensively prepared for a break with the dominant Church before Luther and others called them out. Negative factors undoubtedly aided, such as the extremely low tone of religion and morality in the popes just before the Reformation and the unspeakable abuses of the entire Roman Catholic system as epitomized by the selling of pseudoindulgences. That these alone account for the tremendous revolution of the sixteenth century is difficult to believe.

Luther the Man

Without all of the factors that have been mentioned, even a Luther could not have accomplished what he did. He would have suffered the same fate that had befallen John Huss a century before. Yet a Luther was required to complete or weld together all of the factors which have been mentioned. In a real sense Luther combined all of the motives for reform that had previously been exhibited. Some had wanted reform on the basis of their devotion to the Bible; Luther was their man, for he was an outstanding Bible scholar and attempted to fashion his reform around the Bible. Patriotism had been a motive for reform; and Luther's Reformation gathered up all the love that a German could have for his race and exploited it to the utmost. Many mystics desired reform that would emphasize the ability to approach God without human priests and institutions; Luther read and published their literature and spoke in language that they understood. Humanism clamored for reform on the basis of a new intellectual approach; Luther sympathized with their general point of view.

Beyond these unifying elements in Luther's life, he symbolized a German peasant who had been aggrieved by papal tyranny for half a millennium. Long-standing demands found in him a champion who could speak the language of the people. His personal experience in moving slowly step by step from protest to disputation to condemnation and schism probably formed a mirror of the experience of the average German who followed him. They understood him because they were so much like him. Without the very kind of man that Luther was, reform in the Germanic states would have been handicapped or perhaps impossible at the time. Somewhat similar historical and personal factors thrust forth Zwingli and Calvin in their particular areas. The time was ripe for reform.

Concluding Summary

The fulness of time had come. Reform was in the minds of many and on the lips of a few. A pioneer was required to inaugurate a successful revolt against the Roman Catholic system. Luther was that pioneer. Zwingli and Calvin were not far behind.

17

The Lutheran Reform

A FTER CENTURIES OF preparation began the movement which led to the shattering of the Medieval Roman Catholic system and the formation of some of the principal branches of the Christian movement that exist today. The first of these reforms was that of Martin Luther.

Luther's Early Life (1483–1517)

Martin Luther was born in Eisleben, Saxony, a small Germanic state, on November 10, 1483. It is not surprising that the one who was to break through the heavy crust of the Medieval ecclesiastical tyranny should spring from this geographical area, for the German people were suffering much from papal avarice. Nor is it surprising that he came from peasant stock. This class of people above all others bore the brunt of oppression and mistreatment from both secular and religious authorities.

Luther's parents were like most other peasants—poor and religious to the point of superstition. Luther himself never got away from some of their primitive ideas about witches and goblins. Shortly after Luther's birth his parents moved to Mansfeld, a nearby village, where his father engaged in the new mining industry. The boy attended elementary school here and further prepared for the university by enrolling at Magdeburg in the spring of 1497 and at Eisenach in the following year. In 1501 he entered the University of Erfurt, where he received the bachelor of arts degree in 1502 and the master's degree in 1505.

Up to this point Luther's life had not varied greatly from that of any other young man preparing for a professional career in the field of law. He did not continue in this direction as the result of a tremendous religious crisis. The religious tensions deliberately induced by the Medieval Catholic system worked in Luther, as in every typical man of his day, a constant religious unrest. The Roman Church demanded obedience to the earthly institution as the price of salvation. When man became careless, the pains of purgatory were magnified to bring dread and subservience. The sacramental wealth of the Church was then offered as a means of limiting the sufferings of the nether world. God was pictured as completely inaccessible; Christ was portrayed as a dread judge. Only the benefits sold by the Roman Catholic Church could avail for the trembling sinner. Even the most obedient Catholic must suffer the pangs of purgatory. The best opportunity of escaping divine wrath was to be found in the monasteries.

How long Luther had been pondering these things cannot be determined. By the time he received his second degree at Erfurt, he had an overwhelming feeling that he must get right with God. He had experienced several frightening incidents that caused him to think about eternal things. The climax came on July 2, 1505. While Luther was walking near Stotternheim, he became unnerved when a bolt of lightning struck near him and vowed that if spared from death, he would become a monk. This was the first step of Luther in an effort to find peace with God. Against the wishes of his father he kept his vow and fifteen days later entered the Augustinian monastery at Erfurt.

To his dismay Luther found no lasting peace in this surrender. When he attempted to perform his first Mass in May, 1507, his fear of God almost prostrated him. Following the precepts of the Medieval Church, he sought relief through performing good works. His reputation for self-denial spread across the land, but still he found no peace. Obediently, he opened every door prescribed by the Roman Catholic Church. He sought the merits of the saints; he engaged in almost fantastic confession of every type of sin, whether in thought, word, or deed; he performed regular religious duties feverishly; he even walked to Rome, the center of the Catholic religious world, where the greatest sins of every sort could be forgiven with the least effort—all to no avail. The merits of the saints reminded him of his own need; confession only spoke of unremembered sins not yet forgiven; his work as a priest increased his trepidation at approaching God; and his trip to Rome brought him into contact with cynical and greedy leaders. Through all of these tumultuous experiences Luther was approaching the object of his search.

Luther does not relate exactly when his burden was lifted, but he does indicate how it happened. The human agency was John Von Staupitz, the vicar of the Augustinian monasteries, who counseled with Luther and pointed him to the study of the New Testament. Equally important was the theological study which he found in a new occupation assigned him by Staupitz—that of teaching in the University of Wittenberg. He received the doctorate of theology degree in October, 1512. His lectures during the next five years on Psalms, Romans, and Galatians worked within his heart that which the entire sacramental system of the Roman Church could not accomplish. He discovered the true scriptural insight that salvation is a gift. Heretofore he had tried to deserve salvation; now he learned to accept it by faith without deserving it. He seized upon the text, "The just shall live by faith," believed it, and found the peace for which he had so long sought.

Luther's Reform Movement (1517–46)

Manifestly such a discovery by Luther apart from the religious system that environed him constituted a threat that he would urge others to find peace in the same way. Apparently Luther did not at first recognize the logical conclusion to which he must surely go—to challenge the validity of the system which could not bring him peace. Step by step his experience led him away from the obedience which he had exercised formerly. Luther did not always know when he took these steps and perhaps was not fully aware of the tremendous strides he had taken until he paused to look around. The first of these steps centered in his opposition to the Roman doctrine of indulgences.

Luther's question about indulgences.—It will be remembered that the Roman Church taught that all sins before baptism were washed away in that rite. The sacrament of penance was provided to care for postbaptismal sins. Should a man sin, he must present himself to the priest with sorrow in his heart for the sin, confess his sin to the priest, receive absolution (in which the priest on behalf of God forgives the eternal guilt of this sin), and then perform some good work or satisfaction to take care of the earthly penalty. That is, every sin gave offense in two directions: it brought guilt before God and it wronged the earthly Church. The priest pronounced God's forgiveness; the hurt to the earthly institution must be atoned for by specific prayers, gifts of money, a religious pilgrimage, or some similar act of devotion. To neglect the earthly penalty, it was taught, brought additional suffering in purgatory after death.

The most popular way of paying this earthly debt in Luther's day was through the purchase of writs of indulgence from papal representatives. These indulgences were written statements announcing a specified remission of penalty to the purchaser. They were sought by those who wished themselves to escape extensive residence in purgatory after death, as well as by those who had loved ones supposedly in purgatory already and wished to apply this credit to the account of the one already suffering.

As early as 1516 Luther had questioned the doctrine of indulgences. His own ruler, Frederick, the elector of Saxony, had a vast collection of relics. Should a person view these relics and make the proper offering, a writ of indulgence granting remission of specified canonical penalty was given. The genuineness of Luther's spiritual change was verified as in 1516 he endangered his own livelihood to question the correctness of the doctrine of indulgences, because a part of his own salary came from the proceeds of indulgence sales. In 1517 Luther had reached the point of exasperation. Pope Leo X had sold the archbishopric of Mainz to Albert of Brandenburg. In order to allow Albert to repay the money borrowed for the purchase of this office, and also in order to gain money allegedly for the building of the Cathedral of St. Peter at Rome, Leo declared a special sale on indulgences. To attract buyers the older Catholic doctrine of indulgences was perverted, and it appears that some claimed that pardon for sin could be obtained through them. The Dominican monk Tetzel was given the task of hawking these indulgences.

The thing that infuriated Luther was the suggestion that both guilt against God and the penalty against the earthly Church could be taken care of by the indulgences. Since Frederick, Luther's prince, was also engaged in selling ecclesiastical indulgences to the people, Tetzel was forbidden to enter electoral Saxony for the purpose of selling these new indulgences. However, Tetzel crowded the very borders of electoral Saxony in order that those who might be interested could cross over and buy the indulgences. Whereupon, on October 31, 1517, Luther prepared ninety-five statements for debate and, according to university custom, tacked them on the door of the church at Wittenberg, which was in a sense the university chapel. These statements (or theses) invited debate on three general subjects: (1) the traffic in indulgences, which Luther avowed was unscriptural, ineffective, and dangerous; (2) the power of the pope in the forgiveness of guilt and noncanonical penalties, which Luther denied; and (3) the character of the treasury of the Church, alleged to consist of the merits donated by Christ and the saints. Luther denied that the merits of Christ and the saints constituted such a treasury to be used by the Church.

The widespread storm following this protest seems to have been a surprise to Luther. Printing presses, a new method of intellectual warfare, reproduced Luther's protest, translated from Latin into German, for the eyes of all Germany. Luther's language was plain and direct, written in the vocabulary and spirit of a typical German. From various angles the protest gathered up popular antagonism against the papacy from many classes— biblicists, patriots, mystics, humanists. The pope, Leo X, was not at first alarmed by the protest. When he did take notice specifically, his first direct action was to appoint a new general of the Augustinian order with instructions to discipline Luther. However, at a meeting of Luther's chapter in April of 1518 at Heidelberg, Luther found some support. Thereafter, he began to assume a bolder attitude. He soon began to question the continuous historical primacy of the papacy and then completely denied the power of the pope over purgatory.

In July, 1518, Silvester Prierias, a Dominican official in Rome, attacked Luther as a heretic. Luther's reply went even further toward the evangelical position. He asserted that both the pope and the ecumenical council could err and had done so, and that only the Scriptures are an infallible authority. Luther was ordered to report at Rome to answer for heresy, but through the influence of his prince, Frederick, the consultation was referred to Cardinal Cajetan in Augsburg. This interview in October, 1518, drew from Luther the direct denial of the authority of a papal bull, for Luther asserted that the voice of the Scriptures outweighed the voice of the pope.

In November Luther appealed to a general council as the ultimate earthly authority in Christianity to pass on his views. This constituted a direct act of hostility to the person of the pope, since previous popes had for a century described such an appeal as open heresy. Luther's precarious position, however, was greatly aided by the influence of Frederick. The Holy Roman Emperor died on January 12, 1519, and Frederick was one of the seven men who would elect a new one. The pope earnestly desired to dictate who should be elected and consequently was quite deferential to Frederick. This probably accounts for a reversal of the antagonistic papal policy.

Karl von Miltitz, a German, was sent to conciliate Luther until after a new emperor had been chosen. Miltitz only asked Luther to refrain from debating the question. Luther agreed on the condition that his opponents would do likewise. However, Professor Johann Eck of the University of Ingolstadt did not keep this truce and attacked Luther without calling him by name. Through Eck's influence a debate was arranged and took place in Leipzig in early July of 1519. Here Luther was driven to approve doctrines of John Huss, who had been condemned and burned by the Council of Constance a century before. On July 15, 1520, a bull of excommunication against Luther was issued, commanding him to recant within sixty days. Luther later burned it publicly.

During the remainder of that summer and fall Luther wrote the principal tracts describing his beliefs. In August the *Address to the German Nobility* was published. In this tract Luther urged a reform of the Church by the Christian magistrate. He attacked the claims of the papacy that the spiritual power is above the temporal, that the pope alone can interpret the Scriptures, and that ecumenical councils can be assembled only by a pope. His proposals for reform would strike off the material wealth and possessions of the pope and magnify a spiritual ministry. Luther also attacked monasticism and celibacy. Abuses and corruptions within the Church must be corrected.

In October Luther's tract *On the Babylonian Captivity of the Church* was printed. In this tract Luther denied the efficacy of indulgences and boldly attacked the sacramental system of Rome. He insisted that both the wine and bread of the Supper should be served to the people and dwelt on the necessity of faith by the partaker in order to assure its efficacy. In his discussion of baptism, he created a continuous tension in his theological system by eliminating the necessity for personal expression of faith as a prerequisite to baptism. That is, he demanded personal faith for the Supper but made no provision for such faith before baptism. He continued with a critical discussion of penance, confirmation, matrimony, orders, and extreme unction. He would eliminate all sacraments except the Supper and baptism but praised parts of the sacrament of penance. In the following month his tract on *The Freedom of the Christian Man* appeared. This writing magnified the freedom and priesthood of every believer, whether layman, priest, bishop, or pope.

These writings and others in a similar vein, progressively becoming bolder in their attacks upon the central doctrines supporting the papacy, completely alienated Luther from the Roman Church and made compromise impossible. On April 17, 1521, following a summons by Emperor Charles V, Luther appeared before the Diet of the Empire, meeting at Worms. After two hearings in which Luther boldly defended his views, he was kidnapped by his friends (perhaps under secret orders from Frederick) and on May 4 arrived in disguise at Wartburg. Meanwhile, at Worms on May 26, after Luther's supporters had returned home, the papal forces were able to secure an edict banning Luther as an outlaw. Thus by the middle of 1522 Luther had been excommunicated by the Roman Church and banned by the Empire.

Delay in suppressing Lutheranism (1521–29).—It appeared that the cause of reform was again lost, and history seemed destined to add the name of Martin Luther to the long list of victims of ecclesiastical intolerance. However, the kidnapping of Luther by his friends removed him from possible physical danger for about a year. In addition, Emperor Charles V became engaged in war with King Francis I of France shortly after the close of the Diet of Worms in 1521. This war continued intermittently for the next eight years. Furthermore, the hands of the emperor, the chief opponent of Luther, were withheld from Luther because of the menacing Turks who were driving through the Balkans with the intention of overthrowing the Empire. It is rather interesting that Emperor Charles was also delayed from suppressing the Lutherans by the political maneuvering of the pope himself, who was afraid of the amount of power in the hands of Charles.

During this time, with the aid of Melanchthon and others, Luther prepared a great deal of literature, including an excellent German translation of the Scriptures. Luther also revealed the character of his movement. In 1522 at Zwickau several religious radicals attempted to carry out what seemed to be the implications of Luther's ideas. The Roman Catholic priestly system of conducting the Supper was altered; the common people were given both elements—bread and wine; and Roman liturgy, chanting, and altars were eliminated. The city was in an uproar. Luther voluntarily left his haven at Wartburg to take personal command in fighting these radicals. Thenceforth Luther may be described as a conservative reformer; that is, he retained those elements of Roman Catholic tradition which in his judgment were not specifically prohibited by the Scriptures. Thus infant baptism, robes, candles, and similar Roman Catholic characteristics appear in Lutheranism.

In 1525, the year of Luther's marriage, a great peasant's revolt occurred. For half a century there had been increasing tension between the nobility and the peasants who tilled the soil. The attempt to apply Roman law in the place of the ancient Germanic law, the breakdown of feudal estates with the resultant suffering and confusion, and economic turmoil incident to the rise of the third estate—commercial and financial princes—fanned the flames of dissatisfaction and revolt among the peasants. In addition, Thomas Müntzer, a radical millennarian, accelerated the outbreak of violence by injecting a religious note. "God will not let you fail; on to slaughter!" was his cry. Unnumbered thousands of peasants were mercilessly put to death in the revolt of 1525. Luther lost his faith in the common man and thereafter looked to the nobility as the hope of the reform movement.

Because of the preoccupation of the emperor, the annual meetings of the German diet had practically left the task of adjusting the religious situation in the hands of each prince or ruler for his own hand. By 1529, however, the situation was changed. The Lutherans faced a new crisis. By that time the emperor had soundly defeated King Francis of France, had seen the Turks driven back from Vienna, and had permitted the pope to be imprisoned for a period. The diet met at Speyer in that year. Ferdinand, brother of the emperor and a strenuous opponent of the reform movement, presided. By his direction the diet passed an edict which looked to the complete annihilation of the Lutheran reform and the recatholicizing of Lutheran areas. A minority protested this action, receiving thereafter the name "Protestant." This is the first occurrence of the name in ecclesiastical history. The Lutherans were required to answer the edict within one year.

The crisis (1530).—At the meeting of the diet in 1530 at Augsburg the Lutherans were fearful concerning events to come. In the previous year Philip of Hesse, one of the Lutheran princes, had endeavored to secure a military alliance between the Lutherans of Germany and the Zwinglians of Switzerland. At a meeting in Marburg in 1529, however, Luther refused to have any sort of connection with Zwingli, despite the fact that the only point of disagreement in their theology centered in the interpretation of Jesus' words, "This is my body." Luther, of course, being under the ban of the Empire, could not appear at the diet in Augsburg. He aided Melanchthon in the preparation of the confession which was presented to the diet. The confession and a subsequent defense were rejected by the diet, and the Lutherans were given one year to forsake their heresies or feel the edge of the sword. The Lutheran princes formed a military alliance known as the Schmalkaldic League. The Catholic princes had also joined together for military action. Again Emperor Charles did not find it expedient to attack the Lutherans. The Turks were threatening, the Lutherans were fairly strong, and King Francis I of France was ready to fight again.

Luther's death.—This uneasy truce between Protestants and Catholics was still in effect in February, 1546, when Luther died. The death of Luther was not a great blow to his movement. Other hands had taken up the torch.

The Schmalkaldic War and the Peace of Augsburg (1555)

The Schmalkaldic War broke out in 1546 when Pope Paul III declared a crusade against the Protestant princes. Within a year the Protestants had been utterly defeated. Jealousy between Emperor Charles and the pope prevented the immediate destruction of Protestants, however, and in 1552 after a period of political maneuvering the war erupted again and in a few months the Protestants regained all that they had lost.

The Peace of Augsburg admitted the right of the Lutheran religion to exist within the Empire. Each prince was to determine the religion of his state, and should any of the subjects desire a different faith, the right of emigration without loss of honor or goods was guaranteed. In case a Catholic prelate desired to become a Lutheran he must resign his ecclesiastical position so that it might be filled from Rome. In the free cities where both faiths had adherents, each should be permitted to continue.

The Spread of Lutheranism

Before 1540 most of northern Germany was officially Lutheran. In the border states, such as Bohemia and Poland, and in the earlier years of reform in Hungary, Lutheranism was very strong. Denmark adopted the reformation by 1536 through its rulers and the preaching of Hans Tausen. By the preaching of Olaf and Lars Petersen and Lars Andersen and the work of King Gustavus Vasa, Sweden adopted Lutheranism in 1527. Finland, a Swedish satellite, adopted Lutheranism principally through political action, the most important preacher being Michael Agricola.

Concluding Summary

Martin Luther, then, was the pioneer reformer that broke the power of the Roman Catholic system. He secured sufficient political influence among the Germans to maintain his system despite coercion.

It must not be forgotten that during the latter years of Luther's life, other reform movements were also in progress. Ulrich Zwingli at Zurich, John Calvin at Geneva, the radicals and Anabaptists in various parts of the Continent, and Henry VIII in England present other instances of reform. These will be considered in the following chapters.

18

The Zwinglian and Calvinistic Reforms

THE SECOND OF the attempted general reforms of the Roman Catholic Church during this period began in two Swiss cities but spread extensively and soon was a rival of the Lutheran movement. The Swiss republic offered unusual opportunity for the reform movement, while at the same time it presented unusual obstacles. Almost three hundred years before, the several independent cantons, as the small county-like states were termed, had entered into a confederation, each canton, regardless of size, having one vote in the diet or congress. This made it possible for a minority of the people (in the less populated cantons) to prevent the majority of the people (in the cantons made up of larger cities) from embracing the Reformation movement by political vote. The struggle between the country cantons and the city cantons characterizes the course of the early Reformation efforts.

The country cantons had good reasons for opposing the reform. The Roman Catholic Church had for centuries employed strong young men from the Swiss rural cantons to be used as mercenaries in the papal army. Papal abuses were not burdensome. The rural cantons possessed considerable independence of spirit and little money and so were hardly aware of papal exploitation. The more wealthy city cantons, on the other hand, had long fought papal financial exploitation and political domination. Humanism had made vast inroads into the larger cities, particularly Basel, where educational and printing facilities provided instruments of wide propagation to agitate reform.

The two cities of Switzerland which became leaders in the reform were Zurich and Geneva. Ulrich Zwingli was the principal figure in beginning the reform at Zurich, while John Calvin played the chief role in Geneva. Calvin's movement swallowed up the Zwinglian reform in one generation, so the two will be discussed as one movement.

The Zwinglian Reform in Zurich

Ulrich Zwingli was born in 1484 at Wildhaus in Switzerland. His uncle, a priest in the Roman communion, supervised his education in some of the outstanding schools of the Continent. From 1502 to 1506 Zwingli taught school at Basel while finishing his education. In this active humanist center he was greatly influenced toward enlightened views and was brought to the study of theology. The lectures of the humanist Thomas Wyttenbach, in particular, gave the young teacher a passion to eliminate the superstitious elements in Christianity and to restore the ancient authority—the Scriptures.

Through the influence of his uncle, in 1506 Zwingli was appointed parish priest at Glarus, where he served for ten years. From 1516 to 1519 he was priest at Einsiedeln. Here his pungent preaching and reforming tendencies attracted widespread attention. In 1519 he was appointed the chief preacher at the great cathedral church in Zurich. He had been moving already toward the application of scriptural principles. While at Einsiedeln in 1518, with the approval of his bishop he had opposed the sale of indulgences by Bernard Sampson. Upon beginning his work at Zurich, Zwingli caused a sensation by preaching an exposition of the Gospels in the language of the people, scorning the traditional lessons assigned and the Latin tongue of the Roman Church.

Several experiences apparently kindled his reforming zeal. By 1520 he had become familiar with the reformatory works of Luther. Zwingli always insisted that he was not indebted to Luther for the principles of reform in Zurich. An analysis of the reforms instituted by the two men partly bears out Zwingli's contention. Zwingli's reform was intellectual, biblical, and political. He approached religion as a humanist seeking truth. Luther, on the other hand, was moved by a great experience which convinced him that the Roman system could not bring peace to the soul of a man. So while Zwingli through reform sought to satisfy his *mind* with respect to the truth of Christianity, Luther aimed at satisfying his *heart* through the appropriation of true Christianity. Thus while Luther's writings doubtless gave encouragement to Zwingli, it is possible that Zwingli's reform developed somewhat independently.

In addition to the writings of Luther, other factors turned Zwingli more zealously toward an active reform. The dreaded plague struck Zurich, and Zwingli was laid low. At the very door of death he had a mystical experience in which he was conscious of the strengthening presence of God. From this and the bereavement in the loss of a brother, Zwingli seemed to deepen considerably in his spiritual life. For years he had been receiving a pension from the pope, a retainer for encouraging young men to engage in mercenary military service. In 1520, consistent with his new insights, he resigned this pension and took a more positive stand against the hiring of Swiss lads as mercenaries.

His preaching began to emphasize the authority of the Scriptures alone. Acting upon this principle, some of his followers in Zurich in 1522 refused to fast during Lent on the ground that the Bible did not forbid eating. Zwingli defended them against the strictures of their bishop and wrote a tract *On Choice and Freedom in Eating*.

In July, 1522, Zwingli attacked clerical celibacy. He knew firsthand the terrible evils involved in this system, openly admitting in his writings that he was unmarried but not chaste. In 1524 he announced his marriage to the woman with whom he had been living in common-law relations for some years.

Exercising great influence over the city government at Zurich, Zwingli was able to develop his program of reform. The city council adjudged him to be victorious in two public disputations with Roman Catholic representatives in January and October, 1523. Zwingli presented sixty-seven brief articles of faith, which went beyond Luther toward the evangelical position. In these Zwingli magnified the scriptural position in contrast with the teachings of the Roman Church. Salvation is by faith. Roman sacraments, intercession of saints, and purgatorial sufferings are unscriptural. All believers are priests. Clerical celibacy must be abolished.

At one point Zwingli had disagreement within his own ranks. It has been pointed out that his movement was partly political because he had to work through the government of the Zurich canton. When the question of baptism arose, the political aspect weighed considerably. Zwingli knew that if he denied the validity of infant baptism he would "unchurch" the Zurich city council, for all of them were sprinkled as babies. Apparently this factor caused him, after considerable hesitation, to retain infant baptism. He did not teach that infant baptism brought salvation, after the fashion of the Roman Church; rather, said he, infant baptism simply identifies the child with the Christian covenant, much as the rite of circumcision identified the Jewish child with the Israelitish covenant. He viewed the Lord's Supper as a symbol of the body and blood of Christ. Zwingli was able to justify to the Zurich government the elimination of images, relics, monasteries, and the traditional observance of Mass.

By 1524–25, however, because of the retention of infant baptism, Zwingli was obliged to defend his movement against the attacks of a group which had stood with him in the early days of reform. Conrad Grebel, Felix Manz, and others among his early supporters insisted that Zwingli must abolish infant baptism if he wanted to be consistent in his main principle—to restore the scriptural pattern. Even political circumstances, they said, should not prevent steadfast allegiance to scriptural injunctions. At first it appeared that Zwingli might move in this direction, but soon he vigorously resisted the movement.

Zwingli's reform transformed Zurich by 1525. His influence also aided in the reform of other Swiss and south German cities like St. Gall, Basel, Bern, and Strassburg. The rural cantons of Uri, Schwyz, Unterwalden, and Zug, however, completely satisfied with the old Roman Catholic relationship, formed with Lucerne a league to withstand the reform. Most of the other Swiss cantons and some of the southern German cities confederated in a reform league. Both groups sought outside alliances. In 1529 a civil war seemed imminent, but by negotiation hostilities were postponed in a peace favorable to the Zwinglians.

In the fall of 1529 at Marburg there occurred an important meeting between the Lutherans and the Zwinglians. The second Diet of Speyer had recently condemned all dissent from the Roman Catholic Church. Conformity within one year was demanded. Philip of Hesse, an influential Lutheran, desired to secure a political and military alliance between Lutheran and Zwinglian forces in order to withstand the Catholics. Luther insisted that there must first be agreement in doctrine. On fourteen articles of faith Luther and Zwingli were in general agreement, but in a part of one article Luther rejected Zwingli. The point of difference lay in the interpretation of the presence of Christ in the Supper. Luther contended that Christ's physical body was present for the faithful in the true observance of the Supper; Zwingli objected that a physical body could not be everywhere at the same time. Zwingli said that the bread symbolizes or represents Christ's body. This single point of disagreement outweighed all else. The dream of an alliance was shattered.

Zwingli returned to his task of endeavoring to secure acceptance of his reform throughout all of the thirteen cantons of Switzerland. The five Catholic cantons, however, alert for an opportunity to retrieve the initiative, raised an army in 1531, and in the ensuing battle Zwingli was slain. His successor in Zurich, Henry Bullinger, respected the treaty signed with the Catholics and limited his work to his own canton. In less than a generation the Zwinglian movement was swallowed up by the larger and more influential movement of John Calvin.

The Calvinistic Reform at Geneva

The city of Geneva first felt reform as an indirect result of the Zwinglian movement. The winning of Bern to reform in 1528 brought additional impetus through the increased evangelical interests of this, the strongest Swiss city in the south. It was through the encouragement of Bern that William Farel, impetuous reformer from France, made his way to Geneva in 1533. Geneva had felt already the political pressure of Bern to accept the evangelical reform. Political factors, as a matter of fact, played the most important role in winning Geneva to the reform movement. The city was ruled by a bishop and an administrator, both of whom were controlled by the duke of Savoy, monarch over an adjacent kingdom. The citizens shared in local government through a general assembly and an elected committee known as the Little Council. Larger committees were appointed by the Little Council to resolve questions involving fundamental principles. Beginning about 1527, the ancient hostility between the citizens of Geneva and the duke of Savoy erupted into open war. The citizens were able to beat off the duke's attacks through the aid of Bern and a Catholic neighbor, Freiburg, and establish Geneva's freedom. With the encouragement of Bern, William Farel and Antoine Froment, two French preachers, infiltrated Geneva in the interest of the evangelical cause. About 1535 the reform movement took a strong foothold, and Geneva entered the evangelical fold. In July, 1536, John Calvin paused in the city en route to Strassburg, and Farel enlisted him in the task of making Geneva a strong Protestant city.

The work of John Calvin.—John Calvin was born in Noyon, France, on July 10, 1509. His father was an influential ecclesiastical functionary and secretary of the bishopric. As a result, Calvin's education was provided through benefices in the Roman Catholic Church. In 1528 he received the master of arts degree from the University of Paris. At the request of his father Calvin entered into the study of law at Orleans and Bourges and received the doctorate in law from the former institution in 1532. His first love was literary, not legal, however, and after the death of his father Calvin was free to forsake the practice of law.

Calvin was familiar with reforming ideas. Jacques Lefèvre Étaples, a French scholar living in Paris, had magnified evangelical ideas as early as 1512 in a commentary on Paul's epistles. He also translated the New Testament a decade later. The writings of Luther were circulated freely in France, and Calvin became familiar with them. Calvin's conversion to evangelical views was sudden, his own testimony asserts. Perhaps the complete explanation will never be known, but a number of factors were involved. His father and brother had been excommunicated by the Roman Church, which may have loosened the hold of that system upon Calvin. His cousin, Robert Olivétan, was already a full-fledged reformer. The humanistic atmosphere of Calvin's university training and teachers doubtless moved him toward evangelical convictions. In May, 1534, he resigned his benefices and for some reason was imprisoned for a brief period. This is the first definite indication that Calvin had now entered the evangelical fold. With the outbreak of widespread and severe persecution in France in 1534, Calvin fled here and there in France, thence to Strassburg and Basel. While at Basel in 1536 Calvin published the first edition of his outstanding work, *The Institutes of the Christian Religion,* which brought immediate fame. His dedication of the *Institutes* to King Francis I of France is a masterpiece of argumentation from Scriptures and history. Calvin visited for a short time in Italy and Paris and on the journey to Strassburg passed through Geneva, Switzerland. Here William Farel convinced him that it was God's will for them to set up the evangelical standard in Geneva.

For the next two years Calvin labored in this important city. In January, 1537, he presented to the Little Council of Geneva a series of articles relative to the reform. The Lord's Supper was made central in church discipline. Moral lapses and the neglect of divine services without excuse brought exclusion from participation in the Supper. A confession of faith was submitted to the council for their approval, after which all citizens were required to assent to it. The purpose was to require total conformity to evangelical doctrines. The next step logically was to train the growing children in the doctrine. Calvin provided a catechism for their use. A system of lay inspectors to observe the conduct of the citizens was felt to be necessary. Immediate opposition to Calvin's program came from both political and religious dissenters. Calvin was attacked as a foreigner and a meddler. The annual city election in 1537 favored the Calvinistic supporters, but a year later the opposition succeeded in taking over the reins of government, and in April Calvin and Farel were banished from Geneva.

Calvin went to Strassburg, a city already strongly evangelical, and became pastor of the French refugees. He had a remarkably free hand in his preaching and administration of the church. He was called upon after January, 1539, to lecture to the advanced classes in the schools. He laid the groundwork for his famous expositions of biblical books, which subsequently were printed in commentary form. He also had opportunity to prepare a greatly enlarged edition of the *Institutes*.

While Calvin was absent from Geneva, Cardinal Sadoleto appealed to the city to return to the Catholic fold. Since no one in Geneva felt qualified to answer this appeal, it was finally handed to Calvin in Strassburg. His *Reply to Sadoleto* in 1539, justifying the evangelical position, added to his reputation.

At Strassburg Calvin was married in August, 1540, to Idelette de Bure, widow of an Anabaptist convert. Calvin spoke in highest terms of his wife and their happiness. She died in 1549. Their only child, born in 1542, lived but a few days.

In 1541, after considerable persuasion by his friends, Calvin returned to Geneva. He faced a difficult task. The party which had ousted Calvin had been overthrown in the elections of 1540 but still were formidable. The relations of Geneva with Bern were threatening, and the internal situation was bad. It appeared that rioting and disorder would soon break out within Geneva. Calvin returned with the assurance that he would be allowed to institute his reforms. A committee from the Little Council aided Calvin in the preparation of his *Ecclesiastical Ordinances*. Provision was made for four officers in Genevan church life—pastors, teachers, elders, and deacons. The most distinctive aspect of this program was the office of elder or presbyter, from which the name

"Presbyterian" is derived. Twelve laymen were chosen by the Little Council to serve as ruling elders in the Genevan church. This was a departure from the general idea that presbyters were to be ordained and should preach rather than govern. These twelve presbyters were combined with the regular ministry (at first numbering but six ministers) to form the Consistory, which had supervision over all ecclesiastical discipline. Calvin apparently had desired that the Genevan church exercise her own discipline apart from the secular authorities but was forced into the compromise that allowed the Little Council to take a large hand in this sphere. The Consistory exercised detailed and extensive authority over Genevan ecclesiastical life.

Calvin's system of doctrine, as set out in the *Institutes*, began with the sovereignty of God and, following the general order of the creeds, discussed Christ, the Holy Spirit, and the Church. His emphasis upon the predestination of God was attacked by several, and his retention of infant baptism reflected the importance he placed upon the sociological aspect of the sacramentals. His view of baptism was quite similar to that of Zwingli, and he taught the real spiritual presence of Christ in the Supper.

Despite the entreaties of the Genevan authorities in 1541 for the return of Calvin, many opponents had remained. By 1553 it appeared that Calvin's supporters might be defeated in the popular vote and that another banishment might result. However, in that year Michael Servetus, an exasperating and unorthodox Spaniard, made his way to Geneva. An old opponent of Calvin, Servetus already was under condemnation by Romanists and evangelicals alike for his attacks upon the doctrines of the Trinity and the person of Christ. Calvin vigorously prosecuted Servetus, and the opposition party unwisely gave indications of favoring Servetus. Consequently, when Servetus was condemned and burned in October, 1553, Calvin's victory was complete. The elections of the following year gave him a resounding triumph. From 1555 until his death in 1564 Calvin ruled Geneva with little opposition.

The spread of Calvinism.—It will be remembered that after the death of Zwingli in 1531 his reform spread no farther. The

214

aggressive system of Calvin and his thorough training of preachers soon began to bear fruit in the Zwinglian cantons. By 1566 Calvin's doctrines were acceptable to most of the Zwinglian cantons, and thereafter these became identified with the Calvinistic system.

The government of France was centralized under the control of the king. King Francis I (1515–47) had a working agreement with the papacy whereby each would profit by the maintenance of the Roman Catholic system. In co-operation with the pope, France had warred against Spain intermittently from 1521 to 1529, and for purely political reasons France and Spain had continued the struggle in 1536–38 and 1542–44. These wars required Francis to adopt a policy which would best serve his immediate plans. As a result, a considerable foundation for reform in France was laid without extended persecution.

Reference has been made to Jacques Lefèvre Étaples who spread evangelical views long before Luther. A number of his pupils continued to propagate evangelical views. Reform ideas appeared among the faculty of the University of Paris, long a Catholic stronghold. Calvin fled from France in the latter part of 1534, just as the full weight of royal persecution was beginning. Despite the frequent martyrdoms that occurred, French preachers by the score attended Calvin's school at Geneva and returned to their homeland to preach what was known as the Huguenot gospel. By 1559 there were forty-nine congregations of Calvinists in France, and in that year a synod was held in Paris which formed a national organization and adopted a Calvinistic confession of faith. Within two years the number of congregations had increased to 2,150. Between 1562 and 1598 a series of wars between the Huguenots and the Catholics took place, and on the latter date through the efforts of King Henry IV (who had become a Roman Catholic in order to secure the French crown) the Edict of Nantes was enacted, providing certain "perpetual" liberties for French Calvinists. However, as a result of continued struggle in the seventeenth century these liberties were eliminated in 1685.

The Netherlands consisted of about seventeen provinces in

what is now Belgium and Holland. They had long been known as the center of opposition to Roman Catholic doctrine. The Waldenses, the Brethren of the Common Life, mysticism, and humanism were represented in this section. Between 1517 and 1529 Lutheranism spread rapidly in the Low Countries. The Mennonites made great progress until about 1540, when Calvinism began to become influential. One reason why many left the Mennonite ranks to become Calvinists was that the former demanded pacifism. In this period Spain was waging a determined war against the Netherlands for both political and religious reasons. Consequently, a great number of the inhabitants embraced the militant Calvinistic movement in preference to the pacifistic Mennonite belief. By 1550 the Calvinists began organizing churches in the homes. In 1559 a national synod was held, the Dutch Reformed Church (Calvinistic) was organized, and a Calvinistic confession adopted. From 1566 to 1578 the patriots under William the Silent (1553–84) fought the Spanish overlords and in 1581 the northern provinces declared their independence.

Scotland had been evangelized very early by British missionaries. The Roman Catholic system gained control of Scotland in the eleventh century. The fight with England in the thirteenth and fourteenth centuries, which resulted in Scottish independence under Robert Bruce, brought Scotland into close alliance with France. Reform movements had begun in Scotland under the inspiration of the work of Luther, Tyndale, and others. Patrick Hamilton, trained in the University of Paris, voiced evangelical doctrines and was burned in 1528. As a result many noblemen, both from political and ecclesiastical motives, turned toward Protestantism. In 1546 George Wishart was also burned. His martyrdom inflamed John Knox. Subsequently, Knox attended Calvin's school in Geneva in 1554 and served as pastor there after 1555. In 1559 Knox returned to Scotland and was victorious in establishing the Presbyterian system.

Calvinism did not attain its large influence in the German states in this period. It was excluded from toleration in the Treaty of Augsburg in 1555. Melanchthon became increasingly sympathetic toward Calvinistic doctrine, particularly after 1546, when Luther died.

Neither was England greatly affected by Calvinism in this period, although the regents of Edward VI (1547–53) were familiar with its tenets. Its greatest influence in England came in the next period.

Concluding Summary

Reform erupted in Switzerland under the leadership of Ulrich Zwingli and John Calvin. The untimely death of Zwingli radically turned his reform into different channels. His movement was later swallowed up by that of John Calvin.

Both of the Swiss reformers condemned and persecuted the radicals and Anabaptists. By the time of Calvin's death in 1564, his movement was known in every part of Europe and England and was very influential in Scotland and Switzerland.

Anabaptists and the Radical
Reformation

FOR CENTURIES THE principal historians either ignored or grossly misunderstood what is now recognized as one of the important movements of the Reformation period. This movement was for centuries called Anabaptism, although with some reservations by those most familiar with it. A. H. Newman, for example, recognized—as scholars of other denominations now agree—that the name "Anabaptist" was an epithet of reprobation or condemnation. It was long identified with fanaticism, schism, and lawlessness. As early as the fifth century the Theodosian Code named the death penalty for any who rebaptized another. This law was aimed at the Donatists, who sometimes were referred to as Anabaptists because they insisted upon performing the rite of baptism upon anyone coming from the corrupted Catholic churches, which, said the Donatists, had lost the power to administer saving baptism. With this sort of background, the name "Anabaptist" came to be applied to any religious iconoclast or fanatic.

It is now generally recognized that to find someone referred to as an Anabaptist in the sixteenth century does not necessarily mean that such a person rebaptized; it may simply mean that his views were considered radical. For this reason, the name "Anabaptist"—emphasizing the single doctrine of believers' baptism—can hardly be applied properly to all religious radicals who were threatened or condemned by being classed in this category.

A better classification to describe more accurately the various types of radical thinkers has been attempted recently by many historians. Perhaps, as some have suggested, the word "radical" is the best generic term for all of them, for these groups were radical both in relation to the practices of contemporary religious reformers and in the opinions of both the Roman Catholics and the Protestants of that day. The various groups, then, will be discussed under four categories: radical biblicists, radical chiliastics, radical mystics, and radical rationalists. Before discussing each of these groups, a word should be said about the possible origins of these movements.

Origins of the Radical Reformers

In general, there are two points of view concerning the origin of these reformers and their extensive constituency. One is that they were called forth by the immediate historical situation and the renewed study of the Scriptures. This view would deny that there were any antecedents before the sixteenth century.

It would appear to be more consistent to hold that the sudden appearance of these reformers over such a large area and embodying such varying doctrinal emphases cannot be explained in terms of a single or localized factor. History does not turn corners suddenly or reveal multiform expressions without antecedents. A movement as complex and widespread as this one would seem to demand a multiplicity of factors—the lingering of medieval ideas, the immediate economic and religious commotion of the sixteenth century, the restudy of the New Testament in terms of contemporary interpretations, and perhaps other elements which cannot be classified.

Types of Radical Reformers

It should be recognized that these classifications of the various types of radicals are totally arbitrary. Often one man could be put into several categories and another man would fit into none. There is value, however, in pressing some sort of outline upon the material in order to provide a better context.

Radical biblicists.—This group has recently been termed the "Anabaptists proper" by one author, with good reason, for they

219

demanded personal faith before baptism as a basic element of their belief. They were radical in the sense that they eliminated all traditions in favor of biblical authority, which they counted the source of their ideas about believers' baptism, separation of church and state, the elimination of sacramental and sacerdotal grace, the centrality of the gathered church, the restoration of the primitive Christian spirit of love and the New Testament pattern of organization, and holy living as the result of an experience of regeneration through God's Spirit.

It will be recalled that in his reform at Zurich, Ulrich Zwingli advocated the view that the Scriptures alone must constitute the basis for faith and practice. In 1523 in conferences with Zwingli, Balthasar Hübmaier (then pastor at Walshut, Austria), Felix Manz, and others discussed with him the necessity of rejecting infant baptism. Zwingli at first seemed to look favorably upon the doctrine of believers' baptism, since it followed his avowed principle of following only scriptural injunctions and since already his elaboration of his Sixty-Seven Articles had pointed to the primitive practice of baptizing only after faith and confession.

His theory of Christianity's relation to society, however, finally drew him away from this position. Zwingli felt that he must have the support of the civil authorities in Zurich in order to carry out his reform. The denial of infant baptism would have forfeited that civil support, for the city council itself, upon whom he depended for aid, would have been unchurched. Consequently, on January 17, 1525, in a disputation at Zurich, Zwingli denied the principle of believers' baptism. He was opposed by many of his former associates, stalwart men like the able and respected Conrad Grebel. The city council, acting as judge, decreed Zwingli victorious in the debate and gave orders that all babies must be baptized. The Anabaptists were to be banished or imprisoned. A second disputation in November ended similarly. In March, 1526, Anabaptists were ordered to be drowned if they persisted in their heresy, and Felix Manz, Jacob Faulk, and Henry Riemon were early victims of this sentence.

The Anabaptist movement gained multitudes of adherents in

Switzerland between 1525 and 1529. Upon being banished from Zurich, Anabaptist leaders like George Blaurock, William Reublin, Hans Brötli, and Andreas Castleberg went everywhere preaching. Great numbers were baptized in Schaffhausen, St. Gallen, Appenzell, Basel, Bern, and Grunigen. Not only were numerous Anabaptist churches formed, but the movement aided in purging from other groups unworthy ministers, whose evil lives were rigorously attacked by the Anabaptist preachers.

By 1529 the Swiss Anabaptist movement had greatly declined but did not die out. Men like Pilgrim Marbeck worked extensively in Switzerland and south Germany thereafter. Particularly at Bern the Anabaptist congregations continued their struggle. Like other persecuted movements, Anabaptism went underground, and its influence cannot be judged.

One reason for the decline of Anabaptist activity in Switzerland was the beckoning of an adjacent country. Anabaptism had spilled over into contiguous areas like Austria and Moravia. It was to the latter country that many Anabaptist leaders made their way. Moravia had been sown with radical seed by the Hussite and Taborite revolts. In June, 1526, Balthasar Hübmaier fled to Nickolsburg, Moravia, after being persecuted in Austria and Switzerland. Here he had instant success, within a year baptizing between six and twelve thousand. He was also able to publish several excellent apologetical works in defense of the Anabaptist position. His work in Nickolsburg, however, was undermined by Jacob Wiedemann and others who advocated a strong pacifism (not only refusing to engage in war but declining to pay taxes to support those so engaged) and a communistic sharing of personal goods. Perhaps the bitterness of this controversy may have stripped Hübmaier of friends sufficiently that the Austrian authorities were able to seize and burn him in March, 1528. So died one of the greatest and wisest of the Anabaptists.

The pacifistic and communistic party grew rapidly in Moravia. Leadership was assumed by Jacob Huter, and a large community practicing communal economy became an Anabaptist haven for refugees from all Europe. Despite almost continuous persecution in the succeeding two centuries, Moravian Anabaptists increased and prospered. Their church government was quite similar to that of the earlier Waldenses of this area. The growth of the group in nearby Tyrol and Austria was at first rapid, but because of severe persecution the movement there was drastically curtailed.

The third principal group to advocate a rigid biblicism were the Mennonites, who took their name from Menno Simons (1496–1561). Menno was born and reared in the Low Countries, received a good education, and was ordained a priest in the Roman Catholic Church in 1524. The atmosphere of reform sent him to a careful study of the Bible, especially after the execution of an Anabaptist near his home. The radical fanatics at Münster between 1533 and 1535 repelled him, but also impelled him to leave the Roman Church under the pressure of conviction. In 1536 he received the new baptism and became an Anabaptist minister. With Obbe and Dietrich Philips, Menno gathered and organized the biblicists of the scattered Anabaptist flock. He spent the remainder of his life as a fugitive from Catholics and Protestants alike. Traveling and writing extensively, Menno preserved the heritage of the biblical Anabaptists.

It is noteworthy that Menno Simons, doubtless because of his intense repugnance to the fanatics of Münster, disclaimed any historical connection with early Anabaptism but traced a succession of his movement through the Waldenses back to apostolic days. He also followed the Waldensian pattern in several key doctrines.

Radical chiliastics.—The chiliastic wing of the radical movement turned their faces away from the ideal of restoring the primitive pattern in gathered congregations. Instead, taking their text from apocalyptic writings, securing training and inspiration from earlier fanatical fires still burning in Bohemia, and counting themselves chief actors in God's drama of restoring a millennial kingdom, these men sought to bring heaven to earth by means of sword and coercion.

The Waldensian and Taborite ideas that covered Bohemia were reproduced in many details in the work of Nicholas Storch. Influenced by his early contacts in Bohemia, Storch displayed a fierce,

222

denunciatory spirit toward those dissenting with him. He aligned himself in 1520 with Thomas Müntzer, a highly educated Lutheran pastor at Zwickau, who like Luther was attacking the monastic and priestly establishment of the Roman system. Storch set up a distinctive type of church organization after the model of the Taborite churches which he had known in Bohemia. In the following year Müntzer himself turned up at Prague; apparently the indoctrination he received here put him into the party of irrecoverable radicals.

Storch, meanwhile, who seems to have influenced Müntzer toward Bohemian polity and principles, remained at Zwickau, where he almost made radicals out of several of the Wittenberg faculty, despite the fact that he was holding "Bohemian" errors. Carlstadt, Cellarius, and even Melanchthon were greatly impressed with Storch. The latter confessed himself to be greatly perplexed about how to answer Storch's arguments against infant baptism. After returning from Bohemia, Müntzer settled as pastor at Alstedt. Here his revolutionary preaching against religious and social inequalities did much to prepare the way for the Peasant Revolt. Driven from Alstedt in 1524 by the authorities, he hastened to Mühlhausen, where his doctrine of social revolution, mingled with apocalyptic and fanatical rabble-rousing, hastened the Peasants' War. Here was a radical who was never an Anabaptist. Although Müntzer was put to death shortly, his influence did not die with him. Two other leaders, Hans Hut and Melchior Rinck, attracted by Müntzer's chiliastic ideas, preached millennial ideas far and wide across the German states.

The successor to the spirit of Müntzer, and a man who resembled him in many respects, was Melchior Hofmann (ca. 1490–1543). It is quite possible that some of Hoffman's chiliastic ideas were gained at Strassburg from Nicholas Storch, the teacher of Müntzer. After the disaster of the Peasants' War, many of the radicals made their way to Strassburg in south Germany where a measure of toleration prevailed. Leaders like Storch, Jacob Gross, Hans Denk, and Michael Sattler had given chiliastic coloring to Strassburg radicals. In 1529, after a riotous ministry in

Sweden and Denmark, Hofmann turned to Strassburg and perhaps was baptized there in 1530. Hofmann now boldly set the year 1533 as the date of the beginning of Christ's millennial reign and named the city of Strassburg as the "new Jerusalem." He ordered that baptism be suspended for two years to prepare for the event. For most of the two years he traveled in the Netherlands, meanwhile gaining a disciple in Jan Matthys, who would outdo his master in chiliastic fanaticism. Hofmann was thrown into jail in May, 1533, at Strassburg, where he died ten years later. Matthys announced in 1533 that he was the prophet Enoch who had been promised by Hofmann, and he assumed leadership of the fanatical party.

It was Matthys who set the stage for the Münster fiasco. The people in Münster, a city of northern Germany, had reacted favorably to the evangelical preaching of Bernhard Rothmann between 1529 and 1532. Many radicals flooded the city, and in 1534 John of Leiden and Gert tom Closter, representing Matthys, arrived to take charge. Matthys himself then announced that Münster, not Strassburg, was to be the "new Jerusalem." The seizure of the city by the radicals brought the troops of the Roman Catholic bishop. In the siege and war that followed, John of Leyden, who became leader when Matthys was slain, introduced polygamy and required baptism or banishment. The city held out for almost a year. The few leaders that were captured were tortured and then hoisted in a cage to the tower of the principal church of Münster. Their bones remained there for centuries, a constant reminder of the dire effects of the radical movement.

Radical mystics.—The extreme emphasis upon sacramental observances and the cold, strictly intellectual scholastic theology brought a reaction from those who looked within themselves for the witness and illumination of the Spirit. Moving in an atmosphere that scorned both Roman Catholic and Protestant sacramental systems, these mystics ofttimes found themselves attracted by nonsacramental Anabaptist and radical doctrines.

One of these was Hans Denk (1495–1527), a humanistic scholar and reformer associated with Zwingli for a period. In 1525 he organized an Anabaptist church in Augsburg but was successively driven to Strassburg, Worms, and Basel, where he died of the plague in 1527. His writings link him with earlier mystics. His friend, Ludwig Hetzer (1500–29), had a somewhat similar experience with his persecutors before his execution in 1529. Sebastian Franck (1499–1542) moved from Romanism to Calvinism and was accused of turning to Anabaptism. His pronounced mysticism and defiant admiration of heretics who had dared to follow the truth make it difficult to classify him under any single category. He doubtless influenced Kaspar Schwenkfeld (1487–1541), who moved similarly out of Lutheranism, although Schwenkfeld's doctrines remained closer to orthodoxy than did those of Franck.

Jacob Kautz and John Bunderlin should be classed among these mystics; perhaps even Heinrich Niclaes (*ca.* 1501–60), the founder of the "House of Love" or the "Familists," should be included. Niclaes passed from Roman Catholicism to Lutheranism, finding in neither what he desired. His mystical nature was stirred by David Joris (1501–56), and he seems to have felt that he had been given a special divine revelation beyond anything man had yet known. He spent much time in England, and the influence of his movement was found there during the next century.

Radical rationalists.—Both Catholicism and Protestantism in the Reformation period abhorred the radical rationalists, whose reasoning not only led them out of orthodox churches but also developed doctrinal aberrations that put them "out of bounds." As a matter of fact, all types of radicals (biblical, chiliastic, mystical, and rationalistic) were averse to orthodox symbols and creeds. The mystics in particular often followed recognizable heresy in their doctrines of the church, of salvation, and of Christ. Men like Franck, Hetzer, Denk, Kautz, and Bunderlin approached the views of rationalists, and in some cases went beyond them in their radicalism, but their methods and course of travel were different. One well-known rationalist was John Campanus (*ca.* 1495–1575). Influenced by Erasmus and the atmosphere of the radicals in the duchy of Julich, Campanus moved away from Catholic and Lutheran views and finally fell into anti-Trinitarianism. His influence was widespread in Julich, and many followed his antipedobaptistic ideas. He was jailed about 1555 and died there about twenty years later.

The best known of the radical rationalists was Michael Servetus (1509–53), a brilliant but erratic Spaniard. In 1534 he met John Calvin at the University of Paris, beginning a long relationship of mutual distrust and dislike. From 1546 until his death, Servetus greatly irritated Calvin through provocative correspondence and ill-tempered criticisms. In the year of his death Servetus published his *Christianismi Restitutio,* which asserted anti-Trinitarian and other doctrines abhorrent to Calvin and the rest of the orthodox world. He was seized in Geneva by Calvin and after an ecclesiastical trial was burned.

His influence may have survived in the work of Laelius Socinus (1525–62) and Faustus Socinus (1539–1604). The former was an Italian lawyer whose extensive skepticism about contemporary orthodoxy was not fully known until after his death. In 1547 he left Italy, already being suspected of heresy. He traveled widely and was an attentive observer at the trial of Servetus in Geneva in 1553. At his death in 1562 he left his manuscripts and his skepticism to his nephew Faustus, who became an outstanding propagator of anti-Trinitarian doctrines. In 1579 Faustus moved to Poland, a haven for liberal thinkers, where he met men of similar views like Peter Gonesius, George Biandrata, and Gregory Paulus. Here he founded a college and disseminated rationalistic views over a wide area until his death in 1604.

Some mention should be made of the strong anti-Trinitarian movement in Italy which was snuffed out by the Roman Catholic Inquisition. Such figures as Renato and Tiziano characterize these radicals, who seem to have grasped evangelical ideas in general but held to an adoptionist Christology, with its consequent weak notions of sin and the atonement.

Other radicals.—The principal effort in this discussion has been to furnish a workable outline of the radicals and to name some principal figures. There are many other radicals of this period who have not been mentioned and some important leaders that can hardly be classified. For example, Sebastian Castellio (1515–63), Pierre Paolo Vergerio (d. 1565), and Bernardino Ochino (1487–1564) are typical of those who found themselves out of step in their day. Some continued their seeking pilgrimages all of their lives.

The Significance of These Reformers

Some sober historians believe that twentieth-century Christianity reflects more of the ideas of the Anabaptists and the radicals than of any of the other reforms. In a sense this is true, because in their efforts to restore the primitive New Testament order these radical movements, unfettered by political and social commitments that tied the hands of Luther, Zwingli, and Calvin, simply without inhibition tossed aside hoary and respectable ideas on the ground that the New Testament did not specifically contain them.

From one point of view, most of the struggle between the radicals and the traditionalists, both Catholic and Protestant, centered in the relationship between the Christian and the world or community about him. The true Anabaptists and many of the radicals insisted that the world or community cannot make Christians. This basically was the significance of rejecting infant baptism. Traditional Christianity, including the Protestant reformers, used proxy or community faith—spelled out in terms of "godfather" and "godmother"—to induct the newborn child into the Christian fold. Both Luther and Zwingli faced problems at this point. Luther's theme of "faith alone" was compromised by his final solution. Unwilling to divorce his movement from the traditional community tie of infant baptism, he made laborious efforts to justify it in terms of proxy faith for the infant or subconscious faith in the infant. His final result was to introduce a basic tension into his system by demanding personal faith for the Lord's Supper but eliminating personal faith for the induction of the person into the Christian life.

Furthermore, the world or community cannot constitute a true church. There must be a gathered church in the sense that only believers, those with a faith baptism, may participate. At this point, also, Luther struggled heroically. He earnestly desired in the early days of his reform to separate the church from the world. His theme of "faith alone" demanded it. He finally turned away from this ideal in order to retain the church-community solidarity. In thus turning away from a gathered church, Luther destroyed the possibility of attaining another of his ideals— separation of church and state. A gathered church cannot be a part of the secular state. Abandonment of infant baptism drew a sharp line between world and church. Even heresy was not punishable by the state, because a man is accountable only to God for his spiritual response. Religious liberty could not be simply a privilege but must be a right and a duty. Pope and emperor could no longer rule all mankind in different spheres. A gathered church eliminated the pope as completely as the rising national states eliminated the emperor; a gathered church also eliminated church-community solidarity and brought separation of church and state.

In addition, the world cannot determine the ethics and attitude of Christians. These must come from God alone but are more demanding than secular laws. The concepts of a disciplined community, an ethic of love, and a spiritual brotherhood were common ideas among the radical groups.

Finally, the world cannot satisfy the longings and impulses of the spirit. All of the radicals were to some extent mystics. For them God was near, and his demands were personal. God's purposes seem to have been misinterpreted ofttimes, and eschatological schemes of frightful magnitude were developed. This is partly understandable in the light of the disorderly and violent world faced by these radicals. Withal, however, was the sense of personal participation in the eternal plans of a watchful and omnipotent Lord.

In the large sweep of history these radical ideas, designed to restore the primitive Christian pattern, have come to be understood and appreciated more than they were when they were voiced.

Concluding Summary

The radicals and Anabaptists were the most hated religious groups on the Continent in the sixteenth century. Roman Catholics and Protestants alike persecuted them. They present a complex picture of uninhibited men who in some groups endeavored to reproduce primitive Christianity, in others sought to find God's presence in the temporal order, and in still others tried to bring in the millennial kingdom. Their contributions have been varied and significant.

20

The Anglican Reform

THE LAST OF the great reform movements occurred in England. This large island off the coast of continental Europe proper received Christianity at a very early period, perhaps from the lips of soldiers who had been chained to the apostle Paul in Rome and who, after their conversion to Christianity, had been stationed in the island. The Romans had first invaded the British Isles in 55 B.C. under Julius Caesar. After the withdrawal of Roman troops in the fifth century because tribal invasions threatened Rome, the island was overrun by the Angles, the Saxons, and the Jutes. Seven principal states evolved (the Heptarchy), until they were united under Egbert in 827 into one kingdom—Angle-land, or England.

Meanwhile, the Roman Catholic Church had sent Augustine the monk as a missionary in A.D. 596, and by 664 the Roman type of Christianity became dominant. After a period of struggle in which English and Danish kings intermittently ruled, the island was invaded in 1066 by William I of Normandy, who attained the kingship by defeating King Harold at the Battle of Hastings. William set the pattern for the attitude England would in general have toward papal supremacy. In a letter to Pope Gregory VII he refused to render fealty to the pope, although he agreed to send financial gifts. He carefully limited the influence of Rome upon the English church, almost to the point of denying the ecclesiastical authority of the pope. Between William (d. 1087) and Henry VII (d. 1509), English kings alternately obeyed and defied the popes. During the Hundred Years' War, when the popes were living in France and under the influence of the enemy of England, King

Edward III and Parliament passed the statutes of provisors and praemunire in 1351 and 1353, respectively, limiting papal influence in England. In the same century John Wycliffe and his Lollards actively opposed the Roman papacy. In 1450 the War of the Roses erupted—a civil war among the nobles to determine who should succeed to the throne. The victor in 1485 was Henry Tudor, who attained considerable royal power because the strong nobles had been slain in the civil war and because he married the heiress of the House of York, his principal rival. He became Henry VII and the head of the English line which gave direction to the reform in that land.

Roots of Reform

The reform in England was not caused by the divorce of Henry VIII, as some suggest. That provided the occasion, but as mentioned in the previous paragraph, England had for centuries tugged at the strings binding her to the papal see. The outbreak of reform in England cannot be described as coming from doctrinal conviction. The leaven of the teachings of Wycliffe and the Lollards and the oblique attacks on Rome by the English humanists assisted in the preparation of the people for a non-Roman Catholicism. The strong nationalistic spirit that enveloped England played an important part in preventing strong opposition to the ecclesiastical changes which Henry VIII introduced.

The Occasion for Reform

The principal mover in the English revolt against papal control was the sovereign himself—Henry VIII. Despite his later fondness for changing wives, there were other factors than the flashing eyes of Anne Boleyn that pushed Henry toward a break with the papal see. The trouble began when Henry's father arranged for a marriage between Arthur (Henry VIII's older brother) and Catharine, youngest daughter of Ferdinand and Isabella of Spain. Such a union would strengthen the hold of the Tudor line upon the English throne and was felt to be necessary. The wedding occurred on November 14, 1501, but Arthur died on April 2, 1502. A union between the two nations was still desired, so it was arranged that young Henry should marry Catharine. The pope, Julius II, under pressure from England and Spain, granted a dispensation with serious doubts, and the wedding was celebrated on June 11, 1509. It should be said that Catharine herself later in solemn oath asserted that she had never in fact been Arthur's wife.

Apparently Henry VIII never got away from the feeling that the marriage was a sin, since canon law and the Old Testament forbade one to marry his brother's widow. The only child to survive the marriage was Mary, born in 1516; four children before her birth and several thereafter either were stillborn or died in early infancy. This meant that Henry had no male heir. Since the Tudor line had just won the throne and since England might resent a female sovereign, it was feared that the lack of a male heir would bring revolution. Henry determined to have the pope declare the marriage to Catharine invalid and thus permit another marriage in an effort to secure a male heir. The pope delayed accommodating Henry, since Catharine's nephew was Emperor Charles V of Spain, who refused to permit the pope to take that action. When in 1529 the papal representative gave clear evidence of the papal refusal, Henry moved deliberately to break England away from Roman ecclesiastical control. By false accusation and coercion Henry secured legislation from Parliament in 1534 which separated England from papal control and declared Henry the supreme head of the Church of England. Meanwhile, in January, 1533, Henry had married Anne Boleyn, and as soon as Thomas Cranmer was consecrated as archbishop of Canterbury, the marriage to Catharine was declared invalid.

In addition to Anne Boleyn, between 1533 and his death in 1547 Henry married Jane Seymour (1536), Anne of Cleves (1540), Catherine Howard (1540), and Catherine Parr (1543). The principal events during the closing years of Henry's reform were: the confiscation of monastic property; the publication of Tyndale's Bible and later, through the influence of Thomas Cranmer and Thomas Cromwell, the wide circulation of an English translation of the Bible based upon the works of Tyndale and Miles Coverdale; the preparation by Henry of the Ten Articles, which attempted to wean the people away from Roman superstitions; and the issuance of the Six Articles, which identified the Church of England as entirely Roman Catholic in doctrine although in all things (save ordination) under the headship of the sovereign of England. Such was the condition of the reform when Henry died on January 28, 1547.

The Continuing Reform Under the Tudors (1534–1603)

It will be remembered that Henry VII began the Tudor line in England. The children of his son (Henry VIII) completed that line. These were Edward VI (Henry's son by Jane Seymour), who reigned from 1547 to 1553; Mary Tudor (Henry's daughter by Catharine), who reigned from 1553 to 1558; and Elizabeth (Henry's daughter by Anne Boleyn), who reigned from 1558 to 1603. The beginning of the reform under Henry VIII has been sketched above.

Reform Under Edward VI (1547–53).—Henry VIII apparently looked toward further ecclesiastical reform, for the Council of Regency which he provided in his will for the nine-year-old king, Edward VI, was composed of men known for their reforming views. The new Duke of Somerset was made Lord Protector and moved cautiously in the direction of continued reform. The clergy was instructed to preach against the usurpations of the Roman bishops, and visitation showed a deplorable religious illiteracy among the established clergy, which made it impossible for them to carry on an effective preaching ministry. The Six Articles of Henry VIII were repealed, along with most of the other heresy laws. Clerical marriage was permitted; royal control over the Church in England was tightened. In 1549 the first prayer book of King Edward VI, along with an Act of Uniformity prescribing its use, was prepared and circulated, reflecting Roman Catholic doctrine and ritual. After the replacing of Somerset by the Duke of Northumberland (although without the official title of Protector), a revision of the prayer book was made (1552) which reflected Protestant thinking. In the next month a creed

233

known as the Forty-two Articles was prepared, which was even more Protestant than the prayer book. On July 6, 1553, Edward died and despite plotting by Northumberland, Mary, oldest daughter of Henry VIII, succeeded to the throne as England's queen.

Reform Under Mary (1553–58).—Mary came to the throne determined to take vengeance upon those who had declared her mother's marriage to Henry invalid, to return England to the bosom of the Roman Catholic Church, and to inflict God's judgment upon those heretics who loved England more than Rome. In 1553 Cardinal Pole was sent by the pope to act as legate to England, and under his guidance every vestige of ecclesiastical reform set in motion by Henry VIII and Edward VI was expunged from the law books. England was restored to the Roman Catholic Church on November 30, 1554; suffering and death had already begun. A few months later, Bishops Ridley and Latimer were burned for heresy, and soon thereafter Archbishop Thomas Cranmer suffered the same fate. Historians judge that the burning of these three leaders, along with approximately three hundred others during the five-year reign of Mary, made England a Protestant nation. In July, 1554, Mary married Philip II of Spain, soon to become the Spanish king, but she died without heir.

Reform Under Elizabeth (1558–1603).—Elizabeth, daughter of Henry by Anne Boleyn, was the last of the Tudor line. It is surprising that she remained alive to secure the throne. The reason for sparing her was purely political. Philip of Spain recognized that if anything happened to Elizabeth, then Mary, Queen of Scots, and wife of Francis II of France, would be the successor to the English crown. This would have meant that England, Scotland, and France would unite under one crown, an overbalancing of continental power that Philip feared greatly. His father, the emperor, felt that Elizabeth should be slain regardless of possible succession; and too late to accomplish it, Philip came to the same conclusion. It was a foregone conclusion that Elizabeth would be anti-Roman, since the pope had declared that her mother was not properly the wife of Henry VIII. She was trained under Bishop Hooper, who was strongly Calvinistic in his doctrinal ideas.

Elizabeth moved slowly at first, but in 1559 with considerable opposition Parliament passed legislation acknowledging Elizabeth as supreme governor of the church and possessing even more ecclesiastical power than her father had known. She worked carefully to finish demolishing the entire pro-Roman structure which Mary had built. In 1559, by an Act of Uniformity, Elizabeth required again the use of the second prayer book of Edward VI with a few revisions.

Less than two hundred of the nine hundred Roman Catholic clergy refused to take the oath of allegiance to Elizabeth, but all of the Marian bishops were included in the minority. Cardinal Pole had died shortly after Mary, so for a non-Roman succession Elizabeth secured four bishops who had been consecrated under Henry VIII and Edward VI to lay hands on Matthew Parker and consecrate him as archbishop of Canterbury. The Church of England claims that this continuance of succession was valid under church law, while the pope has officially ruled that this succession is invalid. In 1563 the Forty-two Articles of Edward were revised and issued as the Thirty-nine Articles (although the thirty-ninth article was suppressed until 1571 for political considerations), and these articles have become the official doctrinal statement. They show a tendency toward Calvinism.

In 1570 Elizabeth was excommunicated and deposed by the Roman Church, who declared her kingdom a proper target for crusades by the faithful. In 1587 Mary, Queen of Scots, was executed for alleged complicity in a plot to overthrow Elizabeth. As a result of these events, Philip II, now sovereign of Spain, assembled a fleet of ships, and on July 12, 1588, the Spanish Armada set sail to capture England. They were defeated by the superior seamanship and equipment of the English navy, although storms later assisted in the destruction of many of the invading vessels.

By the time Elizabeth died in 1603, England had a strong Protestant government. This did not mean, however, that dissent would be permitted, for religious dissent could not be differentiated from civil rebellion in a realm where church and state were united in one sovereign.

235

Rise of the Puritans

With the rapid oscillation of the royal religious ideas, it is not surprising that the people did not quickly change their religious convictions to match. This was particularly true in the case of those who had been exposed to continental reform movements where convictions were much deeper and more influential than they were on the English isle.

As early as 1550, Bishops Hooper and Ridley (both later burned by Mary Tudor) revealed their repugnance to popish superstitions and unscriptural practices. The reversal of royal religious demands under the Catholic rule of Mary Tudor (1553–58) sent scores of Protestant leaders fleeing to the Continent for safety. Many of them came into contact with Calvin's system in Switzerland. From this doctrine they were convinced that worship should contain only those elements that were distinctly enunciated by the Scriptures. Such a principle would undercut the many Roman Catholic practices that rested simply upon tradition and would in many cases dispense with some Lutheran retentions, for Luther chose to leave traditional practices and regalia in worship unless they were expressly prohibited by the scriptures. Thus when a Protestant sovereign ascended the English throne in 1558, many of these exiles returned to their own country favoring a more radical Protestantism than the "middle-of-the-road" English reform.

They demanded the elimination of popish elements in worship, such as the adoration of the wafer in the Supper through kneeling, the retention of the priest as over against the minister, and other such barnacles which tradition had added to the scriptural teachings. By 1564 these reformers were known as Puritans in popular vocabulary, because of their desire to purify the English reform. They were encouraged by several of the archbishops of Canterbury who were Puritans in fact, if not in name. One of the Cambridge teachers, Thomas Cartwright, became outspoken in asserting that Calvin's system was of divine origin and authority and, although ejected from his post by Archbishop Whitgift, was quite influential after about 1572 in converting men to Puritan views and in rallying them to the standard.

From this time until many of them were gathered up in the Wesleyan movement of the eighteenth century, the Puritans played a large part in English religious life. They, along with the Separatists and the Baptists, are introduced here because references to them will be made in the reign of the first Stuart king, beginning in 1603.

The Development of Separatism

It was inevitable that some would not be satisfied with efforts simply to purify the established church. Across the channel on the Continent Lutherans had separated from the Roman Church and by the treaty of Augsburg in 1555 were officially recognized in their separation. The radicals, the Zwinglians, the Calvinists, and many others across the Continent had denied the claims of authority by the Roman Church and had appealed to the Scriptures as their sole guide. Already the Scriptures had been provided in the English tongue. In 1525–26 William Tyndale, from his exile on the Continent, made an English translation of the New Testament and smuggled it into England. Apprehended and slain in 1535 by the Roman Catholic Church for this translation, his last words prayed God to open the eyes of the king of England.

The prayer was answered in the next year. Henry had now broken with the Roman Church and permitted Miles Coverdale to translate the entire Bible into English. Matthew's Bible was published in 1537 and the Great Bible in 1539. Fittingly, these last three English translations almost reproduced Tyndale's. Perhaps God had opened the eyes of the king to permit the extensive circulation. The reading of the Scriptures in the English tongue by the common people sowed seeds for what amounted to a second reformation in England.

As early as 1567, after Archbishop Matthew Parker had demanded conformity to the symbols of the established church in England, the authorities apprehended a group of London Separatists under the leadership of Richard Fitz; they were of the

A SUMMARY OF CHRISTIAN HISTORY

congregational type, although it is difficult to estimate how far their organization had progressed. About 1580 an outspoken Puritan minister, Robert Browne, adopted separatist principles and with Robert Harrison founded an independent church in Norwich in the next year. Browne fled from persecution to the Netherlands and published three treatises which have remained an exposition of the basic views of the Congregationalists, although Browne returned to the established church. In 1587 Henry Barrowe and John Greenwood were imprisoned for separatism, and through their tracts Francis Johnson, a Puritan and an enemy of separatism, was won to their principles. In 1592 Johnson became pastor of an organized Congregational church in London, but in the following year, because of increasing persecution that brought death to Barrowe and Greenwood, Johnson was forced to flee to Amsterdam where he became pastor of a congregation.

Soon a second Separatist church came to Amsterdam. A group of Separatists in Gainsborough, England, among the leaders of which were Thomas Helwys and John Murton and later John Smyth, fled about 1607 to Amsterdam and formed another independent church in that city. Out of this group there came a new type of biblicism, which will be discussed shortly under the heading of English Baptists. A third independent congregation to flee from England about 1607 settled at Leyden, after first stopping in Amsterdam. This group had come from Scrooby Manor, not far from Gainsborough, and was led by men with familiar names —William Bradford, William Brewster, and John Robinson. From them came the Pilgrims who emigrated to New England in 1620.

English Baptists

The pastor of the second Separatist church in Amsterdam was John Smyth, who had been a pupil of the pastor of the first Separatist church in the same city—Francis Johnson. Smyth had been reared in the Church of England under Elizabeth and in 1600 had been appointed preacher in the city of Lincoln. After serious study of the Scriptures he decided in 1606 to leave the established church and join the Separatists.

It was a dangerous time to decide that. James I had determined to harry the nonconformists out of the land. Smyth joined the Gainsborough group and with them fled to Amsterdam about 1607. Here Smyth came to the conviction that the Scriptures must be the sole guide for faith and practice and that the Scriptures demanded the baptism of believers only. This, of course, went far beyond what the other Amsterdam independent church believed and helped bring alienation between the two churches. About 1609 Smyth baptized himself (by pouring) and thirty-six others and formed the first English church holding to believers' baptism. Smyth and a small following soon seem to have doubted his authority to baptize, so they appealed for admission to the Mennonite church nearby. Smyth died before being admitted to their communion, but eventually some were received.

On the other hand, Thomas Helwys and John Murton with the majority returned to England to form the first Baptist church on English soil about 1611–12. Here Helwys published his famous plea for liberty of conscience in a little book, *A Short Declaration of the Mystery of Iniquity.* He addressed his dedication to King James I, boldly asserting that the king was a man and not God, and that while political fealty was due him by his subjects, every man was responsible only to God in spiritual things. Helwys was imprisoned at Newgate and probably died there. Murton became the pastor and leader of this first English Baptist church. By the time James I died in 1625 there were six or seven of these early Baptist churches, and by the close of the period (1648) about fifty churches containing perhaps ten to fifteen thousand members. Because of the influence of their environment in Holland they held to what is known as a "general atonement," that is, the doctrine that Christ died for all men, not for just a particular few. For this reason they have been known as General Baptists. They were at first called Anabaptists because of their rejection of infant baptism, but they rejected the name. They were the first English group to champion complete religious liberty. After 1644 they were called Baptists.

English Calvinistic or Particular Baptists generally are dated

239

from 1638. A Separatist or independent church was organized in London by Henry Jacob in 1616. Several schisms came under succeeding pastors. In 1638 a group separated because of their conviction that only believers should be baptized. With others these formed the first Calvinistic Baptist church in England in 1638 under the pastoral leadership of John Spilsbury. They were later called Particular Baptists because of their belief in a limited atonement—Christ died only for the elect. By the close of the period there were more than seven Particular Baptist churches in England. Some of their outstanding leaders were William Kiffin, Hanserd Knollys, and John Bunyan.

Reform Under the Stuarts

James I (1603–25).—Elizabeth reigned for a long time, but it was evident when she died in 1603 that she had not lived long enough to stabilize the religious settlement which she had provided for England. The succession to the crown of England went to King James VI of Scotland, the great-great-grandson of Henry VII of England. Both the restless Roman Catholics and the vocal Puritans were heartened by the prospects of the Scottish king's accession as James I of England. He was the son of Mary, Queen of Scots, and had displayed his rancor toward the dominant Presbyterianism of his native land. Since he had married a Roman Catholic wife, and since his mother was executed by Elizabeth, the Catholics reasoned that their cause would be close to the new king's heart. The Puritans, on the other hand, felt that James' experience with Scottish Presbyterianism had conditioned him to favor them in the new realm. Meanwhile, leaders of the Church of England felt that the subservient character of their church to royal supremacy would recommend them to the new king. The Church of England won the tug of war. The other contenders for royal favor were spurned.

Two plots against the king's life were attributed to the Roman Catholics and led to a demand that papalists conform. The Puritans met James in 1603 with a petition to purify English Christianity from papist superstitions (by adopting Calvinistic doc-

trines), but James curtly refused. In the following year at the
Hampton Court Conference, James again spurned Calvinism but
did grant a request for additions to the catechism and a revision
of the English Bible. From the latter permission came the famous
King James Version of the English Bible in 1611. By 1604 the
king had rejected all Puritan bids and made it his policy to
harass them constantly. An example is seen in the Declaration of
Sports of 1618. James knew that the Puritans were quite careful
to keep Sunday as the holy day of God. As a repressive measure,
he required every clergyman to announce from the pulpit the
sports program for the entertainment of the people on Sunday.
This was a severe trial for any conscientious Puritan.

Charles I (1625-49).—Upon James' death in 1625, his son
Charles, inferior to his father in ability and diplomacy, succeeded
to the throne. He was suspect to the Protestants when he was installed, since his mother was a Roman Catholic and he had married a Roman Catholic princess. He tried to continue his father's
policies, but the mounting resentment carried over to him from
his father's reign was ominous. The situation was not eased by the
persecuting tactics of Archbishop William Laud who through
spies, the Star Chamber, and the Court of High Commission endeavored to suppress all dissent. The Declaration of Sports was
again pressed.

Because they resented his rigorous tactics, Charles dismissed
the Parliament in 1629 and ruled without their aid until 1640.
He called them into session then only because of a crisis which
he was unable to handle without the co-operation of the people
themselves. The crisis sprang from Scotland. The Scots resented
royal interference with their Presbyterianism. Since 1603 (when
James became sovereign of both countries) the Church of England
and the crown had desired to extend the establishment of episcopacy into Scotland. By wily diplomacy James had been able to
make considerable progress in that direction. In 1637, however,
Archbishop Laud attempted to force upon Scotland a replica of
the English establishment, including a drastic revision of the
liturgy. Opposition was immediate. The struggle of the Scots to

maintain Presbyterianism against royal policy became rebellion, but the king had insufficient funds and men to wage war against the Scots. Thus in April, 1640, Charles was forced to call Parliament into session. But these Englishmen were in no mood to acquiesce in the face of royal flaunting of English law and equity. When Parliament demanded political and religious reform, Charles dissolved the body. It had met for just three weeks and is known as the Short Parliament. Then Charles completely alienated his people by illegally holding convocation (the assembly of the clerical leadership) after the dissolution of Parliament. Under Archbishop Laud's direction a number of canons were adopted, declaring that the king had unlimited power over the persons and possessions of his subjects by divine right, without respect to their consent. The clergy were required to sign an oath never to change the government of the English church, and in describing their submission the canon ended a list of surrendered privileges with the words "et cetera" (and so forth), which could be interpreted in almost any sense. This legislation aroused such feeling that Charles suspended it. It showed the people what they might expect from their king.

Meanwhile, the Scots had invaded England, and Charles had no other choice than to call Parliament to secure funds and men. In November, 1640, Parliament assembled and quickly showed that Puritanism was in the majority. Religious and political reforms were begun. When Charles attempted to seize several members of the House of Commons in January, 1642, civil war broke out between the king and Parliament. Drastic alterations then took place. The episcopal and liturgical (prayer book) forms were abolished, and an assembly (the Westminster Assembly), made up principally of Puritans, was summoned to advise Parliament on the creed and government of the new English church. Parliament badly needed Scottish aid in their fight with Charles and agreed to work for uniformity in ecclesiastical organization and doctrine in England, Scotland, and Ireland, and to oppose episcopacy. This Westminster Assembly, primarily Puritan, recommended a Presbyterian type of church government, which was established in 1646 and provided a Presbyterian liturgy for public worship in place of the prayer book. The famous Westminster Confession was adopted by Scotland in 1647 and by England in 1648.

Meanwhile, Parliament's armies were winning substantial victories, bringing into prominence a new leader in Oliver Cromwell. The new Presbyterian establishment and intolerance were no more attractive to Cromwell than the episcopal intolerance. Cromwell and most of his leaders were independents and favored no intolerant government, whether Presbyterian or episcopal. In December, 1648, dissatisfied with the Presbyterian Parliament, the army purged Parliament of those members who refused to carry out the army's wishes. King Charles, meanwhile, had been defeated in the field and had surrendered to the Scots. He convinced them that if they would take his side, he in turn would favor Presbyterianism in England. The Scottish leaders, noting that the army of Cromwell was opposed to the Presbyterian Parliament and fearing that Cromwell would overthrow the Presbyterian reforms which had been made, agreed to support Charles.

However, in August, 1648, the Scottish army, endeavoring to invade England, was soundly defeated by Cromwell. After the purge of Parliament, under the influence of the army Charles was tried for treason and beheaded. The period closes with the temporary defeat of royal power in England; with the Tudor reforms, the work of the early Stuarts, and the Presbyterian revolution swept away through the military power of Oliver Cromwell and his army of independents; and with considerable uncertainty as to the outcome of the struggle in both political and ecclesiastical life in England.

The impact of the events in England was considerable in her American colonies. That story is a succeeding chapter.

Concluding Summary

The occasion of the English reforms was the caprice of Henry VIII (1509–47), but the causes were much deeper. In 1534 the Church of England was established. It maintained Roman

Catholic doctrine in most respects, although denying the headship of the pope. The regents of Edward VI moved toward Protestant doctrine, but Mary returned the English church to the bosom of Rome in 1554. Five years later Elizabeth permanently wrenched it away. James VI of Scotland became James I of England (1603–25) to institute the Stuart line. His son, Charles I (1625–49), was beheaded for treason at the close of the period. The decade before his death was a stormy one. A civil war took place. Episcopacy and Presbyterianism were disestablished successively, and scores of tracts advocating religious liberty and toleration of dissent appeared. Oliver Cromwell and the army assumed control of the government at the close of this period.

The Roman Catholic Revival

THE TERM "COUNTER REFORMATION," sometimes applied to the activity of the Roman Catholic Church during this period, is not entirely accurate. It is better simply to call it the Roman Catholic revival. It is true, of course, that the direction taken by the Roman Catholic Church both responded to, and reacted against, the reform movements by Luther and others. As a matter of fact, it is difficult to judge whether the Roman Catholic Church was hurt or blessed by the movement known as the Reformation. The events of this period may have saved the Roman Catholic Church from complete inner decay and provincialism at a time when the world was expanding rapidly. Certainly, without the stimulation and redefinition that grew out of conflict with the reformers, the Roman Church would have been ill prepared to face what lay in store for it in a new and larger world.

Background of Roman Catholic Revival

National reform movements.—It has been noted that the reforming councils which were aimed at the Roman Church in the fifteenth century failed because of papal opposition. The popes never again have had to deal with antagonistic reforming councils like those of Pisa and Constance. By manipulation of the constituency, the agenda, and the method of voting, the popes have been able to control succeeding councils and their decisions.

A new world was being born in the fifteenth century. Heretofore the principal struggles of the Roman Catholic Church had been with her counterpart in the political sphere, the Holy Roman Empire. The ideal of a universal political empire was dying, however, and in its place came the rise of a strong nationalistic spirit. The papacy was now forced to reckon with sovereign states. The French king during the Reformation, Francis I (1515–47), was able to a large degree to control both church and state in his country. It will be remembered that after the breakdown of the Council of Basel, Charles VII of France, together with the nobles and clergy, had in 1438 enacted the Pragmatic Sanction of Bourges, which provided state control sufficient to offset some papal abuses. England under Henry VIII (1509–47) exercised considerable state control over the Church before her break with Rome in 1534. The German states, honeycombed by ecclesiastical princes and retarded by papal divide-and-conquer tactics, possessed no national political unity and continued to suffer under the papal abuses, all the while observing the more fortunate states about them. No wonder the reform spread like wildfire in this atmosphere.

Perhaps the most significant area in the rise of the national states was that of Spain. It developed rapidly. In 1469 it was united by the marriage between Ferdinand of Aragon and Isabella of Castile and enlarged through their subsequent conquests. Repressing all dissident forces within the peninsula and moving with boldness and firmness in European politics, Ferdinand and Isabella aided in leaving to their grandson, Charles I, the strongest government on the Continent. Although there was no hint of revolt in Spain against papal control, the dual sovereigns recognized the necessity of maintaining the integrity of the state in dealing with the Roman Church. In assuming control of the Roman Church in their state, Ferdinand and Isabella directed their efforts toward purifying and strengthening the clergy and maintaining as far as possible the medieval conception of papal suzerainty. The Spanish king (Charles) became the Holy Roman Emperor in 1519 and declared himself at the Diet of Worms as being determined to maintain the medieval standards of Roman Catholicism which his forefathers had known. The history of the Roman Church during this period was greatly colored by the conflicts between the emperor, determined to protect the ancient Roman

Catholic Church and its pure doctrine, and practically every other power, including the popes.

Preparing the way for Charles, and in many respects constituting the inspiration of the Spanish type of reform, was Ximénes de Cisneros (1436–1517). Trained in Spain and Rome, Ximénes was talented, dedicated, tireless, and ruthless. Picked by Queen Isabella as her confessor, Ximénes, despite seemingly sincere protests against holding high office, was appointed archbishop of Toledo and chancellor of Castile. Uniting ecclesiastical and royal authority, Ximénes founded the University of Alcala (Complutum) and arranged for the production of the Complutensian Polyglot, in which the Old Testament was printed in Hebrew, Greek, and Latin, and the Targum on the first five books of the Bible, while the New Testament had the text in Greek and Latin. Erasmus published his Greek New Testament in 1516, but Ximénes had printed his text by 1515, although papal permission for publication delayed its appearance until 1520.

Ximénes demanded that all of the Mohammedans in Spain— who had settled there after Charles Martel had thrown them back from France in 732—either become Christians or be banished. In addition, Ximénes' rigid discipline is said to have driven over a thousand monks out of Spain before his death in 1517. His zeal inspired a theological revival and complemented the work of Torquemada in the enforcement of the Inquisition, which the crown had begun in 1480. Thus Spain had already instituted a type of reform of the Roman Church in the closing years of the fifteenth century, but it was primarily a nationalistic movement, strongly medieval and intolerant. No Protestant reform movement either began or survived in this realm during the Reformation period.

Humanism and the Roman Church.—Another factor that affected the Roman Catholic Church in its relation to the reform movement was the work of the humanists. Delving as they did into the ancient writings, Christian as well as classical, these men saw the wide differences between the early Christian movement and the contemporary Roman Church. There can be little doubt that humanists in every country helped prepare the way for the Protestant reform. Some of them joined it; more stayed within the framework of the Roman Catholic Church and endeavored to coax it in the direction of eliminating abuses and superstitions. Desiderius Erasmus of Rotterdam (1466–1536), doubtless the outstanding humanist of the Continent, actually suggested a plan for the proper kind of reform. For years he had been assailing the superstitious legends of contemporary Roman Catholicism, and his writings sounded so much like those of Luther that he was later forced to disclaim authorship of some of Luther's tracts. Erasmus wanted a reform without violence or ill feeling. He suggested that the priests simply be trained in the right way and then teach the people a pure type of Christianity. His efforts did not succeed. For the most part, humanism was unwilling to plunge into revolution to attain reform, and apparently revolution was required.

Roman Catholic piety and reform.—Within the top echelon of the Roman Church there was a genuine concern for the strengthening of the spiritual life of that body. In the very year that Luther posted his theses, a group of Italian Catholics formed the Oratory of Divine Love, a devotional type of society designed to deepen spiritual life and eliminate abuses. Among its members were Caraffa (who subsequently became Pope Paul IV) and Sadoleto (who attempted to woo Geneva back into the Catholic fold when Calvin was exiled to Strassburg). This piety, it should be noted, was channeled into loyalty to the ancient institution.

Papal Response to Reform Efforts Before 1540

The strong but unsuccessful efforts to reform the papacy through councils were apparently wasted. The succeeding popes seemed to consider the failure of the councils as a vote of confidence in the unscrupulous methods and careless lives of the previous popes, as well as an evidence that widespread abuses in doctrine and practice were of minor concern. The looseness of Pius II (1458–64), Sixtus IV (1471–84), and Alexander VI (1492–1503) has already been mentioned. Julius II (1503–13) found it necessary to call a general council as a means of defeating a reforming council of the king of France and the emperor in 1510. The council met in Rome in 1513 shortly before the death of Julius. It had happy results for the papacy. The French cardinals who had sharply criticized papal corruptions were pacified. More important, in 1516 a new understanding was reached between Pope Leo X (1513–21) and Francis I of France, by which the Pragmatic Sanction of 1438 was abrogated and king and pope agreed to share the ecclesiastical spoils of France. After approving this agreement, the general council dissolved in March, 1517; in October of that year the Lutheran reform erupted.

Although tardy in appearing, a papal bull on November 9, 1518, corrected some of the worst abuses. It will be remembered that the marrow of Luther's early protest consisted of his denial that indulgences could forgive guilt without repentance. This pivotal point was conceded by the papal bull. It also fixed papal authority as immediate on the earth only, although allowing considerable influence to the petitions of the pope for souls in purgatory, because of the merits of Christ and the saints. This bull did not represent a concession to Luther or a revision of official Roman Catholic doctrine. The reverse was true. The pope had now made explicit declarations of Roman Catholic orthodoxy, and unless he conformed, Luther could be condemned for ecclesiastical anarchy as well as doctrinal defection. Lines began to form for each side in the controversy. A considerable body of literature appeared, some attacking and some defending Roman Catholic government and doctrine. Even Henry VIII of England and, later on, Erasmus wrote as defenders of the faith.

The brief pontificate of Hadrian VI (1522–23) accomplished little but lip service toward reform. Clement VII (1523–34) attempted the time-honored customs of crushing ecclesiastical dissenters by branding them as heretics fit to be burned and of countering Protestant princes by resort to political alignment. His judgment was often poor. His support of King Francis I of France actually tied the hands of Emperor Charles V of Spain, when Charles was willing and able to kill the young and weak

Lutheran movement. Clement's "balance of power" politics directed against the growing Hapsburg influence during the critical period of reform may have saved the Protestant Reformation. In 1527, angered by the tactics of Clement, Charles allowed an army to invade Italy and take the pope prisoner, the hardships from which probably hastened Clement's death.

His successor, Paul III (1534–49), worked carefully. From the ranks of the Oratory of Divine Love and others known to favor limited reform to suppress abuses, he appointed several new cardinals—Caraffa, Sadoleto, Pole, and Contarini—and set up a commission under their leadership to investigate and report on the need for reform. Although their report in 1538 was not immediately effective in obtaining action, yet the preparation of it and the training given these men soon would have the highest places of leadership in the Roman Church made it significant. Many of the ideas in this report were included in the action taken by the Council of Trent.

Final Roman Catholic Decision on Reform

The Roman Church hesitated briefly. Should it attempt to conciliate the Lutherans or condemn them unequivocally? Some, like Contarini, remembering the effort made by Philip Melanchthon at Augsburg to minimize the differences between the Lutheran and Roman Catholic viewpoints and the abortive plan of Philip of Hesse to unite all reform movements against the Roman Church, desired to see if it were possible to work out an understanding that would be satisfactory to Lutheran leaders and still would not compromise the traditional Catholic dogma. Others, like Caraffa (who had been trained in the Spanish reformation), desired simply to condemn the schismatics and organize to meet the challenge of the evangelicals. Besides, argued this party, what could be done with the Zwinglians, the Calvinists, the Anglicans, and others? Conciliation would lead quite far from the historic position of the Roman Church. However, under pressure from Emperor Charles, a series of conferences was held—one at Hagenau in 1540, one in Worms in the same year, and one in Regensburg in

1541. Despite some strong efforts at compromise, these conferences failed to reach common ground for agreement.

After the conference at Regensburg (Ratisbon) in 1541, the Roman Church set its face like flint toward the Protestants and has never swerved from a position of open and complete hostility toward them. This decision made, Roman Church leadership now began to bend all efforts toward halting the inroads of Protestantism and toward getting its own house in order so that it could best wage its war. Again the quarrels between the pope and Emperor Charles V saved the Lutherans. The Schmalkaldic War, begun in 1546, resulted in the early defeat of the Lutherans. The pope then had a vigorous controversy with Charles over the place of meeting for a proposed general council. Perhaps the quarrel was necessary, for the pope might not have been able to control a council under the shadow of Charles. Perhaps the papacy came out as well as it would have otherwise in the "calculated risk" taken by Paul III. At any rate, the Lutherans fought again and were successful.

Two movements greatly aided the struggle of the Roman Church with the reformers: the rise of the Society of Jesus (known more familiarly as the Jesuits) and the Council of Trent.

The Society of Jesus

Ignatius Loyola, founder of the Society of Jesus, was born in 1491 in Spain. At the battle of Pampeluna with the French in 1521, he was so severely wounded that he could no longer pursue military service. While convalescing he read legends about Francis and Dominic, who were described as Christ's soldiers. Loyola determined to become a knight of the virgin Mary. After his recovery he entered the Dominican monastery at Manresa. His deep devotion drove him as a pilgrim to Jerusalem in 1523. Unable to carry on mission work there as he desired, he sought an education and returned to a school at Barcelona at the age of thirty-six to sit in class with boys ten years old. He made rapid progress and in 1528 entered the University of Paris. Here he gathered a small group of like-minded followers, chief among whom was Francis Xavier, and in 1534 the group took solemn vows to work in Jerusalem or anywhere the pope might direct.

Three years later the expedition to Jerusalem began, but because of the Turkish War they were stopped at Venice. Here Loyola met Caraffa and attracted the attention of Contarini. Pope Paul III (1534–49) was impressed by the ability of Loyola and his devotion to the Roman Church, and on September 27, 1540, the Society of Jesus was authorized. A membership of but sixty was permitted originally. Two years later this limitation was removed. Loyola was chosen as the first general of the order and held that position until his death in 1556.

Organization and doctrines.—The tremendous impact of this new order may be seen in the fact that when the Council of Trent met, only five years after the authorizing of the Society, it was Jesuits who played a leading part in this important council. This Society has been at the forefront of some of the Roman Catholic Church's greatest achievements. The organization bore a military simplicity—a general at the head, provincials over geographical districts, and a careful system of recruitment and training. As early as 1522–23 Loyola had begun preparing a series of spiritual exercises for Christian soldiers. The manual outlined a four week's course—twenty-eight general divisions with five hourly meditations covering the entire redemptive drama. Novitiates were to be tested by difficult service for a two-year period, then were promoted to be scholars trained in both ecclesiastical and secular learning. The next step was the coadjutor. This office was given those who were chosen and carefully trained for particular service. It included teachers, priests, missionaries, authors, consultants, and advisers. After long and faithful service, a few coadjutors could be admitted to the inner circle of the Society—the professed, from which the general officers would be chosen.

The thorough training and ethical standards of the Jesuits quickly brought them into places of leadership throughout Europe. As confessors and ecclesiastical lawyers they greatly influenced the Catholic princes in their affairs of state; their schools, their compromising nature at the confessional, their crafty preaching, and their missionary zeal gave them a wide following. Perhaps the word "obedience" is the largest word in Jesuitism. Loyola wrote in his *Spiritual Exercises:*

That we may be altogether of the same mind and in conformity with the Church herself, if she shall have defined anything to be black which to our eyes appears to be white, we ought in like manner to pronounce it to be black. For we must undoubtingly believe, that the Spirit of our Lord Jesus Christ, and the Spirit of the Orthodox Church His Spouse, by which Spirit we are governed and directed to Salvation is the same. . . .

And again, in the Constitution, the statement is made:

And let each one persuade himself that they that live under obedience ought to allow themselves to be borne and ruled by divine providence working through their Superiors exactly as if they were a corpse which suffers itself to be borne and handled in any way whatsoever; or just as an old man's stick which serves him who holds it in his hand wherever and for whatever purpose he wishes to use it. . . .

This blind obedience demanded renunciation of individual conscience. Other unacceptable moral standards of the Jesuits are the doctrine of probabilism (any course may be justified if one authority can be found in its favor), intentionalism (if the intention is good, other considerations may be overlooked), and mental reservation (the whole truth does not necessarily have to be told, even under oath). Two other doctrines have been ascribed to the Jesuits but have been denied by some of their responsible leaders. One is that the end justifies the means; if the result is for the greater glory of God, then any means used to accomplish it are permitted. The other is the assassination of tryants. Despite Jesuit protests, there is evidence that these last two principles were acceptable at an earlier period of the Society's history and, as a matter of fact, are implicit in the first three of these moral standards.

The progress of the Society.—The Society made rapid progress in Italy, Portugal, Belgium, and Poland. Its greatest victories were won in Germany and Austria where, coupled with the Lutheran controversies, the Roman Catholic Church won back almost all of the territory in south Germany which the Reformation had alienated. The Society's activities were only partly successful in France until after the death of Henry IV (1589–1610), but thereafter the Jesuits controlled France until the French Revolution. In Venice, England, and Sweden their program was not at all successful during this period. True to the original purpose for which the Society was founded, the Jesuits entered wholeheartedly into missionary work. Although it was not possible to go to Jerusalem, in 1542 Francis Xavier (1506–52) was sent to India and Japan, where for ten years he labored sacrificially and heroically; in 1581 Matteo Ricci (1552–1610) went to China; in 1606 Robert de Nobili (d. 1656) sailed to India; and in 1685 Jesuits began work in Paraguay.

Council of Trent (1545–64)

Background.—The second great weapon of the Roman Church against the Protestant movement was fashioned in a well-controlled general council. It will be recalled that when Luther was condemned by Pope Leo X, he appealed from the pope to a general council. Such an appeal infuriated the supporters of the pope. The reforming councils of the fifteenth century had only been suppressed by the boldest action and good fortune; and Pope Martin V, after his election by the Council of Constance in 1417 ending the terrifying papal schism, had promulgated a bull condemning any person that appealed from the decision of a pope to a general council. However, Leo X (1513–21) had dealt with an ecumenical council and was confident that the best method of suppressing Luther would be to call such a council and let it under his control repress him. His death in the opening years of Luther's reform prevented this action, and despite clamor for a general council from all sides—Lutheran, Catholic princes, and even the emperor Charles—the popes and their advisers had not felt it to be a propitious time to summon a general council. Paul III (1534–49), familiar with the demands of all groups and confident that he could control a general council, began preliminary negotiations soon after assuming the pontificate. At this stage he still had hopes of conciliating the Protestants, so his legates conferred with both Catholics and Protestants about attending such a council. Neither desired to have a council in Italy where the pope could dictate to it. Twice Pope Paul issued a call for a council to assemble in Italy, and twice he was ignored. Finally, in conference with Emperor Charles, it was agreed that the council should meet in Trent, a small Austrian city, and after a delay caused by another Spanish-French war, the council was set for March, 1545. The emperor was hoping that this council would unite Europe religiously and politically, not through suppressing Protestantism but through conciliation; the pope, on the other hand, had determined by 1545 to have no part in conciliation of the Protestants and looked to the council to define and declare Catholic doctrine for the purpose of confuting and condemning the Protestants.

The sessions.—Seven sessions of the council were held at Trent during the first two years (1545–47). When pestilence threatened at Trent, Pope Paul ordered the council to meet in Bologna, Italy, which aroused the hostility of the emperor. The council met in Trent again in 1551 with some Protestant princes attending by invitation from the emperor, but they saw that papal control of the agenda and committees robbed the council of any autonomous action, so they soon withdrew. Another outbreak of the Schmalkaldic War ended this meeting of the council. Finally, after the death of several popes and a number of Protestant gains, Pope Pius IV (1559–65) negotiated for the reopening of the council as a weapon against Protestantism. In 1561 the council again assembled at Trent and remained until 1564 when its work was finished, mainly under Jesuit leadership.

The results.—The results of the council show that the papal party was in control most of the time. Occasionally uninhibited dissenters raised their voices relating to some of the more fundamental problems, but for the most part it was a complete victory for the ultramontane party. The emperor's hopes for religious and political unification of Europe were shattered. He soon retired from his office. The only elements of reform included in the council's recommendations were aimed at meeting the challenge of Protestantism. Priests must know their Bibles and be able to preach; stronger episcopal control in the parishes was ordered; arrangements were made for better education of clergy and for more care in making appointments; and morality and discipline were emphasized. All of these items were an attempt to gird the Roman Church to fight back at Protestantism.

The doctrinal decrees of the council were aimed in the same direction. Doctrines of Lutherans, Zwinglians, Calvinists, Anabaptists, and other dissenters were specifically anathematized. An authorized canon of Scriptures was announced, which included the Old Testament Apocrypha, and the Latin Vulgate was pronounced inspired in all its parts. The seven sacraments were defined; Scriptures and tradition were combined for authority; good works were judged to aid in justification; and it was reaffirmed that the Church alone can interpret doctrine. These were strengthening measures taken by the Church.

Inquisition and Piety

Two other factors, looking in opposite directions, completed the Roman Catholic response to the challenge of Protestantism. The first was the establishment in 1542 of the Roman Inquisition. This intensive ferreting out of heresy was not effective except in Italy where Caraffa and Loyola, who had charge of the inquisitorial reorganization, strongly enforced it. By driving out or destroying evangelicals like Bernardino Ochino, Pietro Martire Vermigli, Galeazzo Caraccioli, Vergerio, and Aonio Paleario, the Inquisition gave the Roman Church in Italy more freedom from dissent than it had ever known there.

At the same time, there was a revival of a medieval type of piety within the Roman Catholic Church in Spain and Italy. Mysticism and asceticism combined to popularize a sort of oriental "union with God" experience of exaltation in Spain. New monkish orders arose; stringent reform occurred in some of the older orders. Earnestness and zeal were added to the weapons of the Roman Church in her effort to face Protestantism.

Concluding Summary

The sixteenth century brought an active revival of the Roman Catholic Church. Unquestionably the Protestant Reformation provided the stimulus to much of this revival. The Roman doctrine was clarified and standardized. A powerful new order, the Jesuits, became the assault troops against Protestantism. A strong missionary program was launched. Most of the territory wrenched away from the Roman Catholic Church by the Protestant Reformation now became a new ecclesiastical battleground because of revived Catholic strength. As a matter of fact, before 1648 the Roman Catholic Church had won back most of the territory in southern Europe. Generally speaking, that area which had once been the old Roman Empire in Europe was retained or won back by the Roman Church. This struggle by the Roman Church, with other factors, led directly to the wars over religion which will be discussed in the next chapter.

22

The Continuing Conflict

NOTHING COULD ILLUSTRATE better the secularized condition of Christianity in the sixteenth century than the fact that efforts to reform the Roman Catholic system brought two centuries of the bloodiest fighting men had yet known. The antecedents to the use of military force for suppressing religious dissent were many and ancient. There was no support for it in the teachings of the New Testament or in the example of the early Christians. The adopting of Christianity by Constantine in 312, however, brought the use of political methods and weapons for the suppression of religious dissent. On this ground alone the alleged beneficent rule of Constantine proved to be a more deadly blow to true Christianity than the severest persecutions by his predecessors on the Roman throne.

Wherever it could control secular rulers, the developing Roman Catholic Church followed Constantine's example of suppressing dissent with the sword. During the Medieval period it is likely that the secular sword did more for the growth of Roman power than all of Rome's missionaries combined. The Crusades represented on a large scale the foul spirit of military coercion in the name of religion. Heresy-hunting by torture and punishment by burning occupied the attention of most orthodox bishops in the Roman Catholic system until 1243, when special inquisitorial machinery was set up by the papacy for locating and forcibly suppressing religious dissent.

The Hussite Wars of the fifteenth century brought a foreglimpse of the horrors to come in the next century. Julius II (1503–13), the warrior pope who boasted of his prowess with the sword, is a typical figure in an age when might made right—even in religion. In the sixteenth century the attempts to reform the Roman Church brought repressive wars in four countries—Switzerland (against Zwingli), Germany (against Luther), France (against the Huguenots), and the Netherlands (against Calvinism) —while the Thirty Years' War of the seventeenth century ravaged most of the Continent.

Causes of the Thirty Years' War (1618–48)

The first phase of the reform movement was completed by 1555 when the Peace of Augsburg closed the struggle between the Roman Catholics and the Lutherans (now called Protestants). The immediate result was a victory for Lutheranism. The secular empire now recognized the legal right of Lutheranism to exist and expand. This was in marked contrast with the picture two decades before, when the Lutheran movement, its leader officially judged a heretic and an outlaw, continued to exist only because Emperor Charles V was too busy fighting France, the pope, and the Turks to suppress it. Despite vehement protests by the pope, Lutheranism could propagate its faith boldly. It seemed that the use of the sword as a means of settling religious jurisdiction had come to an end.

Glancing back at this period from the present vantage point, however, it can be seen that all factors pointed to another war. In general, the following matters led to the outbreak of a new war between Roman Catholics and Protestants.

Lutheran disunity.—Even while Lutheranism was being threatened with extinction in the Schmalkaldic Wars that began in 1546, the Lutheran theologians were fighting vigorously among themselves in the area of doctrine. It is not surprising that doctrinal controversies occurred among the followers of Luther. The break with the Roman Church led Luther to push out into new directions of thought. Sometimes his impetuous nature prompted him to emphasize certain aspects of theology to an extreme; at other times he might express himself in terms that seemed to contradict what he had previously said. He hardly had time to meditate upon a complete and consistent scheme of theology but was forced to produce it piecemeal in various writings. Furthermore, as he developed and matured in his reforming ideas, he ofttimes changed his views expressed just a few years or even months before.

In addition, the diverse backgrounds and ideas of his prominent followers sometimes did not actually represent Luther. Philip Melanchthon, for example, after Luther's death in 1546 introduced new elements and attitudes into the movement which represented a divergence from Luther's general position. As a result, violent internal controversy rocked Lutheranism in the sixteenth century after Luther's death, various secular princes supporting this or that theologian in his doctrinal views. These Lutheran princes were not adverse to the use of force in suppressing what they believed to be erroneous Lutheran doctrines. No wonder the Romanists were encouraged.

The Roman Catholic resurgence.—Meanwhile, the Roman Catholic Church was busy also. Unified and strengthened by the internal readjustments of the sixteenth century, the Roman Church steadily won back territory and followers. The Society of Jesus provided trained and zealous soldiers who infiltrated into Protestant lands and schools with subversive effect. In addition, the Catholic princes soon began to persecute the Protestants in their lands. This was particularly true in Bavaria, Austria, Bohemia, and Hungary. Not only was the defection of Roman Catholic princes and ecclesiastics to Protestantism halted, but extensive and important gains were made by the Roman Church.

The challenge of Calvinism.—The Peace of Augsburg (1555) had granted recognition to Lutheranism as a legal religion, but no recognition was given to the followers of John Calvin, who were becoming numerous and powerful. Calvinism became a rival not only of Catholicism but also of Lutheranism. While the Roman Catholics were strengthening their forces in the closing years of the sixteenth century, Lutheranism became engaged in a bitter struggle with the Reformed Church (Calvinism). In many instances Calvinism partly supplanted the Lutheran movement, as in Poland, Hungary, Bohemia, and the Palatinate. Perhaps one explanation why Calvinism made such vast inroads was that Lutheranism retained so much of the medieval Roman system. While Calvinism was strongly anti-Roman, it had no Melanchthon to seek areas of compromise with the Roman Catholic system. Rather, Calvin rejected all tradition and insisted upon a fresh start from the direct teachings of the Scriptures. In addition, the Calvinistic system was more nearly self-consistent in its teachings and its methods. Its emphasis upon God's predestination in human experience put iron into the souls of men as they fought the Roman system.

Violations of the Augsburg Treaty.—The pope had never agreed to the Treaty of Augsburg in 1555. Quite naturally his followers were not at all scrupulous to observe the legal right of the Lutherans. Nor was the papacy alone at fault. The Lutherans also were guilty. The union of church and state, practiced through the centuries by the Roman Catholic Church and adopted in Lutheranism, Zwinglianism, Calvinism, and Anglicanism, made it imperative for them that military and political weapons be used in the advancement of any movement which was a part of national interest. Under this philosophy, religious differences were viewed as political and military threats. Flagrant violations of the Augsburg Treaty were excused on the ground of national interest. They led unerringly toward war.

Political rivalry.—When the war finally came, it presented a confusing scene. Ofttimes political interests took precedence over religious beliefs. Catholic France and Catholic Spain could not fight on the same side because of political rivalry. Protestant princes looked first to political factors before taking up arms and choosing sides. Consequently, although the struggle was basically between Roman Catholics and Protestants, the Thirty Years' War brought strange alliances and questionable motives.

Outbreak of War

The immediate occasion for the war occurred in Bohemia. The emperor Matthias (1612–19) forbade Protestants to erect certain churches, despite his initial oath that he would tolerate the numerous Protestant subjects of Bohemia. To add fuel, the dyspeptic Matthias arranged for his cousin Ferdinand, a militant Roman Catholic, to succeed him as the king of Bohemia. The Protestant reform flared into violence in Prague in May, 1618, and war was made certain when the Bohemian Protestants rejected Ferdinand as their king in the following year, choosing instead a Protestant.

The war that followed had four distinct phases.

Struggle in Germany (1618–23).—The Roman Catholic policy of continued preparation was quickly rewarded. By 1620 the Bohemian Protestants were crushed. All Protestant schools and churches were closed in Bohemia, Moravia, and Austria. Their pastors were driven into exile. The Romanists were not generous in victory, taking immediate steps to re-Catholicize the conquered lands. The Calvinistic government of the Palatinate was over- whelmed in 1623, and Protestants were required to conform or leave. This victory was significant in that the prince of the Palati- nate was one of the seven electors of the emperor, and with the Catholic victory in the Palatinate the pope controlled the majority of the electors, guaranteeing emperors subservient to the Roman Catholic Church.

The European phase (1623–29).—Thoroughly alarmed by the rigorous repression of Protestantism by the Catholics in the newly won lands, Lutheran princes of north Germany prepared them- selves for conflict, seeking aid from Denmark, England, and Hol- land, nominally Protestant states. The Roman Catholics, however, defeated the new foes. The Edict of Restitution of March, 1629, continued the severe terms by the victorious Roman Catholics. All Protestants were to be banished from Catholic lands, and it appeared that all of the gains of the Protestant Reformation would be wiped out under the Roman program.

Gustavus Adolphus (1629–32).—In this dark hour for the Prot- estants, two developments changed the picture. The first was the quarrel among the various Catholic leaders, secular and ecclesiasti- cal, over the division of the spoils. The second was the intervention of Gustavus Adolphus, the sagacious and brilliant Swede. In 1630 he began his invasion of Europe. At first other Protestants paid him scant attention, but within two years he had defeated all of the Roman Catholic armies and was master of the Continent. In his moment of victory at Lützen in 1632, however, he fell in battle.

Indecisive fighting (1632–48).—The next sixteen years brought terrible slaughter and great destruction of property, but neither side could secure victory. Germany, in particular, served as the battleground and suffered greatly. Despite the vocal opposition of Pope Innocent X, the exhausted armies on each side agreed to terminate the war.

Results of the War

The Peace of Westphalia in 1648 is a landmark in religious history. It closed the last of the general wars over religion and usually is considered as the beginning of the modern era. By the terms of the treaty, Lutherans, Calvinists, and Roman Catholics were recognized as equally entitled to civil and religious rights. The year 1624 was designated as the normal year; that is, each state or territory would revert to its religious status as of that date.

There can be little question that France won the war. The long battle between that nation and the Hapsburg line was finally resolved. The German states would not recover from devastation of the land for over a generation, and many of her finest leaders were slain. The emperor continued to exist in name only. The pope protested the cessation of hostilities and, in fact, paid little attention to the terms of Westphalia. He continued actively his efforts to re-Catholicize through subversion and diplomacy. Generally speaking, south Europe remained Roman Catholic, north Europe remained Protestant. The German states and Switzerland included both groups. It is ironic that the Protestants in Bohemia and Austria, who had begun the great battle thirty years before, received no relief in the final terms. This exhausting war apparently convinced the Roman Catholic Church that Protestantism could not be defeated with arms.

Other Conflicts

Arminianism in the Netherlands.—The theological system of John Calvin magnified God's predestination. There was widespread objection to this system, because it was felt that it involved human fatalism and compromise of God's character. Jacob Arminius (1560–1609) was the leader of the group opposing Calvin's doctrine. He denied an unconditional election, asserted a universal atonement for all believers, taught that man could cooperate with God in achieving regeneration, insisted that God's grace was not irresistible, and believed that men could fall from grace. These views were condemned in the Synod of Dort in 1618, and dissent was dealt with vigorously.

England and Scotland.—During this period occurred the fierce struggle in England and Scotland over the religious establishment. Although that story is told in connection with the English reformation, it is referred to here to complete the picture of the confused and violent situation during the first half of the seventeenth century.

Concluding Summary

The Peace of Augsburg (1555) did not end the struggle between Roman Catholics and Protestants. Strife continued for half a century. In 1618 war erupted in Bohemia and spread across the continents. The Peace of Westphalia in 1648 marks the close of the last great Roman Catholic-Protestant conflict on the Continent. Legal recognition was accorded to the two most extensive continental reform movements—Lutheranism and Calvinism. Political motivations began to outweigh religious differences, although religious persecution was by no means a thing of the past.

American Christianity

AMERICAN CHRISTIANITY WILL be discussed in three sections. The first covers the period from the discovery of America in 1492 to the year 1648—an arbitrary date in American history but quite significant in the English homeland and on the Continent. The second section covers the remainder of the American Colonial period, while the third section begins with the founding of the American Republic (1789) and continues to the present. This chapter will cover the first of these sections.

Importance of American Christianity

There are several reasons why American Christianity deserves extended treatment. (1) In a comparatively short time—by the standard of continental Christianity—American Christianity developed rapidly into an area of great vitality and influence. The United States is now the strength of the Roman Catholic Church as well as of the Reformation groups. (2) In the twentieth century American Christianity has become the principal base for world missionary efforts. (3) The gradual deterioration of vitality in Christianity on the European continent has accentuated the extraordinary progress made on the North American continent. (4) Christianity in the United States has assumed forms diverging from the historic pattern. Even the physical characteristics of the earth and rivers in what became the United States have tended to unify the nation, minimizing the sharp demarcations that characterized European states and racial groups. This basic unity, along with the tremendous resources of the great expanse of land, providing an economy of plenty, produced a new type of man. Self-reliant, independent, suspicious of coercion, and conscious of the opportunities afforded by personal worth and industrious application, the colonial American was a new factor in the complex religious picture of the world.

Significance of the Time

The discovery and settlement of America came at a peculiarly opportune time. The reformations in Europe and England were working their purifying effects to provide an evangelical base for gospel extension. There was great improvement in the Roman Catholic Christianity that was transplanted, in that many of the medieval abuses of doctrine and morals had been repressed. Most of the Roman Catholic immigrants in the formative years came from the British Isles, where they had been tempered by their minority position and their contact with other persecuted minorities. Roman Catholicism in the United States has not known the harsh and vindictive spirit which it has shown elsewhere. The tremendous growth of Roman Catholicism in the United States (with its different spirit in many respects) into a dominant power in the entire Roman movement gives hope that some day Roman Catholicism everywhere may cease its persecuting and coercive tactics.

Not only the Roman Catholics but all Christian groups in early colonial America had contact with the sweeping religious currents of seventeenth-century England. Thousands had fled to America to escape the intolerable policies of Archbishop William Laud. The avalanche of tracts and books in the last years of Charles I advocating religious toleration and even religious liberty were known in colonial America. The harshness of the reactionary legislation of the restoration Parliament conditioned Englishmen in the colonies for the exultant national and anti-Roman surge that brought William and Mary to the throne and gave homeland and colonies alike the Act of Toleration in 1689.

With this background and the comparative isolation of the American colonies from English interference, the men and women who fled to a new world planted a new sort of Christianity that

266

could not have been understood or tolerated a century or two before.

Characteristics of American Christianity

This new kind of Christianity flowed to a considerable extent from the activity and efforts of the religious dissenters, aided at some points by philosophical and humanistic idealism. A strong democratic spirit and the principle of separation of church and state greatly influenced, and gave direction to, the religious life of the United States. These distinctives encouraged the rise of religious individualism, of denominationalism, of religion by conviction rather than coercion, of competition in religion, of a sharpened sense of lay obligation, of zealous and extensive missionary activity, of the organization of nonecclesiastical ethical and philanthropic bodies or societies, and of the secularization of public benevolences and institutions.

Early Struggle for Domination

The discovery of America was not mere chance. The explorers did not just happen to stumble upon it. Solid financial reasons sent ships from various maritime nations scurrying westward in the closing decades of the fifteenth century. A very profitable trade with the Far East had been funneled through the eastern Mediterranean countries, but in 1453 the Turks seized Constantinople, and their conquests successively swallowed up all of the former points of trade. The development of the compass, astrolabe, and maps, making possible navigation when both stars and land were obscured, provided stimulation for adventurous voyages. In addition, with the increasing conviction by many that the world was round and that the vast ocean bordering China, described by Marco Polo almost two centuries before, was probably the western terminus of the same ocean that washed the shores of Spain, hardy men sailed westward. That there might be lands within that ocean between Spain and China was not at first commonly considered.

Portuguese explorers began poking into inlets and harbors in west Africa, thence southwestward as far as the Cape Verde Islands. Christopher Columbus was possessed with the great dream that he could reach the profitable markets of the East by a voyage, not too hazardous or distant, due west. He sailed on August 3, 1492, arriving on October 11 at what is probably one of the Bahama Islands. This began a number of explorations, laying the basis for Spain, Portugal, France, and England to claim large sections of the Western Hemisphere. The Spanish led the way, a series of explorers touching land from North Carolina south to the Straits of Magellan. Portuguese explorers visited Labrador, Newfoundland, and Brazil. England paid scant heed at first to the explorations of the east coast of the United States by John Cabot (perhaps accompanied by his son) but a century later made them the basis for claims in the New World. France entered the field late, touching the northern section of the continent through the work of Verrazano and Cartier.

Spain first began efforts at colonization. Within half a century after Columbus by their explorations Cortez, Balboa, Ponce de Leon, de Soto, and Coronado made claims for Spain in Florida, Mexico, and what is now the southern United States. Priests and monks accompanied these men and set up the Spanish type of Catholicism; but as soon as the Spanish sword was withdrawn, the movement deteriorated.

It seems providential that France did not capture the entire American continent and institute a zealous type of Jesuit Christianity. Her magnificent plan was conceived by the explorers themselves. It involved no less than the complete control of America by straddling "the core of the continent"—the Saint Lawrence, the Lakes, and the Mississippi to the Gulf. For a century and a half it appeared that this grand scheme would certainly be successfully consummated, since by 1754 the French flag floated unchallenged in the very areas of the grand design. Major diplomatic and military struggles on the Continent in what is called the Seven Years' War (1756–63) blasted this great dream when France surrendered to Great Britain all of her American possessions. There were subsidiary reasons, but the main one was military supremacy on the Continent.

Other Christian Colonies in America (1607–48)

Apart from the Roman Catholic movements established by the Spanish and French, American Christianity during this period may be divided into six groups. As far as possible, as a means of emphasizing the continuity of Reformation movements despite geographical and racial influences, the outline of American Christianity will follow the general pattern of Reformation groups. At times, of course, extensive modifications in a denomination or the dilution of the original influence of one of the Reformation movements may bring a denomination that must be treated as a different group. A denomination in America like Congregationalism, for example, although greatly indebted to Calvinism, is not put under the reformed group but is treated as a separate body.

The six denominations involved in early American colonization were the Church of England (1607), Congregationalists (1620), Calvinists (1623), Lutherans (1623), Roman Catholics (1634), and Baptists (1638).

Church of England in Virginia (1607–48).—English attempts to colonize the American continent began during the long reign of Queen Elizabeth (1558–1603). Adventurous sea captains had discovered a profitable venture in preying on Spanish ships sailing to and from colonial areas with valuable cargos. Meanwhile, the English seafarers explored the lands along the southern coast of the North American continent and published glowing accounts. Sir Humphrey Gilbert and his half-brother, Sir Walter Raleigh, secured patents from Queen Elizabeth to enable them to colonize new lands. After Gilbert's untimely death, Raleigh endeavored to plant a colony on Roanoke Island in Virginia in 1587, without success. Profiting considerably from his experiences, in 1607 the first permanent settlement was established at Jamestown, Virginia. Despite great hardships, the colony survived. Its religious background was the Church of England, and a church was established. It was handicapped, however, by the lack of a resident bishop.

Congregationalism in Massachusetts (1620–48).—The English independents, or Brownists, who had fled to Holland in 1609 under the leadership of John Robinson, William Brewster, and others, determined in 1620 to sail for Virginia in the New World. The ship of these Pilgrim fathers, the *Mayflower,* was driven northward by the elements and landed instead in November, 1620, in what is now Massachusetts. A large colony of Puritans under John Endicott entered the area in 1629, causing misgivings among these Pilgrim Separatists, but through the medical skill and gracious spirit of Dr. Samuel Fuller of the Separatist colony, hostility and misunderstanding between the Separatists and Puritans were removed. From a common council the group united into a single church system in which the authority lay in the congregation, banded together by covenant, guided and instructed by the ministers whom they set apart, and supported as a part of a theocratic government. In 1631 the colony enacted a regulation that only members of the established Congregational churches could be freemen. Thus the ministers in the local congregations were able to regulate suffrage on the basis of religious orthodoxy. By 1648 this colony had increased considerably, swelled by the Puritan exodus from England between 1630 and 1640.

The Massachusetts Bay Colony was completely intolerant of Separatism. The reasons were both religious and political. For one thing, the colony was born with a "divine right" sense which transformed them from the category of dissenters in England to the established church in America (and curiously enough made dissenters out of Church of England followers in the colony). Those dissenting in the American colony were viewed as abhorring God's revealed will and rebelling against God's appointed order. This was to be an ideal theocracy. Furthermore, the colony was schismatic from the Church of England. Noisy strife, particularly any that might seem to favor a radical Separatism in the colony, could have brought the ire of Archbishop Laud and Charles I and had serious consequences. Thus when Roger Williams arrived in 1631 and immediately denounced the Massachusetts Bay theocratic system, every effort was made to silence him. He was banished in 1636 and in 1638 organized Providence plantations. Similarly, when in 1637 Mrs. Anne Hutchinson introduced variant ideas, she too was banished. By the end of this period the Massachusetts Bay Colony was engaged in a struggle to maintain her theocratic nature and political independence.

Calvinism.—The Dutch Republic also made explorations along the North American coast and made subsequent claims of territory. In 1609 Henry Hudson inspected the North American coast from Newfoundland to Virginia in an effort to locate a passage to the Far East. Although he failed in this, he explored the river which bears his name and secured the adjacent area for the settlement in 1623 of New Amsterdam, later to become New York. The Dutch Reformed Church (Calvinistic) was organized here in 1628, although many other different religious groups found a foothold also. Until the close of the period there was little religious persecution. Peter Stuyvesant became governor in 1647 and changed this policy.

English and Scotch-Irish Presbyterianism also began to infiltrate the colonies during the latter part of this period. It is sometimes difficult to distinguish between the Presbyterians, the Puritans from the Church of England, and the Congregationalists, all of whom were greatly influenced by John Calvin's doctrines and organization. Between 1637 and 1639, in fact, there was considerable correspondence between English Presbyterian leaders and leaders of Massachusetts Bay Congregationalism respecting the new type of Calvinistic modification in the American colonies. Sometimes, as in Connecticut generally, Presbyterianism was integrated without friction, and even Massachusetts Bay Congregationalism absorbed some Ulster Presbyterian immigration. Other Presbyterians had considerable trouble over doctrine with Congregational neighbors early in the 1640's but were well received by the Dutch Reformed leaders in New Amsterdam. The large Calvinistic immigration came after the close of this period.

Lutheranism.—The movement of continental Lutheranism to the American colonies came about 1623 when Dutch Lutherans were included among the early colonists in New Amsterdam. In addition, Swedish Lutherans began colonizing New Wilmington, Delaware, in 1638 and established the first Lutheran congregation in America in that year. Lutheran immigration was small during this period.

Roman Catholicism.—The first permanent English Roman Catholic colony was established in Maryland in 1634. Sir George Calvert, a secretary of state under James I (1603–25), embraced Roman Catholicism in 1623. Long interested in colonization and desirous of founding a state for personal affluence and religious refuge for Roman Catholics, Calvert secured grants to Newfoundland in 1622 (under James I) and to what now includes Maryland and adjacent areas in 1632, although he died before the transaction was completed. His son Cecil proceeded with the plan, and in March, 1634, the colony was founded near the Potomac River. Jesuit priests worked actively in settling the colony and in converting the inhabitants to Catholicism. Indeed, Lord Baltimore (Cecil Calvert) became uneasy at the zeal of the Jesuits and their ability to secure land and special immunities; he issued surprisingly repressive orders to them, doubtless because he feared the effect on public opinion in Protestant England should it be learned that the new American colony was dominated by the feared and disliked Jesuits.

A considerable improvement in the treatment of Roman Catholicism in England after the death of James I forestalled the expected immigration to the new Catholic colony. Consequently, Cecil, anxious to guarantee the success of the colony, welcomed settlers of all faiths and refused to establish the Roman Church with civil support. An admirable toleration was provided. However, it was not religious liberty, for the famous Act of Toleration of 1649 at the very close of this period enacted the punishment of death for speaking against the Trinity and assessed heavy penalties for not believing in Jesus Christ, for breaking the sabbath by swearing and disorderly recreation, and for similar offenses.

Baptists.—American Baptists trace most of their early ancestry to England. During the reign of Charles I (1625–49) large numbers of dissenters of every sort fled from the stringent persecuting measures of Archbishop William Laud. One of these was Roger Williams, a highly educated and talented "godly minister," according to the first description of him by Governor Winthrop in Massachusetts Bay Colony. He arrived in February, 1631, about six months after Boston was settled and named. Williams is significant not only as the organizer of perhaps the first Baptist church in America but because of his advanced views. Religious liberty, separation of church and state, and democracy were condemned almost universally on both sides of the Atlantic in 1631, save by a few General Baptists in England and Williams in America. It took a decade more of time and a political and constitutional revolution in England before dissenters there of any sort, apart from the Baptists, championed such ideas.

Where did Williams get such notions? Perhaps a clue is found in his writings. He preserves a story about the second pastor of the first Baptist church in London, John Murton, an early contemporary of Williams. This tale speaks of how Murton wrote Baptist tracts from prison by using milk and paper bottle stoppers for writing paper. A confederate outside browned the dried milk to rescue the writings of Murton. Murton died in London about 1626 when Williams was about twenty-seven years of age. Perhaps there is a larger context for this anecdote which Williams alone remembers from Murton, for some of the ideas of Williams were those of Thomas Helwys, first pastor of the church, and John Murton.

At any rate, Williams was banished in 1636 from Massachusetts Bay Colony for holding such opinions. His critics in America thought that he had "windmills" in his head. In 1638 he founded a colony at Providence based upon his advanced concepts of democracy and religious liberty, and in the following year he organized what was perhaps the first Baptist church in America. He began to doubt the validity of his baptism before long—a question that plagued others of the Baptists in England—and became a Seeker.

No such doubts assailed Dr. John Clarke, founder of the Baptist church at Newport, Rhode Island, perhaps in 1644 or before. His warmhearted and unselfish spirit, expressing itself in extensive and sacrificial labors in behalf of the gospel, religious liberty, and separation of church and state, marks him as the outstanding Baptist of this period.

Baptists appeared during this period in New Hampshire and Connecticut and perhaps elsewhere, in addition to Massachusetts Bay Colony and Rhode Island, but their numbers were few.

Concluding Summary

From the beginning the religious forms and tensions of the Old World were projected into the tiny English colonies scattered along the eastern seaboard of America. Before the Peace of Westphalia (1648) American Christianity was already providing a fore-glimpse of the rich and complex development of denominations that was to characterize her later history. In half a dozen colonies there were that many different religious groups. Already a wide ocean and a seemingly limitless frontier were shaping a new sort of man in America.

BIBLIOGRAPHY

BAINTON, ROLAND. *Here I Stand*. New York: Abingdon-Cokesbury Press, 1950.

BETTENSON, HENRY (ed.). *Documents of the Christian Church*. New York: Oxford University Press, 1947.

BINNS, ELLIOTT. *The Reformation in England*. London: Gerald Duckworth & Co., Ltd., 1937.

GEE, H., AND HARDY, W. J. *Documents Illustrative of English Church History Compiled from Original Sources*. London: Macmillan & Co., 1896.

LATOURETTE, K. S. *A History of Christianity*. New York: Harper & Brothers, 1953.

LINDSAY, THOMAS M. *A History of the Reformation*. 2 vols. New York: Charles Scribner's Sons, 1941.

LITTELL, FRANKLIN H. *The Anabaptist View of the Church*. Philadelphia: American Society of Church History, 1952.

McNEILL, JOHN T. *The History and Character of Calvinism*. New York: Oxford University Press, 1957.

NEWMAN, A. H. *A Manual of Church History*. 2 vols. Philadelphia: American Baptist Publication Society, 1953.

ROBINSON, JAMES HARVEY. *Readings in European History*, II. Boston: Ginn & Co., 1904.

SWEET, WILLIAM W. *The Story of Religion in America*. New York: Harper & Brothers, 1950.

V. PERIOD OF ENCROACHING RATIONALISM (A.D. 1648–1789)

Introduction to the Period

At the beginning of this period the world was badly disorganized. The Thirty Years' War on the Continent had ravaged most of the German states, and the continuation of sporadic struggle projected the misery of the earlier catastrophe. In England the fratricidal war between the people and the house of Stuart ended dramatically in 1649 with the beheading of Charles I and the assumption of power by Oliver Cromwell. Throughout this entire period the Continent was dominated by France, although the political and religious repression of the people laid the foundations for the great revolution at the end of the period which was to sweep France out of her high place among the nations. England, meanwhile, moved toward the democratization of her monarchy. Parliament increasingly assumed more responsibility for government and policy. The Wesleyan revival doubtless saved England from a revolution similar to the one in France.

During this period the intellectual world threw off traditional restraints in its theological and philosophical systems. It will be recalled that the formulations of Francis Bacon (1561–1626) and René Descartes (1596–1650) brought a new emphasis on rationalism in interpreting the world. This emphasis was continued in Spinoza and Leibnitz. The empiricism of John Locke (1632–1704) turned in a different direction, giving inspiration for the idealism of Berkeley and the skepticism of Hume. In this period Immanuel Kant (1724–1804) brought the age of reason to its height. By making man's mind the dominant factor in categorizing the world of experience, Kant demolished older rationalism but introduced a new type. He laid the foundations for later systems of thought that developed more fully the truth that man is not simply a thinking creature but has other facets in his nature.

Points of Special Interest

In this period the student can see the successive thrusts of Christianity against militant rationalism and skepticism. On the Continent this took the form of pietism. This movement was quite important in

275

its immediate contributions, as well as in its influence upon the revival both in America and England in the following century. The dominating theme in English Christianity in this period was the Wesleyan revival. Every part of English life was blessed by it, and the rise of England to a dominant place in world affairs in the next century stems in large part from the saving character of this revival, both in social and political life. The Great Awakening in the American colonies, evidently sparked by Pietistic antecedents, did much to lay the foundations in religious and political life for the rise of the new nation.

Continental European Christianity

THE PEACE OF WESTPHALIA of 1648 marked the close of the period known as the Protestant Reformation. The principal European nations during the Reformation were England, Spain, France, and Sweden, with the loosely confederated Holy Roman Empire and the threatening Turks in southeastern Europe completing the picture. New nations were now beginning to develop—Austria, Brandenburg-Prussia, the Dutch, and Russia. It will be the purpose of this chapter to trace Christianity on the Continent from the close of the Reformation to the French Revolution. England will be considered in a separate chapter.

Political Background

It will be remembered that Francis I of France and Charles V of Spain battled intermittently during the Reformation and, unintentionally, greatly aided the success of the Protestants. These wars were not incidental. National aspirations rose sharply in the sixteenth century. The old order was changing. The empire was decadent, and as though sensing their destiny, each of the several states endeavored vigorously to secure the advantage in the new order. Although Spain, through colonial discovery and early centralization, was the dominant power in the Reformation period, the leadership soon passed to France. A century of exhausting wars, a fatal weakness in maintaining a strong succession to her throne, and the inability to exploit her colonial empire toppled Spain from her high place. On the other hand, King Louis XIV of

France (1643–1715) was a shrewd, heavy-handed man who ruled long enough to carry out an extensive and energetic program of aggression and expansion. The Holy Roman Empire, so potent a factor during the Reformation, was rapidly declining. Political decay and economic stagnation combined to pull down this imposing medieval edifice and deliver its opportunities and duties to the individual German states, principally Bavaria, Saxony, Hanover, Austria, and Brandenburg-Prussia. Italy remained divided into small states.

The Turks, too, soon moved off the principal stage of events. Once more in the latter half of the seventeenth century the armies of the Turks threatened Vienna, as they did during Reformation years, but thereafter the tide subsided. Sweden also, after a brief period of glory through the work of Gustaphus Adolphus (1611–32), was defeated by a coalition of her enemies in 1709.

This was the golden age of the Dutch Republic, for a time undisputed mistress of the seas. In this period also the Russian giant began to bestir itself. Peter the Great (1689–1725) made a start toward westernizing the nation, and under Anna (1730–40) and Catherine the Great (1762–96) Russia added considerable territory and moved toward assuming a larger place in the European family of nations.

Roman Catholic Church

The new nationalistic spirit sweeping the world demanded complete control by the state. The Roman Catholic Church, on the other hand, claimed the immediate allegiance of clergy and people. The replacing of the power of the medieval empire by that of the individual states meant the weary repetition of conflict between overlapping powers. The strife between universal empire and universal church was replaced by the battle between many strong national states and the militant Roman church. Particularly in France and Austria on the Continent was this true. In France Louis XIV (1643–1715) attained absolute authority, while later on Marie Theresa (1740–80) in Austria sought the same ideal.

The principal story of the Roman Church between 1648 and

278

1789 is the interaction between the ecclesiastical and diplomatic aims of France and Rome. The religious attitude of Louis XIV was governed by his nationalistic aims at the particular time, for he apparently had little religious conviction. In 1682 he forced the Roman Catholic clergy in France to issue what are known as the Gallican Articles, a direct strengthening of national interests by limiting the pope to spiritual things only and by putting all ultimate spiritual authority into the hands of ecumenical councils. The pope, Innocent XI (1676–89), was one of the ablest and most conscientious pontiffs of the entire period, but he saw instantly the subversive nature of this legislation and fought it bitterly. In fact, so great was his hatred of Louis XIV of France that he may have consented to the overthrow of Catholic King James II of England partly because of James' friendship with Louis XIV. Innocent's successor, Alexander VIII (1689–91), tried to work out a compromise with Louis but did not quite succeed. However, the next pope, Innocent XII (1691–1700), found Louis in a trading mood, and in return for favors from the pope the French king allowed his bishops to disapprove the Gallican Articles.

Persecution of the Huguenots.—It will be remembered that the Huguenots (French Calvinists) had received the "perpetual and irrevocable" promise of certain liberties in the Edict of Nantes (1598). The Roman Church regarded this toleration as deplorable and worked continually and effectively to undermine it. The Catholic sovereigns of France during most of the seventeenth century were bitterly hostile to the Huguenots and waited only for the opportunity to smite them. In the arena of practical politics the Huguenots improved their situation by standing firm for the government amidst popular uprising and received in turn the commendations of Louis XIV. In 1656 the Catholic clergy remonstrated with Louis XIV about the privileges granted the Huguenots. The king showed his true distrust of the Huguenots by moving against them, particularly after 1659. Persecution began. It was as vicious as the combined shrewdness of Bourbon absolutism and vindictiveness of Jesuit bigotry could contrive.

In October, 1685, the original charter of French Protestant

liberty, the Edict of Nantes, was revoked by the same meaningless words that brought it into being—a "perpetual and irrevocable edict." All Protestant houses of worship were to be destroyed and schools abolished, all Protestant religious services halted, and all Protestant ministers must leave France within fifteen days. If Protestant ministers would become Catholics, they could continue with a substantial raise in salary and other specific rewards. Torture, prisons, and galleys now became the rule. Over a quarter of a million Huguenots fled from France, despite border guards posted to halt them. As a result, France lost perhaps one fourth of her best citizens; those who remained defiled their consciences, and their children were reared as skeptics or actual unbelievers; the established Roman Catholic Church shamelessly exploited state and people in such fashion that the first strong blows of the French Revolution a century later were aimed at the Church; and the monarchy became so impervious to the rights of the people that the foundations were laid for the great deluge.

Persecution of the Jansenists.—The Jansenists received their name from the founder, the French bishop Cornelius Jansen (1585–1638), who revered the theological system of Augustine. Augustine, it will be remembered, magnified the sovereignty of God in all areas of grace and salvation. The Jesuits, on the other hand, were for the most part strongly Pelagian, emphasizing the ability of man to aid in the redemptive transaction.

After the death of Jansen in 1638, his friends published his theological masterpiece lauding the Augustinian system. Naturally the Jesuits did their best to get this work condemned by the pope. The whole matter came to be a test between the Jesuits and their enemies. In 1653 the pope condemned five propositions which apparently contained the marrow of Jansen's views on grace. Prominent leaders like Blaise Pascal and Antoine Arnauld were arrayed on the Jansenist side. Pope Alexander VII and Louis XIV joined hands to require the Jansenists to conform. Persecution and coercion continued for over half a century, finally virtually overthrowing French Jansenism, although it survived in the Netherlands. The significance of this controversy rests in the fact that it represents the Roman Catholic condemnation of the teaching of Augustine, one of its early fathers, and a victory for the Pelagian ideas of the Jesuits. The synergism of the Roman Catholic system is more favorable to Pelagianism than to Augustinianism.

Persecution of the Salzburgers.—In the mountainous areas of upper Austria the people, unaccessible for regimentation, had long been followers of evangelical doctrines. The Waldenses, the Hussites, the Lutherans, and the Anabaptists had disciples there. Outwardly, most of the people conformed to the Roman Catholic Church but met secretly for evangelical worship. By the time of the Peace of Westphalia (1648) many of these had become staunch Lutherans. Since the Westphalian treaty provided that Lutherans in the territory of a Catholic prince had the right of peaceable emigration, the Protestants of Europe were shocked when Lutheran congregations in the territory of the Bishop of Salzburg were harshly imprisoned for their faith. The archbishop conveniently died and stopped both the persecution and the furor. In 1728, however, a new archbishop was appointed who vowed that he would destroy the heretics. Persecution began again, and in 1731 about twenty thousand Lutherans were driven from the country in the midst of winter. Most of them went to Prussia, where they were gladly received.

Suppression of the Jesuits.—The Jesuit order was probably the most influential party in the Roman Church during the first century after Loyola founded the society. Its tightly knit organization, clear-cut objectives, oscillating ethics, and overwhelming zeal brought it to the front rapidly, but these same characteristics also incurred enmity from many quarters.

In the opening years of the eighteenth century the Dominicans charged that the Jesuits in China were allowing the Chinese to continue worshiping pagan idols with a thin veneer of Christian vocabulary. In 1721 one of the men whom the Jesuits had driven from his assignment in Portugal was elected pope and took the name of Innocent XIII (1721–24). He promptly withdrew from the Jesuits the right to conduct mission work in China and nearly abolished the order entirely. Benedict XIV (1740–58) also condemned the heathenish practices of the Jesuits on the mission fields. Clement XIII (1758–69), a staunch supporter of the Jesuits, brought the final blow by the issuance of two bulls praising the Jesuit order. Portugal had already expelled the Jesuits in 1759; France had done likewise in 1764; and in 1767 Spain and Sicily took similar action.

The storm of protest against papal support of the Jesuits resulted in the election in 1769 of an anti-Jesuit pope, Clement XIV (1769–74). France, Spain, and Naples demanded suppression of the Jesuits as a condition of their continued relations with the papacy. After several preliminary steps, Clement abolished the Jesuit society in 1773 in vitriolic language. No Protestant has ever condemned them more unequivocally. Frederick of Prussia, a Lutheran, and Catherine of Russia, a Greek Catholic, gave the Jesuits haven in the hope of profiting by Jesuit resentment. Restoration came forty-one years later.

The approaching storm.—A glance at the history of the popes during this period shows that in the eighteenth century they faced a hostile world. Bitter rivalry with nationalism and the trading of blows with Protestantism account for only part of their struggle; the other part came from what has been called the Enlightenment. The first enthusiasm of discovering an orderly world—one operated on the basis of fixed and determinable laws—was almost uncontrollable. In the minds of many authority was shifted from a sovereign God to a thinking man, who was the measure of all things. In the eruption of the revolution in France, the Roman Catholic Church and Christianity in general were looked on as enemies of human rights and opponents of the highest achievements of mankind.

The Lutheran Church

The Lutheran lands bore the brunt of the war that closed in 1648. The frightful results of this war impoverished these German states for a century. The male population was decimated, and the constant march of armies which lived off the land brought devastation from enemy and ally alike.

282

Doctrinal controversies.—The harsh controversies among the Lutherans following the death of their founder barely subsided before the outbreak of the Thirty Years' War in 1618. War partially stopped most theological disputation, but the torrent of angry words soon erupted again. This time it began with Georg Calixtus (1586–1655), a spiritual descendant of the party of Philip Melanchthon. The training and experience of Calixtus fitted him to play his role. Through extensive traveling and diversified study he learned to appreciate other Christian groups. About 1630 he began to minimize distinctively Lutheran doctrines and to suggest plans for Christian union. His opponent was Abraham Calovius (1612–86), whose temperament and training inspired a strong loyalty to Lutheran confessionalism and made him abhor all that Calixtus advocated. This controversy, foreshadowing a similar but less bitter division among American Lutherans, engaged much of the vitality and attention of continental Lutheranism in this period.

Pietism.—Within Lutheranism one fruit of the depressed economic and religious conditions following Westphalia was an attempt to bring a vital renewal of practical Christianity. Pietism represents a reaction against rigid intellectual scholasticism and an effort to return to biblical principles. It was not an isolated movement. England had somewhat of a counterpart in her Puritan and Wesleyan revivals. The leaders of Pietism among the Lutherans were Philipp Jakob Spener (1635–1705) and August Hermann Francke (1663–1727). Spener was the pioneer, while Francke carried the movement to its greatest success. Neither of these men desired to separate from the Lutheran church but wanted to reform it from within. As a pastor in Frankfort in 1666, Spener saw the difference between the true Christianity of the heart and the rather formal and intellectual acceptance of doctrine that characterized church life about him. He introduced Bible and prayer classes into his church in an effort to revitalize Christian living. In 1675 he published a little work entitled *Pious Wishes,* which urged that Christianity should be more personal, scriptural, practical, and loving. Fellow Lutherans accused Spener of leaning toward Calvinistic doctrines and turning away from the Lutheran faith.

Francke carried forward the work. He had a conversion experience in 1688 and became strongly evangelical and pietistic. His great work was done at the University of Halle. While there he translated Christianity into practical living, founding an orphanage and providing educational opportunities for thousands of boys from grade school through university. From this center came the early gleams of the modern mission movement when in 1705 it supplied the first missionaries for the Danish mission in India. Likewise, Henry M. Muhlenberg, probably the outstanding early American Lutheran, came from Halle in 1742.

In addition, the work of Spener and Francke resulted in the founding of the Moravian Brethren. Count Nikolaus Ludwig von Zinzendorf (1700–60) was reared by his Pietistic grandmother and received his schooling at Francke's institution in Halle. He permitted two families of Bohemian Brethren to settle on his estate in Saxony. Becoming interested, he joined their group and assumed leadership. It is interesting to note that he secured episcopal succession through both Lutheran and Reformed sources. Zinzendorf desired to establish a Christian association of all true Christians of all churches. He was banished from Saxony in 1736 by the state authorities and used the occasion to visit Moravian Brethren, as his group was called, in England and America. In 1742, much to his displeasure, his community in Saxony in his absence organized into a separate church. He was allowed to return to his home in 1749. The zeal and missionary activity of the Moravian Brethren were quite pronounced during the eighteenth century.

Beyond its own organizational life, Pietism had a considerable influence. It gave a renewed emphasis to study of the Scriptures and magnified the place of the conversion experience. In a reaction against its views, some of its opponents prepared the way for rationalism.

Rationalism.—During the Medieval period Christian philosophers had struggled with the question of the relationship between human reason and divine revelation. Particularly when reason seemed to conflict with some area of revelation did this problem become acute. Many Christians looked upon the synthesis of Thomas Aquinas as setting forth the proper relationship. Aquinas took the position that reason should go as far as it could, forming a base for knowledge, and that revelation should then complete the structure, thus providing in a sense a capstone or completion for the whole. Other forces, however, continued to raise the original problem. For one thing, the Renaissance opened up new worlds of knowledge and understanding to men. Furthermore, during the late fifteenth and sixteenth centuries the movement known as humanism turned men increasingly toward faith in their rational powers. In a sense the Protestant Reformation itself, by fighting superstition and appealing to the reasoning of men as well as by formulating rational confessions and debating over doctrine, aided the swing toward reason. Some leaders of the Reformation magnified human reason and drastically attenuated the field of the supernatural, but generally the struggle was in bounds with respect to basic supernaturalism.

In this period, however, the onslaught against supernaturalism in favor of radical rationalism became critical. Strangely enough, the severest blow was doubtless delivered by one who was endeavoring to protect Christianity against the deism of England and the skepticism of France. Christian Wolff (1679–1754) was reared in the tradition of the philosophers Descartes and Leibnitz, who emphasized that all truth is capable of clear demonstration and is basically harmonious. Wolff tried to bring all philosophical concepts into self-evident and incontrovertible clarity and then turned to theology with the same purpose. Believing that he could do so, he asserted that Christian doctrines must be capable of demonstration with as much clarity as a mathematical proposition. This left revelation completely under the sway of human reasoning. Unless revealed doctrines were completely demonstrable to the satisfaction of the mind, they were unworthy of belief.

Because of his views Wolff was driven from his professorship of philosophy in the University of Halle but was restored by the Prussian ruler, Frederick the Great. Liberalism and skepticism were widely scattered throughout Germany. The Illumination—as the movement was called—ruled almost supremely in Germany throughout this period. Revelation became almost meaningless. Rational demonstration only was acceptable in teaching Christian doctrines. The curious religious system of Emanuel Swedenborg (1688–1772) and his New Jerusalem church was a direct result of this background, as he attempted to justify the spiritual world by showing its correspondence with the natural order.

This rational movement reached its height in Immanuel Kant (1724–1804). While often called the father of German rationalism, he introduced some elements that turned away from a strict and final intellectual interpretation of all life. He demolished Wolff's idea that all truths must be demonstrable by clear ideas, and while insisting that the existence of God could not be proved objectively, yet in his *Practical Reason* he introduced a moral imperative into life that suggested a moral governor of the universe. His entire system, however, discarded supernatural revelation and made man's reason the ultimate criterion of truth. This period in Lutheran life closes with rationalism strong and religious skepticism widespread throughout the German states.

Calvinism

Calvin's system of theology was more self-consistent than that of Luther, and as a consequence, there were fewer internal controversies in the century after the death of Calvin. The controversies that did develop were in the nature of radical revolt against the entire system rather than disagreement with one facet. A brief survey of Calvinism in this period can be made in a geographical outline.

Switzerland.—It will be remembered that Calvin began his movement in Geneva about 1534. After Calvin's death in 1564 his emphasis on predestination was taught even more rigidly by his disciple, Theodorus Beza. The movement was not greatly affected by the Thirty Years' War. However, the development of theological liberalism, along with German and French skepticism surrounding the area, greatly undermined the faith of Swiss Calvinists after 1750.

The Netherlands.—The Arminian controversy of the previous period gradually diminished. The dissenters were for the most part permitted to return and propagate their views. Two outstanding theologians lived in this period. Hugo Grotius (1583–1645), ofttimes called the founder of international law, felt the persecuting hand of the extreme Calvinists. He is remembered for his theory of the atonement of Christ in terms of the vindication of the majesty of God's government. The other leader was John Cocceius (1603–69), probably the outstanding biblical scholar of his area. Cocceius popularized the idea of the covenants: the covenant of works in Adam having failed, God gave a new covenant of grace in Christ. In the middle of the eighteenth century, Dutch Calvinism was also adversely affected by deism, skepticism, and rationalism. The Dutch Reformed Church was carried to America in 1628.

The German states.—The Peace of Westphalia recognized Calvinism as having equal civil and ecclesiastical rights with Roman Catholicism and Lutheranism. As suggested previously, however, the Roman Catholic Church vigorously attempted to re-Catholicize as many of the German states as they could reach and were successful in replacing Calvinism in some areas. The German Reformed Church also was greatly affected by materialism and skepticism in the eighteenth century. Some of its members emigrated to the United States in 1746.

France.—France had been fighting constantly (usually with Spain and the Hapsburgs) since the early days of the Reformation. The Thirty Years' War brought victory almost beyond the dreams of the earlier kings. France became the principal power of the Continent. During the long reign of Louis XIV (1643–1715), his chief aim was to establish royal absolutism on the basis of divine appointment. He developed a thorough organization, a strong army, and a meticulously loyal court. His extravagances brought great burdens to the people. He had a lofty conception of his office that brooked no rivalry. He made every effort to destroy Calvinism. After the revocation of the Edict of Nantes in 1685, the Calvinists fled to the Cevennes Mountains and waged guerrilla warfare against the Catholics. For a century the persecution of the Calvinists continued intermittently. The outstanding names that are preserved from this period are those of Antoine Court, the restorer of the Reformed Church of France, and Paul Rabaut, the apostle of the desert. The closing years of this period brought some toleration through the efforts of Robert Turgot.

Concluding Summary

During this period the controversy over Pietism and syncretism divided the Lutherans and encouraged rationalism. The resultant skepticism adversely affected both Lutheran and Reformed (Calvinistic) movements in every part of Europe. Roman Catholic persecution added to the miseries of the period and drove many toward skepticism and revolution.

The hierarchical organization in the Roman Catholic Church forestalled much of the radical rationalistic influence that blighted Protestantism. Internal conflicts brought the suppression of the Jansenists and Jesuits, and persecution of Protestants was widespread and vicious. Politically, the Roman Church made peace with the various states, in particular with France, the strongest power on the Continent.

Other small groups, such as the Mennonites, carried on in this period, but that story cannot be told here.

25

English Christianity

THE STORY OF English Christianity in this period is closely related to the political history because of the union of church and state. At the close of the previous period Charles I (1625–49) had been beheaded by Cromwell to institute what has been called the Commonwealth period (1649–60). A Presbyterian Parliament had become so intolerant that Cromwell purged its membership and sponsored his own parliamentary reorganization.

Church of England

During the Commonwealth (1649–60).—After the beheading of Charles I, Cromwell was faced with armed opposition from Scotland and Ireland who recognized Charles II as the rightful king of England. With his well-trained armies, however, Cromwell overcame the portions of the nation favoring Charles II and in 1653, after dissolving Parliament, declared himself Lord Protector of England. The Presbyterian Parliament had disestablished the Church of England from the support of the government in 1641 and subsequently had put Presbyterianism in that favored position. Cromwell altered this situation by providing that all acceptable ministers should be supported by the state. As a means of determining which ministers were acceptable, he instituted a Board of Triers to test those ministers applying for state support. Views on doctrine and polity were never to be questioned in determining who was fit for employment; only one's character as a godly man and his ability to communicate religious truths were considered. For the most part, religious toleration was provided for all except Roman Catholics and anti-Trinitarians.

Charles II (1660–85) and James II (1685–88).—After the death of Oliver Cromwell in 1658, there was a reaction in favor of restoring the royal house of Stuart to the throne of England. The traditionally poor memories of the people had forgotten the speakable tyranny of Charles I but remembered the harshness of the Presbyterians and the highhanded authority of Cromwell. Perhaps also the promise by Charles II of religious liberty for tender consciences caused many to turn toward him. Upon his restoration to the throne Charles found that he had promised more than he could give. The Church of England party was still entrenched in a powerful position and lost no time in taking the new king in hand. In addition, almost before Charles was settled as king, Thomas Venner and a group of millennial-minded fanatics known as the Fifth Monarchy Men staged an uprising in an effort to seize the throne from Charles and set up a kingdom for the return of Christ. They were repelled without great difficulty but certainly influenced the king against all dissenters.

The Church of England (the episcopacy) was established again in 1660, and in that year persecution against all dissenters began. Five acts were passed. *a.* The Corporation Act of 1661 excluded all dissenters from taking part in local government in England by requiring them to partake of the Supper in the established church, to repudiate the Solemn League and Covenant oath, and to swear not to take up arms against the king. *b.* The Act of Uniformity of 1662 required every minister to believe and follow the Book of Common Prayer in his services. Out of approximately ten thousand pastors in the Church of England at this time, two thousand were driven from the pulpits because they were unwilling to subscribe. The same requirements were prescribed for all teachers in public or private schools. *c.* The Conventicle Act of 1664, aimed especially at the Baptists, forbade all religious meetings by dissenters. *d.* The Five Mile Act of 1665 prohibited dissenting ministers from coming within five miles of any city or town or of any parish in which they had ministered. *e.* The Test Act of 1673 was aimed particularly at the Roman Catholics. Charles had issued a Declaration of Indulgence in 1672 in an effort to spare the Catholics from the effect of some of these acts, but in direct defiance of the crown, Parliament passed the Test Act, which excluded Catholics from all civil and military positions by requiring as a prerequisite for such offices the condemnation of the doctrine of transubstantiation and the partaking of the Supper in the established church.

Although some of these acts were aimed at specific groups, all of them brought great trial to Presbyterians, Congregationalists, Baptists, Quakers, and Roman Catholics.

On his deathbed Charles II was received into the Roman Catholic Church and his brother James II (1685–88), an active Roman Catholic, succeeded him on the throne despite an Exclusion Bill which Parliament had earlier passed in an effort to prevent a Roman Catholic from assuming the crown. Without delay James attempted to aid the Roman Catholics. In 1687, without parliamentary approval, he published a Declaration of Indulgence, granting liberty of conscience and freedom of worship to all his subjects. James also released Catholics from the obligations of the Test Act of 1673. Early in 1688 James again published his Declaration of Indulgence, ordering it to be read in all the churches of England. Seven bishops refused to do so and were tried for sedition. They were acquitted amidst general rejoicing.

The birth of a male child in the home of James meanwhile brought universal fear that Catholicism would be firmly planted on the English throne. On the very day that the seven bishops were acquitted—June 29, 1688—seven leading members of Parliament invited William of Orange, ruler in the Netherlands and a Protestant, son-in-law of James II, to take the throne of England. Partly because William felt that his wife was properly the sovereign of England and partly as a means of circumventing Roman Catholic continental power, William agreed to accept the throne and in November, 1688, with little resistance, invaded England and secured the crown. Parliament regularized his equality on the throne with his wife Mary. Coincident with this, Parliament declared Roman Catholics and those married to Roman Catholics to be forever incapable of wearing the English crown;

all Catholics were deprived of whatever ecclesiastical holdings they might have; and no Catholic was allowed to approach within ten miles of London.

William and Mary (1688–1702) and Anne (1702–14).—One of the first moves of the new sovereigns was to pass the Act of Toleration (1689). This relieved dissenters from most of the persecuting acts of Charles II, although it still left many disabilities to pass away through the influence of public feeling. Catholics and Socinians were still proscribed. Dissenters had few political rights and still were forced to support the Anglican clergy.

Some of the bishops were unwilling to take the oath of allegiance to William and Mary, protesting that the Stuart line (James II) was divinely instituted on the English throne. Nine bishops and other clergy refused to sign the oath and were called the Nonjuring clergy. They fled to Scotland and kept up an independent succession until 1805.

Queen Anne (1702–14) entered into office at a time when Parliament was dealing tolerantly with dissenters, but an event in the fifth year of her reign aroused her ire against dissent. In 1707 Scotland was united with England officially by the admission of fifteen Scots (Presbyterians) into the House of Lords and forty-five into the House of Commons. This, with other acts designed by a tolerant Parliament to conciliate dissenters, led to a violent reaction among the leaders of the established church. In 1709 Henry Sacheverell preached a fiery sermon against toleration. Parliament promptly tried him and punished him for libel. Anglicans were incensed, and through their influence a reactionary Parliament was elected in 1710. Queen Anne favored the repression of dissent, and by 1714 severe laws were prepared against dissenters. Her death ended this movement.

The Hanover line (1714 to end of period).—Through legislation by Parliament, George I (1714–27) was brought from one of the German states as the nearest Protestant relative of Queen Anne. He and his successors, George II (1727–60) and George III (1760–1820), followed the general policy of toleration set out by William and Mary. It was under the last of the three that the

English colony in America protested against taxation without representation and won independence. The Church of England was greatly influenced by the Wesleyan revival during this period, a movement that will be discussed in succeeding pages.

The Roman Catholic Church in England

It will be recalled that Charles I (1625–49) favored Romanism and married a Roman Catholic. His overthrow and execution ushered in a period of stringent persecution for Roman Catholics. Cromwell was tolerant toward most groups but specifically excepted the Roman Catholics from this favor. Charles II (1660–85) was personally favorable to the Roman Catholics but was unable to aid them because of the universal feeling against them in England. He joined the Roman Church on his deathbed. James II (1685–88) vigorously pursued a pro-Roman Catholic policy, which was the cause of his expulsion from the English throne and the declaration that no Roman Catholic should ever wear the English crown. Roman Catholics were excepted from the Act of Toleration of 1689, and their movement was rigorously persecuted. Throughout the entire period Catholicism was also vigorously repressed in Ireland. The rule of the Hanovers brought no relief to the Catholics in England, although prejudice against them was dying out by the time of the French Revolution.

Lutheranism in England

Lutheranism did not gain a foothold in England.

Calvinism in England

Calvinism, appearing in England under the various forms of Presbyterianism, Congregationalism, Independency, or simply Puritanism within the established church, was in control in England at the close of the previous period. A church assembly from Scotland and England, made up principally of Calvinists, was preparing what has become known as the Westminster Confession of Faith, one of the most influential of modern Christian confessions, not only in its relationship to Presbyterians, but in its modification into the basic formulations of Congregationalist and some Baptist confessions of faith as well.

Presbyterian intolerance, however, became insufferable. Their severe laws, developed in the comparatively brief period of parliamentary control, provided the death penalty for errors in doctrine. In 1648 Cromwell purged the Parliament, wresting it from Presbyterian control. Many Presbyterians became pastors of state churches under Cromwell's regime. Like all dissenters from the episcopal establishment, they suffered considerably from the persecuting legislation under Charles II and rejoiced in the coming of toleration in 1689. Unitarianism, however, made large inroads into English Presbyterianism in the eighteenth century.

Presbyterians in Scotland meanwhile were forced to disestablish their church under the restoration policy of Charles II in 1661. The episcopal type of church government used by the Church of England was re-established. Scottish Presbyterians chafed under the whip of persecution. A small group gathered and signed a covenant to continue the fight against episcopacy. From a leader, Richard Cameron, they secured one of their names —the Cameronians. They are also known as the Covenanters and the Reformed Presbyterians. Although comparatively few in number, they were able to survive the vicious persecution that followed. Under William and Mary's Act of Toleration (1689), Presbyterianism was restored to state support.

In the first half of the eighteenth century two struggles took place in Scotland. One was against the inroads of Socinianism and deism, both of which made great gains from Scottish Presbyterianism. The other was against lay patronage. In 1711 Queen Anne restored the principle of lay patronage for Scotland, which permitted influential parishioners to control the appointment of the ministers. Opposing both theological laxity and lay patronage, Ebenezer Erskine (1680–1754) was expelled from the church of Scotland in 1733 and organized the Secession Church. In 1752 Thomas Gillespie was expelled from the state church because of lay patronage and formed in 1761 the Relief Presbytery. These two groups united in the next period.

A very significant movement occurred in Ireland. Even before the stirring events surrounding the seizure of the throne of William and Mary, some Scottish Presbyterians had settled in north Ireland. After the defeat of the Irish in 1691 in the struggle over the accession of William and Mary to the English throne, the English government appropriated a large tract of land in the province of Ulster and invited Scottish Presbyterians to settle there. Thousands came and began a vigorous Presbyterian movement in Ireland. In the first part of the eighteenth century many of these Scotch-Irish Presbyterians were driven to America because of the failure of the potato crop and the raising of rents by English landlords. These Ulster Presbyterians were never an established church and for that reason were much more democratic in spirit than English Presbyterians. From them came some of the outstanding leaders of American Presbyterianism in the early years, principally Francis Makemie.

The Congregational movement in England was greatly aided under Cromwell, who encouraged the calling of a Congregational assembly for the adoption of a confession of faith. The assembly was not convened until after Cromwell's death in 1658. A declaration of faith was adopted, following quite closely the Westminster Confession of Faith of 1648 by the Presbyterians. The Congregationalists suffered with other dissenters during the reigns of Charles II and James II and welcomed toleration under William and Mary.

Other Denominations in English Christianity

Baptists.—English Baptists became vocal during the parliamentary struggles taking place in the fifth decade of the seventeenth century. Their convictions regarding religious liberty had been expressed a generation before in England, and they took the opportunity to urge their point of view. While in England in 1644 Roger Williams published his *Bloody Tenet of Persecution*, detailing the melancholy story of persecution in New England and pleading for liberty of conscience. English Baptists were prominent in the army of Cromwell and at the same time were probably the strongest deterrent to Cromwell's ambition to head a new line of kings in England. Perhaps beguiled by the promise of Charles II that he would allow liberty of conscience, Baptists joined in laboring for the restoration of the Stuart line. With other dissenters they suffered severely in the period between 1662 and 1688.

Strangely enough, after toleration was legislated in 1689, Baptists did not grow rapidly, as would be expected. They seem to have exhausted their strength during the harsh days of persecution. Particular Baptists framed a confession of faith in 1676 on the pattern of the Westminster Confession. A larger assembly adopted this confession in 1689, and it has become the principal English Baptist confession. It was the model for the Philadelphia Confession of Faith adopted in America in the next century. General Baptists were overwhelmed by the Socinian currents in the opening years of the eighteenth century, and many of their churches became Unitarian. Particular Baptists fell under the blight of hyper-Calvinism, hemmed in on every side by what they believed was God's elective limitation.

Quakers.—The Quakers were a product of the mystical experience of George Fox (1624–91). He became opposed to organized Christianity when as a young man he could find no help from the churchmen for a personal problem. Mystical in nature, although trained in Presbyterian background, he had what he felt was an inner revelation from God in 1646. His emphasis upon the inner light, and his defiance of organized Christianity brought much persecution. The movement grew rapidly. The size of his group is illustrated by the fact that in 1661, under the persecuting acts of the Restoration, there were more than 4,200 Quakers in prison. Quaker missionaries went everywhere. In 1681 William Penn founded his colony in America as a haven for the persecuted of his group and others. The central doctrine of the Quakers was the "inner light" from God. Formal worship, singing, the ordinances of baptism and the Supper, ministers and special theological training were rejected—perhaps a reflection of Fox's intense opposition to all that constituted organized Christianity in his day. Pacifism and philanthropy have characterized the Quakers from the beginning, although the movement has lost the radical and condemnatory spirit it first knew.

The Evangelical Revival

One of the most influential movements in the modern period was the evangelical revival of the first half of the eighteenth century. In England it was known as the Wesleyan Revival; in America, the Great Awakening. The Continent, with its Pietistic movement and with historical connections between Augustus G. Spangenberg and John Wesley, deserves some share for the background of the Awakening, although the unwillingness of the Pietists to organize for the perpetuation of their ideals prevented them from the possibility of spreading extensively like the Methodists.

The strong rationalism that brought skepticism in Germany and France, along with the widespread destruction of property and ideals by the Thirty Years' War and its projection, turned the thoughts of men on the Continent away from the things of God. In England this rationalism took the form of deism or naturalism and in its influence upon continental Christianity, particularly in France, was probably more hurtful than a philosophical skepticism. Deism was an effort to minimize special revelation. There is no need for a supernatural revelation, the deists argued; religion is not mysterious and mystical, but the natural expression of man's need for God and virtue. In this sense, all religions of the world have equal worth insofar as they are rational. These ideas were slowly developed from the early skepticism of Lord Herbert of Cherbury (1583–1648) to their more complete description in John Toland (1670–1722) and Matthew Tindal (1653–1733). Along with deism, various other types of philosophical skepticism grew out of English rationalism in the eighteenth century. William Law (1686–1761) and Joseph Butler (1692–1752) were the noteworthy opponents of English deism.

Other elements in English life brought Christianity into general disrepute in the opening years of the eighteenth century.

297

The low state of morals and indifference to religion by earlier sovereigns (especially the later Stuarts), who were supposed to exemplify some Christian ideals as supreme governors of the Church of England, gradually filtered down to the man on the street. Social unrest and economic stringency were everywhere. The rapid industrialization of England, accelerated by continental events, crammed new and old cities with submerged masses of bewildered and frustrated people. Wealth began to concentrate, abject poverty to spread. Reacting equally against Roman ritualism and mystical enthusiasm, the Church of England became even less than lukewarm. Most of the dissenting groups, racked with rationalism or hyperorthodoxy, had little to say to the needy people. Morals and religion alike were at their lowest ebb.

Into this arid country flowed the refreshing streams of the Wesleyan revival. The leaders were John and Charles Wesley, bred in the parsonage of a High-Church rector, and George Whitefield, son of a saloonkeeper. Both Wesleys spent a brief but important period in missionary service for the Church of England in Georgia. There they came into contact with the Moravian leader Spangenberg, from whom they learned the need for a personal experience of faith in Jesus Christ. Both returned to England and in 1738 professed conversion and regeneration. Whitefield, too, had experienced a rebirth, and the three formed the triumvirate of the new Methodist movement.

Of the three, doubtless Whitefield was the ablest preacher, Charles Wesley was the great hymn writer, while John Wesley was the methodical organizer who gave structure and endurance to the movement. It is noteworthy that Whitefield was a Calvinist, while the two Wesleys were Arminian. As a result, two types of Methodists were developed, although the great majority followed the Wesleyan type. These three Methodist leaders preached and sang throughout all of Britain, Wales, and Scotland, while Whitefield made extensive preaching tours in the American colonies. In some instances these men built upon the foundation others had laid. In Wales a layman, Howel Harris, had begun a Welsh revival two years before the Methodist leaders arrived to kindle fresh fire. In America Whitefield built upon the efforts of Frelinghuysen, the Tennents, and Jonathan Edwards.

The Wesleys did not desire to break with the Church of England and between 1738 and 1784 organized Methodist "societies" like those of the Moravians. The rapid growth of these societies and the acquisition of property required additional organization and supervision. In 1744 the first annual conference of preachers was held in London, and two years later England was divided into circuits for preaching. Finally, in 1784, because of the need for preachers in America, Wesley made a radical departure from his former plan. For the first time Methodist preachers were ordained and given the authority to baptize and celebrate the Supper. In addition, Wesley gave form to the annual conference of preachers and transferred to it much of the authority that he had personally exercised over the movement through the years. In 1784, because of the separation of the American colonies from England, the Methodist Episcopal Church in America was organized.

The results of this evangelical movement both in England and in America were phenomenal. Within the Church of England a whole generation of evangelical-minded leaders profoundly breathed new life into the old Anglican forms—men like James Harvey, William Romaine, Isaac Milner, Charles Simeon, and William Wilberforce. In addition, there sprang forth missionary, Bible, and tract societies and other aids to the spread of the gospel. Many historians believe that the Wesleyan revival so thoroughly regenerated English life that it warded off a catastrophe similar to the French Revolution. A permanent evangelical party arose within the Anglican Church. Later on a new and significant phase of Methodism was the Salvation Army.

Among other English groups the revival had profound effects. Its emphasis upon personal experience validated religion for many in the face of skepticism and rationalism. It renewed the zeal of English Baptists, resulting indirectly in the beginning through them of the modern mission movement. Other denominations were similarly blessed. In America the movement heightened the revival already begun, and the whole is known as the first Great Awakening. Practically every religious movement in America felt the surge of the revival fires. A new church—the Methodists—was founded, and other groups that magnified a crisis experience in conversion, such as the Baptists, benefited greatly.

Concluding Summary

England was ruled as a commonwealth from the death of Charles in 1649 until the restoration of the monarchy in 1660. Oliver Cromwell served as protector from 1653 to 1658. This was a period of comparative religious toleration. However, after the restoration of Charles II in 1660, persecution began against all but the established Church of England (the episcopacy). The "bloodless revolution" of 1688 brought the Protestants William and Mary to the throne, and in the next year an Act of Toleration was enacted. Strangely enough, the end of active persecution in 1689 seemed to bring lethargy to all Christian groups in England. The Wesleyan revival, which began about 1738, profoundly affected all England and beyond.

American Christianity

THE PRINCIPAL STORY in the Americas during this period concerns the area now forming the eastern part of the United States. The western area was still a wilderness. Latin America and Canada were being colonized slowly. Because of lack of space, most of the story in the Americas during succeeding periods will be devoted to Christianity in the United States.

Rapid growth characterized the Colonial period in the principal area to be discussed. From less than fifty thousand colonists hugging the Atlantic seaboard in the opening years, the population increased to almost four million by the time the first census was taken in 1790. Able now to provide for their own needs, the colonies began a brisk trade. New England exported grain, livestock, cloth, fish, rum, and lumber products; the Middle Atlantic states shipped rice, tobacco, and lumber products; the South provided rice, indigo, tobacco, lumber products, and cotton.

General Survey of the Period

Political background.—It should be kept in mind that the American settlements of England were simply colonies during the main portion of this period, and each was more directly related to the crown than to corporate life with one another. That they would become an independent nation was a thought that was comparatively late in finding popular support. France and England were strong rivals for control of the North American continent. For a long while it appeared that the French might be victorious. However, the English won the last battle, this time in

Europe. England and France had ranged themselves on opposite sides in a series of conflicts in Europe during the eighteenth century. Particularly in the War of Austrian Succession (1740–48), known as King George's War in America (1744–48), the English colonies in the New World played a significant role. After a valiant expedition from New England captured Louisburg, the strong French fortress on Cape Breton Island, the European treaty between England and France in 1748 returned the fortress to France. Americans resented this move after they had risked so much to capture it.

The Seven Years' War on the Continent—known in the American phase as the French and Indian War (1756–63)—prepared the way for American independence. In it France was forced to surrender her claims in America. This eliminated a possible rival in America for a new nation and provided an important ally against England when war for independence came. In addition, the important part played by the colonials in this war brought to them a feeling of self-consciousness and unity. The unwise policies of King George III brought rebellion in America; the European nations defeated by Britain in the Seven Years' War—France, Spain, and others—combined against Britain to help bring about victory for the Americans by 1783.

Colonization by other Christian groups.—During this period several additional Christian groups emigrated to the new land.

The Quaker movement that began in England in 1647 soon had adherents in the American colonies. They were roughly handled. Massachusetts executed four in 1659, while Virginia and New York enacted rigorous laws against them. Quaker zeal and courage, despite erratic behavior at times, carried the day, however, and they continued as a part of the wonderfully rich and complex religious heritage of America. The haven of the American Quakers became Pennsylvania, founded in 1681 by William Penn, although already in New Jersey the Quakers had developed their characteristic organizational forms. Penn had been granted a large tract of land by Charles II of England, and he specifically appealed to those suffering from religious persecution, both in

England and on the Continent, to flee to "Penn's woods" in the New World. Large numbers of dissenters responded, particularly the Quakers, with whom Penn had identified himself.

Mennonites from Germany also sought Penn's colony and settled at Germantown in 1683. This constituted the first organized congregation of the group, although occasional Mennonite emigrants (Dutch, Swiss, and German) had appeared in America almost fifty years before. A substantial number of Mennonites from the several parts of Europe flowed into Pennsylvania during this period.

The Moravians found Pennsylvania a welcome haven. They had first entered Georgia in 1735, but in five years most of them had moved to Pennsylvania. The founder of their movement, Nikolaus Ludwig von Zinzendorf, spent about a year in the colonies in 1741 when exiled from Saxony and visited Moravian settlements in Pennsylvania and in North Carolina.

American Methodism took its start about 1766 from the work of Philip Embury, Barbara Heck, and Captain Thomas Webb in New York, and Robert Strawbridge in Maryland. Growth was slow at first. The first American conference of 1773 reported a few over a thousand members; by 1775 there were about three thousand; and by 1783, about fourteen thousand. It will be remembered that John Wesley desired to keep Methodism within the framework of the Church of England and that Methodist organization was first effected so that none of the prerogatives of the Anglican Church would be assumed. Consequently, in both England and America during the first half century Methodism had no ordained preachers. All baptizing, marrying, communion, and other acts requiring ordination were administered by Church of England priests. American Methodists followed the English pattern for forming local classes of about a dozen members who would meet to pray and worship under the supervision of a class leader. Several of these classes constituted a "society," which subsequently became the local Methodist church. Each of the early American preachers had a circuit of societies which he would visit regularly for preaching. This simple type of organization was both thorough and productive of great zeal and personal enlistment.

Since the Methodist movement was a part of the Church of England prior to the Revolutionary War, it was looked upon by American patriots with considerable suspicion. The situation was not improved when Wesley himself urged his followers to be faithful to the crown. Practically all of his preachers returned to England during the Revolution, the notable exception being Francis Asbury. After the war Wesley was convinced that Methodist preachers must have ordination. He first approached the Church of England with a request that they ordain Methodist preachers for America. When they declined, Wesley, himself a presbyter in the Church of England, ordained Richard Whatcoat and Thomas Vasey as presbyters on September 2, 1784, while Dr. Thomas Coke was ordained as superintendent for America. Francis Asbury, already in America, was to be ordained as joint superintendent with Coke. Upon their arrival, Asbury insisted that he would take office only if elected by the Conference of American Methodist preachers. He was so elected and was ordained. In December, 1784, at Baltimore the Methodist Episcopal Church was organized and continued to grow rapidly during the remainder of the period.

Other less numerous groups settled in America during this period, such as the German River Brethren and the Shakers. At the very close of the period the first Protestant Episcopal church in New England became the first Unitarian church in America.

The first Great Awakening (1726 on).—One of the formative factors in American Christianity was the great revival of the early eighteenth century which swept across the colonies. The roots of this revival seem to have sprung from Europe. The warmhearted evangelistic movement there known as Pietism had prepared the hearts of many of those emigrating to America. Several groups of Germans in Pennsylvania who had come under its influence were among the first to experience revival. By 1726 the preaching of Theodore J. Frelinghuysen, a deeply spiritual minister of the Dutch Reformed Church in New York, became peculiarly effective in winning men to Christ and moving his hearers toward God. He inspired others during the next several years, one of the most important of whom was the Presbyterian minister, Gilbert Tennent, who became a zealous (and not always wise) promoter of the revival.

By 1734, in what seems to have been a separate movement, Jonathan Edwards, Congregationalist pastor of Northampton, Massachusetts, found a deepened spiritual sensitiveness in his congregation and in the whole community, so that (he wrote) the town seemed to be full of the presence of God. A great revival followed. The entire revival movement was characterized by the conversion experience of those seeking God for themselves. It spread rapidly to every part of the colonies. Even John Wesley in England, as yet unturned, learned about it in 1738 and marveled.

Another great name associated with this awakening was that of George Whitefield, colaborer of Wesley in England, who had a conversion experience in 1735 and in 1738 arrived in Georgia to take up the work the Wesleys had left. Returning to England to raise money for his orphanage in Georgia and for ordination in the Church of England, he was delayed because of military operations but spent his time in evangelistic preaching throughout Britain. After the ship embargo was lifted, Whitefield sailed for Philadelphia en route to Georgia. His fame had spread, and multitudes flocked to his ministry. In all of the American colonies he trumpeted the gospel message. Utilizing the fires of religious revival already evident in the work of Frelinghuysen, Tennent, and Edwards, he led the revival movement to its highest point.

The results of the revival were many. They will be seen more particularly in the survey of the important American denominations in this period. In general, the results normally to be expected from a widespread spiritual awakening were present—many conversions, strengthening of churches, ethical gains in the personal lives of the people, and moral and benevolent institutions founded or strengthened. Christian education was advanced. Two rather unexpected results also were important. (1) The great strengthening of the minority groups and the interdenominational character of the spiritual visitation combined to lay the groundwork for religious liberty in the New World. (2) A sense of spiritual unity was engendered among the colonists in America at the very time the political relations with the mother country were being strained to the utmost. The tours of Whitefield from Maine to Georgia tied the colonies together; his converts were found in every colony; his preaching was a common bond that united diverse groups. In their struggle toward the great destiny which they knew not, the colonies were being unified in a most fundamental way.

Skepticism and religious decline.—In some parts of the South the Great Awakening continued almost unabated until the close of this period. In general, however, the Revolutionary War marked the beginning of a rapid religious decline. In addition to the loss of church property and the difficulties confronting the holding of religious services, the war brought the customary callousing of spiritual sensibilities and encouraged moral looseness. Along with these factors, the entire intellectual and theological atmosphere was discolored by the deistic speculations from England, the atheistic assertions of France, and the rationalistic systems of the German thinkers. Many of the outstanding leaders and patriots during the Revolutionary War were infected by such currents. Skeptical and atheistic literature circulated extensively. Even the church-fostered schools became hotbeds for infidelity. Less than 10 per cent of the population were professing Christians just before the close of this period in 1789. A new revival was greatly needed, and it came shortly after the opening of the next period.

The Older Denominations (1648–1789)

The Church of England.—The Church of England had accompanied the English settlements in Virginia (1607) and the Carolinas (after 1665). It was also established in Maryland in 1692, after that colony, founded by the Roman Catholics, was assumed by the English crown following the accession of William and Mary in England. New York was captured by the English from the Dutch in 1664, and in 1693 the Church of England was at least partially established there. The Society for Propagating the Gospel in Foreign Parts (established by the Church of England in 1701) was instrumental in planting missions and churches in New England after 1702.

The progress of the established church in the colonies was slow. It faced many foes. The quality of ministers sent from England was generally low, with notable exceptions. The lack of an American bishop made discipline next to impossible. The increasing number of dissenters and the aversion to ecclesiastical authoritarianism which had driven many to America militated against the popularity of the leaders. In Virginia in 1619—when the Church of England was established—there were only five clergymen, two of whom were deacons. A century later the number had increased only to about two dozen, although there were forty-four parishes in the colony. The constant political and religious turmoil in England during the seventeenth century was bound to bring confusion to the American colonies and neglect of the churches established there.

Although George Whitefield was a member of the Church of England when he came preaching with power in 1739, he was not welcomed by the colonial establishments of the Church of England. For one thing, he was preaching a strongly evangelical gospel, magnifying conversion and denouncing many in the ministry as "unconverted." Furthermore, he had been denied the use of churches in England and had gone to the fields for preaching. In addition, the enthusiasm and emotionalism of the Great Awakening were not to the liking of the orderly and staid episcopal adherents. In fact, Whitefield was called for trial before an episcopal ecclesiastical court in Charleston, South Carolina, and was convicted and suspended from the ministry by Commissary Alexander Garden for irregularities. Whitefield paid scant attention to the proceedings.

The Revolutionary War brought crisis to the Church of England in the colonies. She was a part of the English system and as such was distrusted by many and hated by some. Two thirds of her clergy were loyal to England during the war. In Virginia in particular there was much loss. Only fifteen of ninety-one clergymen could remain at their posts in that state, and much of their property was destroyed. The losses were not so great in Maryland, where out of forty-four parishes, each with a minister before the Revolution, almost two dozen of the clergy remained and the property loss was comparatively small. There was great opposition to the Anglican Church in New England, New York, New Jersey, and Pennsylvania, where organized efforts had been made prior to the Revolution to prevent the appointment of a bishop in America. At the very close of this period, steps were being taken to organize the Protestant Episcopal Church, a new body holding to doctrines of the Church of England but disentangling itself from English control.

Congregationalism.—By 1648 the Congregational churches in Massachusetts and Connecticut had developed a theocratic government. Right of franchise was limited to members of Congregational churches, and no new Congregational churches could be formed without permission from the old. A college (Harvard) was flourishing at Cambridge, Massachusetts, and the clergy was supported from tax funds. Dissenters like Baptists and Quakers were rigorously persecuted.

The work of the Westminster Assembly in England inspired New England Congregationalists to prepare a doctrinal statement, which was adopted at Cambridge, Massachusetts, in 1648. One of the important provisions was the requirement that any person admitted to the Lord's Supper must have made a public profession of faith (even though he had been baptized as a baby) and have given evidence of a Christian experience. Unless the parents of a child fulfilled these conditions, their child could not be baptized. Controversy began immediately. Unless one could relate a conversion experience and pursue an orderly walk, he could not partake of the Supper, he could not have his children baptized, he was disfranchised and disqualified for civil office, he knew the odium of religious ostracism; yet he must give money to support the Congregational ministry and churches. Finally, in 1662 the Half-Way Covenant was enacted, providing that children of moral and baptized persons might also be baptized, even though the parents could not qualify for admission to the Supper. This action increased controversy and practically eliminated any requirements for church membership.

In an effort to regularize and stabilize the practices of the various Congregational churches, a strengthening of external authority in the associations was attempted in Massachusetts, but the movement failed. A similar program in Connecticut, the Saybrook Platform in 1708, was successfully introduced there.

It can be recognized that a movement like the Great Awakening would agitate again the divisive question about a conversion experience. Jonathan Edwards was one of the outstanding figures of the revival. His deep piety, mingled with profound philosophical thought, made him one of the foremost American religious thinkers. His church at Northampton, Massachusetts, was the center of revival in 1734. Not all Congregationalists followed Edwards, however. In churches which did not favor the revival, some minority groups, insisting upon a conversion experience, withdrew and formed "New Light" churches or "Separate" churches. Some of these later adopted immersion and became Baptist churches.

The Congregationalists were strong patriots during the Revolutionary War period. They emerged from the war with considerable prestige because of their noble service for the new nation. Skepticism and infidelity played havoc with many of their churches, however. In addition, the lack of organization beyond the local level hindered larger denominational development and to some extent made it difficult to resist growing Unitarianism that was soon to rob New England Congregationalism of much of its church property. Despite these factors, as well as controversy and schism, the number of Congregationalist churches in New England—to which this denomination was generally confined—increased greatly during this period.

Calvinism.—Those following the teachings of Calvin came to America in various national groups during this period. The Dutch Reformed Church had been begun about 1628 in what became New York, and even after the colony fell to the English in 1664, the small Reformed group of Holland carried on their worship.

Scottish and Scotch-Irish Presbyterians had emigrated quite early to the New World. At the opening of this period, small Presbyterian churches could be found in many of the colonies along the coast. The important name in this early period of Presbyterian life was that of Francis Makemie, who came from Ireland in 1683. By his work American Presbyterianism organized the first presbytery in 1705 at Philadelphia with seven ministers. Eleven years later the first synod was formed, consisting of seventeen churches, three presbyteries, and nineteen ministers. Some French Reformed refugees (Huguenots) fled to America and settled principally in the South during the critical days after the Edict of Nantes was revoked in 1685.

The first German Reformed church was formed in 1719 at Germantown, Pennsylvania. Through the efforts of Michael Schlatter and the Dutch Reformed group, a synod was formed for the German Reformed Church in 1747, consisting of forty-seven congregations and but five ministers.

The Great Awakening brought dissension and schism among the Presbyterians. Gilbert Tennent, a young minister at New Brunswick, New Jersey, influenced by the pietistic spirit of Theodore Frelinghuysen, his neighboring preacher, delivered fiery evangelistic sermons. After 1728 revival occurred among the Presbyterians, and many were converted. In 1741 Tennent and his followers were ejected from the synod for unauthorized and censorious activities, causing an extensive schism which continued until 1758. Meanwhile, in 1745 the New York Synod established a college, which was to become Princeton University.

After internal peace was restored, Presbyterian growth, principally from immigration, was rapid until the Revolution. Almost without exception the Presbyterians were patriots and supported American independence. They aided greatly in the successful struggle in Virginia for separation of church and state and religious liberty.

Lutheranism.—It has been seen that Lutheranism was first planted in what became New York. While this colony was under Dutch rule (1623–64), persecution of Lutheranism was carried on, but after 1664 the English permitted relative liberty. The Swedish Lutherans who settled in Delaware faced difficulties as their colony was seized by the Dutch in 1655 and ceded to England in 1664, but a measure of religious liberty was permitted under the rule of each. Lutheran growth was accelerated with the coming of the Germans in the opening years of the eighteenth century. William Penn had visited the war-torn and suffering Germanic areas in 1681 and invited them to emigrate to his colony in America. The response came principally after 1708, and large numbers of German Lutherans settled in New York, Pennsylvania, and the Carolinas. In 1734 many Lutherans from the province of Salzburg in Austria, driven out by rigorous Roman Catholic persecution, settled near Savannah, Georgia. The first Lutheran synod was formed in 1735 in New Jersey, representing sixteen congregations.

The patriarch of Lutheranism in America was Henry Melchior Mühlenberg, who was sent from Germany in 1742 to aid the struggling American Lutheran churches. His wise and capable leadership united and organized the early American Lutheran movement.

The Great Awakening did not greatly affect American Lutherans. The Germans were somewhat responsive. Their rallying around Mühlenberg and their active zeal probably stemmed in part from the revival. The Swedish Lutherans, on the other hand, did not enter into the movement. Lutherans almost to the man supported the American Revolution, furnishing outstanding leadership and support. The two sons of H. M. Mühlenberg, Peter G. and Frederick A. C., became eminent military and political leaders. Like all other denominations, the Lutherans suffered from the loss of manpower and interest during the Revolutionary War, but after its cessation rapidly recovered.

The Roman Catholic Church.—By 1648 the Roman Catholic Church had moved into America through the work of English, French, and Spanish immigrants. The English colony in Maryland in 1634 has already been described. French missionaries and explorers continued the work of Jacques Cartier (1534) and Samuel de Champlain (1613). La Salle (1676), Marquette and Joliet (1673), and many other lesser figures established missions and forts in the northern and central sections of the nation. The vast mission program of French Catholics, begun and continued under severe difficulties, was abandoned when defeat in the Seven Years' War (1756–63) brought cession of French claims in America. Spanish missionaries and monks were very active also in this period.

The Spanish missionary work in Florida in its early history was accompanied by coercion and the sword. By 1634 there were forty-four missions with thirty-five priests under the Bishop of Havana. In 1701, during the War of Spanish Succession, the English in the Carolinas and Georgia attacked Spanish Florida and burned St. Augustine in 1702. At the close of the war Florida was given to England, ending Spanish missions there.

Spanish priests striking northward from Mexico planted missions in New Mexico about 1598. By the opening of this period about sixty Franciscan monks were serving in this area. Internal bickering over authority, raids from wild Indians, and the recurrence of what a Roman Catholic author calls "cryptopaganism"—the reverting of the Indians to ancient pagan worship despite a claim of being Christian—brought problems. In 1680 the Pueblo Indians revolted and drove the Spanish from New Mexico for twelve years. Between 1692 and 1700 the area was reconquered, and missionaries were restored by force of arms, although the two principal tribes (the Moqui and the Zuni) refused to allow Catholic missionaries among them. At the close of the period the work was termed unsuccessful, partly because the missionaries refused to learn the language of the people.

A Spanish Jesuit monk toured Arizona about 1687, and in 1732 others arrived to begin missions in what is now Arizona. Jealousy between them and the Franciscans brought rivalry and strife, hindering effective results.

A Spanish missionary expedition was sent into Texas in 1689, and in 1716 work was begun; but Catholic historians call the work a failure, partly due to the large number of different tribes and dialects in the area.

Lower California had been explored and mission stations established in the late sixteenth century. Upper California had no mission work until 1769 when, doubtless to forestall the Russian advances down the coast, a Mexican military and missionary expedition entered that area. Junípero Serra led in the hard and perilous work of establishing Roman Catholic missions here. At the close of the period there were perhaps a dozen missions operating, although friction between the missionaries and the Mexican military leaders hindered the effectiveness of the work.

The Catholic colony in Maryland suffered from the political revolution in England in 1688. The overthrow of James II was the signal for the Protestants in Maryland to seize the government, and the Church of England was established under a new charter with Maryland as a royal colony (not proprietary) in 1692.

As might be expected, the Roman Catholic Church felt none of the impulses toward revival during the Great Awakening beginning about 1739. American Catholics played an honorable part in the Revolutionary War, although they were still comparatively few in number. At the close of this period it is estimated that there were approximately twenty thousand Catholics in the former English colonies of America.

It should be mentioned that Spain and Portugal had for a century been sending military forces and missionaries to almost every part of South America. Missions were established in the West Indies and Mexico, as well as Brazil, Peru, Chile, and Argentina. In this period the Roman Catholic missionaries touched almost all of Central and South America.

Baptists.—The handful of Baptists that organized Providence Plantations as a colony in 1638 increased slowly in this period. Congregations were formed throughout New England, the middle states, and the South before 1700. In 1707 Baptists around Philadelphia formed the first association in America—the Philadelphia Association. It stood alone until 1751, when the second was organized in South Carolina. Thereafter the growth of associations of Baptist churches was rapid.

Before the Great Awakening Baptist progress was slow. There were fewer than fifty Baptist churches in all America after one hundred years (by 1739) . The Great Awakening multiplied American Baptists. At first New England Baptists were reluctant to have any part in the revival, partly because those engaged in it were their persecutors and partly because of the Arminian reaction against a movement among the Calvinists. However, the conversion to Baptist views of Isaac Backus, a Congregationalist New Light, began a movement that brought many New Lights into Baptist life. Between the revival and the Revolution, Baptist churches in New England increased from twenty-one to seventy-eight.

The middle and Southern colonies also felt the impact of the Great Awakening. Shubael Stearns and Daniel Marshall, converted under the preaching of George Whitefield, became Baptists and, aided by men like Colonel Samuel Harris, Elijah and Lewis Craig, and many others, led in the formation of new Baptist churches throughout Virginia, the Carolinas, and Georgia. Whereas there were only seven Baptist churches in the South before the Great Awakening, by the close of the Revolution Virginia had 151 churches, in addition to supplying Baptists for over forty churches in Kentucky; North Carolina had forty-two Baptist churches; South Carolina had twenty-seven; and Georgia, where Baptist work had begun in 1772, had six churches.

In addition, Baptists had a principal part in the struggle for religious liberty in Virginia and had established Brown University in Rhode Island in 1765 for the education of the ministry.

Baptists took a prominent part in the Revolution, several rising to important places in the chaplaincy and in the army. Hezekiah Smith, John Gano, and others were outstanding in New England and the middle colonies; in the South Richard Furman had a price put on his head by the British as one of the outstanding patriots. At the close of the period Baptists were active and growing.

Concluding Summary

During most of this period France and England were rivals for control of the vast North American continent. England emerged victorious in 1763, but the American colonies won their independence in twenty years. A steady flow of immigrants came from England and the Continent. Their religious background had an important bearing on Christianity in the new nation. The First Great Awakening, beginning after 1726, profoundly influenced both religious and political life in the American colonies. The Revolution brought a rapid religious decline, accelerated by skeptical and rationalistic currents from England and the Continent. At the close of the period, Christianity in the United States was at a low ebb, and its prospects were dark.

BIBLIOGRAPHY

BETTENSON, HENRY (ed.). *Documents of the Christian Church.* New York: Oxford University Press, 1947.

GARRISON, W. E. *The March of Faith.* New York: Harper & Brothers, 1933.

LATOURETTE, K. S. *A History of Christianity.* New York: Harper & Brothers, 1953.

NEWMAN, A. H. *A Manual of Church History*, I. Philadelphia: American Baptist Publication Society, 1953.

NICHOLS, JAMES H. *History of Christianity 1650–1950.* New York: Ronald Press Co., 1956.

ROBINSON, JAMES HARVEY. *Readings in European History*, II. Boston: Ginn & Co., 1904.

SWEET, WILLIAM W. *The Story of Religion in America.* New York: Harper & Brothers, 1950.

VI. PERIOD OF GENERAL
SECULARIZATION (A.D. 1789 to present)

Introduction to the Period

This has been a period of revolution. The American nation was organized under a constitution in the opening year of this period, after throwing off the political yoke of England. France entered into her revolution at the very beginning of this period, also. The Congress of Vienna (1815) endeavored to restore traditional boundaries, but revolution had not yet ceased. New nations developed both in Europe and in the Americas.

There were revolutions in other areas also. Mechanical and industrial developments created a new sort of economic and social life. Scientific advance in the twentieth century has made almost every decade a startling and challenging era.

The modern mission movement helped to inaugurate this period. Its impact in the widespread enrichment of life and general humanitarianism can never be fully computed. Many extensive humanitarian movements in England and America sprang directly from missions and the revivals of religion of this period.

This has also been a period of extensive secularization of culture. By that is meant, as one writer expresses it, the development of the "religiously neutral civilization." This situation is not altogether good or completely bad, but is essentially true. To some extent this accounts for the extensive spread of denominational Christianity. The divorcing of church and state (one aspect of this secularization) has resulted in religion by conviction rather than by coercion. The second reformation in England during the first half of the seventeenth century developed numerous types of polity and doctrine. These were transplanted to America by immigration. The older movements on the Continent also moved toward America, but the tendency has been toward diversity in organization, even in those groups following a single system of theological thought. Calvinism, for example, was organized in America piecemeal by different groups. Scottish Calvinists not only did not join Calvinists from other nations but reproduced in America many other schisms which had taken place in Scotland. English, French, Dutch,

316

Swiss, German, and Scandinavian Calvinists retained their own separate types of organization, reflecting racial and language distinctions when they moved to America. As a result, the Christianity in colonial America was amazingly complex and has continued to develop new forms in the centuries that have followed. Doubtless a reaction against undue proliferation gave impetus toward the ecumenical and church union movements which came into considerable strength in the first half of the twentieth century.

In religious thought, this period has witnessed the high mark of rationalism, followed by a reaction in an attempt to retain elements of the older supernaturalism. There have been vigorous and numerous attacks on traditional supernaturalism during the first half of the twentieth century. The ultimate effect of the accelerated attacks must await description by a later pen.

Points of Special Interest

The student should notice the recurring cycles in religious thought. Generally the pendulum swings to one extreme, depending a great deal upon historical conditioning, and then away from it. Extreme views are basically self-destructive. This fact brings some comfort in periods of uninhibited speculation and corruption.

A related observation concerns the nature of man. As a self-conscious and spiritual being, man will never be satisfied with any religious system that appeals only to his intellect. Sterile scholasticism has no more vitality in the twentieth century than it had in the second. Ofttimes it will bring spiritual reaction and revival.

The secularization of culture and politics, which has occurred not only in the West but almost universally, is not an unmixed evil. A "neutral" state and culture will remove elements of harmful influence on Christianity, eliminate Christianity as a tool of low motivations, and minimize religious coercion. It should emphasize the spiritual nature and independent worth of true Christianity.

317

Continental European Christianity

A FULL DESCRIPTION of any aspect of this last period is manifestly impossible. Progress in technological development can hardly be believed or understood, not to speak of trying to describe it. Iron, steel, aluminum, and plastics successively brought great thrusts in the manufacture of basic commodities. Coal, steam (on both land and sea), electricity, petroleum, and atomic fission have provided power for transportation, communication, illumination, warfare, and many other uses. The industrial revolution mobilized and exploited these resources. Astounding research has been made in all the sciences from anthropology to zoology. The body, the mind, and the soul have been made the subject of intense study. Every part of man and his world has come under observation.

Strong intellectual currents have accompanied this physical progress. Charles Darwin (1809–82), after first making basic assumptions in an effort to explain change and progress in human history, developed a theory of evolution based on the survival of the fittest. The projection of this theory into the areas of religion and philosophy brought considerable controversy, which has not yet ended. Karl Marx (1818–83) propounded the belief in the necessity of the ultimate victory of a "scientific socialism"—the elimination of all economic classes and the final millennium of an equalitarian society. His communistic ideas are still being tested on a large scale. Representing just a cloud on the horizon at that time, Hegel (1770–1831) idealized the state and Nietzsche (1844–

1900) the "super race," laying the foundations for the twentieth-century totalitarian movements.

The political atmosphere of the world is reflected in the history of Christianity in Europe during this period. In general, it has been a period when national states have fought for their autonomy and demanded self-expression. The German empire was founded in 1870; Italy was unified and France became a republic in the same year; China, Japan, and the Orient were opened to Western culture; South American colonies became independent republics; and all across southeastern Europe new independent states sprang up. Popular government has almost universally dethroned hereditary sovereigns. Almost all the world has been explored, and improved communication and transportation have made it much smaller.

The principal Christian groups on the Continent in this period were the Roman Catholics, the Lutherans, and the Calvinists. These will be viewed briefly during the three chronological sections into which this period falls.

The French Revolution (1789–1815)

The history of Europe is bound up with the French Revolution during the first portion of this period. In the eighteenth century there came an increasing recognition by the common people across Europe that absolutism and oppression in state and church were largely responsible for their depressed economic and social condition. The corruption and luxury in high places in church and state contrasted greatly with the want and suffering of the lower classes.

This was particularly true in France. The Roman Church owned half the land of France and were as reprehensible as the secular state in their dealings with the people. There was general resentment against the various tithes imposed by the Church, against the rigorous repression of religious dissenters, and against the nonproductive monkish orders. The arbitrary national policies and the lavish personal habits of Kings Louis XIV, XV, and XVI (from 1643 to 1793) brought France to the verge of bankruptcy.

319

In order to levy additional taxes, the king was forced to call a meeting of the Estates General, a congress made up of the clergy, the nobility, and the commons. The representatives of the common people, known as the Third Estate, seized control and by their audacity and accurate representation of the temper of the times were successful in beginning a radical reform. On September 21, 1792, France was made a Republic, and four months later the king was executed.

In a reaction against the intense opposition of the Roman Church, the new republic was erected on atheistic lines at first but gradually relaxed to permit religious worship. Napoleon Bonaparte, a French general, was victorious in defeating a coalition of other powers attempting to put down the French Revolution. In 1798 Napoleon invaded Italy and dissolved the papal state, imprisoning Pope Pius VI in Paris, where he soon died. Napoleon was crowned emperor in 1804. His victories and diplomacy changed the map of Europe. However, he was finally defeated by a coalition of powers and exiled to St. Helena Island in 1815. The Congress of Vienna (1815) endeavored to restore the world which Napoleon had disarranged. It began a period of reactionary conservatism politically and romanticism in literature and religion.

The Roman Catholic Church.—In France itself the Revolution stripped the Roman church of her property, her establishment, her tithes and papal assessments, and her monastic system. The reorganization of religious life in France in 1790 by the National Assembly in effect ignored religious differences. In the Reign of Terror of the following two years, hundreds, perhaps thousands, of faithful Roman Catholic priests were slaughtered. In the reaction after 1795, however, Catholics and others were allowed privileges of worship. In 1795 Pope Pius VI joined with European leaders to put an army in the field against France. Napoleon Bonaparte defeated the coalition, captured Rome in 1798, and imprisoned the pope in France, where he died in 1799.

In 1801 the new pope, Pius VII (1800–20), secured an agreement with Napoleon to restore the Roman Church in France under radical limitations, but Napoleon abrogated most of this by his arbitrary interpretation. In 1809 he annexed the papal state to France. When the pope protested, imprisonment followed. In 1813 he coerced the pope into signing an agreement to allow annexation, but with his Russian debacle Napoleon lost his power to coerce. The pope repudiated his signature and in 1814 restored the Jesuit order. Although the suppression of this order in 1773 had theoretically meant total abolishment, it was found to be completely organized and at almost full strength to take up the battle. Cardinal Consalvi represented the papacy at the Congress of Vienna in 1815 and was able to secure the return of all that Napoleon had taken from the Roman Church.

Lutheranism.—The French Revolution greatly affected Lutherans in the German states. War and suffering revealed that skepticism and infidelity were not sufficient to meet the needs of the human spirit, and multitudes turned again to religious faith. The old Holy Roman Empire was dissolved in 1806, stimulating the strengthening of independent states like Austria, Prussia, and Bavaria. Later in the century this contributed to the unification of the German people under the leadership of Prussia.

Calvinism.—Calvinism in Europe also felt the shock of the French Revolution. Already skepticism had weakened this group in France, Switzerland, the German states, and the Low Countries. The unsettled political conditions that continued through the Congress of Vienna in 1815 brought disorganization and uncertainty to continental Calvinism.

Reaction and Continued Conflict (1815–70)

For a decade after the Congress of Vienna the reaction against revolution and democratic movements was apparent in the diplomacy and activity of the great powers. National feelings, however, could not long be suppressed. Twice more France set off explosive nationalistic movements in 1830 and 1848 in her search for a responsive and stable government. Holland (1815), Belgium (1830), and Greece (1832) established autonomous governments, and others began their journey toward statehood.

The German states provided the key to the momentous events in the latter part of this period. The Congress of Vienna had aided in the formation of a German union (*Bund*) composed of thirty-five states, and later a North German union headed by Prussia was organized. In 1870 Prussia declared war on France, and victory brought the organization of the modern German nation. Curiously enough, during the Franco-Prussian War, the French government took the step that led to the founding of a unified Italian state. French soldiers had been employed by the papal court to protect the papal state. When Paris was being threatened in 1870, France ordered these troops home, and the Italian patriots were able to overcome Rome and unify the several sections of the peninsula.

The Roman Catholic Church.—The reaction against the excesses of the French Revolution brought great prestige to the Roman Catholic Church as a conservative and stabilizing factor. Leo XII (1821–29) was able to negotiate favorable concordats, or agreements, with most of the important nations, including Protestant states. Catholics were given complete freedom in England in the year of Leo's death, and during the entire period accessions to the Roman church from the Church of England took place.

Another characteristic of this period was the continuance of anti-Protestant outbursts from the papacy. In 1816 Pius VII denounced Bible societies as fiendish instruments to undermine religion. In May, 1824, Leo XII published similar views and called their translations the "devil's gospel." In 1826 he announced that "everyone separated from the Roman Catholic Church, however unblamable in other respects his life may be, because of this sole offense, that he is sundered from the unity of Christ, has no part in eternal life; God's wrath hangs over him." Pius VIII (1829–30) also included liberty of conscience and Bible societies among other evils. Gregory XVI (1831–46) termed religious liberty as craziness or insanity. These utterances formed the background for the sweeping "Syllabus of Errors" of Pius IX, which will be considered shortly.

In this period, also, the movement known as "ultramontanism" reached its height. The word is a geographical reference to papal domination. The restoration of the Jesuits in 1814 was a large step in that direction. The conservative reaction after the Congress of Vienna favored it also. The movement came to its height during the pontificate of Pius IX (1846–78). Singularly enough, his doctrinal victories within the Roman Church and his political defeats from the outside paired up to exalt him and the papacy to heights heretofore unattainable. His strategy in his doctrinal victory was carefully planned and well executed. Pius became pope in 1846 during a very stormy political period. In 1849, taking advantage of the widespread Catholic veneration (and in some cases actual worship) of Mary, the mother of Jesus, Pius sent communications to all Roman Catholic bishops asking them if they desired the pope to set out an authoritative pronouncement with reference to Mary, showing his own opinions by saying, "Ye know full well, venerable brethren, that the whole ground of our confidence is placed in the most holy Virgin . . . God has vested in her the plenitude of all good, so that henceforth, if there be in us any hope, if there be any grace, if there be any salvation, we must receive it solely from her, according to the will of him who would have us possess all things through Mary."

After receiving the approval of the vast majority of the bishops, on December 8, 1854, Pius defined the official dogma. It will be recalled that a canon is a church law that may be changed subsequently if circumstances warrant, but a dogma is an official declaration of truth which cannot be changed or altered and which must be believed by all the faithful as a condition of salvation. This was the first time that a dogma had been promulgated by a pope without the authority of general council. Pius claimed that this dogma was revealed by God and must be believed firmly and constantly by all the faithful. It asserted "that the most blessed Virgin Mary, in the first instant of her conception, by a singular grace and privilege of Almighty God, by the intuitive perception of the human race, was kept immune from any contamination of original sin." Mariolatry was thus brought officially one step further. The Roman tradition had successively declared her a perpetual virgin, then freed her from sin after Christ's conception, then extended that freedom from sin to her own birth, and this dogma declared her without hereditary sin. It remained for the twentieth century to proclaim her bodily assumption to heaven at death.

In 1864 Pius IX issued his "Syllabus of Errors," which summed up encyclicals of immediately previous popes and brought the list up-to-date. In addition to condemning Bible societies, public schools, and freedom of conscience, he specifically denounced separation of church and state, insisted that the Roman pontiffs and ecumenical councils have never erred in defining faith and morals, and claimed the right to use force in carrying out papal policies. The succeeding pope (Leo XIII) declared that this syllabus denouncing these so-called errors was issued under conditions of infallibility.

In 1870 what may have been the last of the ecumenical councils of the Roman Catholic Church was held. Practically every detail was arranged by Pius IX before the council convened. Despite vigorous protests by a respectable minority of bishops who refused to be coerced, the council passed four decrees. The first asserted that Simon Peter was made by Christ to be the visible head of the Church, both in honor and jurisdiction. The second identified the Roman bishop as perpetual successor of Peter, endowed with all Peter's privileges. The third claimed that the Roman pontiff has immediate and full power over all the Church throughout the world. The last one asserted that when the pope speaks ex cathedra (from the throne) in defining a doctrine concerning faith and morals to be held by the universal church, he is infallible. The statement closed with the assertion that any such definition of the pope (without a council) is irreformable.

The strategy that had occupied the thinking of Pius IX for many years had been accomplished. By shrewd diplomacy he had declared a popular teaching to have dogmatic force, without the concurrence of an ecumenical council. It prepared the way for continuing papal domination. This infallibility declaration of 1870 rendered other ecumenical councils useless. All ex-cathedra definitions of faith and morals by the Roman pope now have the force of dogmas. The statement of this infallibility is quite ambiguous, which exactly suited the purpose of the Jesuit proponents of the action. When the succeeding "infallible" pope, Leo XIII, declared the "Syllabus of Errors" of 1864 to be an ex cathedra, however, he may have placed the Roman Church in such a position that there will be continual embarrassment, particularly to American Catholics who claim to accept the doctrine of separation of church and state and some who give lip service to liberty of conscience—basic American ideals.

All of this doctrinal development occurred during a period of political revolution. The papal state had separated the northern and southern sections of the Italian peninsula for over a thousand years. Italian patriots like Victor Emmanuel and Garibaldi fervently desired to unify the entire peninsula and make Rome the secular capital of the unified nation. The papacy vigorously resisted. However, popular revolution in the peninsula had already broken out when Pius IX came to the papal throne. In an effort to placate the people, Pius granted some reforms in the papal government, but nothing less than full surrender would satisfy the patriots in the south. Between 1859 and 1866, through diplomacy and war, Victor Emmanuel was able to secure four-fifths of the papal lands, leaving only Rome and its environs in papal hands. When France was forced to withdraw her troops from Rome to defend Paris, Emmanuel overcame the remaining resistance and captured Rome, making it the national capital of a united Italy.

The Italian patriots tried to placate Pius, but he was never reconciled to the loss of temporal administration and refused to leave the Vatican which, although a defeated combatant, he was permitted to retain. He plotted for the return of the papal state until his death in 1878. Succeeding popes maintained the pretense of being a prisoner in the Vatican until 1929.

In spite of the personal humiliation in this temporal loss, the papacy was greatly forwarded by it. Many friends of true religion had urged the papacy for five hundred years to get out of temporal competition with other nations in the interest of spiritual influence and well-being. Gifts now began to pour into the coffers of the pontiff, all the machinery of the Curia was turned toward ecclesiastical advancement rather than secular administration, and relations with the various national states were greatly improved in view of the diminishing secular power of an ambitious and coercive papacy.

One interesting result of the papal declaration of infallibility was the secession from the Roman Church of a large party who denied papal infallibility, including some very able scholars. The group took the name of the Old Catholic Church and reached a membership of perhaps a hundred thousand, but it has gradually decreased in size and has never gained the popular following that many supposed it would.

Lutheranism.—The history of European Lutheranism during the heart of the nineteenth century concerns principally the movement toward church union and philosophical developments.

The desire for unity by King Frederick William III of Prussia after the desolation caused by the French Revolution led him to listen sympathetically to suggestions by Schleiermacher and other leading clergymen that some sort of church union be attempted. Union of Lutherans and Calvinists in Prussia was decreed in 1817 and met with approval of the large majority of the Prussians. By 1827 many of the German states had followed this example. The University of Wittenberg and Halle united in one institution at Halle. A vocal minority protested against this general drift, particularly among the Lutherans. Klaus Harms led what was known as the Confessional School in opposition to union with the Reformed Church, and in 1841 a number of Lutherans seceded from the state church and organized the Evangelical Lutheran Church of Prussia. Lutheranism in other parts of Europe, particularly in the Scandinavian countries, continued to be infected with rationalism.

It will be recalled that rationalism had brought skepticism and atheism to the forefront during the last period in European Christianity (from 1648 to 1789). Immanuel Kant (1724–1804), although a product of the Illumination (as rationalism was called),

modified the crass intellectualism of Wolff by limiting the area
of philosophical data to phenomena and by conceiving of man as
more than a mind. Hegel (1770–1831) turned in other directions
but, essentially, by his philosophical optimism and theory of
development gave great impetus to a mediating position. F. E. D.
Schleiermacher (1768–1834), early profoundly affected by German pietism, took a large step toward healing antagonism between
rationalism and supernaturalism by making religion an inner
experience—the consciousness of absolute dependence upon God.
His system left much to be desired for those who believed in the
objective reality of a personal, loving God but gave a certain
respectability to the general tenets of Christianity. Soren Kierke-
gaard (1813–55), the "melancholy Dane," laid the foundations
for a new theological formulation during this period, but he was
not discovered for another century.

Calvinism.—The dire effects of rationalism are seen in the
struggles of this period by the churches following the teachings of
Calvin. In Geneva itself, the birthplace of Calvinism, the "venerable company" of the clergy refused to ordain candidates in 1817
if they believed the very things which Calvin emphasized—the
deity of Christ, original sin, and predestination. The result was
a schism, the conservatives organizing free and independent congregations. This movement spread throughout the remainder of
Switzerland and beyond during the rest of this period. The leaders
of this conservative movement in the Swiss cantons were Alexan-
dre Vinet (1797–1847) and Frederic Godet (1812–1900).

French Calvinists had the same experience. Theological liberalism so prevailed in the French Reformed Church that the French
Reformed Free Church was organized in 1849 by Frederic Monrod
and Count Gasparin.

In the Netherlands a similar story may be told. Before 1834
nearly all the Reformed churches were included in the established
church. Liberalism and religious skepticism reigned. Izaak da
Costa (1798–1860), a convert from Judaism, became an evangel
of orthodox Calvinism. From 1834 on, large numbers of churches
left the established Reformed Church and joined with the con-

servative congregations, which were finally recognized in 1869 as the Christian Reformed Church. Many conservative Calvinists remained within the older establishment with the hope of leading it back. However, after half a century of struggle, these also separated from the established church and later united with the Christian Reformed group. Another party growing out of the rationalism of this period was known as the Groningen school, which placed emphasis upon love as central in religion. They were indifferent to orthodox Calvinistic doctrines.

The New Century (1870 to the present)

This final period has been marked by the rapid rise of Germany and Russia to the forefront as world powers. World War I (1914–18) grew directly from closely woven military alliances designed to maintain the balance of power. Hotheaded nationalism, ancient hatreds and rivalries, armament races, and irresponsible impulses completed the explosive picture in 1914. The spark came in a Balkan incident, and war began in the summer of 1914. Germany and her allies were finally defeated. After the war Germany became a republic for a decade. The manifest inequities of the peace treaty and the hard economic depression of the early 1930's encouraged the rise of Adolf Hitler and the national socialistic party in Germany. World War II began in September, 1939. The German coalition was defeated in 1945. The use of atomic bombs late in the war marked the beginning of a new era.

The Roman Catholic Church.—Despite the fact that World War I seriously crippled the strongest Roman Catholic continental powers, that church fared amazingly well in the conflict and appeared to be stronger in some respects after the war than before. The rise of the Nazi party under Hitler in 1933 marked the beginning of repression of the Catholics in Germany, which continued until the end of this period. At the same time, the threat of Russian communism came clearly into focus. At the very close of this period Russia enveloped many of the small Slavic border nations into her sphere of influence, in each case repressing the Roman Church in favor of the Eastern Orthodox Church.

Internally, the activity of the Roman Church may be summarized under three heads—struggle with modernism, strictures against Protestantism, and relations with secular states.

Leo XIII (1878–1903) succeeded Pius IX and was one of the ablest popes in this period. Although he is sometimes termed the "modern pope" because he displayed an interest in classical and scientific studies and permitted liberal clergymen to lead in social reform, a careful examination of his life and work shows that he continued the medieval dogmatism of his predecessors. In 1897 he set forth an encyclical censoring all books condemned before 1600, even though they might not have been included in later lists of prohibited books. Leo permitted only biblical and scientific studies that did not impugn the dogma of the Catholic Church.

Pius X (1903–14) was probably elected as a reaction to Leo. He had little appreciation of scholarship and higher education. Much of the work of Leo was virtually destroyed because of the personal and cultural hostility of Pius X. In 1907 he issued a new syllabus condemning modernism. His encyclical in the same year vigorously attacked modernism within the Roman Church. Pius advocated a return to scholastic philosophy and demanded the rejection of all who desired to study canon law except those with scholastic background. Any taint of modernism was sufficient for the rejection of a teacher in Catholic seminaries or universities and the expulsion of those already in these institutions. Bishops must attempt to prevent the publication of modernistic books and to eliminate them from the schools. All meetings of priests must be checked to see that modernism had no place. Benedict XV (1914–22) continued the fight against modernism, as have Pius XI (1922–39) and Pius XII (1939–1958).

This has been a period of continued attacks by the papacy against Protestantism. Leo XIII went out of his way to approve the Spanish Inquisition of the Medieval age, calling the flames "blessed." He praised the infamous Torquemada, the vicious leader of the Spanish Inquisition, for his "most prudent zeal and invincible virtue." In 1896 Leo denounced Anglican ordination and succession, condemning both the form and the intention. He set forth the typical Roman point of view relative to religious toleration, which asserts that when Protestants are in control of a nation, Catholics are to be tolerated according to the Protestants' general policy of religious toleration; on the other hand, when Catholics are in control, the Catholic policy of no toleration is to be followed. Pius X disapproved vigorously all Bible reading and study. His attack in 1910 on the Reformers and their followers as "enemies of the cause of Christ" aroused considerable antagonism. Benedict XV continued the papal fight against Protestantism.

Pope Leo XIII was quite successful in establishing friendly relations with some of the states. Through tactful diplomacy and laborious efforts by the Jesuits, the papacy made friends of Belgium, Spain, France, England, Russia, and the United States. His successors were not so fortunate. Under Pius X and Benedict XV severe blows were struck at Rome. In 1905 France enacted legislation separating church and state. Church property was confiscated, and all financial aid to religion was withdrawn. Revolutions in Portugal and Mexico further reduced the prestige of the pope. The blow was particularly radical in the Republic of Mexico. Their new constitution of 1917 separated church and state and confiscated church property. All Roman Catholic officials and priests were driven into exile.

It had been hoped that the Concordat of 1929 between Pius XI and the Italian government would bring peaceful relations between the parties. It will be recalled that in 1870 the Italian patriots seized Rome, the last of the papal territories outside of the few acres constituting the Vatican. Thereafter the popes refused to leave this area, calling themselves prisoners. In 1929 Mussolini agreed to pay the papacy an indemnity of $87,500,000, added a few acres to Vatican grounds, and recognized Vatican City as a free state. However, the bitterest controversy was carried on subsequently because each side was unwilling to keep the agreement. In 1946 the monarchy was overturned and a republican government was adopted. Theoretically, the Roman Church was no more favored than any other religious group, but in practice the Catholic background of the people gave the Roman Church a favorite place.

In Spain in 1931 a republic also replaced the monarchy, and the constitution provided for separation of church and state, giving hope that religious equality for all groups would be practiced. Civil war began in 1936, and in 1939 pro-Catholic General Franco became dictator. The Roman Catholic Church again became dominant as the established religion.

In France the Roman Catholic Church, the only religion of a large majority of the state, is ignored by most of its adherents and has little vitality.

Between the two wars, the Roman Church fought valiantly with the Nazis without much success.

Lutheranism.—Lutheranism in Europe has undergone severe trials in this period. Luther's reform was planted in an environment of farmers and peasants and had looked to the benevolent prince of a comparatively small state to maintain the purity and well-being of the Lutheran Church in his area. After 1870 radical changes came. The late unification of Germany into a single nation required considerable readjustment at the point of Lutheran organization and control. The rapid industrialization of Germany and the mechanical revolution also thrust upon European Lutheranism new social and economic patterns that demanded rapid, radical response. At the very time of this challenge militarism and war paralyzed or drafted Lutheran leadership. The Weimar Constitution adopted by the German Republic after World War I provided for separation of church and state, further adding to the woes of traditional Lutheranism. The vitality of Luther's movement slowly diminished in the first decades of the new century. It has been estimated that 75 per cent of the nominal Christians in Germany in the early twenties were indifferent to religion.

The rise of the Nazis in 1933 brought additional problems. Hitler's efforts to control both Lutheran and Reformed churches for the benefit of the state brought schism and conflict. Attempts were made to paganize Christianity in order to magnify racial and national factors. Hitler himself was willing to see a national church organized by a group called the Faith Movement of German Christians, but the opposition of men like Martin Niemöller, Berlin pastor, offered stiff resistance. A Confessional Synod opposing this Faith Movement was organized and included both Lutherans and Calvinists. World War II drastically curtailed all Christian work. In the Scandinavian countries Lutheranism has maintained itself as the religion of the majority.

Calvinism.—The turbulent years of two wars and an almost continuous ideological tussle in Europe added to the bitter modernist-confessional struggle within European Calvinism and sapped the vitality of the Reformed Churches on the Continent. It is true that Calvinism was better prepared by its general outlook to meet the industrial and mechanical revolutions of the new day than was Lutheranism. The disestablishment of the Roman Church in France in 1905 also aided Calvinism in its struggle. The same blows that shocked Lutheranism fell upon Calvinism. General disestablishment occurred in the cantons of Switzerland, partly because of Roman Catholic influx, mainly because of indifference.

From Switzerland, however, at the close of World War I came a strong protest against theological liberalism. Karl Barth (1886–   ), pastor of a small Reformed church in Switzerland, deeply moved by the violence of a world at war, formulated a theological system which has sometimes been called the theology of crisis because it interpreted contemporary problems and world convulsions as stemming from man's confidence in himself and consequent neglect of God's will; sometimes called dialectical theology, which refers to man's total inability to search out God and the necessity of allowing God through his sovereign grace to speak to man; and sometimes called neo-orthodoxy, which relates the movement to earlier Christian orthodoxy. Barth magnified God's sovereignty as transcendent and man's sin as overwhelming. Although Barth's system had elements unacceptable to many traditional supernaturalists, it was in marked contrast with the arrogant rationalism of a previous generation and has been greatly influential in contemporary theology.

Concluding Summary

The last period has been one of almost constant war and political revolution on the Continent. The Roman Catholic Church has been hit hard in what has been traditionally the area of its greatest strength. Indifference and secularism have been greater enemies of Rome than has modernism.

The tumultuous events of the period have rained heavy blows upon continental Protestantism. Internal decay because of widespread rationalism had more to do with the loss of vitality than have the frequent wars. Neo-orthodoxy, a reaction against humanistic optimism and aggressive theological rationalism, has provided the starting point for new theological formulations of various sorts.

English Christianity

THE NINETEENTH CENTURY belonged to England. Just as France became mistress of the Continent after the Thirty Years' War because of the severe losses of the other combatants, so England vaulted into leadership when France was overwhelmed in the backwash of her Revolution at the turn of the century. Queen Victoria (1837–1900), continuing a Hanoverian tradition for longevity, provided the setting for England's rise to world domination in the nineteenth century. No small part of this achievement was made possible because of the ability of England to profit from history.

The lessons of her own "Bloodless Revolution," the American Revolution (when one of her colonies secured political independence), and the French Revolution (when revolt against a nonrepresentative government occurred) were not wasted upon England. A program to bring increased responsiveness to the voice of the people was begun. In 1832 a sweeping Reform Bill was passed, one of the provisions of which was to increase greatly the number who could vote. The Second Reform Act of 1867 doubled the number of voters, while legislation in 1918 and 1928 brought almost total suffrage to the people. The policy of home rule for colonial possessions was established, Canada in 1867 receiving practically independent status in all domestic affairs; while other colonies moved in that direction. Exceptions to this liberal treatment were Ireland and India.

The twentieth century brought serious problems to the empire. The very areas not granted a measure of independence took matters into their own hands. India and adjacent colonies took large strides toward complete independence. Most of Ireland withdrew from the empire and by 1949 became completely separated. An imperial mercantile policy providing abundant and lush fruits was no longer feasible. Two expensive world wars brought heavy and varied burdens to the people and the nation.

Survey of Principal Religious Events

There were four extensive religious movements that affected England during this period.

Modern foreign mission movement.—The momentous victory of England over France in 1763 sent explorers scurrying to find new shores touched by the ocean now controlled by England—men like Commodore Bryon, Captain Wallis, and Captain Cook between 1764 and 1768. The field preaching of Wesley and Whitefield had to some extent divorced the gospel from buildings and had stirred the hearts of Christian people to compassion for those without salvation. Men like David Brainerd in America were seeking out the Indians for Christ. It remained for William Carey, a young Baptist cobbler, to inaugurate and exemplify the modern foreign mission movement. A Baptist society for foreign missions was formed in 1792. Carey and others were sent to India. Inspired by Carey, English independents and the Church of England organized foreign missionary societies. In the next two centuries almost every section of the inhabited world received missionaries from all parts of English Christianity.

Religious revival and humanitarian movements.—The fires of revival, diminished during the wars with the American colonies and with France, burned brightly for a brief time after the defeat of Napoleon in 1814. The ending of several exhausting wars with the peril of imminent invasion was marked by a genuine recognition of divine blessings. As was true a century before, a revival in the United States preceded the spiritual emphasis in Britain. As a matter of fact, the extent and effects of the revival in America in the opening years of the nineteenth century were far greater than were evident in England. Again after 1859 revival took place in all of Britain, receiving impetus with the preaching of Dwight L.

Moody more than a decade later and the influential ministry of Charles Haddon Spurgeon in London.

Along with this religious sensitiveness—perhaps occasioned by it—were a number of moral and humanitarian reforms. The large increase in the number of those in denominations other than the established Church of England, along with the general democratization of legislative processes in England and the enlargement of franchise, guaranteed that existing religious disabilities upon dissenters could not continue. By the 1860's the battle was almost entirely won, as one by one most of the radical discriminations were either eliminated or minimized. The unjust penal laws were slowly replaced, and the treatment and housing of prisoners were greatly improved. Slavery was abolished in 1833. Legislation curbed abuses in the factory system involving the long hours of women and children. The nation accepted additional responsibility for the education of its children and youth. A new sensitiveness to the public good brought legislation for various types of aid to the common welfare—police, cheap postage, public health, commerce and navigation, etc. The twentieth century brought the increasing consciousness of governmental responsibility for the citizens in the problems beyond the local level.

Skepticism and materialism.— The Wesleyan revival in the previous period turned the hearts of the masses from infidelity and skepticism, but a strong core of antisupernaturalism was never touched in this or later revivals. Several factors in the nineteenth century helped to swell the ranks of this group. One was the development of an articulate Socinian movement, appealing mainly to the intellectual classes and magnifying the Christian ethic as the principal contribution of the Christian Scriptures. Both in England and in America the development of organizational structure brought new adherents, particularly in the upper strata of society. Furthermore, in this period continental philosophers made radical attacks upon the Scriptures. The tendency to expurgate, negate, or modify Christian revelation, evident in the work of men like David Strauss (1808–74) and Julius Wellhausen (1844–1918), undercut the faith of some who had not been firmly moored.

Another factor inducing skepticism was the evolutionary hypothesis proposed by Charles Darwin (1809–82) in 1859. His ideas, ofttimes misinterpreted and misapplied, were enlarged from a theory based upon observation of biological phenomena to encompass social, ethical, and metaphysical pronouncements. Such projections of his theory were thought to undermine the possibility of a divine revelation (particularly one handed down from a less advanced state of society) and to minimize the need for divine creative activity and providential supervision.

Still another subversive factor could be termed "sciencism." Technological developments buttressed the older materialism and brought to many folk a blind sort of faith in the dynamic nature of human progress and ingenuity. The trying days of adjustment between wars, severe economic depression, the great human loss and physical destruction of war itself, the immediate social problems involved in wartime morality and displaced persons, and a thousand other stresses as well turned the thoughts of England away from spiritual things. There have been unmistakable evidences of religious decline in the present century. Financial support has decreased, church attendance has been quite poor, and except for the Roman Catholics, it has been difficult for the various religious denominations to find candidates for the ministry.

Ecumenicalism.—English Christianity as a whole has entered heartily into the ecumenical (universal) movement. To some extent, ecumenicalism rooted in the burst of enthusiasm for world missions that followed the inception of the modern mission movement by William Carey. The London Missionary Society of 1795 was made up of members from the Church of England, Scottish Presbyterians, Methodists, and independents. The British and Foreign Bible Society of 1804 was interdenominational; so were many other co-operative efforts in Britain, America, and on the mission fields during that century. Perhaps the principal antecedent of the movement was the formation of the World's Evangelical Alliance in London in 1846 after a preliminary meeting in 1845. The purpose of this body primarily was to promote unity rather than to carry on some immediate joint task. Subsequent conferences were held in Britain, on the Continent, and in the United States. In addition, interdenominational movements among young Christians increased the influence of the movement, including such organizations as the Young Men's Christian Association, begun in London in 1884, and other bodies both in Britain and in the United States.

The immediate antecedents of the modern movement were found in the interdenominational missionary conferences. Foreign missionaries, wrestling with mutual problems, met together in conference, sometimes official, sometimes unofficial. Well-known conferences were held in London in 1854, in Liverpool in 1860, and various parts of England intermittently until the turn of the century. Almost all denominations, other than the Roman Catholics, took some part in this movement.

A large forward step in the movement was the meeting in 1910 at Edinburgh, in which for the first time a conference composed of officially delegated representatives from mission boards and societies was held. The general motif was a united Christendom, and a Continuation Committee insured further conferences. Other conferences were held at Stockholm (1925), Amsterdam (1948), and Evanston (1954). The World Council of Churches was constituted at the 1948 meeting.

Survey of Principal Christian Bodies

The remainder of this chapter will be devoted to a brief survey of each of the principal Christian bodies in England during this period in the light of the general background.

The Church of England.—The Church of England in the modern period has been consistently missionary-minded. After the modern mission movement was begun by the Baptists, the London Missionary Society, formed in 1795, contained many Anglicans, while the Church Missionary Society in 1799 was made up solely of Anglicans. Anglicans also were a part of the Religious Tract Society of 1799 and the British and Foreign Bible Society in 1804.

It could be expected that the Anglican leadership, particularly

338

those who favored the sacramentalism inherited from the Roman Catholic Church, would look with disfavor upon the sweeping evangelical revivals of the eighteenth century and the increasing strength of evangelicals within the established church. The progressive growth of the dissenters and the removal of religious disabilities against them, together with the developing co-operation between evangelicals within the Anglican Church and the dissenters, was of grave concern to the older party. This general background, along with the skeptical intellectual currents sweeping across England in the nineteenth century, led to the development of three distinct parties within the Church of England.

One group of churchmen within the Church of England favored the doctrines of the Roman Catholic Church but allowed the English sovereign to be head of the Church instead of the pope at Rome. They were strict sacramentalists, desiring the retention of monks and nuns, emphasizing the vital nature of apostolic succession, and insisting upon the establishment of the Church within the English state. The success and increase of dissenters aroused them to feverish activity. They began in 1833 the publication of a series of *Tracts for the Times* covering church history and doctrine. The most important tract was the last one, written in 1841 by John Henry Newman (1801–90), attempting to show that the Thirty-nine Articles of the Church of England, heretofore considered as the most Protestant portion of the Anglican system, could actually be interpreted in a Roman Catholic sense.

Newman also favored other elements of the Roman Catholic system and in 1845 was received into the Roman Catholic Church. Many others of this party followed him. After his departure the leadership of the High Church party was assumed by E. B. Pusey (1800–82). In general, the High Church movement has Romanized many aspects of Anglican liturgical and devotional life. Monastic life for men and women has been encouraged. Auricular confession has been introduced. The High Church party received a blow in 1896 when the bishop of Rome declared that all Anglican episcopal succession was invalid. Nevertheless, the party has maintained a strong position in the Anglican Church.

The evangelicals in the Church of England have been termed the Low Church group. Many evangelicals left the Church of England with the Methodist movement, but the Gorham case proved that evangelicalism still may exist within the Anglican Church. In 1847 a High Church bishop refused to install G. C. Gorham, an evangelical in doctrine, because of Gorham's views. The case was taken to court, where the final decision favored Gorham, determining that evangelicalism had legal standing within the Anglican communion.

The Broad Church party favored the widest possible flexibility in the doctrinal and ecclesiastical standards of Anglicanism. This party has also secured legal standing in Anglicanism. In 1860 a collection of seven somewhat radical essays by liberal Anglican clergymen aroused the orthodox viewers, and two of the authors were tried for heresy in ecclesiastical courts. They were finally acquitted. The case revealed that the utmost freedom would be allowed in theological thinking and writing within the Anglican Church, outward conformity to the Thirty-nine Articles and the prayer book being the principal requirement.

The Church of England has been quite active in the ecumenical movement. It has looked upon itself as being the halfway station between Roman Catholicism and Protestantism and has felt that in such a position it would be the ideal place and pattern for reunion for all Christendom. The Lambeth Conferences—a world meeting of all bishops of the Anglican communion which has met in London about every ten years since 1867—explored the possibilities of union with others. In 1888 it approved four items which it considered minimal for union, as follows: the Old and New Testaments as the rule and standard of faith; the Apostles' Creed and the Nicene Creed as the doctrinal statements of faith; the observance of the two sacraments of baptism and the Lord's Supper; and the historic episcopate to preserve the continuing unity of the church. The Anglican Church has looked toward closer union with all Christian groups—Protestants, the Eastern Orthodox Church, and even the Roman Catholic Church. That the four items set out in 1881, known as the Lambeth Quadrilateral, were the very minimum is evident from the fact that when local groups attempted to establish union in South Africa in 1913, in Canada in 1925, and in South India in 1947, the Church of England stood aloof because the proper episcopal ordination was not uniformly secured.

The Church of England was greatly hurt by the two world wars that occurred in the first half of the twentieth century, accompanied as they were by a period of secularism and economic depression. There was a marked decrease in vitality and influence, the number of candidates for the ministry declined radically, church attendance and religious interest were curtailed sharply by war activities and weariness, and there was a continuation of skeptical literature and secular thinking.

In some measure this decline, along with the depleted resources of the nation and parliamentary disapproval of the revised prayer book in 1927 and 1928, brought demands both from within and without the Church of England that the church be disestablished. Those within felt that the vast endowments of the church, accumulated over four centuries, could probably provide for the financial needs of a disestablished church. However, others felt that disestablishment would soon be followed by disendowment. The High Church party, in particular, has opposed any plan for disestablishment.

In Wales the Church of England was established at the opening of this period, although a large majority of the people were dissenters. A series of revivals, particularly among the dissenting group but also entered into by the established churches of Wales, helped dissipate the lethargic and disinterested situation at the opening of the period. The Anglican establishment ended in Wales in 1920.

Until 1949 all of Ireland was a part of England. The parliament of Ireland had been dissolved in 1800, and representatives were given seats in the English body. The Church of England was established as the state church in Ireland for a small minority, despite protests by a large Roman Catholic majority and a vigorous Presbyterian minority in Ulster County. However, the Roman

Catholic Emancipation Act of 1829 removed many disabilities from the majority, and in 1868 the Anglican Church of Ireland was disestablished.

Australia was first colonized when Great Britain made it a penal colony in 1787. The outstanding name in the formative years was Samuel Marsden, chaplain of the Church of England from 1793 until his death in 1838. Through his efforts Christianity was forwarded not only in Australia but in New Zealand and the other Pacific islands as well. The large British immigration began in the first quarter of the nineteenth century, the majority being the Church of England adherents, while Irish Catholics, Scotch-Irish Presbyterians, and English Methodists formed most of the remainder.

New Zealand was about a decade behind Australia in colonization. Samuel Marsden took the lead here also in calling for an active missionary program. The English immigration came about 1840 and was principally Anglican.

Canada's history, predominantly French until 1763, then English, is reflected in her Christianity. That story will be briefly sketched in the chapter on American Christianity.

India and other colonies of England during this period were the recipients of much labor from the many missionary societies of Britain.

The Roman Catholic Church in England.—At the opening of this period there were severe disabilities against the Roman Catholics in England. They were unorganized on the higher level and not numerous. In 1829, however, the Roman Catholic Emancipation Act removed many of the civil disabilities. In 1850 the pope restored the hierarchy in England with the appointment of an archbishop of Westminster. This created quite a furor among those who feared the Roman Catholic movement.

The failure of the potato crop in Ireland shortly before the middle of the nineteenth century caused many of the Roman Catholic peasants of Ireland to emigrate to England, greatly swelling the number of that group there. Some joined the Roman Church from the Tractarian movement, while others emigrated from the Continent. As a result, the familiar institutions of Romanism soon appeared throughout England, Scotland, and Wales—churches, schools, monastic orders for both men and women. The large Irish Roman Catholic immigration provided an increasing number of that faith in England during the first half of the twentieth century, increasing the Roman Catholic population to about two and a half million. This group has grown more rapidly and withstood loss of vitality better than any other English denomination. The new nation of Eire, wrenched loose from the remainder of Ireland to become a republic in 1949, is predominantly Catholic.

English Calvinism.—Presbyterianism, so active in England during the Cromwellian period and shortly thereafter, practically disappeared after the Restoration, some falling into Unitarianism and others joining the Congregational movement. In the next century the only Presbyterians in England were the small congregations of Scottish Presbyterians who retained ties with their home base. These slowly increased during the nineteenth century and in 1876 organized the Presbyterian Church of England. By the first quarter of the twentieth century this group numbered almost 85,000.

Irish Presbyterians settled in northern Ireland in the opening years of the seventeenth century. When the Protestants William and Mary came to the English throne in 1688, the hard lot of the Presbyterian minority in Ireland was improved. By 1691, through subsidies provided by the English government, large numbers settled in Ulster County. Immigrants from these Scotch-Irish Presbyterians played a very important part in the rise of American Presbyterianism. In the opening years of this period Irish Presbyterians were struggling with the Unitarian views current in England at the time and finally triumphed. In 1860 the General Assembly of the Presbyterian Church in Ireland was formed. The disestablishment of the Anglican Church in 1868 gave impetus to the Presbyterians in Ireland, along with the fresh spiritual awakening about that time. Missions and education advanced, and the twentieth century found them numbering over one hundred thousand, although they suffered from the two wars and religious skepticism.

In the twentieth century efforts have been made to unite English Presbyterians with English Congregationalists.

Presbyterianism was the established church in Scotland at the beginning of the period. Scottish Presbyterians were not greatly influenced by the evangelical revival of the eighteenth century, perhaps a reaction against the Arminian doctrines of Wesley. A genuine spiritual awakening did occur, however, in the opening years of the nineteenth century, spearheaded by the Haldane brothers. This new spiritual life agitated an old problem, the question of secular control as seen in lay patronage. Do noble and wealthy patrons in a community have the right to name the minister of the church there? Doughty Scots had twice opposed this, bringing schisms in 1733 and 1760.

The nineteenth century movement was led by Thomas Chalmers (1780–1847). The General Assembly of the Church of Scotland took the side of the churches, declaring in 1834 that no pastor should be forced upon an unwilling congregation. In 1842 the matter reached the English House of Lords, who decided that a church must take a minister appointed by a patron, whether to their liking or not. In the following year, in an act of drama and sacrifice, nearly half the Presbyterians of Scotland left the salaries and buildings of the Church of Scotland in protest against lay patronage and formed the Free Church of Scotland. Most of these groups seceding over lay patronage came together by 1900 under the name United Free Church of Scotland, and in 1929 this body united with the established church again, the principle of lay patronage being eliminated.

Presbyterianism was carried to Australia and New Zealand in the wave of English immigration in the 1820's. Although fewer in number than the Anglicans and the Roman Catholics, they have considerable influence. The Canadian story will be told in connection with American Christianity.

English Congregationalism in this period was closely related to Presbyterianism, receiving many of its members and influencing the thinking of those who did not make the change. The Congregational movement was greatly blessed by the Wesleyan awakening in the eighteenth century, as well as by the modern mission movement and the brief revival after the Napoleonic wars. One evidence of the increased vitality in the early nineteenth century, in addition to growth in constituency and churches, was the development of a vigorous interchurch fellowship. First came the county unions, principally inspired by the challenge of home missions. In 1832 the Congregational Union of England and Wales was formed. By the present century English, Welsh, and Scottish Congregationalism, numbering perhaps half a million in 1928, carried on a vigorous program of education and other benevolences, although two wars and depression have taken their toll.

English Methodists.—English Methodism grew more rapidly than any other of the dissenting groups during this period, at the same time having considerable difficulty because of the great number of schisms. After the death of John Wesley in 1791, Methodism quickly separated from the Anglican Church. The rigid ecclesiastical organization and discipline of English Methodism brought a number of protests. The great leaders after Wesley were Thomas Coke (1747–1814), Jabez Bunting (1779–1858), and the contemporary John Scott Lidgett. The movement, of course, had an original divergence, one group becoming Calvinistic and the other Arminian. The latter became the dominant group. Among this group came schisms in 1797 over lay representation (the Methodist New Connection), in 1810 over camp meeting methods (Primitive Methodist Connection), in 1815 over zealous evangelism (the Bible Christians), and in 1828 over music (Wesleyan Protestant Methodists). By 1907, however, the organization of the United Methodist Church brought several of these together, and in 1932 most of England's Methodists, totaling over a million, united into one body. Methodists in New Zealand in the third decade of this century numbered near 30,000 and in Australia about 166,000. English Methodists also were dealt hard blows by two wars and the accompanying spiritual decline.

English Baptists.—This final period in church history is marked off in part by the English Baptists as they began the modern foreign mission movement. The Wesleyan revival brought new life into English Baptists. General Baptists benefited greatly by the work of Dan Taylor, founder of the New Connection of General Baptists. Particular Baptists were inspired to begin the modern mission movement. William Carey, a journeyman cobbler, became a Baptist in 1783. Unschooled, he became well educated through private application, mastering Hebrew, Greek, Latin, and Dutch in his spare hours. With the help of Andrew Fuller, John Sutcliffe, Samuel Pearce, and John Ryland, Jr., Carey organized a Baptist missionary society in London in 1792. In the following year Carey went to India as a missionary and with his companions translated the Bible into eighteen languages and published tracts in twenty tongues in nineteen years. In addition, more than seven hundred converts had been baptized and a dozen nationals had surrendered for the Christian ministry.

English Baptist work, both home and foreign, grew rapidly under the inspiration of this example. Schools were founded, and various social reforms were entered into in co-operation with other Christians. Preachers like Robert Hall (1764–1831), Charles Haddon Spurgeon (1834–92), Alexander Maclaren (1825–1910), John Clifford (1836–1923), and John H. Shakespeare (1857–1928) gave new respectability to the Baptist cause. In 1891 the division between General and Particular Baptists which had existed from the beginning of English Baptist life was healed, principally through the work of John Clifford. In 1953 there were 202,361 Baptists in England proper, about 100,000 in Wales, 20,000 in Scotland, and 5,000 in Ireland. Skepticism and two wars have slain their thousands among English Baptists in the twentieth century.

In the dominions, with the possible exception of Canada, Baptist work has been fed principally from England. Australian Baptists number over 30,000, New Zealand Baptists number about 11,000, while Canadian Baptists total almost 150,000.

Other Groups

There are many other smaller groups in England which cannot be discussed, although some of them have made vital and enduring contributions by their distinctive views.

Concluding Summary

In the opening years of this period, English Baptists inaugurated what has been termed the modern mission movement. During the nineteenth century practically all denominations in England carried on foreign mission programs in almost every part of the world. Skepticism and secularism have made large gains in England in the last two centuries, however, and the general picture is one of religious decline and lowered vitality. During the last century the ecumenical movement has gained favor with a large majority of English denominations. The Church of England has defined the four minimal points for church union, and it is apparent from developments in various parts of the world that each of these points is counted significant.

The churches and the Christian faith in England, along with the remainder of the nation, have suffered greatly from the two world wars in which England has been a principal combatant.

American Christianity

CHRISTIANITY IN THE United States during the modern period has had phenomenal growth. The tremendous expansion of the country in extent and population partly accounts for this. In 1789 the territory of the United States was confined to the area of what is now east of the Mississippi and north of Florida (which included a strip of land across the Gulf coast to the Mississippi). By means of purchase, annexation, and war the remainder of the present nation was added—the vast area west of the Mississippi known as Louisiana in 1803; Florida in 1819; Texas in 1847; the Oregon-Washington area in 1848; California, Arizona, and New Mexico by the Mexican Cession of 1848; Alaska in 1867; and in 1898 the several insular areas of the Philippine Islands, Guam, Puerto Rico, Hawaiian Islands, Samoa Islands, and Wake Island. The American population in 1790 was about four million, in 1880 about fifty million, about 1915 it neared one hundred million, and by 1957 it reached almost a hundred and seventy million.

During this time the principal occupation of the nation changed from agriculture to commerce and industry. Large cities and a highly industrialized society have altered the complexion of daily life. Unbelievable advance in technology and mass production have brought wealth with its accompanying social and economic problems. The organization of labor and extensive governmental supervision have brought checks and balances to unlimited industrial empire. The impressive contributions of the United States to World Wars I and II have brought her to a place of world leadership.

During these years as a nation the environment in America

has been peculiarly suited to the religious development of the people. A number of important factors mark the religious history from 1789 to the present. They are listed in approximately the chronological order in which they occurred.

Factors in American Religious History

Relation of church and state in the United States.—Some have judged that the greatest contribution of the United States to the science of government has been her development of the separation of church and state. It will be remembered that through the centuries the Roman Catholic Church maintained her strength and molded her system through the aid of the secular powers. It was only through the help of the state that Rome could enforce uniformity, repress heresy, and spread her system. Lutheranism, Calvinism, Zwinglianism, and Anglicanism were not averse to accepting aid from the state. In America it appeared that perhaps the government might find itself in the same dilemma of religious establishment. New Hampshire, Massachusetts, and Connecticut had Congregationalism established by law at the time of the American Revolution, while Maryland and Virginia had the Church of England so established.

The national pattern in relation to religion, however, followed none of these states but rather the system of Rhode Island—separation of church and state, much despised when first set up, but constantly winning adherents. For one thing, the American Revolution undercut the establishments of the Anglican Church on patriotic grounds, for it was not then known that the American followers of this system would set up an independent and national episcopal body. Furthermore, in the very area where this establishment was involved the strength of dissent was considerable, especially among the Baptists, Presbyterians, and Methodists. The democratic nature of the Great Awakening had deeply impressed the population, and these revivals were still occurring in Virginia and nearby states. The New World had been sought as a haven from religious persecution, and the spirit of democracy of the frontier and religious revivals resisted a national establishment.

In addition, at this very time the educated class was drinking deeply from cups of French philosophical and political liberalism. Democracy and liberty were large words. The dignity of the common man demanded respect and recognition. The unquestioned corruption and malignity of the Roman Catholic religion in France, which had fastened itself to the state and was slowly sapping its life, brought to American skeptical intellectuals in key political places additional reasons why there should be no religious establishment. The Revolution of 1776 itself was in the vanguard of religious liberty. The casting off of monarchy and the surge of democracy was the triumph of the theology of dissenters who in the revivals of the past generation had seen the spirit of God move freely among all people.

The victory of religious liberty began in Virginia. Here amidst stringent disabilities imposed by the established Church of England, the Baptists, strongly aided by the Presbyterians and the Methodists, began an active program to throw off the establishment. This was accomplished by 1787 through the political aid of James Madison. In addition, the new Constitution was approved by Virginians, with the understanding that there would be added immediately a bill of rights guaranteeing religious liberty. This promise was carried out, and the first of the rights protected the infant nation from the evils of an established church. It was, of course, a matter for the states to reflect this same spirit by eliminating establishments. The last of these, New Hampshire, Connecticut, and Massachusetts eliminated support of Congregationalism in 1817, 1818, and 1833 respectively, principally through the efforts of John Leland, a Baptist. To the present day there are still problems involved in the separation of church and state, but the continued stability of the American nation itself is wrapped up with the preservation of this principle.

Early infidelity and skepticism.—During the American Revolution and immediately thereafter, most of the colonies experienced a wave of infidelity. Part of the reason was the bitterness and cynicism that war always brings. Both the French and Indian War (1756–63) and the Revolutionary War (1775–83) had brought widespread suffering and moral decline. Close contact with English intellectual currents ᵇbefore the Revolutionary War and with France during that war had brought considerable amounts of their skepticism and infidelity to American shores. The anti-Christian writings of Voltaire (1694–1778) in France and Thomas Paine (1737–1809) in America were widely read and approved.

At the close of the Revolution it has been estimated that less than 10 per cent of the American population were professing Christians. The various "Christian" schools were filled with unbelievers and atheists. Only two of Princeton's student body professed to be Christians in 1782, and the other schools were quite as bad. Rationalistic and atheistic societies flourished. This was not so completely true in the lower South, where revivals of religion had continued from the days of the first Great Awakening (1739). The second Great Awakening in the opening years of the nineteenth century turned America again toward faith. Christians began to multiply much more rapidly than the population. While perhaps only about 275,000 out of 3,929,214 were Christians in 1790, over 83,000,000 were professed Christians out of a population of over 165,000,000 in 1956.

The second Great Awakening.—In New England, probably the area of greatest spiritual need, a second Great Awakening occurred in the opening years of the nineteenth century. It was quite different from the first Awakening of half a century before. There was less emotional excitement and less immediate controversy over methods of revival. Single outstanding leaders were fewer, and the power of the revival was channeled into benevolent objects. Because of it, practically all denominations were aroused to the importance of spreading the gospel, both at home and abroad. Increased efforts were made to Christianize the Indians, and plans were made for sending the gospel to the ever-receding frontier to the west. The Congregationalists organized the American Board of Commissioners in 1810 to carry on foreign mission work. Baptists developed the General Missionary Convention of the Baptist Denomination in the United States of America for Foreign Missions in 1814.

351

The American Bible Society was formed in 1816 on an inter-denominational basis, as were also the American Sunday School Union in 1824 and the American Home Mission Society in 1826. Baptists formed their Tract Society in 1824, one year before the interdenominational American Tract Society. Baptists also formed their Home Mission Society in 1832. The inspiration for the founding of these various benevolent societies doubtless sprang principally from the spiritual revival at the turn of the century. It is also true that the growing sentiment both in the North and in the South in favor of the abolition of slavery was accelerated by these revivals, especially those of Charles G. Finney.

Meanwhile, a revival of a different sort was experienced west of the Alleghenies in Tennessee and Kentucky about the same time. All denominations seem to have engaged in it, although the initial movement developed under the leadership of the Presbyterian, James McGready of Kentucky. In this revival the camp meeting became popular. Settlers drove from miles around to make camp in some central area. Ministers of different denominations preached at the same time at various parts of the campgrounds to crowds as large as their voices could reach. Great emotional and physical excitement were evident in the meetings. Shouting and weeping alternated with barking, shaking, running, crawling on all fours, and in some cases, the appearance of complete loss of consciousness. As a direct result of this revival, the Presbyterians refused to countenance the action of one of their presbyteries in ordaining new men for evangelistic work without the proper prerequisites, and a schism took place, resulting in the Cumberland Presbyterian Church. In general, the revival added great numbers to the churches in Kentucky and Tennessee, and practically all of the frontier denominations profited from renewed spiritual interest.

Flood of immigration.—One of the important factors in the religious history of the United States was the gigantic tide of immigration that flowed into the country. It brought repercussions in many directions. The religious characteristics of the immigrants gave color to American Christianity; the holding of these immigrants constituted a vast challenge to the religious denominations

THE DEVELOPMENT OF THE AMERICAN NATION

THIRTEEN COLONIES
AND
WESTERN LANDS
1776

FLORIDA 1819

From Spain 1795

From Spain
1810-13

●●● line indicates the frontier of about 1740

LOUISIANA PURCHASE
(FROM FRANCE)
1803

TEXAS 1845

Disputed 1845-48

OREGON
TERRITORY
1846

MEXICAN CESSION
1848

Gadsden Purchase
1853

to which they belonged; large communities from a single nation greatly influenced others in the immediate area; the large accessions to those denominations in America to which the immigrants belonged brought them not only immediate problems but also a rapid increase in wealth and prestige; and when large numbers of immigrants landed and settled near the coast, the settlers in communities along the seaboard were influenced to move to the west where there was more room.

The number of immigrants was accelerated by many factors. The westward migration after the Louisiana Purchase in 1803 and the return of peace in 1815 brought immediate demands for laborers along the coast, especially for the extensive programs of building railroads, canals, and roads. Unrest, famine, and economic crises in various countries abroad served to drive many to American shores. The American Revolution and the War of 1812 discouraged immigration in the opening decades of the nineteenth century. By 1820, however, the immigrants began arriving at the rate of over 9,000 a year; between 1825 and 1835 they averaged over 30,000 a year; in the following ten years they averaged 70,000 a year; while between 1845 and 1885 almost 12,000,000 immigrants flooded the country, about 25,000 a month for forty years.

In the first half of the century the largest number of immigrants came from Ireland, where the failure of the potato crop in the 1840's brought virtual famine to millions. It is estimated that nearly two million of the Irish emigrated to America, practically all of them avid Roman Catholics. Not quite as many Germans made the journey, while a smaller number came from practically all the countries of southern Europe, also strongly Roman Catholic. This avalanche of immigrants greatly influenced the history of the several denominations in America.

Westward expansion and war.—The American frontier, an outgrowth of a great new continent of virgin land slowly becoming settled, had an unbelievably significant place in the religious life of the nation. It shaped the economy to one of plenty rather than of scarcity in the ownership of land. European land space had been exhausted or pre-empted for centuries, and land meant stability and wealth. In the virgin country the presence of a constantly expanding frontier gave every man a sense of financial independence and of worth. It provided a fluid society, for a person could move to the frontier for any reason or for no reason. It stimulated new immigration by pulling manpower, particularly the marginal laborer or unskilled worker, to the opportunities of the virgin country. It encouraged a democratic spirit inasmuch as every man must stand on his own worth in the harsh and rigorous areas of frontier life. It gave encouragement to those denominations of Christians which magnified democracy in church life—the Baptists, Methodists, and similar bodies. The rough, and many times immoral, frontier life challenged the Christian denominations in the older communities of the east to send missionaries to the frontier to encourage Christians and to win the lost. The camp meeting type of revival was developed for the preaching of the gospel to large numbers.

Another aspect of the importance of the frontier and the west concerned the political effect of newly settled states. The avalanche of westward emigration that brought a constant projection of the frontier line resulted in the settling of new states. One of the crushing problems of the new nation concerned Negro slavery, introduced in 1619 to the Virginia colony, impressed upon them by England against their protest, spread through the South by Northern importation and financing, and gradually embraced by the South through the devastating choice of a one-crop economic system. A climatic and geographic determinism limited Negro slavery almost wholly to the South in a feudal and anachronistic system. Without doubt the institution would have crumbled of its own weight, because it was economically unsound as well as morally wrong. It became a political issue, since those states denominated as "slave states" usually formed a united coalition. Had the older states remained as the sole members of the national union, the slave question would not have become politically explosive, but the question of state rights and sectional jealousies, combined with differences in the interpretation of the meaning of the Constitution, were sparked into conflict by the spread of slavery.

Many of the denominations divided over the slavery question. War came in 1861 and brought sorrow and loss to every part of the nation. The Union victory in 1865 assured the unity of the nation politically and sounded the death knell to American Negro slavery. Troops were stationed throughout the South until 1878, adding to the bitterness engendered by the war. The schisms caused by this issue in some of the denominations have not been healed to the present time.

New denominations.—It is not possible, of course, to sketch the entire story of American Christianity in a brief summary of this sort. The surge of freedom of choice in the area of religion brought a rich and uninhibited variety to denominations in America. Several of the more important are mentioned here.

Thomas Campbell and his son Alexander were a part of a widespread movement which desired to restore primitive Christianity by eliminating all creeds and denominational organization. Doubtless, the two received strong impressions in this direction by their contacts with Scottish Christianity, and especially with Greville Ewing, John Glas, and Robert Sandeman. Practically every distinctive doctrine of the movement was patterned after the Scottish practices. In America both of the Campbells left Presbyterian ranks and in 1812 joined the Baptist fellowship. About 1830 Alexander Campbell and his group left the Baptists, differing from them in several particulars, and took the name "Disciples of Christ." Campbell taught that baptism completes salvation, observed the Supper each week, and frowned upon any distinction between ministers and people, as seen in such titles as "clergy" and "laity." Walter Scott of Ohio and Barton W. Stone of Kentucky joined with Campbell in this "restoration" movement and greatly aided in its growth. Instead of eliminating denominational movements, Campbell began a new one, which slowly developed the characteristics of other denominations. Its total membership in 1956 was 1,897,736 in 7,951 churches. The conservative Church of Christ movement stems from Campbell also. In 1956 its membership was shown as 1,600,000 in 16,500 churches.

The Church of Jesus Christ of Latter-day Saints was founded in

1830 by Joseph Smith, who reported seeing celestial visions and receiving the *Book of Mormon* on gold plates. The westward trek in 1847 and the founding of Salt Lake City is a dramatic epic of American history. The portion of the movement which settled at Independence, Missouri, took the name of the Reorganized Church of the Latter-day Saints and now numbers 137,856 members in 808 churches. The Utah branch has spread and is quite active in propagating their tenets. Because of their belief in the continuation of prophetic gifts through their president and the sacred nature of the *Book of Mormon,* some have questioned whether Mormonism should be counted as a part of the Christian movement. They now report 1,230,021 communicants in 2,624 churches.

The Germans who settled in Pennsylvania and adjacent areas were influenced by strong personalities to form new denominational groups which combined the older traditions. Philip William Otterbein (1726–1813) and Martin Boehm (1725–1812), the one a Reformed minister and the other a Mennonite, joined in the holding of evangelistic meetings among the Germans in Pennsylvania and adjoining states during the Revolutionary War days. In 1800 they formed the United Brethren in Christ. This group united in 1946 with the Evangelical Church (organized by Jacob Albright on Methodist principles in 1816), and the combined body was called the Evangelical United Brethren Church. It now reports 737,489 members in 4,370 churches.

In 1831 William Miller (1782–1849), by carefully counting the symbolical numbers in the book of Daniel, concluded that Christ would return within the next few years and gathered a group known as the Adventists. Despite the failure of this principal prophecy, the denomination still perseveres, now numbering 277,-162 constituents in 2,858 churches.

A distorted type of apocalyptic speculation by Charles Russell in the late nineteenth century resulted in the International Bible Students' Association. It now claims 187,120 members in 3,484 churches. Mary Baker Eddy set forth a sort of modern Gnosticism and founded the Church of Christ, Scientist in 1879 in Boston, and her followers now operate 3,100 branches of the mother church.

The national churches of the East which broke fellowship with Rome in 1054 were slow in developing in the United States, but by immigration and birth the number has grown steadily. The various national groups formed their own churches, such as the Greek Orthodox, the Rumanian Orthodox, the Serbian Orthodox, and others. These have perhaps a million constituents in America at present.

Many other smaller, though important, Christian groups are found in the United States, but these cannot be discussed in a work like this one.

In addition, American Christianity has been characterized by many benevolent and semi-Christian movements, such as the Young Men's Christian Association, first organized in 1844 in London, and the Young Women's Christian Association, also organized in London in 1855. The English Salvation Army, founded by Methodist William Booth in 1878, has widely expanded in the United States, now numbering 249,641 adherents in 1,323 churches.

Resurging rationalism.—The older European systems of rationalism, illustrated by the philosophy of men like Christian Wolff in the seventeenth century, were confounded by Immanuel Kant, Schleiermacher, Ritschl, and others, who showed that man is not simply a thinking creature but is as well a moral, feeling, and choosing person. The last half of the nineteenth century, however, brought a rationalism of a newer sort. Physical science was added to philosophy, sociology, and psychology to raise doubts concerning the being of God or to oppose steadfastly the idea of a special revelation involving supernaturalism. The material world became very real. Even philosophy began to classify values in terms of whether they could successfully operate in a workaday world. Religion and spiritual matters were viewed in humanitarian terms and channeled into social betterment. In this milieu it is possible to mark off several attitudes in relation to traditional Christianity.

These are: (1) A definitely nontheistic or agnostic party. Despite the phenomenal advances of Christianity in America since the Revolution, a hard core of skepticism and unbelief was never touched. It denies the existence of God and scoffs at any idea of revelation. (2) A theistic party, but not distinctively Christian. This group is in the succession of English deism, which affirms that there is a God but that he has no special revelation. Hinduism thus is as valid a revelation as Christianity; every prophet in every religion has been inspired and adds something to the total revelation of God. (3) The nonsupernaturalistic Christian party. This group claims to follow the Christian tradition but denies many of the older beliefs. Revelation becomes meaningful only as it is reasonable. The Christian Scriptures in the main are historically unreliable and must be sifted carefully by human reason in order to find truth and significance. What is not reasonable in the human frame of reference is discarded. A substitutionary atonement is impossible because Christ was simply a good man. The immediate confrontation of God may be sensed by the human spirit and constitutes the only valid religious authority. For this group the principle value of religion comes in broad humanitarian channels. Perhaps the chief exponent of this party in America has been Harry Emerson Fosdick (1878–   ). (4) An American neo-orthodox party. This group, differing in some aspects from the thinking of Karl Barth but agreeing generally with him in basic approach, emphasizes the essential sinfulness of man. Like Barth, its followers are quite liberal with respect to many doctrines of traditional supernaturalism but cling to older orthodoxy at the point of man's sin and God's transcendent sovereignty. Perhaps the outstanding figure in this school is Reinhold Niebuhr (1892–   ). (5) The party of traditional supernaturalism. This group endeavors to make the traditional Christian message relevant in a materialistic and scientific age, holding to the basic tenets of New Testament revelation and accepting the "unreasonable" supernaturalism of Christianity as exemplified in spiritual regeneration of the individual by the work of the divine Spirit.

Perhaps a sixth group should be included—what is commonly

known as fundamentalism, which in some cases goes to the other extreme from rationalism; that is, it completely eliminates the rational element from Christian revelation and religion in general.

Church union and ecumenicity.—For the most part, American Christianity has entered heartily into the movement toward church union and ecumenicity. The reasons are many and include: a basic desire for unity; the influence of English interdenominational movements, particularly in missions; the uniting of "family denominations"—those believing the same things and in the same tradition and needing union for strength and enlargement of work; the challenge of the foreign mission field, where there was need to place a united Christendom before a pagan world; the sweeping humanitarian movements, such as abolitionism, that crossed denominational lines; the cry for efficiency; the secular moves toward unity in the world, as seen in the United Nations; the need for a non-Catholic united front to match the organizational unity in the Roman Catholic Church; and the effect of liberal theology, where the toning down or denial of traditional Christian convictions makes lesser denominational distinctions seem relatively academic.

The specific antecedents of the modern ecumenical movement in America may be seen in the interdenominational missionary, tract, and Bible societies organized shortly after the turn of the nineteenth century. The American branch of the World's Evangelical Alliance, an interdenominational organization for the promotion of Christian unity, was organized in 1867 and for almost half a century promoted the cause of church union and ecumenicalism, although in the context of conservative evangelicalism. Other important organizations looking to the minimizing or eliminating of denominational lines were the Student Volunteer Movement (1886) and the World's Student Christian Federation (1895). The interdenominational missionary conferences, beginning in 1854 in New York, produced the Foreign Missions Conference of North America. The Federal National Council of Churches of Christ in America (now the National Council) was organized in 1908. Most major American denominations, with the exception of

Southern Baptists and the Lutheran Missouri Synod, have participated freely in the world conferences at Edinburgh (1910), Stockholm (1925), Lausanne (1927), Jerusalem (1928), Oxford (1937), Edinburgh (1937), Madras (1938), Utrecht (1938), Amsterdam (1948), and Evanston (1954).

Two world wars.—The two global conflicts in the twentieth century in which America has participated have had significant effects. The aftermath of the first was a resurgence of liberal doctrine and an optimistic humanitarianism. Many believed that the last war had been fought and that there would soon come the millennium of universal peace and total prosperity. Man's capacity for achieving these things was hardly doubted. The cataclysmic financial depression and the bewildering rise to power of European dictators set the stage for a second world conflict. With it came a realization of man's need for God, and there is now widespread evidence of interest in spiritual things. Whether history will see this as the first religious revival of the atomic age, no one can know, but the adversities of mid-passage can be counted blessings if they deepen faith in God and encourage dependence upon him.

A Résumé of Older Denominations

Episcopalianism.—The American political revolution represented a religious revolution also for the members of the Church of England in America. There was no bishop in all America for this church, and the break with England politically left its status uncertain. After a period of indecision, a general convention was held in 1789 by representatives from all of the colonies, and the Protestant Episcopal Church in the United States of America was formed. It was based upon the doctrine, discipline, and worship formerly observed in the Church of England. Episcopal ordination for American bishops was received from Scotland and England between 1782 and 1790. The General Convention, consisting of a House of Bishops and a House of Clergy and Lay Deputies, was constituted as the governing body for the church.

Many factors combined to make the first four decades most disheartening for the new church. Its historical and doctrinal ties with England (again in a war with the United States in 1812) brought it unpopularity. Its formal type of worship was not effective on the frontier in America, so it was confined generally to the more inhabited areas. The shock of disestablishment, along with the lack of effective discipline and national leadership, brought many types of problems. The general skepticism and infidelity which pervaded the American colonies immediately after the Revolution greatly crippled this church also.

This lassitude was overcome, however. As a rule, the members of this church were of the educated and upper economic group. The several revival movements involving emotionalism and physical excitement were of no interest to them. Seminaries and missionary societies were organized in the second and third decades of the nineteenth century. After 1835 there was an increased zeal for converts, and under the leadership of men like William A. Mühlenberg a good growth was begun. Immigration from England brought many. As a matter of fact, the American Episcopal Church has been greatly influenced by trends in the Church of England. The High Church, Low Church, and Broad Church parties of England were reproduced in America. The effect of the Tractarian movement in England was also felt in America, when Bishop Ives of the Episcopal Church in North Carolina submitted to the Roman Catholic Church. There was actually no schism in this church during the Civil War. The Southern bishops were simply marked absent at the meeting of the General Convention in 1862, and after the war they were seated again.

The awakened rationalism that emerged in the last half of the nineteenth century affected the Protestant Episcopal Church. The first American Unitarian church came from their ranks. There was a rapid growth in the Broad Church party, which placed considerable emphasis upon social implications of the gospel and a liberal theological interpretation.

This church has been active in the ecumenical movement. Negotiations for church union have been carried on with the Russian and other Orthodox churches of the east, as well as the Old Catholics who left Rome after the promulgation of the infallibility decree, and others. In 1886 the General Convention suggested the plan for Christian reunion, which later became the Lambeth Quadrilateral.

At present this church has 2,757,944 constituents in 7,271 congregations in America and carries on a strong program of missions, theological education, and social service.

Congregationalism.—Congregationalism emerged from the Revolutionary War with bright prospects. Her leaders had supported enthusiastically the war for independence, and her American history was long and stable. The state support of her clergy in Massachusetts, Connecticut, and New Hampshire constituted a sore spot for those in other churches; however, particularly through the efforts of the Baptists (Isaac Backus and John Leland), by 1833 Massachusetts eliminated the last of American establishments.

The early skepticism probably affected Congregationalism more than any other denomination in America. Unitarianism (denying the essential deity of Christ) took large numbers from their churches. In some cases entire churches became Unitarian, including the first Congregational church in America—the Old Pilgrim Church of Plymouth. Through a legal technicality a minority of Unitarians were able to secure the church property in many cases from a Congregational majority. Harvard University became Unitarian in 1805. Within twenty years the Unitarian group organized and became vocal. At the present time the Unitarian Church reports 96,715 constituents in 378 churches.

Congregationalism was greatly blessed by the second Great Awakening at the opening of the nineteenth century. Many new churches were founded; schools and seminaries were begun; and societies for home and foreign missions, the publication of tracts, and the advancement of education were formed.

The westward movement challenged Congregationalists. Some thought that all of New England was moving to the west in the first half of the nineteenth century. However, Congregationalism lost many of their constituents who moved westward. A comity agreement was made with the Presbyterians in 1801, which planned co-operative efforts in founding new churches. The majority was to decide whether the church should be Presbyterian or Congregational, but in practice almost all of the Union churches became Presbyterian. Many hundreds of Congregational churches were probably lost to the Presbyterians before the plan was abandoned.

As a group Congregationalism strongly opposed slavery and aided the abolitionist movement, particularly in the early years of the movement. Civil war did not affect the fellowship of the churches, because this group did not have churches in the South. The renewed rationalism after the war profoundly affected Congregational leadership. Many became liberal theologically and magnified the social aspect of the gospel. Ecumenicalism and church union have been quite appealing. Congregationalism united with the Evangelical Protestant Church of North America in 1925 and the Christian Church in 1931 and now bears the name of Congregational Christian Churches. Their present constituency numbers 1,342,045 members in 5,561 churches.

Calvinism.—Calvin's religious system, altered in some ways by the various national groups of Europe who adopted it, is represented in America by the Presbyterians and the Reformed (and Evangelical) churches. In a sense, the Congregationalists belong to this family, but their independent background and type of church government differentiate them enough to discuss them under separate heading.

The Presbyterians acquitted themselves nobly on the patriotic side during the American Revolution. The physical damage and general disruption of war were more than offset by the heightened prestige after the founding of the new nation. In 1790 there were about eighteen thousand members, but several factors contributed to a rapid increase in constituency. They gained considerably from the sweeping revivals in Pennsylvania, Kentucky, and Tennessee in the opening years of the nineteenth century. Immigration added some. The completing of organizational structure doubtless gave impetus to growth also. At the very close of the previous period there came the organization of the General Assembly, which was the capstone of the local and territorial organizations. Thereafter

Presbyterian growth was accelerated. Another factor unintentionally worked to the growth of Presbyterians. The Plan of Union of 1801, seemingly fair enough for both sides, added many Presbyterian churches in the west at the expense of the Congregationalists.

Several schisms have divided American Presbyterians. In 1810 a small group in Kentucky withdrew over the question of prerequisites for ministerial ordination and organized the Cumberland Presbyterian Church. The schism lasted about a hundred years, although at the reunion in 1906 a minority refused to return. Doctrine and organizational forms brought separation in 1838 between the old and new school groups, while slavery also caused a schism which has not yet been healed.

Extensive benevolent work has characterized American Presbyterianism. Home and foreign mission societies were organized in the first half of the nineteenth century. Many schools and seminaries have been founded. At present there are about ten bodies of American Presbyterians, the largest of which are the Presbyterian Church in the United States of America with 2,645,745 members in 8,282 churches, and the Presbyterian Church in the United States (Southern Presbyterianism) with 810,917 constituents in 3,852 churches.

The opening years of the modern period saw the ending of schism among the Dutch Reformed and the adoption in 1792 of a constitution. Two years later the General Synod was organized. This denomination is similar to the Presbyterians in organization, for they have a common source in Zwingli and Calvin. The session they call a "consistory"; the presbytery they call "classes"; the synod they call a "particular synod"; and the General Assembly they call a "general synod." At present they have 804 churches with 205,323 members.

In 1934 the Reformed Church in the United States (German Reformed) united with the Evangelical Synod of North America as the Evangelical and Reformed Church. At present the number of this body includes 774,277 constituents in 2,732 churches.

Lutheranism.—The Lutherans were loyal to the colonies and active participants in the American Revolution. Although there were fewer than eighty ministers of this denomination in America at the close of the Revolution, the next several decades brought rapid growth, mostly by immigration. Both the growth itself and the type of growth brought problems of languages, organization, and doctrine. The strength of continental Lutheranism was in Germany and the Scandinavian areas. The semicongregational system of organization made it difficult to secure uniformity. Immigration from the Continent transplanted to America many of the divisive problems found in Europe. In the nineteenth century controversies arose over confessional and liberal points of view, as well as over differences in language, racial distinctions, and organizational forms.

In general, American Lutheranism has stressed the authority of each congregation, although some autonomy has been surrendered to the developing general organizations. The local church is governed by pastor and a church council. The larger organizational forms are the conference and the synod. Before 1820 American Lutheranism did not have a general body. In that year the General Synod was organized, although it did not receive widespread support for many years. Because of immigration and the development of general organization, American Lutherans by 1833 could count more than three hundred ministers serving 680 congregations with almost sixty thousand communicants.

The nineteenth century controversies have been succeeded in the present century by a spirit of increasing unity among Lutherans. The Synodical Conference was organized in 1872 for conservative or "strict" Lutherans, its largest constituent body being the Missouri Synod, which now numbers 2,006,110 members in 4,805 churches. The United Lutheran Church in America was organized in 1918 and now numbers 2,175,726 members in 4,050 churches. The American Lutheran Church was organized in 1930 and now has 836,485 members in 1,919 churches. An American Lutheran Conference was loosely organized in 1930 for fellowship and matters of common interest, but it was dissolved in 1954. American

Lutherans engage in all benevolent enterprises, including over three dozen theological seminaries and all levels of Christian education and an extensive missionary program. The latest statistics show that American Lutherans now total over seven million constituents in about twenty bodies.

Roman Catholicism.—At the beginning of the modern period the Roman Catholic Church had about twenty thousand constituents. Many of its members played valiant roles in the Revolution. The disorganized state of the new nation offered great opportunity for growth. The Great Awakening of 1800 had little influence upon this body, but immigration from Catholic countries of Europe provided unbelievable growth. In 1820 Roman Catholics in America were estimated at almost 250,000; in 1830, over 350,000; in 1840, 1,000,000; in 1860, 3,000,000; in 1890, over 10,000,000; and at present, 33,396,647 in 21,086 churches. Practically all of this growth has come from immigration and birth.

The Roman Catholic Church was quick to complete its organization in America, mainly because of the sagacity of John Carroll of Maryland, who became the first American bishop in 1790 and the first archbishop in 1808. For a brief season this church was plagued by a movement called "trusteeism," which in effect was the application of congregational authority. Language and racial issues also transplanted tension from the Old World. During the nineteenth century Catholicism was harassed by accusations of anti-Americanism. The present century has been comparatively free from such problems.

Two distinctive organizations have been developed on American soil. Elizabeth Ann Seton (1774–1821) began the parochial school system in the United States, which has become an outstanding institution for the Roman Church. The second influential organization founded by American Catholics was the fraternal society for Catholic men known as the Knights of Columbus, begun in 1882. This has become an aggressive and militant propagator of the Catholic faith.

The organization of the Roman Catholic Church in America is directly subordinate to Rome through an apostolic delegate at

Washington, D. C., as well as the offices of various cardinals and the regular organizational forms of parishes, dioceses, and more than a dozen archbishoprics.

Baptists.—American Baptists were wholeheartedly patriotic during the American Revolution, many of their ministers serving as chaplains in the army. This denomination took the lead in the movements in Virginia and New England that broke the shackles of state religious establishment, and it performed a similar service in securing the constitutional guarantees of religious liberty in the new nation.

Baptist organization and doctrine were peculiarly fitted for the extensive American frontier, and a large portion of the Baptist story deals with intrepid men who pioneered with their fellows during the day and preached to them at night and on the week end. The great revival along the frontier in the opening years of the nineteenth century added many to Baptist ranks. Simply the mention of the large numerical growth of American Baptists in the modern period gives evidence of their vitality and activity. They numbered less than 100,000 in 1789; at present they total over 18,000,000.

There may be several principal reasons for this tremendous increase. (1) The Baptists preached a simple gospel, minimizing theological formulations and emphasizing a life-changing experience. (2) As a rule, preachers sprang from among the common people. Problems of ordination, organization, and ecclesiastical authority were overshadowed by the necessity of trumpeting the story at the command of God. There was fire in the bones of the simple farmers and pioneers which transformed them into preachers. The fire spread. (3) The economic aspect of the ministry offered no difficulty. Most of these early preachers labored during the week along with their congregations and preached without remuneration at the end of the week. Whether by making tents or tilling the soil, the gospel was preached. (4) Each Baptist church was completely independent. This sort of principle appealed to frontier democracy. It gave opportunity for free expression of dissent as well as assent and stripped away the possibility of ministerial immunity when it came to consistent living and morality. (5) From the first, American Baptists have been missionary-minded. Both foreign (in Canada) and domestic mission work were done before the organization in 1814 of the first national foreign mission society and of the first national home mission society in 1832. A tract or publication society was organized in 1824 as a missionary aid.

Remembering the Baptist principle that each person is a priest of God through faith and regeneration and has the right to interpret the Scriptures for himself, it should not be startling to note that the American Baptist family has had some divisions. There have been controversies over organization, over the mission enterprise, over slavery and abolitionism, and over modernism. The last issue, in particular, has caused much controversy in the last half century.

Despite these problems, American Baptists have engaged in an active program of missions, education, and every other benevolence. Their growth in numbers and organization has been accompanied by an increasing sensitiveness to all the needs of their constituency and the world. The largest bodies in American Baptist life are the two national organizations of Negro Baptists now numbering 7,168,190 in 36,894 churches, the American Baptist Convention (Northern Baptists) with 1,513,692 members in 6,490 churches, and the Southern Baptist Convention with 8,467,743 members in 30,340 churches. The Baptist World Alliance was organized in 1905. Many Baptists in the North have been active in the ecumenical movement.

Methodism.—The close relationship of Methodism with English life, particularly during the lifetime of John Wesley (who died in 1791), and the fact that many Methodist ministers in the colonies were loyal to England during the American Revolution made the task of American Methodists quite difficult in the opening years of this period. Several factors soon altered this picture, however. The organization of the Methodist Episcopal Church in America in 1784 brought a new unity. The great leader of these early years was Francis Asbury (1745–1816), who introduced the office of bishop into Methodism. By his example as a tireless itinerant minister and his stern demand that his preachers follow this pattern, Asbury had a large part in the phenomenal growth of American Methodism. The simple type of organization and the singing, experiential salvation that was preached was ready-made for the extensive American frontier. The sweeping revivals in the west in the opening years of the nineteenth century brought Methodism a large ingathering.

There have been several schisms. Because it was a people's church, Methodism was among the first to feel the impact of the slavery-abolitionist controversy in the fourth decade of the nineteenth century, and schism came in 1844–45. Other important excisions from organizational unity came because of disagreement over church government and the doctrine of holiness. The new rationalism prevalent in the second half of the nineteenth century greatly affected Methodism and brought considerable controversy over the modernistic issue.

The schism over slavery ended in 1939 with the reuniting of the northern and southern divisions. American Methodism now numbers 9,292,046 constituents in 39,854 churches, most of whom are members of the new united body. This denomination has always been active in missions, education, and other benevolences and has taken an outstanding part in the ecumenical movement.

Canadian and Latin American Christianity

Canada.—In the opening years of this period Canadian Christianity was principally Roman Catholic of the French type. Following the Seven Years' War (1756–63) Canada was ceded to Great Britain by France, accompanied by an unusual religious settlement. By the Quebec Act of 1774 the Roman Catholic religion was guaranteed free exercise, and the Constitutional Act of 1791 practically gave Catholicism control of what became Lower Canada. As a result, Roman Catholicism is in a dominant position in Canadian religious life.

The considerable Protestant immigration to Canada from the United States and England during and after the Revolutionary

War gave the Church of England a foothold in Canada. After a period of trial and error with respect to state support and ecclesiastical organization, the Church of England in Canada was organized in 1861, although it was not supported or controlled by the government. In 1893 a general synod was formed to govern the Canadian Church of England.

In the twentieth century this denomination has not kept pace numerically with other groups, a dwindling immigration from England being part of the reason. Although favoring the establishment of an interdenominational church union in Canada, the Church of England refused to enter the United Church of Canada when that body was organized in 1925 by the Methodists, Presbyterians, and Congregationalists because the other parties refused to continue the historic episcopate.

Although one of the earliest groups to begin work in Canada, Congregationalism never really became a prominent part of Canadian Christianity. Baptists and Presbyterians profited by excisions from this denomination. Despite valiant work by a joint home missionary society organized by Congregationalists, Baptists, and Presbyterians in 1827, and the work of the Colonial Missionary Society formed in England in 1836, Canadian Congregationalists numbered but 12,586 when the United Church of Canada absorbed them in 1925.

Canadian Presbyterian life before 1875 was unbelievably complex, representing a melting pot of Calvinistic thought from various racial and doctrinal groups. Foreign quarrels and problems were transplanted from every part of the world. The formation of the Presbyterian Church in Canada in 1875, representing a merger of several bodies, brought increased vitality in all benevolences and education. In 1925 this denomination reported over 400,000 constituents at the time the majority entered the United Church of Canada. However, about 180,000 of these refused to participate in the union, continuing as the Presbyterian Church of Canada.

Canadian Methodists also had an almost infinite variety in organization and thought before 1884. In spite of gathering up all of the organizational, political, and doctrinal tensions of American and English Methodists and adding some problems distinctly their own, Canadian Methodists made amazingly good progress despite diversity. When the Methodist Church of Canada was formed in 1884, its constituency numbered over 157,000. This denomination took the lead in working toward church union, and in 1925 when it became a part of the United Church of Canada, its membership numbered over 415,000.

Not long after the issuance of the Lambeth Quadrilateral (1888) interest was aroused in Canada over the possibility of church union. First efforts were not encouraging because only the Church of England desired to perpetuate the historic episcopate. At the turn of the century, however, Methodists, Congregationalists, and Presbyterians laid the groundwork for union. The Baptists declined an invitation to become a part of the movement. The final organization adopted elements of all three denominational types, and in 1925 the union was completed, bringing together 609,729 constituents from the three merging denominations. Growth since 1925 has been slow.

The Roman Catholic Church has made the greatest strides of all Canadian groups in the modern period. From constituting about 40 per cent of the population in 1911 and about the same in 1931, the Roman Church outstripped the population in the next decade and rose to about 44 per cent of the population in 1941; and because of the high birth rate among the predominantly French and rural members, the ratio doubtless has risen even higher in the last decade.

In addition to these principal groups in Canada, smaller denominations include the Baptists, Lutherans, Greek Catholics, Mennonites, and others.

Latin America.—At the opening of the period in 1789, Latin American Christianity—embracing principally Mexico, Central America, and South America—was almost wholly Roman Catholic, although the papacy had less control than the secular powers of Europe which claimed the different areas. This picture had been altered radically in the last century. It has been a century of revolution and change. French, Spanish, and Portuguese political

372

control has been eliminated, and practically all of the Latin American states have become independent republics. Along with political revolution has come religious turmoil. Because the Roman Catholic Church was so closely related to the political powers, it suffered considerably from anticlericalism and from some patriotic movements.

In the second half of the nineteenth century, evangelicals (principally from the United States) began an active missionary program. Practically all American denominations have had a part in this missionary task, which has made great gains from the nominal Roman Catholic population. However, dominant Roman Catholicism still makes religious liberty an ideal rather than a reality.

Concluding Summary

Christianity in the United States was separated from the secular authority by the Constitution. After 1833 all state establishments were abolished. The revival in the opening years of the nineteenth century, known as the Second Great Awakening, greatly strengthened the Christian movement in the young nation. It established the dynamics for the extensive development of benevolent work. Societies for missions, publications, and Bible distribution sprang up quickly.

To a considerable extent the large immigration from abroad and the westward thrust of the frontier in the homeland shaped the characteristics of Christianity in the United States. Missionary zeal was forwarded, new denominations were founded, older denominations grew and in some cases divided, increasing financial stability provided support for churches in each community, and a distinctive type of Christianity in general took shape. The "grass roots" denominations grew most rapidly.

During this national period in the United States, Christianity has faced problems of industrialization, the rise of cities, extensive immigration, severe world wars, and both financial prosperity and depression. Perhaps none of these has been as serious as the inroads of rationalism and materialism.

The Contemporary Outlook

THE PRINCIPAL PORTION of this study has involved the dominant forms of Christianity in the geographical areas of their strength. This naturally means that many forms of Christianity in large portions of the world have been either completely neglected or sparsely treated. That is inevitable in a work of this kind. An effort will be made in this last chapter to survey briefly the course of Christianity in sections of the world other than Europe proper and North America. Many of these areas are looked upon as mission fields, although some of them have developed so far that they should be included in any history of Christianity. This rapid survey will be followed by several observations about some contemporary problems of Christianity.

The Near East and Africa

The birthplace of Christianity has been under Mohammedan control for over a thousand years. The Near East, including what was Palestine and contiguous areas, now consists of over a dozen small countries, the largest of which, populationwise, are Turkey, Egypt, and Iran. The story of the eclipse of Eastern Christianity by the westward push of the Saracens after A.D. 632 has already been told. This did not mean the utter destruction of Christianity. After the immediate shock of conquest the Moslem conquerors took a practical attitude toward the Christians. Although no Moslem could become a Christian, the Christians were permitted to remain true to their faith, inasmuch as the tribute of money—and sometimes of boys for military service—levied against them would have been diminished or eliminated if the Christians had been destroyed. For this reason no great effort was made to proselyte Christians to the faith of Islam.

It will be remembered that the Mohammedan invasion in the seventh century overwhelmed Alexandria, Jerusalem, and Antioch, disposing of them as episcopal rivals to the bishop of Rome. Constantinople, on the other hand, withstood the assaults of the Mohammedans and in some ways was strengthened as a rival to Rome. The schism between Rome in the West and Constantinople in the East in 1054 grew out of ceremonial, social, racial, political, and ecclesiastical differences, goaded by the burning ambition of the crafty patriarch of Constantinople.

The emperor at Constantinople meanwhile faced a new crisis. A civil war of terrible proportions had been draining the strength of the Eastern world for twenty-five years. The Seljuk Turks, a new revolutionary segment of the Mohammedans, were threatening to burst out of Asia into Europe. Their barbarous treatment of Western pilgrims desiring to visit the Christian relics at Jerusalem, along with the political and ecclesiastical developments in the West, prepared the way for the Crusades which, with the contemporary overwhelming of Russia and eastern Europe by Genghis Khan (1162–1227) and his successors, checked for three centuries the further advance westward by the Turks. Efforts were made to reunite Rome and Constantinople in religious matters in the hope that the West would drive the Turks away from the siege of Constantinople. Union of Greek and Roman Catholicism was twice proclaimed, once in 1274 and again in 1439, but in each case the East subsequently repudiated their representatives, apparently preferring the cruel Turks to Roman fellowship.

In 1453 Constantinople fell to the Moslems. The patriarch (archbishop) of Constantinople became a pawn of the Turkish sultan and has continued so to be until the present time. Eastern Christianity, loosely confederated in the Greek Orthodox Church, consists of many independent national or racial churches in eastern Europe, Asia, and Africa, including patriarchates in Constantinople (the first among equals), Alexandria, Antioch, Jerusalem, and Cyprus, and the abbotship of Sinai, along with the Russian church.

Meanwhile, the Moslems advanced up the Balkans in the fifteenth century but were defeated just before reaching Central Europe. Gradually they were pushed back into what was formerly called Asia Minor. After throwing off the yoke of the Turk, the various Balkan states generally adopted state churches affiliated with the Greek Orthodox movement.

The Moslems have been difficult to reach with the Christian gospel. As early as the fourteenth century Raymond Lull became a missionary martyr among them. Individuals worked among them in the sixteenth and seventeenth centuries, but organized work did not commence until early in the nineteenth century.

The large core of Mohammedan culture in the Near East at present makes the mission task more formidable. Iraq and Iran (Persia), as well as Arabia (the birthplace of Mohammedanism), have hardly been touched by Christian missions because of strong Moslem resistance. Strenuous missionary efforts have been made in Turkey, principally by American missionaries, despite many governmental restrictions. The Church of England has led in the Egyptian field, their efforts mainly looking toward the reactivating of Greek Orthodox Christianity in the areas where they work. Some important and significant schools have been planted in the Near East.

The majority of the people across the northern part of Africa, once possessing a thriving Christianity, are now fanatically Moslem. The same thing is true toward the south in Africa proper. From Alexandria to Capetown the threatening shadow of the Moslem crescent hangs over the country. The overwhelming Islamic infiltration from the north and east still continues. Mohammedanism now has ten times as many followers in Africa as all Protestant missions combined. The field has been actively worked by both Roman Catholic and Protestant missionaries, the former beginning in the late fifteenth century, principally from Portugal, and the latter mainly from America and England in the nineteenth century, in the inspiration of the Negro emancipation movement. Africa is bound to become a battleground between Mohammedanism, Christianity, and secularism in this her day of awakening and new awareness. The situation has been aggravated by the political events which brought the nation of Israel into existence. This has drawn the Moslem world closer together, and resentment toward outsiders, even missionaries, has been growing.

Russia

Sprawling over portions of both Europe and Asia is the extensive territory of the Russian giant. The beginnings of Christianity in Russia are shrouded among apocryphal tales and traditions. Perhaps the missionaries Cyril and Methodius planted the seed in the ninth century. The extreme illiteracy of the masses of the people for many centuries thereafter insured a sacramental and liturgical type of Christianity plagued with much superstition. The continuous internal warfare of the eleventh and twelfth centuries, followed almost immediately by the destructive invasion of Genghis Khan and his Mongolian hordes, inhibited Russian Christianity until the middle of the fifteenth century. After the fall of Constantinople in 1453 Russia became a stronghold of the Orthodox tradition, developing a Russian patriarchate in 1589. The Russian Church was completely subservient to the state. Peter the Great (1689–1725) abolished the patriarchate and established the Holy Synod under his control. Catherine II (1762–96) completed the humiliation of the Church by confiscating its extensive lands and serfs.

It should be said that the Church was doubtless as corrupt in every respect as it could possibly be. The serfs confiscated with the land, estimated to number over a million, probably received better treatment in secular hands than they had known from the ecclesiastical tyrants. The defeat of Russia by Japan in 1905 and the catastrophe of their fiasco in World War II contributed both to the Revolution of November, 1917, and the militaristic sensitiveness of the Bolshevik regime.

In January, 1918, not only were church and state separated, to the disparagement of the former, but after 1922 an effort was made to destroy Christianity, which had been identified for a thousand years with imperial cruelty and domination. The contemporary policy of the Communist Party in Russia is to stamp out all Christian influence for the young but to let the older folk carry it with them to their graves.

Asia and Related Areas

The earliest mission field in the modern period was that of India, which now has more than 400,000,000 people living in an area of a little more than a million and a half square miles. The first missionary work was done by Pietistic Lutheran missionaries sent out by Denmark in 1705 to Tranquebar on the west coast of India. The Society for the Promotion of Christian Knowledge, organized in 1699 in England, also aided this work in the eighteenth century, as did the Moravian missionaries.

It was to India that William Carey went in 1793 to institute the modern mission movement. Since that time practically every major denomination has worked in India. Despite striking advances and sacrificial labors, the total of nominal Christians in India now does not exceed six and a half million, of whom less than half are Protestant. The nationalistic movement of the twentieth century which brought Mahatma Gandhi to the fore has, strangely enough, actually helped Christian missionary activities, because Gandhi made practical use of some of the principles of Jesus. There are more Moslems in India than anywhere else—almost one hundred million of them. About half of the entire population claim Hinduism.

China, with a population a little larger than that of India, became a Protestant mission field in 1807 when Robert Morrison entered Canton. Roman Catholics had worked in China since days of Francis Xavier in the sixteenth century. The Opium War of 1841 pried open five important port cities to foreign trade, and into these cities Christian missionaries poured. However, it took England two additional wars in the middle of the nineteenth century to convince the Chinese of their best interests. Most of the early mission stations dotted the coast. In 1866, however, J. Hudson Taylor and his China Inland Mission, operating through voluntary offerings on the faith principle, pushed into interior China.

Internal wars greatly disrupted missionary activity between 1900 and 1927. In 1931 the undeclared war with Japan was begun. World War II and the Communist regime in China have practically cut off all missionary work in continental China. Before the war there were about 750,000 Protestant adherents and over two million Roman Catholics. Ceylon, the island just off the southeastern edge of India, is strongly Buddhistic. Two-thirds of the population, numbering perhaps ten million, follow this religion. Roman Catholic missionaries began work there in the sixteenth century, while Protestants from England followed two centuries later. Before World War II Roman Catholics numbered about four hundred thousand and Protestants about fifty thousand.

Burma was entered by Christian missionaries from William Carey's Baptist mission at Serampore in 1807, but the first permanent work is credited to Adoniram Judson, American Baptist missionary, who arrived in 1813. Other denominations, principally the Anglicans and Methodists, have also opened missions here. It is estimated that there are about 175,000 Christians in Burma.

Christian missionaries are also working in Thailand; in Indochina, where French Roman Catholics almost pre-empted the field and claim about one and a half million adherents; in Malaya, where half of the population of over five million is Moslem; in Indonesia, where over two million adherents in a population of over 65,000,000 claim to be Christians, mainly Protestant, although the Moslem movement provides strong opposition; in Borneo; and in the Philippine Islands, where American missionaries claimed a following of about 330,000 before World War II.

Japan was first entered by Roman Catholic missionaries in the middle of the sixteenth century. For fifty years they worked with unusual success, but severe governmental persecution cut them short. Although Commodore Perry opened Japan to the outside world in 1853, missionary activity was retarded until 1873, after which scores of denominational bodies began work in Japan. The rising spirit of Japanese nationalism after 1900 created problems for Christian missionaries, as did the industrialization of the nation, which provided the background of Toyohiko Kagawa. Before World War II there were fewer than four hundred thousand Christians in Japan in a population of eighty-five thousand. After the war it appeared that many opportunities for Christianity beckoned from this island, but many of these doors are now closing.

The Dutch began mission work in Formosa in the first half of the seventeenth century, but with the overthrow of Dutch control this work stopped. Roman Catholic missionaries began their work two centuries later, as did Protestants. The number of missionaries has increased since the closing of China and the militarization of this island.

Korean Christianity, after a period of unusually rapid growth before 1910, felt the blighting effect of Japanese domination. Protestant communicants numbering a few less than 150,000 were reported before World War II.

Oceania

The various islands in the southern Pacific Ocean known as Oceania have also been the object of Christian missions. Adherents before World War II numbered almost half a million.

Some Concluding Observations

The Christian movement today faces major decisions and problems. Some of these will be discussed briefly to complete the story.

Supernaturalism amidst rationalism.—For over a thousand years Christian thinkers have wrestled with the problem of supernaturalism. Does it transcend man's rational powers? Is it complementary to logical thinking processes, or is there a basic antagonism between the two? Is it possible to hold to both rationalism and supernaturalism?

Eighteenth and nineteenth century Protestant continental philosophy and theology increasingly attacked belief in supernaturalism as being unnecessary and untenable. In the twentieth century a new approach has been made. This attempts to conserve the idea of a transcendental God and recognizes man as being a needy creature. However, the radical view of the person of Christ and the denial of the reality of a divine historical revelation which have characterized the liberal wing of this movement brings almost the same dilemma that faces continuing rationalism of the older sort —namely, does this world order know any historical, supernatural intervention of God? Many liberals are emphatically denying that the world does or can know such a supernatural intervention.

What is the logical conclusion to a denial of supernaturalism? It demands an acknowledged departure from the New Testament Scriptures and the historic Christian movement. To deny the supernatural resurrection of Christ from the dead is to refute a basic doctrine of Christianity (see 1 Cor. 15:13 ff.). There can be no Christianity without a supernatural resurrection. The same thing is true with reference to a supernatural spiritual regeneration. When this point has been reached—the reduction of Christianity to a nonsupernatural account of the ethical teachings of a man who had delusions about his own relations with God and deceived others at this point—it seems only fair to deny that such a theological system should be called Christian. Many will term such conclusions as naïve, but that cannot settle the problem. Undoubtedly this century will witness a bold effort to separate Christ from the Christian movement. An existential confrontation by a mysterious and unincarnated deity, who is prevented by either a limited sovereignty or a limited love from aiding the needy people in the temporal order of this world, would seem to be the general direction of contemporary liberal theology.

Missions amidst nationalism.—The extensive missionary program of the last two centuries has been among the heroic movements of human history. There is a serious question, however, whether the pattern that has been followed in these two centuries will be permitted to continue. The development of a strong nationalistic spirit among the newer nations of the world constitutes a challenge to the established order of missions. In some cases missions already are being viewed as an effort to supplant a native culture with a foreign one and are resented as such. Despite the sacrificial lives of previous missionaries, some still suspect that the missionary movement is a prelude to political and economic infiltration. In addition, the fact that America is giving extensive aid to all sections of the world has indirectly reacted against missions. American funds are now provided in many foreign countries for various services once carried on exclusively through missions. Governments that formerly allowed missionaries in their lands in order to reap the advantage of these services and institutions are now finding that they can provide their own services and institutions without permitting foreigners to work in their countries.

Faith amidst secularism.—The preoccupation of mankind with things has always been a deterrent to Christian progress. It has never been more of a threat than in this generation. Men have become increasingly indifferent to spiritual things. Even hostility toward Christianity has in many cases been replaced by a blithe ignoring of all religious values. This, basically, constitutes the subversive nature of Communist Russia. Her religious policy has stemmed principally from reactionary and political motivations. The indifferentism of Russia to spiritual things may in the long run be more harmful in the nations under her domination than the earlier policy of persecution.

One of the inviting elements to the areas of the world now awakening is crass secularism, whose gospel is simple and whose materialistic rewards are contemporary. America has been badly infected with this virus. How much it will sap the vitality of American Christianity in days ahead cannot be known, but without doubt it will contribute to crime and corruption through the elimination of spiritual support for moral and ethical values.

Denominationalism amidst ecumenicalism.—The ecumenical movement has made great strides during this century. Whether it will replace denominationalism is open to serious question. There is still considerable division among adherents of the movement as to whether federation or organic union is the ultimate goal. Organic union is not desired by many who are willing to federate or co-operate in areas where that is possible.

Minimal requisites for union cannot be compromised. The Lambeth Quadrilateral, for example, represents the very minimum requirements of the Church of England and Episcopalianism with reference to church union. Several historical examples in the past fifty years have shown that the omission of any one of the four items set forth in this statement renders union impossible. While other denominations have not specifically set out their minimal requirements for union, it is certain that there are doctrinal or ecclesiastical boundaries beyond which they will not go.

Many "family" denominations, split by historical agreements over matters not basically doctrinal or ecclesiastical, have been unable or unwilling to unite, despite the fact that the various groups involved pay lip service to the ecumenical movement generally.

The Roman Catholic Church has made it plain that they have no interest in church union, unless all other Christians desire to affiliate with them on their terms. This sounds a death knell to any ultimate goal of a united Christendom.

The wide gulf between sacramentalists and evangelicals in the basic interpretation of Christianity constitutes a major problem. In the area of life and work these groups can co-operate together and with many non-Christian bodies whose ethical and moral aims are similar. When the problem of Christian conviction is injected, however, as the Evanston meeting clearly showed, there must be freedom to follow that conviction in the spirit of love.

Concluding Summary

The twentieth century is fraught with more opportunities and more peril for Christianity than any century in a thousand years. Rapid communication and extensive enlightenment have put new burdens on the missionary; he is now forced to offer a Christianity to those who see it lived very imperfectly in the missionary's own land. Mohammedanism increasingly is challenging Christianity for the allegiance of mankind. The increasing influence of the Russian giant is a religious, as well as political, challenge.

BIBLIOGRAPHY

BETTENSON, HENRY (ed.). *Documents of the Christian Church.* New York: Oxford University Press, 1947.
CAREY, S. P. *William Carey.* London: Carey Press, 1934.

FERM, VIRGILIUS (ed.). *The American Church of the Protestant Heritage*. New York: Philosophical Library, Inc., 1953.

GARRISON, W. E. *The March of Faith*. New York: Harper & Brothers, 1933.

KIDD, B. J. *The Church of Eastern Christendom from* A.D. *451 to the Present Time*. London: Faith Press, Ltd., 1927.

LATOURETTE, K. S. *A History of Christianity*. New York: Harper & Brothers, 1953.

NEWMAN, A. H. *A Manual of Church History*, II. Philadelphia: American Baptist Publication Society, 1953.

NICHOLS, JAMES H. *History of Christianity 1650–1950*. New York: Ronald Press Co., 1956.

ROBINSON, JAMES HARVEY. *Readings in European History*, II. Boston: Ginn & Co., 1904.

SWEET, WILLIAM W. *The Story of Religion in America*. New York: Harper & Brothers, 1950.

Index